Ethical Issues in Social Work Practice

Antonio Sandu
Ştefan cel Mare University of Suceava, Romania

Ana Frunza
LUMEN Research Center in Social and Humanistic Sciences, Romania

A volume in the Advances in Human Services and Public Health (AHSPH) Book Series

IGI Global
DISSEMINATOR OF KNOWLEDGE

Published in the United States of America by
IGI Global
Information Science Reference (an imprint of IGI Global)
701 E. Chocolate Avenue
Hershey PA, USA 17033
Tel: 717-533-8845
Fax: 717-533-8661
E-mail: cust@igi-global.com
Web site: http://www.igi-global.com

Library of Congress Cataloging-in-Publication Data

Names: Sandu, Antonio, editor. | Frunz?a, Ana, 1987- editor.
Title: Ethical issues in social work practice / Antonio Sandu and Ana Frunza, editors.
Description: Hershey : Information Science Reference, [2017]
Identifiers: LCCN 2017013845| ISBN 9781522530909 (hardcover) | ISBN 9781522530916 (ebook)
Subjects: LCSH: Social service--Moral and ethical aspects. | Social workers--Professional ethics.
Classification: LCC HV10.5 .E8854 2017 | DDC 174/.936132--dc23 LC record available at https://lccn.loc.gov/2017013845

This book is published in the IGI Global book series Advances in Human Services and Public Health (AHSPH) (ISSN: 2475-6571; eISSN: 2475-658X)

British Cataloguing in Publication Data
A Cataloguing in Publication record for this book is available from the British Library.

Advances in Human Services and Public Health (AHSPH) Book Series

ISSN:2475-6571
EISSN:2475-658X

Editor-in-Chief: Jennifer Martin, RMIT University, Australia

MISSION

The well-being of the general public should be a primary concern for any modern civilization. Ongoing research in the field of human services and public healthcare is necessary to evaluate, manage, and respond to the health and social needs of the global population.

The **Advances in Human Services and Public Health (AHSPH)** book series aims to publish high-quality reference publications focused on the latest methodologies, tools, issues, and strategies for managing the health and social welfare of the public. The AHSPH book series will be especially relevant for healthcare professionals, policy makers, government officials, and students seeking the latest research in this field.

COVERAGE

- Health policy
- Public Welfare
- Poverty
- Domestic Violence
- Healthcare Reform
- Access to Healthcare Services
- Medicare and Medicaid
- Social Work
- Public Funding
- Youth Development

IGI Global is currently accepting manuscripts for publication within this series. To submit a proposal for a volume in this series, please contact our Acquisition Editors at Acquisitions@igi-global.com or visit: http://www.igi-global.com/publish/.

The Advances in Human Services and Public Health (AHSPH) Book Series (ISSN 2475-6571) is published by IGI Global, 701 E. Chocolate Avenue, Hershey, PA 17033-1240, USA, www.igi-global.com. This series is composed of titles available for purchase individually; each title is edited to be contextually exclusive from any other title within the series. For pricing and ordering information please visit http://www.igi-global.com/book-series/advances-human-services-public-health/102256. Postmaster: Send all address changes to above address.

Titles in this Series

For a list of additional titles in this series, please visit:
https://www.igi-global.com/book-series/advances-human-services-public-health/102256

Health Information Systems and the Advancement of Medical Practice...
Kgomotso H. Moahi (University of Botswana, Botswana) Kelvin Joseph Bwalya (University of Johannesburg, South Africa) and Peter Mazebe II Sebina (University of Botswana, Botswana)
Medical Information Science Reference • ©2017 • 350pp • H/C (ISBN: 9781522522621) • US $200.00

Examining the Role of Environmental Change on Emerging Infectious Diseases...
Maha Bouzid (University of East Anglia, UK)
Information Science Reference • ©2017 • 327pp • H/C (ISBN: 9781522505532) • US $200.00

Sexual Misconduct in the Education and Human Services Sector
Christopher Schwilk (Shippensburg University, USA) Rachel Stevenson (Shippensburg University, USA) and David Bateman (Shippensburg University, USA)
Information Science Reference • ©2017 • 291pp • H/C (ISBN: 9781522506577) • US $190.00

Public Health Genomics and International Wealth Creation
E. William Ebomoyi (Chicago State University, USA)
Information Science Reference • ©2015 • 463pp • H/C (ISBN: 9781466685598) • US $235.00

Transforming Public Health in Developing Nations
Mohamud Sheikh (The School of Public Health and Community Medicine, The University of New South Wales, Sydney, Australia) Aziza Mahamoud (Sidra Medical and Research Center, Qatar) and Mowafa Househ (King Saud Bin Abdul Aziz University for Health Sciences, College Of Public Health and Health Informatics, Saudi Arabia)
Information Science Reference • ©2015 • 416pp • H/C (ISBN: 9781466687028) • US $215.00

Innovative Collaborative Practice and Reflection in Patient Education
Jennifer Lynne Bird (Florida Atlantic University, USA)
Medical Information Science Reference • ©2015 • 308pp • H/C (ISBN: 9781466675247) • US $225.00

For an enitre list of titles in this series, please visit:
https://www.igi-global.com/book-series/advances-human-services-public-health/102256

IGI Global
DISSEMINATOR OF KNOWLEDGE

701 East Chocolate Avenue, Hershey, PA 17033, USA
Tel: 717-533-8845 x100 • Fax: 717-533-8661
E-Mail: cust@igi-global.com • www.igi-global.com

Table of Contents

Detailed Table of Contents

The chapter proposes to philosophically ground the ethics expertise in social work, starting from a series of ethics theories: utilitarian ethics, deontological ethics and ethics of virtues. During the foundation of ethics expertise we made conceptual distinctions between the theoretical and practical nature of expertise, between the ethical and the moral one, in order to justify the need for a new model of ethics expertise. In our approach, we debate the influence of such theories in the field of social services, which we consider to be representative in the context of the construction of a new model of ethics expertise, which underlies the constitutive values of social practice. The normativity of the ethical theories is extended to the level of certain different behavioural models and moral reasoning, summing up in practice the frameworks of the moral conduct the individuals can apply, when making an ethical decision, in social or organisational context, namely to determine whether the decision is morally acceptable or not.

Ethical dilemmas are conflicts that arise when two or more ethical principles clash. As social work practitioners often grapple with ethical dilemmas in their practice, it is important and informative to explore how they address them, especially in different cultural contexts. Drawing on data from a qualitative exploratory study of social work practitioners in different settings in Botswana, this chapter identifies and discusses several ethical dilemmas that social work practitioners in Botswana come across in their practice in both government and non-governmental organizations and how they address them. The chapter also examines the struggles practitioners deal with such as ethical stress, as they try to address and deal the ethical dilemmas. The chapter brings forth recommendations that social work ethics should be part of the educational curriculum and the importance of practitioners' self-awareness.

The purpose of this study is to present the ethical dilemmas that social workers in various institutions in Turkey encounter as well as the factors that influence their decisions in case of ethical dilemmas. 234 social workers participated in the research. Statistical analyses were performed in the SPSS program and $p<0.05$ was considered statistically significant. Three out of four social workers who participated in the research (76.5%) indicated having experienced ethical dilemmas in their practices. When we look at the causes behind the emergence of ethical dilemmas, clients' request or need for service conflicting with legislative regulations comes to the fore among the responses given (77.6%). More than half of the social workers who participated in the research (54.1%) stated that they decide primarily according to the principle of client's best interest in case of an ethical dilemma. Social workers often encounter ethical dilemmas due to legal and institutional causes and in case of an ethical dilemma, they usually make a decision in favor of the client.

The purpose of the research is to identify the ethical and axiological perspectives that underlie the process of social construction of the probation practice, and also aim at the ways in which the theoretical perspectives that underlie practice become constituents of the discourse of probation counsellors. The probation practice in Romania derived from social work practice with deviant groups. In the probation practice a large amount of case management instruments are still connected with social work practices. The results lead to the construction of a model of probation that integrates restorative elements with the restitutive ones, but also with elements of utilitarian justice, or centred on humanistic values. The ethical values identified as being constitutive for this model are co-responsibility, dignity and justice.

Social work acts at within the public and private fields. From an ethical point of view, the first one is governed by the society's right to information and the social worker's obligation for transparency. The second one is the beneficiary's right to private life and the social worker's obligation of confidentiality. The two sets of competing rights and obligations define the dual nature of social work to act both in the public sphere, as well as the private one. Starting from the case of Tarasoff, the American instances stated that the obligation of the therapist to protect the possible victims is a priority to that of confidentiality. The current chapter follows the meaning of this obligation in the practice of social work, as well as the clarification of the importance and limits of applicability of the principle of confidentiality in social work.

The profession of social work promotes the social change, the resolution or diminution of social problems and contribution to the development of social autonomy of the individual in order to increase his/her welfare. One of the most efficient ways of professional improvement of social workers is represented by implementing a complex process of supervision which involve the analysis and observance of the whole activity of social work. In this context, the accreditation of the providers of social services is the identification of their capacity to provide qualitative social services to people and to increase the responsibility for respecting the minimal standards of quality, regardless the type of property, legal form of organization and administrative subordination. In this work, we will present the experience of the Republic of Moldova in the development of the mechanism of supervision in the context of social services integrated and the process of accreditation of the providers of social services.

Unethical employee behaviors pose a grave challenge for organizations today. Research has established that every year organizations lose millions of their dollars along with their valuable reputation due to immoral conduct of their employees. Practitioners and researchers in the past have undertook such instances very seriously and analyzed various antecedents to these employee behaviors. While various personality and attitude related variables have been held responsible for counterproductive work behaviors, the role of social learning was often overlooked in this pursuit. Current chapter address this gap and presents a logical framework for establishing social learning as potential antecedent of employee deviance in organizations.

Foreword

The book *Ethical Issues in Social Work Practice*, coordinated by Antonio Sandu and Ana Frunză, presents the ethical framework of social work, as well as the ethical approach to the various issues raised by this field.

The volume brings together relevant professionals in the field of social work, with various cultural background, coming from different countries worldwide - Romania, Republic of Moldova, India, Botswana, Turkey, and the USA. They all come together to share their professional experiences with the readers, as they are shaped by the social and cultural environment they belong to.

The authors provide a holistic analysis of the ethical framework of social work, starting by deepening some of the ethical challenges of the field, both individually and organizationally.

The volume has a fluent structure that starts from the philosophical foundation of ethics in social work, familiarizing the reader with the main ethical theories and central moral values, demarcating the theoretical and practical nature of the ethical expertise, while offering arguments for the need to identify a model of ethical expertise that can determine whether a decision in a social or organizational context is acceptable or not, ethically.

The authors place ethical awareness in the context of the fundamental values of social work, which shows that respect for human rights and the promotion of social justice are the foundations of this field all over the world, dedicated to addressing human needs and developing human potential.

The general ethical framework underlying social work throughout the world is gradually tailored to punctual concepts and case studies illustrating the issues addressed.

Thus, social justice is analyzed in relation to state decision-makers, showing that the state has the obligation to create a social work component of the national social protection system designed to protect individuals and avoid marginalization or exclusion of individuals and families in difficult situations.

Social work services are placed in the context of the strengths-based approach, which brings to the fore the respect for the value and dignity of each person, and the promotion of each individual's ability to achieve their potential. This transforms the social worker from authority into a collaborator who tries to emphasize each client's strengths and resources, but also raises ethical issues related to customer self-determination and informed consent.

Another ethical issue brought to the attention of the reader concerns the limits of confidentiality and the right to privacy. The discussion about these issues is placed in the context of the dual nature of social work that takes place both in the public domain - governed by the right of the society to be informed and the obligation of transparency of the social worker and the private domain - in which the beneficiary's right to privacy and the social worker's duty to keep confidentiality prevails. Starting from the famous Tatiana Tarasoff case, in which the US court ruled the therapist's obligation to protect potential victims beyond confidentiality, the authors stress the need to clarify the limits of the confidentiality principle in the field of social work.

The authors also look at social work from an organizational perspective under the aspect of the supervision of ethics in this field, starting from other forms of ethics expertise, in order to act as a gatekeeper in transferring political theories to public good and to make it possible for professional values to be compatible with the organizational ones. The discussion is particularized by the case of the Republic of Moldova, where this process is recently being implemented, being considered useful and necessary to ensure quality support, professional safety and burnout prevention among social workers. On the same line, the authors also analyse the ethical audit in organizations and its particularities in the field of social work.

The case studies presented in this volume bring to the reader's attention the ethical issues in social work, in different social and cultural environments. Thus, the individualist versus the collectivist approach and the particularities of the probation system are approached in the context of the Romanian social work system. Also, the authors analyse the ethical dilemmas faced by the social work systems in Botswana and Turkey, while proposing solutions and recommendations aimed at improving the social work in these countries.

The reading of this volume shows that the authors have taken the difficult task to customize the general ethical principles to the field of social work, which they have succeeded in, providing a multi-cultural vision on the issues addressed and making the book *Ethical Issues in Social Work Practices* an internationally relevant work.

Ethical Issues in Social Work Practices is a book that recommends itself, by the importance of the topics under discussion, as well as the rigorous and inspired approach, which come to consecrate it as a reference in the field of social work.

Beatrice Gabriela Ioan
"Grigore T. Popa" University of Medicine and Pharmacy, Romania

Preface

Social work profession should be characterized by a reflective equilibrium based theory, the professional experiences being triggered by the values that give the nature of this profession. The ethics literature in social work is dominated by the normative approach centred on underlying the codes of ethics and the secondary ethical legislation involved in the professionalization of social workers (Butler, 2002; DiFranks, 2008; Greif, 2004; Reamer, 2005; Strom-Gottfried, 2000).

The preoccupation for developing codes of ethics in social work has been consistent throughout the profession, basically since Mary Richmond and the stage of pioneering in social work (Bulgaru, 2013; Dolgoff, Harrington, Loewenberg, 2012). The code emerged in 1920 under the name "experimental draft code of ethics for social case workers" (Agnew, 2004).

Currently, most of the professional national associations of social workers operate on certain codes of ethics internally developed, starting generally from the ethical values of the profession. The interest for these codes is given by the possibility of their development, through a management of ethics and the construction of certain personal ethics policies, specific for organisations providing social services (Congress, 2000, 2006; Valentine & Godkin, 2016).

The codes of ethics usually include professional values and principles of practice that derive from it (NASW, 2008; The Policy, Ethics and Human Rights Committee, 2014; Australian Association of Social Workers, 2010). The social workers' obligations to the beneficiaries, colleagues and organizations are encoded from an ethical perspective. The systematic analysis of the codes of ethics in social work led to the identification of two types of such codes. A type of code based on minimal standards, interdictions and sanctions, and a type of codes based on values, principles of good practice and the appreciation of the professionals' results. The two directions correspond to the two different approaches of ethics: a normative minimal one, focused on strengths and oriented towards professional excellence and high standards of practice. Another major direction in the literature on ethics in social work is the analysis of professional values based on which the social workers operate (Brenden & Shank, 2012; Drower, 1996; Kreitzer, 2006).

The social workers' interest on ethics can be attributed to the fact that the fundaments of the profession are profoundly infused by the ethical values. Social work can be seen as a professionalization of charity (Agnew, 2004; Sandu & Caras, 2013).

A series of other ethical values are involved in substantiating social work: social justice, equity, and equality as constitutive values (Frunza, 2016).

In our opinion, the professional values are operational, correlating the organizational constitutive values with the effective practice of the professionals. Professionalization in social work implies a powerful adherence of the professionals to the values that are deeply human, and internalize them, thus bringing their contribution to the development of the profession, in the spirit of the constitutive values of justice and the public good.

Ethical decisions are the result or ability developed in the context of previous moral development, the interest for ethics inside the organization being determined by a series of social factors.

THE CHALLENGES

In the process of development, ethics in current social work stopped to a theoretical understanding from the perspective of the professionals, the very transposal into practice being blocked at the formal level of the organizations' constitutive acts, in reproducing the values and principles into codes of ethics. The literature consulted is limited in the normative and axiological dimensions, with very few references to the field of ethics management and ethics expertise practice, while being required to ensure the transfer of know-how from knowledge to practice. The current ethical reflection tends to theorize what exists in social practice, at the level of values, principles and good practices, without having a prospective dimension, referring to the ethical needs of the beneficiaries that would grant the development of new adequate welfare practices.

Elaine P. Congress synthesizes the ethical elements we consider most important for the practitioner social worker. In the author's opinion, mere knowledge of the codes of ethics does not turn the social worker into an ethical practitioner. The knowledge of a series of ethical principles, such as those of beneficence and non-maleficence, is also insufficient, being necessary to have knowledge of certain instruments of the ethical decision (Congress, 2000). Aside this knowledge, we find it necessary to collaborate with a counsellor or supervisor of ethics, and introduce the ethics expertise as an area of training in social work, dedicated at least to social workers with role of supervisor. Trainings of ethics, but also individual counselling of ethics, as well as supervision of ethics of the activity of case management are only few of the solutions that can transform the social worker from a simple practitioner, into a practitioner with a predisposition towards ethics.

Establishing an act of ethical practice is based, according to Congress (2000), on a process which involves: examining the personal, social, organisational and professional values; thinking about the ethical standards supported by the code of ethics and the relevant legislation in the field; hypothesizing certain possible consequences of different decisions; identifying the consequences of the beneficiaries and the potential harmful actions and consulting the colleagues or the supervisor before taking a decision.

The practice of social work is infused by ethical values – which within the volume will be discussed from their perspective of constitutive values, the social worker following to guide his/her practice according to the operational values.

One of the core values of social work the practitioners must turn to in order to operationalize it, is the responsibility towards the individual, towards the Other. This type of responsibility is considered to be an imperative one, and asked to be manifested with sensitivity and empathy (Gehrke, 2010). In a process of deconstructing charity into responsibility (Sandu & Caras, 2013), in both a wide sense, and a specific one for social work, we observe how a charity-based ethics is funded on the duty towards the Other, while the ethics of moral agency is funded on responsibility, the operationalization of responsibility as ethical value becoming one of the forms of professionalization of social work (Frunza, 2016; Sandu & Caras, 2013). In the field of welfare we turn to the theory of care, whose object is the professional's duty to maintain the beneficiary's status-quo and its integration in the society, but also the theory of social chage, which follows the beneficiaries' empowerment. Transposed in the context of ethics of care, responsibility is treated by Diedrich, Burggraven, and Gastmans (2003) as a parallel between the ethics of care (of the model of Joan Tronto), and the potential transposal of responsibility towards the alterity (Levinas, 1969), into an ethical model centred on the third party's responsibility in inter-social relationships. In the ontological approach of responsibility, Levinas refers to the status of the *third party* through the fact that each of the Others we report to represents a third party in relationships with the Others, starting from the assertion according to which the individual's responsibility for all others can be manifested through Self, by its limitation.

This volume includes, in the third part, namely the "Ethics Expertise in Social Work Organizations", references to the role the ethics expert (as a significant third) has in the relationship of supervision in welfare practice, to ensure the affective and reflective balance, and the moral intensity in the relationships between the practitioner and the beneficiary (Frunza, 2016). Therefore, the call to Levinas and the significant third allows us to ontologically justify the relationship of supervision in social work, as a triad: beneficiary – supervisee – supervisor.

SEARCHING FOR A SOLUTION

In fulfilling the model based on social action, we propose the communicative action as a fundament of a particular type of ethics expertise.

The character of the communicative action of social work is given by the relationship beneficiary – social worker centred on social change, based both on behaviour modification, as in the influence of the social services on the social environment of the beneficiary, in order to facilitate their social integration.

In our vision, the social services are grounded in social action because they are directly interested in the efficiency of transforming the social space, while supervision, both the classical professional one and the supervision of ethics, is based on the communicative action.

Each organisation has a set of values that has generated the very existence of the organisation. The constitutive values generally target the public good and are those values that led to the need to establish an organisation.

The constitutive values can be found in the mission of the organisation and are beliefs shared by all the members. Generally, the members of an organisation, or at least its founders, share a preference for a certain style of business conduct compared with all other competitors. We frequently encounter values such as: performance, satisfaction, competitiveness, efficiency, fairness, justice, fidelity or honesty. We could consider these to be operational values that will generate ethical principles. The transition from the value to the principle is the acting out of an interpretative consensus. If the values are fundamental to the need of an organisation, the principles punctuate the directions of development, and the future programs to be developed.

The development of ethics in social work should be based on its detachment under the empire of axiology and political philosophy, rather following an orientation towards the management of ethics and the ethical expertise. The exit from the spectrum of theoretic towards the applied ethics without abandoning the meta-ethical fundaments can only be done, in a first stage, by similar developments to those of applied ethics in medicine. The professionalization of respect towards the patients' rights, either through means of bioethical principle, or through ethics of care, can underlie a *bioethics of the social intervention*.

In a further stage of development, the ethics of social work should overcome the principle level. For example, if the principle of autonomy in bioethics targets the specialists' respect towards the patient and his/her right to make an informed decision, in social work the autonomy and obtaining the quality of moral agent of vulnerable people is the very purpose of practice, and not a modus operandi. In other words, if for the medical practice, the autonomy is an operational value which guides how should the medical act take place, it becomes a constitutive value for the social intervention, as it guides the purpose of the social worker's practice.

THE STRUCTURE OF THE VOLUME

This volume aims to provide a new perspective of developing a social work profession and (ethical and professional) values-based practice. The volume will strengthen the knowledge in the social work field, contributing to the development of a professional and ethical axiology. Throughout the chapters, the reader will discover topics such as: Ethical values in Social work practice; The principle of justice in social work practices and resources; Governing principles of social work practice; Social work supervision; Supervision of ethics; Ethics audit in social practice.

Section 1: Philosophical Approach of Social Work Ethics

Chapter 1 focuses on the philosophical ground of ethics expertise in social work. Throughout the chapter, the author made conceptual distinctions between the theoretical and the practical nature of the expertise, between the ethical and the moral ones, in order to finally justify the need for a new model of ethics expertise. The deontological, utilitarian and virtue perspectives, as models of theoretical ethics that underlie the professionalization of social work.

Chapter 2 approaches the functioning of social work from an ethical perspective. The chapter focuses on the ethical values of social work, especially of certain series of values with untraditional nature, such as: tolerance, respect for "difference", empathy, own lifestyle, etc.

Chapter 3 aims to fundament the activity of social workers from the perspective of collectivism and individualism, and the way in which these values co-exist in welfarist practice. The author refers to individualism and collectivism as being mutually non-exclusive, both being embodied in the idea of social solidarity.

Chapter 4 emphasises the importance of the professionals' awareness of the ethical dimension of social work. The ethical values approached in the chapter, *Respect for human rights, social justice, equality* – are considered to be central for social work.

Chapter 5 discusses the values considered central for social work, (social) justice in the context of the legislation of soft law, and the European practices which consider ensuring the equality of chances, fighting discrimination and promoting equal treatment for all citizens, especially those belonging to the vulnerable population.

Section 2: Applied Ethics in Social Work Practice

Chapter 6 explores social work centred on strengths and ethical particularities of such an approach. The strength-based social work approach focuses on transforming the social worker, from his/her position of authority into facilitator of client's social and personal development. The ethical aspects raised include questions regarding the beneficiary's self-determination and the issue of informed consent.

Chapter 7 addresses a series of ethical dilemmas the social workers in Botswana encounter in the everyday practice. There are approached both difficulties and ethical challenges encountered by the practitioners, so that in the end, a series of recommendations and solutions for overcoming them and improving practice are being outlined.

Chapter 8 continues the approach of ethical dilemmas, starting from the Turkish practitioners' experience. The aspects the Turkish practitioners most frequently confront with, according to the chapter, are associated with the institutional, legal and ethical causes.

Chapter 9 aims to identify the ethical and axiological frameworks of the process of development of probation practice. The author identifies a series of theoretical perspectives based on which it highlights the speech on the practice of probation counsellors. This practice is a profession related to social work, in the area of deviance and delinquency at least in the Romanian welfare environment, where the research is conducted.

Chapter 10 pursues the significance of the obligation of confidentiality and the respect for the right to a private life in the practice of social work, as well as the clarification of these principles' applicability limitations.

Section 3: Ethics Expertise in Social Work Organisations

Chapter 11 focuses on the reconstruction of ethical expertise in the field of social services, starting from its philosophical grounding and the ethics of medical practice. This chapter approaches a series of models of ethics expertise – counselling of ethics, ethics audit, whose functions are complemented by a new model of ethics expertise – supervision of ethics, as it is proposed by the authors.

Chapter 12 approaches the issue of ethics audit of the organisations of social work, from a theoretical perspective. Within the chapter, there are discussed the theoretical origins of ethics audit as a model of ethics expertise, as well as the values and ethical principles that underlie this model.

Chapter 13 focuses on the approach of supervision as practice with strong ethical fundaments in ensuring the quality of certain social work services, in dedicated institutions in the Republic of Moldova. The chapter comes to support the practice of supervision, in the context of a welfarist system, which will face difficulties in implementing the practices of ensuring the quality of services.

Chapter 14 focuses on the lack of credibility and the loses of resources generated by the unethical practices of the employees.

The volume will have an impact on the field of social work and applied ethics through the novelty it brings in approaching social work as an appreciative, ethics-based profession. The current work will be of interest for students, practitioners and scholars in the field of social work and applied ethics, while being used as a reference source in both schools and organisations that develop professional training for their experts.

Antonio Sandu
Stefan cel Mare University of Suceava, Romania

Ana Frunza
LUMEN Research Center in Social and Humanistic Sciences, Romania

REFERENCES

Agnew, E. N. (2004). *From Charity to Social Work: Mary E. Richmond and the Creation of an American Profession* (Vol. 13). University of Illinois Press.

Australian Association of Social Workers. (2010). *Code of Ethics.* Retrieved July 14, 2017, from: https://www.aasw.asn.au/document/item/1201

Brenden, M. A., & Shank, B. (2012). Social work for social justice: Strengthening social work education through the integration of catholic social teaching. *Social Work & Christianity, 39*(2), 128–150.

Bulgaru, M. (2013). Deontologia asistentei sociale [The deontology of social work]. *Studia Universitatis Moldaviae. Seria Ştiinţe Sociale, 8*(68), 3-15. Retrieved from http://studiamsu.eu/wp-content/uploads/01.-p.03-15.pdf

Butler, I. (2002). A code of ethics for social work and social care research. *British Journal of Social Work, 32*(2), 239–248. doi:10.1093/bjsw/32.2.239 PMID:12774784

Congress, E. (2000). What Social Workers Should Know About Ethics: Understanding and Resolving Practice Dilemmas. *Administration in Social Work, 1*(1), 1–26.

Congress, E., & McAuliffe, D. (2006). Professional codes in Australia and the United States. *Social Work Ethics, 49*(2), 151–164. https://doi.org/10.1177/0020872806061211

Diedrich, W.W., Burggraeve, R., & Gastmans, C. (2003). Towards a Levinasian Care Ethics: A Dialogue between the Thoughts of Joan Tronto and Emanuel Levinas. *Ethical Perspectives: Journal of the European Ethics Network, 13*(1), 33-61.

DiFranks, N. N. (2008). Social workers and the NASW code of ethics: Belief, behavior, disjuncture. *Social Work, 53*(2), 167–176. doi:10.1093/sw/53.2.167 PMID:18595450

Dolgoff, R., Harrington, D., & Loewenberg, F. M. (2012). *Ethical Decisions for Social Work Practice* (9th ed.). Brooks/Cole Cengage Learning.

Drower, S. J. (1996). Social work values, professional unity, and the South African context. *Social Work, 41*(2), 138–146. doi:10.1093/sw/41.2.138 PMID:8851353

Frunză, A. (2016). *Către o nouă expertiză etică. Deconstruind valorile etice* [Towards an ethics expertise. Deconstructing the ethical values]. Iasi, Romania: LUMEN Publishing.

Gehrke, P. J. (2010). Being for the Other-to-the-Other: Justice and Communication in Levinasian Ethics. *Review of Communication, 10*(1), 5–19. doi:10.1080/15358590903248769

Greif, G. L. (2004). When a social worker becomes a voluntary commissioner and calls on the code of ethics. *Social Work, 49*(2), 277–280. doi:10.1093/sw/49.2.277 PMID:15124968

Kreitzer, L. (2006). Social work values and ethics issues of universality. *Currents, 5*(1).

Levinas, E. (1969). *Totality and Infinity: An Essay on Exteriority* (A. Lingis, Trans.). Pittsburgh, PA: Duquesne University Press.

NASW. (2008). *Code of Ethics*. Retrieved from http://www.socialworkers.org/pubs/code/code.asp

Reamer, F. G. (2005). Documentation in social work: Evolving ethical and risk-management standards. *Social Work, 50*(4), 325–334. doi:10.1093/sw/50.4.325 PMID:17892242

Sandu, A., & Caras, A. (2013). Deconstruction of charity. Postmodern ethical approaches. *Journal for the Study of Religions and Ideologies, 12*(36), 72–99.

Strom-Gottfried, K. (2000). Ensuring ethical practice: An examination of NASW code violations, 198697. *Social Work*, *45*(3), 251–261. doi:10.1093/sw/45.3.251 PMID:10803079

The Policy, Ethics and Human Rights Committee. (2014). *The Code of Ethics for Social Work. Statement of Principles*. Retrieved from http://cdn.basw.co.uk/upload/basw_95243-9.pdf

Valentine, S., & Godkin, L. (2016). Ethics policies, perceived social responsibility, and positive work attitude. *Irish Journal of Management*, *35*(2), 114–128. doi:10.1515/ijm-2016-0013

Section 1

Philosophical Approach of Social Work Ethics

Chapter 1
Philosophical Grounding of Ethics Expertise

Ana Frunza
LUMEN Research Center in Social and Humanistic Sciences, Romania

ABSTRACT

The chapter proposes to philosophically ground the ethics expertise in social work, starting from a series of ethics theories: utilitarian ethics, deontological ethics and ethics of virtues. During the foundation of ethics expertise we made conceptual distinctions between the theoretical and practical nature of expertise, between the ethical and the moral one, in order to justify the need for a new model of ethics expertise. In our approach, we debate the influence of such theories in the field of social services, which we consider to be representative in the context of the construction of a new model of ethics expertise, which underlies the constitutive values of social practice. The normativity of the ethical theories is extended to the level of certain different behavioural models and moral reasoning, summing up in practice the frameworks of the moral conduct the individuals can apply, when making an ethical decision, in social or organisational context, namely to determine whether the decision is morally acceptable or not.

INTRODUCTION

The issue of ethics in the organisations is a current and increasingly developed topic, involving all social actors responsible for their good functioning, however, the theoretical and empirical evaluation of the ethical decision are less exploited.

The role of ethical theories was the subject of different researches, aiming to apply certain ethical procedures in the practices of human resources (Schumann,

DOI: 10.4018/978-1-5225-3090-9.ch001

2001), of implementing the policies of corporatist social responsibility, or checking the ethical evaluations undertaken by managers within the organisation (Reidenbach & Donald, 1990; Södergren, 2014). The majority of the research conducted in the field of ethics have the main purpose of identifying those rules, principles, values, that the professionals adopt and translate into practice. Another important aspect in the field of ethics of the professions is drawing the frameworks of the ethical principles, on whose considerations and implications the process of ethical decision-making can be developed. The models of making ethical decisions are grounded on a series of central ethical theories, further presenting a few basic characteristics of certain ethical theories, such as those of welfare/good – *the utilitarian ethics*, and ethical theories of justice: *deontological ethics, ethics of justice* (Rawlsian theory of justice as equity), as well as the *theory of ethics of virtue.*

BACKGROUND: ETHICS EXPERTISE AND SOCIAL COMMUNICATION

Theoretical Foundations

As a theory of good, *the utilitarian ethics* is based on the idea according to which a good thing must serve as many people as possible, not just one, and the way in which it is useful should be clearly outlined. Utility, understood in broad terms, as what is useful, opposes to the aesthetics or the religious dogmas, just as Jeremy Bentham shows in his work, since the very introduction, being against the ethical principles which are not based on usefulness (Bentham, 1970).

In the analysis of the theory of usefulness, Robert E. Goodin (2006) highlights a series of features specific for utilitarianism, even the early one, the hedonist, whose principles where criticized and parodied by the followers of other ethical theories. Therefore, under the specific of hedonist utilitarianism, which targeted people's natural tendency towards happiness and pleasure, Jeremy Bentham proposes utilitarianism as an ethics theory derived from psychological premises. Goodin (2006) argues that "utilitarianism can be defined as an exercise of deducting certain possible ethical conclusions (…), starting from potential psychological premises.

Substituting Bentham's hedonist utilitarianism, through the idea of satisfying the preferences, fulfilling the first theory, or even including it, its followers had to turn to satisfying the options of major importance, and less the priorities of pleasure in relation to suffering (Goodin, 2006). When referring to the satisfaction of preferences, the followers of the modern theory of usefulness are influenced by a micro-economic optics. For the individual whose preferences oppose to certain hedonist pleasures, or even exceeds them, satisfying those preferences will be useful for him. The theory however puts *good* and *desire* on the same level, usefulness being reduced to the need for consumption.

Madison Powers is developing an incursion in the field of bioethics, approaching it as a representation of the policy, at the same time exposing the limits of the moral expertise. The author's premise is that in the context of the practice of bioethicists, there are political or social influences that intervene in the decision-making process. The situation of American bioethics is compared to the British jurisprudence of the XVIIIth century, Jeremy Bentham being cited as the critic of the system at that time, and the initiator of the development of a new decision-making model in ethics, that would be applied beyond the influence of policies.

Jeremy Bentham (1970) considers that the methods of decision defended by William Blackstone, in the field of jurisprudence, as rather being the manifesto of personal preferences. The interaction between law and moral theory is a subject approached ever since the XVIIIth century, in debating the British jurisprudence, regarding the methods the judges should use in deciding over cases. Bentham (1970) was to express his concerns on the fact that the judges used to manipulate the arguments in favour of their own favourable results. Bentham's criticisms were amplified, considering that the treaty of Blackstone was actually a catalogue of wrong or non-arguments, insufficiently transparent, also lacking any kind of standards of action, that would serve certain valuable public purposes (Powers, 2005).

Jeremy Bentham (1970) wanted to develop a practical ethics, an algorithm through which all laws could be publicly evaluated, an approach which, according to Powers (2005), results in the utilitarian method of evaluating the benefits and the harm produced by any law. Bentham's (1970) approach has only yet extended to the area of legislation, the hedonist calculation being defined as promising, being based on the idea that both the advantages and the disadvantages can be reduced to a common currency. Bentham's (1970) enterprise to symmetry all contributions to the individual's state of welfare and bring it to a mutual denominator, was criticised by both the critics and the followers of utilitarianism. Powers (2005) advocates the philosophers' support of the idea of intuitive plausibility, according to which certain things are intrinsically good, for example friendship. For that reason, in contrast with Bentham's (1970) utilitarianism, there is a better formulation of the utilitarian perspective in defending the *usefulness* conceived from distinct, separate elements, which are not reduced to it, nor substitutable to other constituents of usefulness (Powers, 2005, p. 309).

Utilitarianism is considered to be both the ethical theory whose fundaments are worth being considered in the decision-making process, as well as the theory which, independent from other ethical paradigms, could not be accepted as a method of applying ethics. Starting from Bentham's intention (1970) to develop a model of applying ethics within the laws of the state, Powers (2005) focuses on the ancient beliefs, intending to argue that the way in which ethics could become a sufficient instrument for guiding the action, is originated in two, at least controversial, hypotheses. The first hypotheses supported by Bentham (1970) is the one according to which the moral conflicts, which would have chosen utilitarianism as an ethical method, would be easily solvable for the simple reason that utilitarianism is grounded on an "old belief", that supports the existence either of a harmonious pattern in whose development all the values come to agreement, or there should be objective answers to normative questions, to which a principle or algorithm would have contributed to (Berlin, 2002, p. 47).

The second hypothesis supported by Bentham in favour of utilitarianism as a sufficient ethical method refers to morality as a subject of science. Therefore, it was considered that as long as whe can discuss the development of a science of morality, we will argue the development of certain technical solutions to the issues of law and public policies would replace the confrontations born among the political ideologies and their competing visions on good life and the optimal form of social organisation (Powers, 2005, p. 309; Elliot, 2016). Bentham's vision (1970) is considered by Powers (2005, p. 310) as being different from other approaches, precisely by rejecting the ideas supported by the theorists of the common law, according to which a coherent structure could be achieved without a method of public evaluation of its rationality.

Beyond the influences the utilitarian theory has been experience since its release, utilitarianism is a filter in the analysis of the public activity, as Goodin (2006) argues. Public activity is what extends beyond own person, and can widely influence, regardless of the social actor who is developing it. Goodin (2006, p. 273) argues that within the public area, when our actions affect the other, one conclusion of utilitarianism would be that the correct action will be the action that minimises the global usefulness, resulting from summing up the individual utilities belonging to those involved. Goodin (2006) refers to the global usefulness of the collective actions, the approach being applied to the public policies, justified by the author as being the very orientation of the utilitarian theory proposed by Jeremy Bentham (1970) and John Stuart Mill (1871), with the purpose of guiding the construction of public policies, as strong ethical and legal guide. The principle of usefulness is perceived as a source of orientation of the ethical public decision, the utilitarians involved in the process of making decisions within the public institutions being requested to estimate the effect and utility of each alternative, reported to all the parties involved, seeking to maximize the good for as many as possible.

Utilitarianism is a consequentialist ethical theory, supporting the idea that the correct actions are those that generate the best consequences, which, in a form of classic utilitarianism, would represent maximizing pleasure to the detriment of pain.

The *deontological ethics* is grounded on Immanuel Kant's theory of pure reason, where the supreme Good is identified in the individual's good will, but also in the sum of morally correct actions, undertaken under the considerations of duty. In Kantian deontological ethics, it is not the consequence of good actions what is important, but the individual's good intentions, beyond the action. The Kantian teaching according to which all rational beings should be subject to the categorical imperative resulting from the universal law of reasoning, was and still is the subject of numerous philosophical criticisms. The Kantian ethics targets the respect for the individual, the categorical imperative knowing different formulations, such as "the formula of universal law" or of the "Purpose itself", which imposes us to treat the "humanity in our person, or someone else's, always as a purpose and never only as means" (the second formulation) (Kant, 1972; O'Neill, 2006).

In the virtue of respecting the second formulation of the Kantian imperative, at the level of the ethics of professional relationships, the individual should not be used, constrained or determined against his will. The organisations and its practices should contribute to the construction of the individual's autonomy, and develop his capacities of moral and social agent (Morar, 2006). The organisational practices of professional and ethical training can contribute to the development of the individual as autonomous moral agent by the awareness and promoting of certain relationships based on ethical principles, such as that of respect for the person, respect for the individual's autonomy.

The *ethics of virtue* is originated in the Aristotelian philosophy, mainly manifesting in the western moral philosophy, previous to Kantian philosophy. The virtue has benefited from a rebirth in the moral philosophy, along with the interested manifested by Elizabeth Anscombe and Alasdair MacIntyre, who between '50s – '60s, brought back into discussion the issue of virtue. Moral, as moral duty, experiences a loss of meaning and influence, but the moral effects continue to be felt, converging in the development of certain principles that transformed virtue into purpose, without taking into account the individual's needs, as Anscombe states (Pence, 2006). The followers of a theory of virtue will argue that the theories of justice, utility, or those based on rationality and the individual's independence, are adopted by the individuals without considering the virtues and moral implications of the individual, beyond the ethical behaviour "programmed" through education. Or, the theory of virtue involved a more detailed knowledge of the person, its humanity, and goes beyond the behaviour, studying politically and socially, the way in which the different virtues – and vices, at the same time – are promoted and encouraged in different social structures (Pence, 2006, p. 285). The theory of virtue refers to that development of the individual's character, the modern philosophy including intense concerns on personal responsibility and character formation, connections between the character and friendship or manners, or the analysis of certain personal traits (Pence, 2006, p. 286).

We consider morality as belonging mainly to the private area, while the ethical behaviour defines action in the public space. Morality belongs to the individual, even if it is shared by the community from the perspective of accepted values, and the ethical conduct rather justifies the collective action, which although is based on individuals that act, is not resumed to a simple conjunction of individual actions (Jonas, 1984).

We formulate the hypothesis that, from the perspective of the ethics of professions, morality should be re-evaluated as good practice. A social worker, for example, when acting responsibly towards his/her client, transposes into the professional plan the value of responsibility, which is good practice, applying responsibility, helping him reach professional excellence. Being responsible is a virtue in itself, related to the individual's personality when applied in the private area, and to its professional reason, when manifested in the public, professional area. However, developing professional activities, as much as one would pursuit professional detachment, cannot be completely deprived of personal involvement, through which the professional expresses his own nature. The responsibility towards the client reveals the responsible nature of the individual, and at the same time, his high professional competence. When responsibility is constantly part of the individual's professional conduct, it represents an interiorised competence, with the nature of virtue. For this reason we can talk about professional virtues, in the sense of applying a behaviour impregnated with ethical value, in the professional practice. However, the consequentialist objection is maintained, according to which it is easier to promote an ethical value, than to apply it in your own behaviour, and more than that, is even more efficient from the point of view of the cost-benefit relationship (Pettit, 2006).

In these conditions, the ethics expert aims to promote the ethical behaviour of the professional, empowering him to act virtuously in exercising his own profession.

In the foreword, "*Introduction in Areotology. Small ethics treaty*", Cozma (2001) supports the necessity of a thorough reconsideration of virtue and its study, as "excellence of the human being", in the context of reconsideration, of ethical thinking with the purpose of valuing the theory of virtue – theory which is considered to be summing up real solutions to the contemporary moral crisis. *Virtue* "represents the capacity of a human being, or a thing, to fulfil well his essential function", in the sense of morality, designating "human – elevated synthetic expression of defining intrinsic human features" (Cozma, 2001, p. 34). *The human* is treated as a synthesis of the features accessible to man, their value being acknowledged, resulting in their act by own will and action; the virtuous man will develop his good, beautiful, useful and commendable skills for his/her own good, and of the others, in general (Cozma, 2001, p. 43). Virtue is considered to be demonstrating a vast instrumentalisation in the field of ethics, being at the same time ground and purpose, quality and rule of action, but also condition, framework and way of moral accomplishment (Cozma, 2001, p. 68).

We have identified the approach of virtue in relation with duty, value approached in the deontological theory and the postmoralist Lipovetskyan ethics. Cozma (2001, p. 159) sees the relationship between the two reference concepts – virtue and duty – as being the adaptation of ethics to a post-moral society, the ethical duty becoming "instant virtue". Duty is analysed, in this context, as an ethical value, with obvious role in defending and conserving the humane, the responsibility the postmodern society is reaching to not being precisely the desiderate of the followers of moral philosophy. The relationship between duty and virtue is advocated as a "mobile for freedom through awareness and respect for necessity, order" (Lipovetsky, 2007), the virtue being approached in the form of duty as acknowledged and accepted imperative.

ON THE POSSIBLITY OF ETHICS EXPERTISE

In the 70's America, the research of ethics in medical sciences began to evolve, starting from the necessity of making the best informed and ethical decisions. The professional ethicists became those experts confronting complicated questions, resulting from the biomedical practice. The ethical dilemmas or problems arising in practice were approached by trained researchers who developed conceptual and methodological instruments in order to address the specific cases, based on ethical principles. An example Hub Zwart offers in his paper *Ethical Expertise in Policy* refers to the principles adopted by the University of Georgetown (Zwart, 2012), found in the scientific literature in bioethics as principiism. Beauchamp and Childress (2001, p. 338) proposed four principles: the principle of respect for autonomy, of non-maleficence, of beneficence and justice – and a series of rules of enforcement, which involved truth, intimacy, confidentiality and fidelity.

From Bioethics to the Ethics of Welfare Professions

Hub Zwart (2012, p. 160) argues that the medical ethics has evolved towards the field of bioethics, being a scientific area controverted by both philosophers, who accused the vulgarisation of the philosophic language, as well as doctors, who emphasized the lack of justification for new philosophical theories reaching the medical space. We assume the medical ethics was and remains a particular area, transdisciplinary, rather belonging to medicine. This one uses knowledge in the humanistic fields – especially in theoretical ethics – but also in the field of social research, influencing them with the epistemological specifics of the medical field.

Bioethics is, at the same time, a field of philosophical research which analyses from theoretical perspectives, the particular realities of the field of health, environment, emerging technologies, social practices, etc. Just as other philosophical reflections on the results of particular sciences are being infused by the knowledge in that science, as such bioethics reflects upon the meanings of social, medical and technological practices, using in the specific language terms coming from the medical area (organ transplant, nanotechnologies, etc.), interpreting them in the sense of philosophical reflection.

Precisely the quality of experts in ethics is being challenged, both from philosophical and medical perspective. The area of the ethics expert's particular knowledge is still delimiting, those who support the ethics expertise referring to abilities such as analytical power, conceptualization, familiarity with the history of moral debates and different ethical perspectives.

Schicktanz Schweda & Wynne support the need for differentiating the terms of moral and ethical expertise (2012). The morality is a set of principles and values with role in guiding the individual life and the social interactions, while ethics involves normative reflection, justification or criticism, in terms of validity, desirability or legitimacy of an action. Therefore the ethics expertise as a theoretical competence involving methods specific for reflection and justification is different from moral expertise, as sensitivity and specific moral authority, which doesn't necessarily involve theoretical reflection, but is rather grounded in education, practice and experience. Even so, the clear distinction between ethics and morality is at least questionable, since a clear delimitation between secular morality (of non-expert individuals) and the ethical reflection (philosophic and academic), can not be fully accomplished. An inter-connectivity between them is rather supported, on grounds of the involvement of normative reasoning and discussion, even if it is developed at different levels, and in a different theoretical depth (Schicktanz Schweda & Wynne, 2012, p. 131).

The field of applied ethics enjoyed a gradual but rigorous development, especially in the social and economic western field. Ethics in the scientific and technological field (Long, 2017) has become, ever since the 90's, an intensely studied subject, being beyond the theoretical discourse in moral philosophy, also academic discipline, label for a relatively new typology of procedures which manage the relationships between the public actors.

In the social sphere, professional ethics has become a referential field. In the second half of the XXth century, the increased interest manifested by the organisations for professional ethics was due to the variety of factors, such as the development of certain controversial technologies, mostly in the field of medical care. The professional responsibility of the specialists in different professions has become an important subject, spread by the contemporary media. The call to ethics in social practices has significantly influenced the development of ethics applied in this field. Starting with 1980s, with the help of a small group of researchers, the American scientific literature starts to include scientific papers that argue over ethical problems and dilemmas, starting from the literature, theories and concepts of moral philosophy and applied ethics. The first volumes and articles that discuss the relationship between ethical dilemmas in social services and making ethical decisions, are connected to the researches of Frederic Reamer (2006, p. 10).

Ethics Expertise or Moral Expertise?

Ethics and moral expertise are controversial subjects, mainly due to the difficulties in labeling ethics as practice, and not necessarily as theory. We will highlight a series of different perspectives on what moral and ethical expertise involves for the theoreticians of the two concepts.

Karen Jones and Francois Schroeter (2012) presents two models of moral expertise which are diametrically opposed. A first model highlighted by them starts from the idea according to which moral expertise is practically a sum of facts with relevance on certain specific issues in the context of a moral theory. Therefore, it is considered that the people with moral expertise are capable of ordering the principles they operate with into an hierarchy, and deduce, from he specific of the ethical issue they confront with, what needs to be done, by simply following the rules/principles in accordance with the situation under debate. Such a model of moral expertise can be characterized by the individual's capacity to reason correctly, the capacity to identify errors, knowledge over the ethical principles and paradigms, and the prioritization of the principles (Singer & Wells, 1984, p. 200). These capacities are tributary to a paradigmatic knowledge, obtained by philosophical study of the ethical theories, which is why this model of ethics expertise (Abrudan, 2011) comes to support philosophers as being the most justified to be considered experts, to the detriment of other specializations (Jones & Schroeter, 2012, p. 218).

The second model of ethics expertise contrasts with the first one, being defined as a model of practical wisdom that highlights perception. The central point of the model is the contemporary approach of the ethics of virtue, being grounded on the capacity of discern the moral prominence of the considerations in a given context. The expert must possess himself a series of virtues in order to be considered entitled to act as an expert. Possessing a virtue will be the starting point in developing other capacities necessary for the decision-making process.

Jones and Schroeter exemplify the virtue of honesty, and he who possesses such virtue will act in favour of truth. The situation, however, is not as simple as it may initially seem. There is the possibility of conflict between two virtues, therefore *kindness* can conflict with *honesty*. It is necessary for the expert in morality to possess all virtues, so possessing them would lead to practical wisdom; in this model, the philosophers are no longer privileged to be ethicist experts (Jones & Schroeter, 2012, p. 219).

Ben Eggleston (2005) addresses in *The Ineffable and the Incalculable: G. E. Moore on Ethical Expertise,* the issue of ethics expertise in Moore's perspectives. Eggleston (2005) reflects upon the nature of ethics expertise, in its philosophical approach of defining ethics expertise starting from Moore's ethics: is ethics expertise theoretical or practical knowledge?

Reffering to Aristotle's *Nichomaniac Ethics* (1988), Eggleston (2005) supports the pragmatic nature of ethics, even if the concept of expertise rather has a theoretical connotation. In ancient times, Aristotle supported the interest and purpose of philosophical examination, as not being to identify what virtue is, but how to become better, how to apply virtue. In modernity, opposed to Aristotle's vision, Moore argues that the main purpose of ethics is the knowledge of virtue, and not its practice (Moore, 1993). Eggleston (2005) adheres to the idea according to which ethics expertise is rather theoretical, arguing the choice by exemplifying the fact that, in a hypothetical situation, a person who does good deeds, without expressly focusing on its virtuous behaviour, or is capable of teaching others how to make good deeds, will be perceived as virtuous, but not as having ethics expertise. Associating the concept of *expertise* with that of *philosophy* justifies Eggleston (2005, p. 90) to support the epistemic nature of ethics expertise, rather than the pragmatic one.

Another aspect that questions the nature of the ethics expertise refers to two possible approaches of the field: the preoccupation of ethics expertise to do *Good,* or the second one, to commit *Justice.*

Both orientation will launch questions on what is determined as *good* or *right,* and endorsed by the ethics expertise. The orientation towards doing *good* will place the ethics expert in incapacity to offer consultancy to agents on what is *correct* or *incorrect* in the situations he is facing, while the expert's orientation towards *justice* will determine him/her to use the expertise explicitly in an action of guidance (Eggleston, 2005, pp. 90-102). Moore's ethics (1993), as a successor to John Stuart Mill, is an ethics of good, arguing in *Principia Ethica,* that Good is a notion all ethics depend on (Moore, 1993, p. 192), and the work of ethics determines those things that have intrinsic value, and to what extent they have it (Moore, 1993, p. 78). Moore acknowledges the importance of using the judgment of good in order to determine judgments on what is right, claiming that it is the object of ethics to inform us of our duties as individuals (Moore, 1993, p. 219).

Synthesizing Moore's approach on ethics, Egglestone exposes a series of characteristics specific for ethics expertise, represented by: the capacity to differentiate the judgments on what is good or bad in good or bad judgments, and judgments of cause and effect; the capacity to use intuition in order to make necessary judgments of good and bad; the capacity to use the empirical investigation in order to make judgments of cause and effect. These abilities are considered to be necessary for a person to determine whether a certain act is *right/good* or *bad.* Considering the ethics expert's abilities indicated by Moore as raising problems of implementation into practice, Egglestone brings certain clarifications to Moore's approach (Egglestone, 2005, p. 99).

The ethics expert described by Moore, a follower of the consequentialist ethics, will not have to investigate the agent's intention, or make sure his future actions will not compromise the ethical act. The real consequences of the ethical act will be those that matter for the practice of Moorean ethics expert, regardless of the tendencies or generalisations associated to the act. Also, Moore focuses his attention to determining the ethical rules desirable for developing such a society, the action underlying these ethical rules also promoting meanings and arrangements such as life, liberty, property security, considered as intrinsic good, regardless of the social circumstances (Eggleston, 2005, p. 100).

The academic discourse on ethics expertise offers at least three different approaches. Peter Singer claims that the ethics expertise constitutes a profound familiarization of theories, models and ethical arguments, as well as their application in different situations (Singer, 1979), while Cheryl Nobel (1982) considers it to include the manifestation of moral wisdom. The third perspective on ethics expertise is identified with the ability to justify moral judgments in a coherent way (Yoder, 1998). Schicktanz et. al. considers that trust given to ethics expertise, as well as using it, depends on the meta-ethic approach of the one using ethics expertise (Schicktanz, Schweda & Wynne, 2012, pp. 130-131).

The Theoretical and the Practical Ethics Expertise

The expertise is understood by Schicktanz and his collaborators as a form of knowledge and superior and/or exclusive competence, in a certain field, which can be obtained through training and experience.

The practice of ethics experts, but also the activity of the ethics committees are developed locally, regionally, nationally or even internationally (Schicktans, Schweda & Wynne, 2012, pp. 130-131). Their legitimacy follows an expertocracy model, as it is used in many contexts of elaborating contemporary policies (Reck, 2003). The influence of the frameworks of ethical normativity is not given by democratic procedures, through majoritarian vote, but through expertise.

Minou Bernadette Friele (2003) shows that the roles of the ethics expert are mainly the analysis and subject to tests of logic and ethical validity of different arguments used in supporting the idea of ethics decision and observing their use as means of discursive argumentation. The roles of the ethics experts are mainly found in the ethicists professional activities, practiced by teaching professional ethics, participating as expert witnesses in the field, to certain processes, are members in different executive and legislative committees, in consulting committees, offering analysis of moral argumentation or consultancy in ethics of research.

Schicktanz and its collaborators trace a series of demarcations on ethics expertise, referring to the critical evaluation of the expertise, to the dialectics between social sciences and ethics, in the field of applied ethics, also approaching the inclusion or exclusion of the audience's perspective on the ethics. We discuss about this "ethics understood by the broad audience" that Schicktanz starts from, in explaining its fundaments as a participatory paradigm, and its normative motives. The concept of "public understanding of ethics" involves the public preoccupation regarding the scientific and technological process, including all other forms of argument, justification and normative judgment on moral issue in the medical system, such as questions on the morality of using human embryos in medical research, on the patient's respect in medical practice, etc. The concept of "public understanding of ethics" can be used to call the social research of the wide audience's vision on the role of ethics and ethicists in different social and political contexts, fields whose ethics is still insufficiently studied (Schicktanz, Schweda & Wynne, 2012, p. 132).

The models of the ethics expert and the ethics committees, as determinants of obtaining consensus, may constitue a driving force in implementing the ethics policies. The advantages are constituted by the facilitation of the cooperation between experts in different fields, engaged in deliberative processes, avoiding as much as possible the controversies generated by the religious or metaphysical beliefs, impossible to reconciliate.

Valentin Mureşan critically reflects upon the relationship between purely theoretical philosophical ethics and applied ethics, initially constituted as application of great ethical theories. The philosopher mainly targets the meanings of applied ethics, which are outlined in parallel with a process of extreme specialization both in ethics itself, as well as the particular fields of reflection on applied ethics.

The context presented by Mureşan (2007) is ambivalent, having plausible arguments both in favour of the necessity of knowledge on traditional ethical theories, as well as on the futility of such theories in the practice of the decision and the ethical consultancy. In favour of the importance of ethics theory in applied ethics, Mureşan (2007) appeals to theories such as *deductivism* – which he defends against reductionist criticism, *weighing the grounds* - used in pluralist theories, such as intuitionism, *specifying norms* – which involves committing in a process of specifying and customizing norms, *the theory of virtue* – seen as an alternative to the dispute between deontologism – consequentialism, *reflected balance* – coherent-Rawlsian theory of justification which requires testing the theoretical principles applied in an ethical case, etc. Mureşan (2007) criticizes the anti-theoretical opinions of certain radical critics ethicists, of the possibility of the existence of certain universalist and grounding ethical theories, of which he refers explicitly to Levinas, Foucault and Lyotard. Considering their vision, Mureşan (2007) argues the existence of a pragmatic substrate of the deconstructive vision on ethics.

The criticism of the aforementioned philosopher doesn't omit Richard Rorty, whom he reproves the confusion of different meanings offered to the phrase "applied ethics", and the possible confusion between the other's moral understanding, and the moral communication and complex appliance of ethics expertise in the construction of a code of ethics (Mureşan, 2007, p. 89).

We adhere to Mureşan's opinion (2007) according to which applied ethics is a complex transdisciplinary field, which requires a collaboration both between the ethicist who is familiar with the great theoretical constructions, as well as the specialist in the particular domains. The mentioned author proposes a focus on areas between pure moral philosophy and the practical application of ethics, area in which the theory of ethical decisions and its models is actually situated, as well as the principiism, the ethical matrix, Hare's utilitarianism, moral casuistry, narrative ethics, but also contemporary ethics of Christian inspiration.

The "Ethics Void" and the Need for Ethical Reflection in Social Work

Undefined standards, internal and external policies of the unclear organization, the lack of supervision and the fear for consulting a professional instance of expertise, lead the social workers to a fragile territory with complex ethical issues, described by McAuliffe (2002) as an "ethical void". Aside these aspects identified by Donna McAuliffe (2002), following certain research conducted in the field of ethics in social work in Australia, the researcher concluded that the subjects of the research, autonomous social workers of first line, were capable of concealing problematic unethical practices, since from the communication between the specialist and the organization it would lack the call to a responsible and ethical behavior. The author, however, did not specify whether she refers to a behaviour caused by the lack of information of specialists, which would result in a potential capacity of identifying the unethical practices.

"The ethical void" identified by McAuliffe (2002) is, from our point of view, an ultimate redoubt of the categorical imperative. In our opinion, there are two levels of professional ethics, one in which the professional is autonomous in a Kantian sense, meaning his professional judgment is his standard of practice, including the ethical standard, and another one in which the professional, not being an ethicist, should comply to certain standards of good practice defined by either a legislator, or ethics experts requested by the professional corpus.

The autonomous professional has full confidence in his own moral judgment, therefore he may not acknowledge the need for ethics expertise, other than when the practical situation makes them face an ethical dilemma. The current situation of generalization of politically correct practices makes certain professional behaviours, performed with good will, to go beyond the "imposed ethics" through the deontological codes. The overconstruction of deontology tends to eliminate the very Kantian fundaments, the moral autonomy and the categorical imperative. A possible role of the ethicist expert, including the ethics supervisor, would be of (re)construction of professional autonomy, and the practitioner's capacity of moral agent, by matching his/her own moral standards with those of the organisation, namely of the professional community.

The qualitative study on ethical dilemmas in the practice of social work conducted in Australia, focused on the way of understanding, evaluating and reacting to an ethical climate, within the staff in the organisations, with specific in the social services, as well as on the way in which the professionals can protect their clients, but also themselves, of the risk of injury or legal and disciplinary liability, being based on ethical considerations.

FUTURE RESEARCH DIRECTIONS

We support the need for awareness of the need for ethics expertise. In this regard, the future research directions can target the ethical acceptability of the professional behaviour. Such a research can be approached in a deconstructive manner, under the idea of *moral minimalism* and ethical standards with universalist claims.

In our efforts to develop a new model of ethics expertise to successfully apply in the area of social services, we find it important to establish ethics committees in organisations of social services. We here refer to the ethical analysis of instruments and strategies of intervention that the case managers apply to the beneficiaries, the central ethical issue being represented by the analysis of conditions of ethical acceptability of social intervention.

CONCLUSION

We briefly outlined some of the ethical theories that can underlie the development of ethics expertise models, in order to offer a perspective on the relationship between ethical theories and ethical issues that may emerge in the practice of any professional field, namely in social work. The ethical dilemmas can appear in the professionals' everyday practice, when the specialist faces at least with two systems of ethical reasoning, being necessary to choose the system of beliefs that optimizes the given situation.

Each of the theories or ethical practices that practices or systems are grounded on, may also be a point of reference in the ethical reasoning and judgment of specialists in different fields of expertise, the final ethical decision being able to be based on one or more of the ethical theories.

REFERENCES

Abrudan, E. (2011). Ethical Expertise and Bioethics. *Journal for Study of Religions and Ideologies*, *10*(30), 399–402.

Aristotle. (1988). *Etica Nicomahică* (S. Petecel, Trans.). Bucharest: Ştiinţifică şi Enciclopedică Publishing House.

Beauchamp, T. L., & Childress, J. F. (2001). *Principles of Biomedical Ethics* (5th ed.). New York: Oxford University Press.

Bentham, J. (1970). *Introduction to the Principles of Morals and Legislation* (2nd ed.). London: Athlone Press.

Berlin, I. (2002). *Liberty: Incorporating Four Essays on Liberty* (2nd ed.). Oxford: Oxford University Press. doi:10.1093/019924989X.001.0001

Cozma, C. (2001). Introducere în aretelogie, Mic tratat de etică [Introduction in aretheology. Small ethics treaty]. Iasi: "Alexandru Ioan Cuza" University Publishing.

Eggleston, B. (2005). The Ineffable and the Incalculable: G.E. Moore on Ethical Expertise. In L. M. Rasmussen (Ed.), *Ethics Expertise: History, Contemporary Perspectives, and Applications* (pp. 89–102). Springer, Netherlands. doi:10.1007/1-4020-3820-8_6

Elliot, E. A. (2016). Craft consumption and consumer transformation in a transmodern era. *Journal of Business Research*, *69*(1), 18–24. doi:10.1016/j.jbusres.2015.07.016

Friele, M. B. (2003). Do Committees Ru(i)n the Bio-Political Culture? On the Democratic Legitimacy of Bioethics Committees. *Bioethics*, *17*(4), 301–308. doi:10.1111/1467-8519.00347 PMID:14567389

Goodin, R. (2006). Utilitatea şi binele [Usefulness and good]. In P. Singer (Ed.), *Tratat de etică* [Treaty of ethics] (pp. 268–276). Iasi, Romania: Polirom.

Jonas, H. (1984). The Imperative of Responsibility. In *Search of an Ethics for the Technological Age*. Chicago: University of Chicago Press.

Jones, K., & Schroeter, F. (2012). Moral Expertise. *Analyse & Kritik*, *2*, 217–230.

Kant, I. (1972). *Critica rațiunii practice* [The criticism of practical reasoning]. Bucharest: Ştiinţifică Publishing.

Lipovetsky, G. (2007). *Fericirea paradoxală. Eseu asupra societățiide hiperconsum* [Paradoxal happiness. Essay on the society of hyperconsummerism] (M. Ungurean, Trans.). Iasi: Polirom.

Long, J. E. (2017). Beyond Bathsheba: Managing Ethical Climates Through Pragmatic Ethics. *The Journal of Values-Based Leadership*, *10*(2), 14. doi:10.22543/0733.102.1194

McAuliffe, D. (2002). *Social Work Ethics Audits: A New Tool for Ethical Practice*. Retrieved from http://citeseerx.ist.psu.edu/viewdoc/download?doi=10.1.1.202.1345&rep=rep1&type=pdf

Mill, J. S. (1871). *Utilitarianism* (4th ed.). London: Longmans, Green, Reader, and Dyer.

Moore, G. E. (1993). *Principia Ethica*. Cambridge, UK: Cambridge University Press.

Morar, V. (2006). Etica şi afacerile. Morală elementară şi responsabilitate socială [Ethics and business. Elementary morals and social responsibility]. Bucharest: Universității Publishing.

Mureşan, V. (2007). Este etica aplicată, o aplicare a eticii? [Is applied ethics and appliance of ethics?]. *Revista de Filosofie Analitică*, *I*(1), 70–108.

Nobel, C. (1982). Ethics and Experts. *The Hastings Center Report*, *12*(3), 7–8. doi:10.2307/3561822 PMID:7107239

O'Neill, O. (2006). Etica lui Kant. In P. Singer (Ed.), *Tratat de etică* [Treaty of ethics] (pp. 204–215). Iasi: Polirom.

Pence, G. (2006). Teoria virtuții. In P. Singer (Ed.), *Tratat de etică* [Treaty of ethics] (pp. 277–288). Iasi: Polirom.

Pettit, P. (2006). Consecinţialismul. In P. Singer (Ed.), *Tratat de etică* [Treaty of ethics] (pp. 258–268). Iasi: Polirom.

Powers, M. (2005). Bioethics as Politics: The Limits of Moral Expertise. *Kennedy Institute of Ethics Journal*, *15*(3), 305–322. doi:10.1353/ken.2005.0023 PMID:16250118

Reamer, F. G. (2006). *Social Work Values and Ethics* (3rd ed.). New York: Columbia University Press.

Reck, B. (2003). *Between Democracy and Technocracy. The Role of Expertise for the European Parliament*. Stuttgart: Ibidem- Verlag.

Reidenbach, R. E., & Donald, P. R. (1990). Toward the Development of a Multidimensional Scale for Improving Evaluations of Business Ethics. *Journal of Business Ethics*, *9*(8), 639–653. doi:10.1007/BF00383391

Schicktanz, S., Schweda, M., & Wynne, B. (2012). The Ethics of Public Understanding of Ethics—Why and How Bioethics Expertise Should Include Public and Patients Voices. *Medicine, Health Care, and Philosophy*, *15*(2), 129–139. doi:10.1007/s11019-011-9321-4 PMID:21448745

Schumann, P. L. (2001). A Moral Principles Framework for Human Resource Management Ethics. *Human Resource Management Review*, *11*(1-2), 93–111. doi:10.1016/S1053-4822(00)00042-5

Singer, P. (1979). *Practical Ethics*. Cambridge, UK: Cambridge University Press.

Singer, P., & Wells, D. (1984). *The Reproductive Revolution: New Ways of Making Babies*. Oxford, UK: Oxford University Press.

Södergren, C. (2014). *Organisations: A Battle for Life, in the Name of Globalisation. Communication for Development One-year Master, 15 Credits, Spring 2014, Supervisor: Michael Krona, Faculty of Culture and Society*. Malmö University.

Yoder, S. D. (1998). The Nature of Ethical Expertise. *The Hastings Center Report*, *28*(6), 11–19. doi:10.2307/3528262 PMID:9868604

Zwart, H. (2012). Ethical Expertise in Policy. In R. Chadwick (Ed.), *Encyclopedia of Applied Ethics* (2nd ed.; pp. 157–164). San Diego, CA: Academic Press. doi:10.1016/B978-0-12-373932-2.00006-5

KEY TERMS AND DEFINITIONS

Ethical Acceptability (Interdictive Acception): Who wishes to establish minimal criteria accepted for social action, which once violated, lead to the moral refection of that action.

Ethical Acceptability (Minimalist Acception): Those limitations in which a certain practice cannot be ethically accepted. The concept of acceptability can be seen from many perspectives.

Ethical Acceptability (Utilitarian Acception): A balance between subjective welfare and discomfort generated by social action.

Chapter 2
The Role of the Core Moral Values in Social Work

Sorin-Tudor Maxim
Stefan cel Mare University of Suceava, Romania

ABSTRACT

We consider it appropriate to examine, within the social work act, under the new circumstances, the importance of other than traditional values which tend to become central, that human intervention relates to. In this particular context, tolerance, understood as a respect for different, but human lifestyles, and the empathy, as a way to meet real, not "presumed" expectations, of individuals and groups, have the ability to restructure the system of values of social work able to allow a different approach in order to achieve the human condition.

INTRODUCTION

The changes taking place in the contemporary world have an unprecedented effect on the society as a whole, but in particular, on the value system to which the individual relates. This implies that, in a society whose fundamental feature is the change – in which the stability only seems to be an "accident" – are imposed new standards and criteria for assessing the importance of a values system, axiological accepted, as well as in value hierarchies of a certain field of social action.

BACKGROUND: ON THE ROLE AND IMPORTANCE OF CENTRAL VALUES IN SOCIAL BECOMING

The materialistic thinking seeks for the mechanisms of social progress in an objective determinism in which the economic dimension, the "relations of production" – in the

DOI: 10.4018/978-1-5225-3090-9.ch002

Marxist interpretation – are revealed as decisive. An opposing view is supported by spiritualist philosophy, which accredits the idea that the dimension of consciousness is responsible for the development of the society, and not that much of the material factor of social life.

Both perspectives can be penalized if we reject the above-mentioned unilateral explanations, considering that the radical restructuring of the hierarchy of values– values that belong to the objective-subjective are causing social progress and give its measure. The restructuration of the axiological system of a society around new "core values" is likely to also impart a new direction to the progress of humanity as a whole.

In such an understanding of social becoming, we support the idea that: a) during Greek and Roman civilizations, the central values were the moral ones[1]; b) the axiological system of Middle Ages is built around religious values[2]; c) the values of the reason are capital in the modern period- "Knowledge becomes otherwise the supreme ethical value and the central value of the system of values" (Boboc, 1984, p. 380); d) the establishment of economical values corresponds to the affirmation of capitalism, centred on efficiency and entrepreneurial spirit, as dominant values for the axiological system and, consequently, for the entire social becoming; e) political values, as essential values, are related to the communist period from the history of humanity; f) for the knowledge society, in which we entered and which we intend to develop in the foreseeable future, is characterized by moral and religious values. A whole axiological system is restructured around these ones, which also determines a new configuration of the structure of social action (Sandu, 2016a).

The undeniable feature of contemporary theoretical discourse is recovering the moral thinking, as the central concern of any systematic reflection on the social dimension: "A name, an ideal, unites consciousnesses and animates again the Western democracies in this end of millennium: the ethics", stated Gilles Lipovetsky (1993) ever since the last decade of the last century.

How could it be otherwise when in a knowledge-based society, where everyone knows what is essential about the others, both at the individual and organization level, the fact of having an attitude devoid of morality is revealed to be even "counterproductive" in the medium and long term, for personal development and, consequently, for the overall success of social action.

By accepting this understanding of the decisive role of moral values in the value system of our society, we must assume that for the social assistance as well, the core values, to which one should relate, must be searched for in the field of morality (Sandu, 2016b, pp. 28-47).

CORE VALUES OF SOCIAL WORK IN A CHANGING WORLD

We will hereafter try to support the idea that certain core values (Sandu, 2015), around which social action is structured in a field, are responsible for defining the direction and success of this action in the context of the social ensemble.

One remark: I consider *the core values of the action of social assistance*, as part of the social action system and not the values of *the profession of social assistant.*

In this second case, of professional values, the social assistance builds its value system on "two essential prerequisites: a) the belief in the uniqueness and dignity of every person; b) the belief in the customer's right to self-determination" (Alexiu, 2011, p. 536). As a matter of fact, in the same remarkable work, George Neamțu (2011) also identifies *two core values,* that represent the support of both the professional values and principles of intervention of any social assistant, in about the same register, starting from the respect of the human being's dignity and integrity, namely from the recognition of democracy as an essential requirement of social life (Apostu, 2012; 2013). Nevertheless, both authors note that for a human activity to be recognized – as a profession also – it should relate to the society in general, and this necessary connection is only possible by searching their own *core values* through the values which are determinant for the axiological system of the society under scrutiny.

Some Concerns Regarding the Core Values of Social Work

By accepting that the core values of our society are moral-religious (neither moral nor religious, and not even religious-moral), with emphasis on the ethical aspect and noting that many of the challenges of the new society are other than those of societies that belong to the past history of mankind, we look at the possibility of supporting tolerance and empathy as core values for the entire approach of social action.

In other words, social assistance in a society dominated by economic values, seeks its own core values in this dimension, focusing on efficiency or on what is financially sustainable; as in a society centred on political values, is understandable that the core values of this activity will target what is politically desirable, promoting, for example, the activity of support, not that of assistance (of subsistence, not of prevention) (Terec-Vlad & Cucu, 2016).

Thus, reporting to other core values, derived from the dominant values of a particular axiological system of a society, can change the meaning and perspective of human action in a specific area of social intervention.

An examination/assessment of the present situation, and of the one towards which our society is evolving, is likely to potentiate the theoretical project proposed.

1. A key feature of the current society is change. This is *the new normality*, and stability seems to be just an accident. Then, it seems natural that social assistance efforts (fundamentally centred on prevention), prepares the individual not for integration in a given society, but for change.
2. The models of existence become themselves fluid and are in dissolution, and the acceptance of other options, or thinking of different ways of expressing the human condition, becomes acceptable provided they are kept within human limits.
3. The knowledge-based society is likely to promote a new type of information colonialism: who has the information has the power – so prevention in social assistance must move toward those who, realistically, will not be able to cope with the change. Some because they cannot do it; others because they lack the necessary means – getting excellent knowledge involves holding exceptional resources – finally, others because they do not want to do it either they do not want to give up their own way of life, or do not accept the globalizing, but also levelling world which is coming into play.
4. Finally, we are faced with phenomena likely to generate deep uncertainty and insecurity: the large gaps in the developing countries of the world, as well as the planetary distribution of financial resources, is enhancing; the sources of conflict are multiplying; there is a danger of a new information warfare, in which the threats do not come by air any longer, by bombs but through the floor, through the networks which transfer and modify information; fundamentalist threats of all kinds are multiplying, and they accentuate the risk factors to the limit of endurance; insecurities are amplified, along with a predictive quasi-impossibility, even in the short term. There is a not very attractive picture that stands in front of us; and it is a picture in relation to which we are not only viewers, but even main characters. The stress and the exhaustion, the dissatisfaction generated by never fulfilled expectations, the requirements that emerge for all the social partners seem to always accompany our way towards individual and collective development, in the new society.

The solution? "In order to survive and succeed, everyone will have to turn into an agent of change. The most effective way to generate change is to determine it" (Drucker, 2004, p. 283). In order to determine the change, we need to act at the level of mentalities, behaviours, attitudes, all of them arising from the restructuring of the system of values and norms which individuals and groups adhere to (Terec-Vlad, 2016, pp. 79-89).

Contextually, tolerance and empathy are revealed as two central values in relation to which the entire axiological system of social assistance must reconsider its position.

A. Tolerance. Prejudices about the so-called civilized ways of living compared to other rated as marginal or unacceptable are not likely to facilitate the dialogue, nor to identify solutions through which everyone who is in need would be supported, to be performed in the manner that *he* finds acceptable, of course – I repeat – if kept within boundaries of humanity. "Our world is characterized by the multiplicity of languages, religions, cultures and traditions which, despite the rationality grounded in science, valid for all – ultimately, even because of it – is a problem of tolerance" (Gadamer, 1999, p. 86).

It is not the authority of a society – which the perverse effect of continuous changes deprives of the legitimacy provided by customs and traditions – that will impose unique cultural patterns of life and the inoculation through education, both institutionalized and within the community, of the respect for values correlated to the tolerant spirit: mutual trust, responsibility for each other, prudence and temperance, solidarity and humanity, desire for dialogue and collaboration.

All this must begin with a joint effort to promote "a certain style, characterized by kindness, courtesy, caution, a style required by the weakness of human self-consciousness that we have to assume for each and every one of us" (Gadamer, 1999, p. 86).

The demand that the central value of tolerance in the system of social assistance, correlated with the value of empathy, imposes to human action, is to adopt a different way of being, more authentically human and more adjusted to the need to face the change: being for the others.

B. Empathy is the ability to resonate with the desires, likes and aspirations of the other. Even if it is ambiguous and leaves room for multiple interpretations in Romanian, the concept suggests the individual's ability to put himself in someone else's place, in order to better understand what this latter expects from life, not what you believe it is good for him. The correlative values are compassion, empathy, sympathy, generosity, kindness.

However, within the charitable actions proper to social assistance, all these virtues acquire significance of value only if revolves around the central value of empathy. Otherwise, compassion turns into a sterile personal interpretation of the other's unhappiness; sympathy, into a vague and devoid of solutions attitude of "being close" to the aspirations of the other; generosity becomes a pointless exercise to give to the other something that is yours, but that he does not need; not least, good will not keep the human action away from danger, knowing that "the road to hell is paved with good intentions".

Specifically, reported to empathy, generosity does not mean anymore to assign what you have to the other, as Spinoza argued, speaking of social justice, but to offer him what is yours and he really lacks (translated into goods or in the need of care or sympathy capital). Empathy is *the foundation* of agreement because otherwise we are almost never ready *in both directions* to face the meeting between us.

CONCLUSION

In our moments of complete lucidity, we are aware that the truth does not belong to us, and it does not belong to the other either, but it is *the meeting* between us which enriches us both. Then, empathy is the path that brings us together. Otherwise, we will always be loneliness near loneliness, isolation besides isolation, increasing, until difficultly acceptable limits, the stress and inadequacy in front of changes of all kinds. The society of "together" is the only response to the challenges and uncertainties of the future. It is the world of tolerance and empathy.

REFERENCES

Alexiu, T. M. (2011). Values and Phases of Action in Social Assistance. In *Treaty of social assistance*. Iasi: Polirom Publishing House.

Apostu, I. (2012). Consensual Union in Romania. Legalization, Value, Conflict and Consequences. *European Journal of Science and Theology, 8*(Supp. 1), 303-312.

Apostu, I. (2013). The Traditionalism of the Modern Family – Social and Legal Directions and Contradictions. *Procedia: Social and Behavioral Sciences, 92*, 46–49. doi:10.1016/j.sbspro.2013.08.635

Boboc, A. (1984). *The History of Modern and Contemporaneous Philosophy* (Vol. 1). Bucharest: Academiei RSR Publishing House.

Drucker, P. F. (2004). *Management of Future*. Bucharest: ASAB Publishing House.

Gadamer, H. G. (1999). *The Eulogy of Theory. The Heritage of Europe*. Iasi: Polirom Publishing House.

Lipovetsky, G. (1993). *Le Crépuscule du devoir: l'éthique indeloire des noveaux temps démocratiques*. Gallimard.

Neamțu, G. (2011). *Treaty of social assistance*. Iasi: Polirom Publishing House.

Sandu, A. (2015). Philosophical Practice and Values Based Ethics: Rethinking Social Action and Core Values, Philosophical Practice. *Journal of the American Philosophical Practitioners, 10*(3), 1618–1631.

Sandu, A. (2016a). *Social Construction of Reality as Communicative Action*. Cambridge Scholars Publishing.

Sandu, A. (2016b). A Levinasian Opening on the Affirmative Ethics of Care. *Journal for the Study of Religions and Ideologies, 15*(43), 28–47.

Terec-Vlad, L. (2016). The Principle of Responsibility towards the Human Non-Presence or the Non-Human Presence. *Postmodern Openings*, *7*(2), 79–89. doi:10.18662/po/2016.0702.06

Terec-Vlad, L. & Cucu, M. (2016). Ethics and Organizational Culture – Key Elements regarding the Development of Economic Activities. *Ecoforum Journal*, *5*(8), 192-198.

ENDNOTES

1 Stoics still noted that all the other values must render an account to moral values; these ones do not have to render an account to anyone.

2 The cross and the sword (itself cross shaped) are prominent symbols of the era.

Chapter 3
Social Work Between Individualism and Collectivism

Dan Ioan Dascalu
Stefan cel Mare University of Suceava, Romania

ABSTRACT

The purpose of this chapter is to present several viewpoints concerning the way in which the individualism and collectivism as ideologies or ethic options meet, confront, and complete each other in the social work activity. We consider that a debate on this subject is all the more necessary in Romania at present time, when our country has transitioned, in the past few decades, from the communist collectivism to the market economy and democracy, namely to an economic and political system that intrinsically implies the predominance of the values of individualism. We aim at bringing some arguments in favour of the idea that, in social work, both the individualism and collectivism are not two antagonistic perspectives, that are not mutually exclusive but can coexist, and even complete each other. The social work contemporary systems are based on a different type of social solidarity, which does not exclude the individualism but integrate it as one of the fundamental values of social work.

INTRODUCTION: INDIVIDUALISM AND SOCIAL WORK

At a first glance, it would seem that individualistic thinking is contradictory to the idea of social assistance. It is a viewpoint that has been theorized since the nineteenth century, by H. Spencer (1876; 1884). The extreme individualism of the English sociologist has undergone, ever since that time, very severe criticism (see, for example, Durkheim, 1987; 2007). We believe

DOI: 10.4018/978-1-5225-3090-9.ch003

that, in the contemporary world, such a viewpoint is totally outdated, and that, on the contrary, the values of individualism can be a starting point for building up social assistance systems. We have in view, on the one hand, the transformations individualism has undergone as a social worldview, which G. Lipovetsky called the second individualistic revolution (1983), the conception of individualism as a real humanism (De Singly, 2007), but also the fact that, ultimately, the objectives of individualism are fully compatible with those of social assistance.

We are witnessing today, all around the world, debates over the social assistance system and attempts to reform it. Of course, these efforts are also related to the fact that the model of the welfare state has proved that it has pretty serious limitations, and to the fact that the current economic and financial crisis leaves an increasingly oppressive mark on the whole world. The sovereign debts of states have skyrocketed, sometimes over the limit to which they can still be bearable, and the requirement to reduce public expenditures has become a command widely accepted by most governments. In this context, the rethinking of the social assistance system and reducing costs in this field are major concerns in the field of public policies.

We think that the reforming of the social assistance system should also include a resumption of the debate on the values that underpin this system. But the issue we want to focus on is part of this very topic. More specifically, we try to express some views on how values of individualism can be a starting point and a support in reshaping the social assistance system. We believe that the relationship between individualism and social assistance has, in Romania, and in other former communist countries, a particular meaning, which is related to the profound transformations from the post-communist transition period, transformations that obviously affect the social assistance system as well.

On a general level, it seems we can speak, in the late twentieth and early twenty-first century, about a revival of individualism. Some call it "second individualistic revolution" (Lipovetsky, 1983, p. 19), different from the modern era. It is a new individualism, with a system of values and behavior patterns which are slightly different. To the process of rethinking individualism and its expansion have contributed a series of processes that marked society in recent decades. Among them, we can mention globalization, the imposition of consumerism all over the world, the affirmation of the knowledge-based society, but also the fall of communism in Eastern Europe.

BACKGROUND: INDIVIDUALISM AND SOCIAL SOLIDARITY TO THE CLASSICAL SOCIOLOGISTS

When it comes to common knowledge, the contradiction between individualism and social assistance seems obvious, because individualism is usually mistaken for selfishness and it is, therefore, the opposite of altruism, which is a constituent of social assistance. We are dealing with a social representation of individualism that gives us actually an impoverished image of it, if not a completely erroneous one. Individualism does not necessarily mean selfishness, just as collectivism does not necessarily imply altruism. It is a deliberate confusion, dating, it seems, from Plato, which is linked to the defence of collectivism as a system of political values (Popper, 2000). However, this does not mean that in certain individualistic visions on society, selfishness does not have an important place. Moreover, some representatives of individualism reject the idea of social assistance. This is the case of H. Spencer, for example, one of the fathers of sociology, an advocate of individualism inspired from British classical economists, but also of social Darwinism. Spencer wrote, in 1884: "The sympathy for someone suffering, suppresses, as long as it lasts, the memory of their mistakes... When talking about the miseries of the poor, we think of the miseries of the unfair poor, instead of thinking about the miseries of the poor who deserve their fate, way in which we should behave to a great extent... They are simply people living on the backs of hardworking people – tramps and drunks, criminals, young people who are the burden of their hard-working parents, men who depend on their wives' wages... Is it not obvious that there must be, among us, a great iota of misery that is the normal result of wickedness and the proof that misery cannot disassociate itself from mischief? There is nowadays the idea that any social suffering can be eliminated and it is the duty of everyone to remove it. Both these beliefs are false" (Spencer, 1996). We have given this large quote, even if it may seem odious by its cynicism, in order to understand a certain position in front of social assistance, a position that belongs to a representative of individualism, of an individualism that we could call extreme.

In fact, Spencer's position was heavily criticized ever since it appeared. Durkheim is one of those who did that, based on a thorough analysis of the sociological underpinnings of Spencerian individualism.

The two classical sociologists suggest, in fact, two different theories on social solidarity and try to show the differences between modern society and traditional societies. Two different paradigms come out of it for the understanding of social solidarity, and for the understanding and acceptance of individualism. And in terms of the topic that we proposed in this paper, the two positions, that of Spencer and that of Durkheim, seem to be located at the extremes of a continuum that includes theories on individualism.

Universally recognized as a value and as a general principle in social work practice, solidarity refers both to a state of affairs, to the cohesion of a particular society or social group, and to a subjective state, the awareness of the individual belonging to the whole social branch under scrutiny (Alexiu, 2003). Of course, there are different theories on what forms the social "glue", which unites people and makes them feel that they belong to the same social body. Obviously, the social assistance, supporting, helping individuals or groups in need of that society is done on behalf of their belonging to the social body, respectively, in the name of maintaining its cohesion (Norbert, 1991). In this way the effort made by society as a whole can be justified, or by each member of it in order to solve the social problems of those in need (Rosanvallon, 1998). Moreover, solidarity can and should be linked to other values involved by social assistance, altruism, for example, or generosity, and, not least, it is also the basis of individual and collective responsibility and configures the dimensions of the debt.

Both collectivist and individualist visions on the society tried to define social solidarity, to find the social glue that underpins it. Individualism, as an ideology, is wrongly perceived as "a cause of refolding on oneself, of selfishness, of indifference to the other, of impoliteness" (De Singly, 2003), therefore it is believed to be opposed to the idea of social solidarity.

Herbert Spencer, in *Principles of Sociology*, and then in *The Individual against the State*, tries to distinguish the manner in which traditional and modern societies are constituted. The first ones are called military societies, and the other ones industrial societies. In both cases, the English sociologist explains how the social structure is formed, how people cooperate to achieve common goals. "The cooperation preserving the life of military societies is a mandatory cooperation. The social structure that can handle hostile neighbouring societies is dominated by a centralized regulator, to which all parties are completely subordinated" (Spencer, 1891). The social glue is thus fear, threatening, the state of war, and social unity is nothing compared to the whole. In the case of industrial societies, the cooperation is autonomous and spontaneous, based only on the interests of the society. In both types of society, the basis of the aggregation, the binder, is cooperation, so, it is, in fact, the social division of labour. What is different is the way in which it is imposed, either from outside, in a compulsory manner, as in the case of military societies, over the will of their members, or from inside, from the particular interests of members of society, without being imposed by anyone in industrial societies.

Durkheim, in his turn, talks about two kinds of solidarity, the mechanical solidarity and the organic solidarity, corresponding to the two types of society, the traditional one and the modern one. In the first case we deal with solidarity deriving from similarities. There is a more or less organized set of beliefs and feelings common to all group members. It is a collective society. "Ideas and beliefs common to all members of the society exceed in number and intensity those belonging personally to each and every one of them" (Durkheim, 2007). "The social molecules that would be consistent only in this manner could not move together unless they have their own movements, as the molecules of inorganic bodies do" (Durkheim, 2007). In the societies where this solidarity is highly developed, the individual does not belong to himself, it is an object held by the society. The second type of solidarity is produced by the division of labour. If in the first case, individuals must be alike, in the second, they must be distinguished from one another. In the first case, the individual personality is absorbed by the collective personality, in the second one, solidarity is not possible unless each one has its personality, its own sphere of activity. The collective consciousness should also let a part of individual consciousness be revealed. The higher this part is, the stronger the cohesion is. "On the one hand, each one depends more on society as labour is more divided, and on the other hand, everyone's activity is all the more personal as it becomes more specialized" (Durkheim, 2007). This movements of social molecules resembles the ones that we see in superior animals' behaviours, hence the name of organic solidarity. To the two types of solidarity correspond two types of societies, that develop contrarily, while the one is regressing, the other is progressing.

The French sociologist makes a thorough critique of Spencer's theory. Even if both start from the fact that individual's role in society increases, even though they admit that the division of labour is the one that produces solidarity in developed societies, the conclusions are different. One of the most criticized aspects is the issue of selfishness and the one of altruism. Spencer believes that selfishness is the starting point of humanity, whereas altruism is seen as a recent acquisition, with the influence of Darwinism, applied to society, seeming obvious. Durkheim shows that wherever there is a society, there is altruism, because there is solidarity, and he says there is even more noticeable in primitive societies, where it is excessive at times, and in more developed societies there is more selfishness.

As regards Durkheim, we deal with a "paradoxical individualism" (Jankélevitch, 1987). In a paper, he summarizes this paradox in the following way: to be individualistic and to say, however, that the individual is a product of society. Both his sociological theory and his method are, obviously, holistic. He rejects utilitarism and also the concept of Smith's "invisible hand". Individualism of this kind is denied as an incorrect theory about the genesis of society, as an ideology that generates moral anarchy and threatens social harmony, but at the same time, it claims to represent a different kind of individualism, "the one of Kant and Rousseau, the one of spiritualists, whom the Declaration of Human Rights tried, more or less happily, to translate into formulas, the one that is taught in our schools and which became the basis of our moral catechism" (Durkheim, 1987). Individualism interpreted in this way is "the praise, not of the ego, but of the individual in general. It does not imply selfishness, but sympathy for all that is human, a wide mile for all the human pain and misery, a more ardent need to combat them and sweeten them, a greater thirst for justice" (Durkheim, 1987). Obviously, we can add that such individualism is fully consistent with what social assistance intends to be.

The debates over individualism have a fairly long history and they run across the entire modernity. As Georg Simmel showed, a century ago, individualism is a feature of modern Western thought. That does not mean that there is a unique insight upon it. We can rather talk about individualisms. Modernity has imposed individualism as an ideology, as the foundation of economic and political thought. It is politically bound to the capitalist market economy and democracy. The classical economists (Adam Smith, for example) felt that the full affirmation of the individual and of his interests in the economic life, a minimized state involvement in economic life, very few limitations, ensure the individual and collective progress and welfare. The invisible hand acts to achieve individual interests in order to accomplish collective interests. Modern theories of democracy give to the individual and to his interests the central role in the political system. In this perspective, individualism is linked to ensuring political participation and the respect of human rights (Comte-Sponville, 1995). The whole history of democratization, from classical modernity to recent modernity (we prefer this term to the one of post-modernity), is actually dominated by these requirements.

THE CONTEMPORARY INDIVIDUALISM

There is, in the twentieth century, which is largely dominated by collectivist ideologies, a certain lack of theoretical benefit for individualism. The failure of totalitarian political regimes, purely collectivist, but also the changes in the economic, political and social life, the increased democratization, the stronger affirmation of the need to respect human rights, the consumerism, the technological development, the general rise in welfare, lead, in the second half of the twentieth century, to a revival in the interest in individualism.

Given the goal we have proposed in this paper, we believe it is necessary to accept a "broader" definition of individualism. Such a definition is given to us by L. Dumont: "We designate as individualistic, as opposed to holism, an ideology that values the individual and neglects or subordinates the social complexity" (Dumont, 1983).

The contemporary individualism, G. Lipovetski writes, is characterized by the "personalization process" (1983). This customization involves, at the level of society, the minimum of constraints for the individual and, at the same time, ensuring as many choices as possible, as little coercion and as much understanding as possible. The customizing "promotes and embodies a fundamental value, of the personal fulfilment, of the respect of objective singularity, of incomparable personality, whatever forms of control and homogenisation we may be talking about" (Lipovetsky, 1983).

Such a way of looking at individualism excludes the opposition often practiced, especially at the level of common sense, between individualism and humanism. "With the model of an emancipated individual, individualism is humanism, projecting an ideal world, wherein each human being is able to develop and to become himself" (De Singly, 2003).

Even if individualism apparently emerged as the dominant ideology in contemporary society, even if it is no longer mistaken for mere selfishness, even if we talk about the diversity of "individualisms" and about the variety and complexity of individualism of the past few decades, we should not see individualism as a vision of the world able to solve all its problems, as a redemptive ideology, which does not create any negative social effects. We talked, and we are still talking about these negative effects on man and society. There is no place here for a review of their impact. Let us remember, however, the "positive individualism" and "negative individualism" that J.-P. Fitoussi and P. Rosanvallon wrote about. According to them, modern individualism is, at the same time, "a vector of emancipation of individuals, developing their autonomy and making the individuals to rightfully bear it and a factor of insecurity, making each one responsible for their future, compelling them to give life a sense that no one else organize" (Fitoussi & Rosanvallon, 1999). We are, therefore, talking about "the individualization-emancipation which is also doubled by an individuation-embrittlement" (Fitoussi & Rosanvallon, 1999).

CONCLUSION

Beyond these negative implications of individualism, and we refer here to the individualism of contemporary societies, we can conclude that the values proposed are not conflicting with values and principles that underpin social assistance. Moreover, some of the values promoted by individualism are included in the system of values and principles of social assistance.

Individualism does not exclude social solidarity, even if individual interests are the main binder ensuring social cohesion. In fact, from the nineteenth century so far, the forms of social solidarity evolved, the principles and the mechanisms underlying them are evolving as well. The erosion of the welfare state model, at the end of last century, imposes a rethinking of the values and mechanisms of social solidarity. Some talk about a dual solidarity. "For taxpayers – economically and socially useful – solidarity is based on insurance, involving reciprocity between equals. For non-taxpayers, solidarity takes the form of welfare services, the allocation of goods and services is made from taxpayers to non-taxpayers, the latter having a condition that does not allow reciprocity. Human Rights constitute the core value of this solidarity" (Soulet, 2004).

If as regards social solidarity, the core value is social assistance, we can see that it is in no way contradictory to the values of individualism, and even current forms of solidarity are based on these values, for others (such as: the respect of dignity and uniqueness of the individual, the customer empowerment, the non-discrimination, the individual approach etc.) we can say they are either expressly considered as being values promoted by individualism, or that they are derived, by default, from the economic and political context imposed by individualism, that is the market economy, the democracy, the human rights.

If the values of individualism seem to impose themselves in our country in this transitional period, they obviously put their mark more and more on the social assistance system and on the reforms that this system implements.

REFERENCES

Alexiu, M. (2003). Valori şi faze ale acţiunii în asistenţa socială [Values and phases of action in social work]. In *Tratat de asistenţă socială* [Treaty of Social Work] (pp. 319–365). Iaşi: Ed. Polirom.

Comte-Sponville, A. (1995). *Petit Traité des grandes vertus*. Paris: P.U.F.

De Singly, F. (2003). *Les uns avec les autres. Quand l'individualisme crée du lien*. Paris: Ed. Hachette.

De Singly, F. (2007). *L'individualisme est un humanisme*. Paris: Éditions de l'Aube.

Dumond, L. (1983). *Essais sur l'individualisme. Une perspective anthropologique sur l'idéologie moderne*. Paris: Éditions du Seuil.

Durkheim, É. (1987). L'individualisme et les intellectuels. Paris: Ed. Mille et une nuits. (originally published 1898)

Durkheim, É. (2007). Diviziunea muncii sociale [The division of social work]. Bucharest: Ed. Antet. (originally published 1893)

Fitoussi, J.-P., & Rosanvallon, P. (1999). Noua epocă a inegalităţilor [New era of inequalities]. Iaşi: Institutul European. (originally published 1996)

Jankélevitch, S. (1987). Un individualisme paradoxal? In E. Durkheim (Ed.), L'individualisme et les intellectuels (pp. 45-64). Paris: Ed. Mille et une nuits.

Lipovetsky, G. (1983). *L'ère du vide. Essais sur l'individualisme contemporain.* Paris: Galimard.

Norbert, E. (1991). La société des individus. Paris: Librairie Arthème Fayard. (originally published 1939)

Popper, K. R. (2000). Individualism versus colectivism. In K. R. Popper (Ed.), Filosofie socială şi filosofia ştiinţei [Social philosophy and philosophy of science] (pp. 362-374). Bucharest: Trei Publishing. (originally published 1945)

Rosanvallon, P. (1998). *Noua problemă socială* [The new social problem]. Iaşi: European Institute. (Original work published 1995)

Soulet, M.-H. (2004). Ce valori, ce practici ale solidarităţii? [What values, what practices of solidarity?]. In A. Vilbrod & I. Ionescu (Eds.), *Asistenţa socială în tranziţie* [Social work in transition] (pp. 23–33). Iaşi: European Institute.

Spencer, H. (1891). Principes de sociologie. Paris: Ed. Felix Alcan.

Spencer, H. (1996). Individul împotriva statului [The individual against the state]. Iaşi: Timpul Publishing. (originally published 1884)

Chapter 4
Ethical Grounding of Social Work Practices

Liranso G. Selamu
Mangalore University, India

Mohan S. Singhe
Mangalore University, India

ABSTRACT

Ethical awareness is fundamental to the professional practice of social workers. Their ability and commitment to act ethically is an essential aspect of the quality of the service offered to those who engage with social workers. Respect for human rights and a commitment to promoting social justice are at the core of social work practice throughout the world. Social work grew out of humanitarian and democratic ideals, and its values are based on respect for the equality, worth, and dignity of all people. Since its beginnings over a century ago, social work practice has focused on meeting human needs and developing human potential. Human rights and social justice serve as the motivation and justification for social work action. Therefore, this chapter included the ethical grounds in social work practices in a deep manner.

INTRODUCTION

Social work bases its methodology on a systematic body of evidence informed knowledge derived from research and practice evaluation, including local and indigenous knowledge specific to its context. It recognizes the complexity of interactions between human beings and their environment, and the capacity of people both to be affected by and to alter the multiple influences upon them including

DOI: 10.4018/978-1-5225-3090-9.ch004

bio-psychosocial factors. The social work profession draws on theories of human development and behavior and social systems to analyze complex situations and to facilitate individual, organizational, social and cultural changes.

On the other hand, social work practice addresses the barriers, inequities and injustices that exist in society. It responds to crises and emergencies as well as to everyday personal and social problems. These include counseling, clinical social work, group work, social pedagogical work, and family treatment and therapy as well as efforts to help people obtain services and resources in the community. Interventions also include agency administration, community organization and engaging in social and political action to impact social policy and economic development. Moreover, social work by its engagement with specific values and ethics determines the kind of social change that the profession wants to bring. Thus, by the use and interpretation of the professions values, the purpose of the profession is not abstract and could be identified in exploring practice. Through our common values and ethics we gain a common vision and a common identity that no one can take from us or criticize us for being unspecific. Through the professions common values and ethics a vision for change and its identity emerges. Thus criticisms aimed at suggesting social work lacks specificity or remains undefined are unfounded.

Although social work is not the only profession that is dedicated to the promotion of important values, its relationship with social policy, its holistic approach to human needs and its engagement with mutually opposed values create complicated ethical dilemmas. There is an apparent agreement in the literature that social work tries to practice among conflicting interests, and therefore complicated ethical dilemmas are common in every day social work practice (IFSW, 2005).

Furthermore, social works ethics and values are not a matter for finding goodness as Briskman (2001) says a place of innocence in social work practice. Rather, by focusing on ethical social work issues we acknowledge and identify a special characteristic of our professional identity, and we confirm the criteria by which effective or good social work practice is judged. In addition, we acknowledge the process of decision–making as a critical element of professional practice, which thereby necessitates that social workers have the knowledge and skills necessary to interpret the ethical underpinnings of practice.

BACKGROUND

Social Work and Ethics

There is a different form of social work entail different kinds of ethical problems. An approximate picture of the diversity of social work can be gained by asking what aspects the work covers. Social work can also be described from the viewpoint of how regulated it is by law, i.e., whether and to what degree there are elements of the exercise of public authority in the work. Another classification that mirrors a frequent discussion in social work can be made on the basis of methods and ways of working (Erik, 2006).

On the other hand, situations arise in social work that involves ethical dilemmas. Often these concerns the social worker professional's own self-understanding and appear in different variations in different fields of activity, some of them related to the matter of which aspect of the work ought to be the primary one. Dilemma is the risk of becoming insensitive, of exhibiting insufficient empathy or plain cynicism, arising from the problem culture encountered in social work, the stress and strains of the job, or disappointment over the behavior of clients. Another common dilemma is the objectifying of the client, who becomes merely another in the endless line of problematic citizens each day encountered, with the risk that each person's unique conditions and role as subject is reduced to a diagnosis to be cured or a case to be dispatched.

In addition, social work values are embodied in the profession's national and international codes of ethics. The Code comprises statements of values and ethical principles relating to human rights, social justice and professional integrity, followed by practice principles that indicate how the ethical principles should be applied in practice (BASW, 2012).

Besides, social work's identity has been commonly characterized as ambiguous; its role in the promotion of social justice questioned and its effectiveness lacking evidence. At the same time, there are others who argue that social work is a victim of an inhuman political and economical system which systematically structures an unjust society to undermine human rights. Ironically, social work as a part of the political mechanism is obligated to contribute to securing these. Ethical awareness, as a professional and/or personal skill, is thought to enable social workers to appropriately answer the question "who receives the benefit of social work practice" as a mechanism to evaluate practice, and defend social work's humanitarian character (Bowles et al., 2006; Feather, 2002; Clark, 2000; Fritzche, 1995).

However, multiple ethical barriers or obligations create dilemmas in social workers" efforts to pursue their professional purposes. Ethical dilemmas reflect the complexity of the social work profession in terms of several factors such as its purposes and the multiple loyalties of social workers. This section presents fundamental ethical dilemmas of social work practice in relation to ambiguities and ethical obligations of the profession. In addition, ethical decision-making is also presented as an inherent part of social work practice, especially when social workers act upon their dilemmas in the form of moral judgments or decisions.

Moreover, people who need social work services are often among some of the most vulnerable in society. This is one of the main reasons that social workers must be sensitive to the ways that they provide their services. Social workers" decisions often have far-reaching consequences for peoples" lives. Therefore, social work practice must be guided by transparent, understandable principles (Parker, 2004). In this sense, social work education should be approached in an ethical, reflective and value based manner so as to ensure that people are not exploited, manipulated or made more vulnerable by social workers" actions. Consequently, social workers must be able to develop a competence in value based and ethical practice that includes values as a core element of their practice (Parker, 2004).

Social Work Values and Ethical Principles

Professional values are those embraced by the consensus of a body of practitioners given their relevance to the profession. This formulation of values is commonly expressed by a stipulated ethical code. They are used to characterize the practitioners" behavior in practice and outline the responsibilities in particular interventions. They also give a common sense of professional identity since practitioners, through values, can talk about similar entities (Dominelli, 2002). In reference to social work, Payne (1996) proposes that values are important to understanding the profession because they reflect the ways that social workers currently think and practice with difficult cases or problems.

Social work values and ethical principles are integrated into codes of ethics. "Codes of ethics are documents that aim to identify the broad values, principles and standards of ethical conduct on which a particular profession is based" (Bowles et al., 2006, pp.75-76).

Moreover, as Banks (1995) argues, a code of ethics binds social workers under a common professional identity and publicizes its ideals and intentions. She also identifies four general functions of codes of ethics. In particular, she argues that codes of ethics are a guide for: conduct and ethical decision-making; protection for users from malpractice or abuse; the professional status of social work; and establishing and maintaining professional identity.

However, protecting users from day-to-day social work practice and avoiding the misinterpretation of ethics is not a tangible achievement through the sole usage of a code of ethics. Ethical standards and principles should be seen in reference to a specific context, otherwise serious harm can result (Bowles et al., 2006). Additionally, Sonnenberg (2004) argues that very general codes like those of IFSW and BASW encourage reflection and debate, but give little guidance. On the other hand, very detailed codes tend to be prescriptive and limit the professional freedom of judgment. Therefore, codes of ethics can never ensure ethical behavior because integrity and morality are qualities that cannot be coerced. Bowles et al. (2006) suggest that in order to attain an adequate response to the social work code of ethics, social workers should be able to see ethical principles as interrelated. Following an ethical principle at the cost of another is seen as misinterpretation of the code and can lead to the fragmentation of the social work profession.

There are several difficulties in conceptualizing the social work identity including the range and types of problems social workers address, settings in which they practice, levels of practice, interventions and methods used, and populations served (Gibelman, 1999; Banks, 1995). Policy and the nature of welfare are also factors related to the social work identity. Policy changes and underpinning ideologies and values pertaining to the welfare state are reflected in the nature of social work. For example, Banks (1998) notes that social work is enormously affected by globalization, neo-liberalism and the ideology of new management. Specifically, she argues that greater bureaucratic accountability and greater specialization and fragmentation of professional roles are the results of the current political state.

However, as noted previously, social work is also a part and an expression of the welfare state. As the welfare state functions under the capitalistic economic and political systems, it also serves to ensure survival of this system and its values. The welfare system is underpinned by the value of competitive individualism as it functions within capitalism. Therefore, the welfare state supports the existing economic and social order by enabling private capital to remain profitable (Banks, 1995). On the other hand, the welfare state and the social work profession are developed in order to express the social concern for values such as justice and equality. Consequently, social work has an intrinsic role of social controller, and its primary aim to work in the best interest of users falls on the contradictory principles of the welfare state (Clark, 2000; Banks, 1995).

Human rights and social justice function as a leading pathway of social workers to give a specific meaning to human well-being. Therefore, the elaboration of such fundamental social work values enables the specification of professional purposes, and moreover, these values are a basic part of the social work identity. Human rights are universal and they apply to all people regardless of their race, circumstances or any other characteristic. IFSW (2005) code of ethics identifies all international human rights declarations as guidance that should lead to ethical conduct and the professional purposes of social work. In particular, social workers should respect the inherent worth and dignity of all people. Similarly, social workers should uphold and defend each person's physical, psychological, emotional and spiritual integrity and well-being.

According to Reamer (1982) argues that social work has ethical and unethical aspects. The ethical aspects of the profession include questions about the obligations and duties of practitioners, and questions about what is ethically right and wrong conduct. The unethical aspects of the profession include questions about the effectiveness of particular intervention techniques, the proper way to prepare process notes, methods for assessing the nature of a client's problems, or ways of carrying out a cost-benefit analysis. However, Clark (2000) believes that standards of ethics in professional practice are not a separate question from standards of technical knowledge and skill, but rather intimately related. Practice that fails to reach reasonable standards of technical skill is just as much unethical as practice that does not respect general principles of professional morality. In fact, Timms (1983) argues that ethics are the source from which social work techniques derive. Moreover, some argue that science and its theories about human behavior and related intervention techniques are never value free. Therefore, perceptions of what is "good" or "bad", and what we call value judgments are always intertwined in so called scientific activity (Seedhouse, 2005; Rhodes, 1986).

Philosophy and Social Work Ethics

In fact, the word philosophy derives from the Greek language and means "love of wisdom". In reference to moral philosophy, Socrates, Plato and Aristotle were those who contributed most to the development of what is currently known as virtue theory. For instance, the basic assumption of Socrates was that all men, if they could, would do what was "good" and that the sole reason for not doing so was some form of ignorance. Therefore, he believed that all people must have certain capabilities that reflect an excellent knowledge for something. Thus, Socrates perceived wisdom as being identical with the notion of virtue. Socrates regarded notions like courage or justice as debatable, and his well-known arguments were attempts to find a satisfactory definition.

Furthermore, Plato, the most important of the Socrates" determinant followers, tried to establish virtues that would have concrete and absolute meaning, eternal in their duration and universally accepted. He argued that the source of moral values was not based on empirical reality, but on a virtue reality that could only be seen in our minds and souls. Plato believed that only a virtuous person could be really happy because only a virtuous person had his/her soul in such a condition so as to be happy. Justice, courage, moderation and wisdom were the central aspects of a virtuous person according to Socrates and Plato (Huby, 1974).

The theory of virtue ethics provides us with a different meaning of effectiveness in professional practice. Therefore, social work and its effectiveness take on a special meaning as virtue theorists place a special emphasis on virtues and vices and give relatively little explicit attention to moral rules and principles. Virtues are not just statements of principles. Rather they are dispositions to choose well; they are states of character. According to Banks (1995), a virtue is a character trait which contributes toward some ideal of the good life, both for individuals and the society they belong. The majority of character traits are currently considered as virtues originate from the ancient Greek philosophy of the virtuous human being. For example, current virtue ethics theorists have embraced some of the virtues of Aristotle's and Socrates ethical theories, including justice, courage and temperance.

Likewise, Aristotle believed that to lack virtues was to lack happiness which was the absolute evil. However, Aristotle developed a completely different approach on ethics and challenged the ideas of Plato and Socrates. Particularly, he argued that nothing is good in its own right and everything is good in relation to something else. He also argued that wisdom or the knowledge of something could be used both for good and for bad purposes; therefore, he was the first who separated the notions of means and ends. For Aristotle, virtues could be reached only if we choose the right means, and the choice of means was within our power.

Regarding the social work profession, virtue theorists argue that virtues have an important role in the formation of the social workers" professional identity. In particular, McBeath and Webb (2002) argue that ambiguity in the social work profession due to our complex socio-political world could be resolved by placing virtues in what we perceive as the social workers identity. Moreover, they believe that doing a task well is not merely a matter of following rules; rather it involves the skills and virtues of a person. Virtue ethics give a moral meaning to the social work profession because social workers" actions are not driven by abstract obligations based on deontological rule books.

Contrarily, social workers actions take on a real moral worth as they reflect the importance of the values that the social work profession is supposed to promote. Nevertheless, there is one problematic area based on how social work virtues are established and defined in the first place (Houston, 2003). This idea becomes more complicated when we consider Aristotle's doctrine on means, whereby a good life is the means between vice and virtue and that too much virtue could be a bad thing (Benn, 1998). In response to this challenge, McBeath and Webb (2002) propose that virtues must be developed from a conscious analytical process rooted in dialogical exchanges between committed inquirers. They also explicitly suggest several virtues for social workers based on the Aristotle's ethical theory: justice, reflection, perception, judgment, courage, prudence, liberality and temperance.

Therefore, virtue ethics and particularly Greek philosophy was always a part of the education in Greece and integrated not only in philosophy courses but also in history, mathematics, science, and literature. More importantly, there are a series of quotes originated by the Greek philosophers that are part of the folk language and verbal expression of the Greeks. Therefore, it is anticipated that Greek philosophy has deeply characterized the Greek culture as it is reflected in everyday language.

In this sense, Greek social workers are culturally informed about virtue ethics even if virtues are not considered as a special social work skill or approach.

Ethical Values in Social work

According to Erik (2006), there are many different issues and themes to explore. We will here make a division into three fundamental ethical questions and areas of discussion: human value, what is right, and what sort of person we should to strive to be.

A fundamental question is how we view human worth and the value of human life. We are then faced with the established position constituted by the principle of human dignity, which maintains the equal and eminent worth of every human being. This worth is inherent and not dependent on how useful we are, what status we have or how great our sense of well-being. The principle of human dignity can be seen as a declaration of love for human life and entails showing respect towards and taking responsibility for our own and others' lives. Respect for every person's dignity and integrity is an established norm, as is respect for every person's freedom and right to self-determination. Values such as justice and equality are also central in the assessment of actions and rules, along with the principles of human rights, humanity and solidarity. Such values and norms can be seen as valid in themselves so need no justification. But they can also be recognized as leading if we utilize them to best outcomes for human lives and societal conditions.

A professional should be well grounded in the general ethical values most strongly entrenched in our society. Ethical values and norms in social work are mainly the same as for other professions, but the choice of these values and the emphasis placed on them varies between different professions, organizations and activities. The following brief overview comments on those viewed as generally applicable, but with special reference to the social work professional role.

Moreover, human rights are a core principle both on ethical grounds and on grounds of juridical relevance. By this principle the individual has the right to certain living conditions and resources which in turn puts demands on nation-states, but also on organizations and other individuals. In social work the concern is mostly for those types of resources and measures that correspond to social rights, e.g. an adequate standard of living, dwelling, work and access to health and sick care. Humanity is another central ethical principle that denotes that one ought to be particularly observant and sympathetic towards persons in a vulnerable and difficult situation. We then see others as fellow beings whom we shall meet with empathy, sensitivity and compassion.

Likewise, Dignity-integrity is an important ethical principle of huge relevance in social work. This is a composite concept and it is not entirely self-evident what it real-ly means to safeguard people's dignity and integrity. However, there is cultural agreement on some of the central aspects of dignity. For example, that we are treated with respect and shown interest, that there is space for us to exert influence, i.e. that we can make our voices heard and that what we say is paid due regard. Further, we have the right to a private sphere. We need to be protected from other people's curiosity and from simplified judgments about ourselves, and we experience any infringement of these aspects of our personal dignity as an offence.

In addition, treating all clients equally, equality emphasizes the importance of having a significant portion of needs and similarity-based justice in any social work operation. This concerns not least the matter of equivalence in the reception and treatment of clients, which shows respect for the equal and high worth of each individual. The endeavor to give an equal reception does not mean, however, that we ought to ignore the imbalance that exists between social work professionals and their clients with regard to the preferential right of interpretation and the exercise of authority. There is indeed a marked asymmetry in such a relationship; one does not meet on equal terms. Equal reception is especially therefore a necessity. This means that a social work professional must receive and treat the client-citizen as an equivalent human being.

SOLUTIONS AND RECOMMENDATIONS

The exploration of social work ethical enhances our understanding in relation to the underlying values that guide social work practice. However, it appeared that the contextual orientation of this study enabled to further this understanding from the nature of social work practice to the nature of social policy. The cases that social workers described as ethical dilemmas and problems provided a detailed illumination of how policy issues have an enormous effect on human suffering. Beyond the ability of social workers to deal their ethical dilemmas it is important to understand the implicit decisions of social policy to act or not towards the elimination of social problems which frame human suffering.

Furthermore, critical social work practice would also be liberating for social work clients who would be acknowledged not as "those who need therapy", but as citizens. Moreover, through critical analysis and reflection their oppression would be reframed by appreciating the political and social context in which they live. In this way, social workers would also be able to gain insight into how their own values and beliefs may contribute to dominant power relations and the oppression of vulnerable people.

Therefore, the critical approach could advance the potential for a genuine partnership between social workers and people. Then, critical knowledge would be shared and the power relationship between experts and clients would be transformed into a powerful union of citizens against injustice. Besides, the exploration of social work ethical dilemmas is meaningful only because their core element is human suffering which must be eliminated.

There were some limitations while writing the chapter, special ethical dilemmas. One dilemma is the risk of becoming insensitive, of exhibiting insufficient empathy or plain cynicism, arising from the problem culture encountered in social work, the stress and strains of the job, or disappointment over the behavior of clients. Another common dilemma is the objectifying of the client, who becomes merely another in the endless line of problematic citizens each day encountered, with the risk that each person's unique conditions. These things were not included in the chapter. However, a lot of social grounding practices, philosophies, ethical values, and principles were discussed in an excellent manner.

FUTURE RESEARCH DIRECTIONS

The exploration of factors affecting the choice of social workers to blow the whistle on the unethical practice of professionals is also a potential for further research. This study provided some initial findings that social workers may have a negative attitude towards whistle blowing. However, a more focused and deep exploration of further research is needed. Social work is also practiced in a variety of placements, is formed in a different way and structured according to specific local contexts. It is anticipated that organizational differences will alter the way that social work ethics are perceived or applied by the social workers.

Moreover, by bringing together the research knowledge and techniques with the efforts of social work practitioners to provide effective and value based services, studies can have an immediate contribution to the scientific development of social work practice. As Lees and Lees (1975) argue, researchers must meet the challenge to communicate their findings with practitioners and crucially to build their research questions according to what practitioners want answers for.

Therefore, further research should be focused in the examination of social work ethics in placements and in the public hospitals. In particular, the exploration of psychotherapy as a system of values that guide professional practice could be explored in more detail and provide more information to those who are interested in exploring what forms ethical practice and ethical decisions of the practitioners, and policy makers.

CONCLUSION

In conclusion, the aim of our chapter writing is to assess the aspects of inevitable ethical values and social work practices. Studies have consistently found that social work is forced to make decisions that involve ethical judgments. There will be difficult choices to make that will have important consequences in ethical values of social work practice. Moreover, this makes it important to be aware the ethical values of social work profession have long been given scant attention ethical foundation as important knowledge and theory in social work practice. Ethical theory building will strengthen the moral fiber of the profession and it will contribute to the current knowledge relating to social work practices.

Social workers often appeared to make a decision by "putting themselves into their client's shoes". The individualistic character of social work practice and the absolute ethical commitment of practitioners to act for the benefit of their clients particularly affected this decision. The underlying value of this behavior appeared to be the ethic of care. However, if social workers were determined to take the place of their clients, they possibly ignored their multiple loyalties. This is what Meagher and Parton (2004) described as the "dark side" of care as practice is detached from policy theory and a communal concern for equality and justice in terms of power and resources in society. Therefore, social work, in other words, demands observance of ethical behavior and different perspectives of ethical values of social work practices addressed in this chapter.

REFERENCES

Banks, S. (1995). *Ethics and Values in Social Work*. London: Macmillan. doi:10.1007/978-1-349-24145-3

Banks, S. (1998). Professional Ethics in Social Work - What Future? *British Journal of Social Work*, *28*(2), 213–231. doi:10.1093/oxfordjournals.bjsw.a011324

BASW. (2012). *The Code of Ethics for Social Work: Statement of Principles*. BASW.

Benn, P. (1998). *Ethics*. London: UCL Press.

Bowles, W., Collingridge, M., Curry, S., & Valentine, B. (2006). *Ethical Practice in Social Work*. Open University Press.

Briskman, L. (2001). A Moral Crisis for Social Work: Critical Practice and Codes of Ethics. Critical Social Work, 2(1), www.uwindsor.ca/units/socialwork/critical.nsf, (Accessed on 23 October 2008).

Clark, C. (2000). *Social Work Ethics*. London: Palgrave.

Csikai, E. L. (2004). Social Workers Participation in the Resolution of Ethical Dilemmas in Hospice Care. *Health & Social Work, 29*(1), 67–76. doi:10.1093/hsw/29.1.67 PMID:15024920

Dominelli, L. (2002). Values in Social Work: Contested Entities with Enduring Qualities. In R. Adams, L. Dominelli, & M. Payne (Eds.), *Critical Practice in Social Work* (pp. 15–27). London: Palgrave.

Erik, B. (2006). *Ethics in Social Work. An ethical code for social work professionals*. Ersta Sköndal University College, SSR.

Fraser, K., & Strang, V. (2002). Decision-Making and Nurse Case Management. A Philosophical Perspective. *ANS. Advances in Nursing Science, 27*(1), 32–43. doi:10.1097/00012272-200401000-00005 PMID:15027660

Fritzche, J. (1995). Personal Values: Potential Keys to Ethical Decision-Making. *Journal of Business Ethics, 14*(11), 909–922. doi:10.1007/BF00882069

Gibelman, M. (1999). The Search for Identity: Defining Social WorkPast, Present, Future. *Social Work, 44*(4), 298–310. doi:10.1093/sw/44.4.298

Houston, S. (2003). Establishing Virtue in Social Work: A Response to McBeath and Webb. *British Journal of Social Work, 33*(6), 819–824. doi:10.1093/bjsw/33.6.819

Huby, P. (1974). Greek Ethics. In W. D. Hudson (Ed.), *New Studies in Ethics, Classical Theories* (pp. 1–71). London: Macmillan Press LTD. doi:10.1007/978-1-349-02396-7_1

IFSW. (2005). *Ethics in Social Work, Statement of Principles*. Available from: http://www.ifsw.org/en/f38000032.html

Lees, R., & Lees, S. (1975). Social Sciences in Social Work Practice: The Case for an Action Research Approach. *British Journal of Social Work, 5*(2), 161–174.

Lyons, K. (2006). Globalization and Social Work: International and Local Implications. *British Journal of Social Work*, 36.

Mcbeath, G., & Webb, S. A. (2002). Virtue Ethics and Social Work: Being Lucky, Realistic, and not Doing ones Duty. *British Journal of Social Work, 32*(8), 1015–1036. doi:10.1093/bjsw/32.8.1015

Parker, J. (2004). *Effective Practice Learning in Social Work*. London: Learning Matters Ltd.

Reamer, F. G. (1982). *Ethical Dilemmas in Social Service*. New York: Columbia University Press.

Rhodes, M. L. (1986). *Ethical Dilemmas in Social Work Practice*. London: Routledge and Kegan Paul.

Seedhouse, D. (2005). *Values-Based Decision-Making for the Caring Professions*. Chichester, UK: Wiley.

Timms, N. (1983). *Social Work Values, An Enquiry*. London: Routledge and Kegan Paul plc.

Chapter 5
Social Justice in Social Work:
Preliminaries

Tatiana Focsa
Free University of Moldova, Moldova

ABSTRACT

The actuality of the given topic comes from the approach of the concept of social justice in relation with factors of decisions and power of the state. One of the solutions identified by the state organization is the creation of the system of social work, which represents a component of the national system of social protection, within which the state and civil society is engaged to prevent, limit or remove the temporary or permanent effects of some events considered as social risks that could generate the marginalization or exclusion of the persons and families in difficulty. In our vision, the social justice represents the equality of chances of each individual in relation with the equity and equality as fundamental principles of social coexistence. In a "healthy" state, any person, regardless of experience or life circumstances, succeeds to achieve the maximum potential. We believe that there is no human society that is entirely based on social equality or equity, but this is only an additional motive to make efforts in this direction.

INTRODUCTION

In this paper we intend to reflect the social justice as value and principle of the practice of social work. The process of globalization and the enactment of the Codes of professional conduct of the social worker at the international, regional and national level, determined the unification of the human values defended unanimously by the state through the professionals in the social field – social workers. Social

DOI: 10.4018/978-1-5225-3090-9.ch005

justice constitutes a value, as well as a principle according to which social workers perform their job.

The goal of the chapter consists in identifying the role of social work in assuring the equality of chances of all social actors without discrimination, in order to assure the respect of social justice as human value.

The objectives emerged in order to accomplish the given goal, are the following:

- To discuss the concept of *social justice.*
- To analyse the *soft laws* of assuring the respect of social values.
- To expose the European social practice of assuring the equality of chances of people from the European space.

BACKGROUND

In the last decade, as indicator of the social changes are the significant changes of the social norms and values that are insistently imposing themselves as economic values. The values which were unacceptable some decades ago, are today seen as something normal. There is the impression that we are on the verge of birth of a new type of culture based on completely different ideas regarding good and evil, beautiful and ugly. Everything is transferred in monetary value, everything is sold and bought. The strategies for clients inspire the idea that with money, all values could be bought. Or, besides the economic crisis, the contemporary world risks a more serious crisis – that of its values (Buzducea, 2009, p. 3).

Borțun (2010, p.13) states that in the last two decades, there is a current which could be called *the ethical criticism of the capitalism,* that proposes a new vision on the contemporary capitalism accused of suffocating the democracy, changing the citizens into customers, and which is unable to block the wave of greed and egoism in favour of the compassion and solidarity. The author sustains the approach to capitalism from the ethical positions and considers that it is responsible for the present and future societies.

The social position represents a complex factor that contributes to the state of health of people by its components: age, sex, socio-economic statute, educational level, occupation, income (Nemțoi & Ignătescu, 2014). Components of social status are an important factor in determining the health of the population (Business Integrity, 2013, p. 80).

In this context, Jean-Claude Mignon, the President of the Parliamentary Assemble of the Council of Europe (PACE) declares that “Europe is in period of great uncertainty. The citizens don’t’ believe the policy, they are disoriented, while the unscrupulous leaders take advantage of this weakness in order to obtain political advantages by inciting to hatred and promising miracles that underestimate all social, economic and political achievements of our continent". Today it is required to work more than ever, in order to consolidate the democratic values, to reaffirm the importance of the basic values of the European Convention of human rights. In a moment of uncertainty, we need more Europe – the Europe of the universal values" (InfoEuropa, 2012).

ARGUMENT OF THE PAPER

An important factor that increases the interest for studying the social justice in the context of social practices is the process of globalization, which influences all societies and domains, inclusively the systems of protection and social work. If until recently we couldn't speak about the international social work due to the fact that the policies of supporting the people were related to each state apart, than at that moment, people more often began to operate with this phenomenon caused mainly by the process of globalization and trauma, lost and sufferings that don't take into consideration the geographical placement of states or certain categories of people

We consider that the problem of social responsibility in a state of law is related to the behaviour and vector taken by the political class that adopts policies based on sustainable development of the state and society. The elaborated policies should promote a social behaviour based on social values, generally accepted by the international and national community. In this era of accelerated globalization, the continuous moral perfection of the community members is necessary, which could not be perceived as a state culture in a broad sense. In other words, a state cannot manifest itself as a good citizen if the people are not good citizens, but vice versa, a citizen cannot be devoted to the state if the state doesn't take into account its interests.

SOCIAL JUSTICE AND SOCIAL WORK: CONCEPTS

Regardless of the domain of intervention and debates around values, in the practice of social work we have a common set of values that should be respected, among which we would like to mention *the social justice.*

The acceptance of the concept of social work on international plan doesn't involve the acceptance of any international system of social work.

The definition of social work, approved by the International Federation of Social Workers (IFSW) and of the International Association, form the Schools of Social Assistance (IASSA) during the common meetings from Copenhagen, occurred on May 2001, from which the common documents of IASSA and IFSW starts – "Ethics in social work. Declaration of principles" shape the principle of social justice as the basic principle in social work (IFSW & IASSW, 2004).

In the ethical Code of the Britain Association of Social Workers (BASW, 2012), the principles are defined as essential norms in the system of thinking or beliefs that form the rational basis of this system (BASW, 2010). The basic values of the social work in the XXIst century emphasized by the ethical code BASW, and are the following:

1. *Human rights, respecting the inborn values and the dignity of every people;*
2. *Social justice;*
3. *Professional integration* (Qreferat, 2006).

In the Ethical Code of the National Agency of Social Workers USA (NASW), is mentioned the fact that the mission of social work is rooted in a set of essential/ fundamental values, such as: services, social justice, dignity and persons value, the importance of the inter-human relations, integrity, competence (NASW, 2008).

In Clark's opinion (2002), social justice implies that social workers contribute to the elimination of social injustice felt by the beneficiaries, by discrimination and unequal access to the community resources (Buzducea, 2009, p. 58; Clark, 2002).

Most ethics codes present some form of legal legitimacy of the provisions of codes of ethics, even if there are certain differences between those provisions (Buzducea, et al., 2011). The social transfers by the people in difficulty or risk situations, as well as the interventions of the social worker by pleading the case of the beneficiaries in front of the state institutions, takes place by facilitating the access to community resources, by mediating family and community conflicts, by specialized services, that contribute to the social justice.

Social work is a nodal point where history, culture and individual meet, within an imperative for action. Given the mission of working with marginalized people, this particular nexus is a place of crushing ambivalence. It is the place where larger cultural and social conflicts and contradictions regarding independence and dependence, deserving and undeserving, institutional and residual, difference and likeness, individualism and collectivism, authority and freedom, meet unresolved but expressed through the contradictions that inhere in practice. No wonder we cling to the fantasy of the smooth trajectory of practice (Rossiter, 2005).

The term of social justice, invented by the priest Luigi Taparelli in 1840, designate the way in which justice is applied in a certain society in relation with the social classes in it. In essence, it is referred to the concept that all people should have the same rights and economic, political and social opportunities. For the followers of social justice, the most important role of the state is to ensure the welfare and respecting of the rights of its citizens, regardless of the social class they are taking part in (Business Integrity, 2013).

The social justice as an essential value in social work is recognized by all ethical/deontological codes of social work: the Ethic Code NASW (2008), the Ethic Code BASW (2012), Deontological code of the social work profession in Romania, (The Official Monitor of Romania, 2008), Deontological Code of the Social Worker of the Republic of Moldova (***, 2005).

The common document of IFSW and IASSW, "Ethics in social work. Declaration of principles", provide that "social workers have the responsibility to promote the social justice in relation with the society in general, and in relation with the persons with whom they are working" (IFSW & IASSW, 2004).

Concerning social justice, the responsibility represents an important problem. Equity of access to resources can be a source of diminishing the responsibility towards its own social condition (Frunză, 2016, p. 126). Miftode (2011) shows that the strongest injustice promoted by inequity through the lack of power, is the serial oppression. The marginal and vulnerable groups are subject to a parallel process of self-vulnerability and self-marginalization, being agents of the perpetuation and transfer of oppression (Sandu, 2016, p. 51; Miftode, 2011).

Mike O'Brien (2013) finds that the social work literature is replete with definitions, going back as far as the early professional and academic literature of a century ago. Core elements of these definitions are covered in both the academic literature, and in recent Aotearoa New Zealand theses (Nash 1998; Staniforth, 2010); the debates do not need to be traversed here. For current purposes, it is worth noting that social justice is a fundamental element in many (but not all) of the definitions and descriptions of social work. IFSW definition states, inter alia: „the social work profession promotes social change, problems loving in human relationships and the empowerment and liberation of people to enhance well-being" (IFSW & IASSW, 2004; Campanini, 2013). Principles of human rights and social justice are fundamental to social work (International Federation of Social Workers, n.d.:1). That definition highlights the social justice components of the practice of social work as one of the central elements in performing effective practice (O'Brien, 2013, p. 51). Underpinned by theories of social work, social sciences, humanities and indigenous knowledge, social work engages people and structures to address life challenges and enhance wellbeing.

THE EUROPEAN SOCIAL PRACTICE IN ASSURING THE SOCIAL JUSTICE

In our vision, the social justice represents the equality of chances of every individual in relation with the equity and equality of fundamental principles of social coexistence.

By social justice we don't understand an equality of social statute between all persons, but an equality of treatment. In a "healthy" state, any person, regardless of the experience or life circumstances, succeeds to achieve the maximal potential.

The social justice refers to the way in which the society distribute the available resources to its members, and presupposes the elimination of discrimination against any person or any group according to race, skin colour, gender, sexual orientation, age, religion, marital status, political convictions, of the discrimination according to the mental or physical handicap or any other preference or personal characteristics, conditions or statute. The social worker should act in order to make sure that all people have access to the resources, services and opportunities they need (Bulgaru, 2013, p.10).

The state, as a political-geographic identity, engages itself to solving the social problems by creating the system of social work that represents the component of the system of social protection.

Being supported by the phenomena of economic and socio-cultural globalization, after the change of the manner of government, in the space of Central and East Europe social problems have appeared, denied until that point, thus leading to the necessity of elaborating social strategies of work.

Buzducea, analysing the European systems of social work mentions that at the European level, we meet different ways of organization of the social protection system, according to the state's history, its administrative-territorial organization, its traditions, the level of its financial institutions, etc. (2009, p. 89). A social movement that represents a common domain in the profession development is being developed.

In Europe, we find:

- **Anglo-Saxon System**: Great Britain;
- **North System**: Swedish, Denmark and Finland;
- **Mediterranean System**: Portugal, Greece and Spain;
- **Continental Model**: Germany.

The criticism subjected mainly to the European systems of social work is related to bureaucracy. This criticism comes from the comparison of European systems and the system of North America, where the services of social work are very well developed, but in Europe, social provisions are predominant (Buzducea, 2009, p. 73).

All these led to the development, in time, of certain visions or paradigms of the European social work, according to which administration should make investments in social work in such a way that the society will be able to absorb the social problems.

Bulgaru sustains that the multiplicity of the interdependence between different populations, nations, ethnicity brings in the globalization conditions a set of issues related to the necessity of permanent comparison with others, the identification of differences and similarities of the cultural and axiological problems, etc. (2012, p. 59).

At the same time, with the strong integrating processes at all levels, in the last decades, the interest towards the international social work was reborn. Ahmadi (2003) considers that the international social work can, and should play, an important role in consolidating the democracy, social justice by implementing international conventions related to human rights, to the elimination of women's discrimination, to children's rights, etc., as well as preventing conflicts and maintaining peace by promoting the global cultural integration (Ahmadi, 2003, p.14).

Littlechild mentions: „Social workers have a responsibility to promote social justice, in relation to society generally, and in relation to the people they work with. This means: Challenging negative discrimination - Social workers have a responsibility to challenge negative discrimination based on characteristics such as ability, age, culture, gender or sex, marital status, socio-economic status, political opinions, skin colour, racial or other physical characteristics, sexual orientation, or spiritual beliefs" (2012, p. 63). While social workers value social justice, we can take a more integral perspective (Larkin, 2006).

Cojocaru (2005) performs a study of ethics and discipline in the governmental and non-governmental social system. The research revealed that in the governmental system, the disciplinary authority functions better than the ethical principles, and in the non-governmental system of affiliation, membership and attachment to the organization makes the social worker be involved in activities and responsible for his/her own actions. Deontological norms should originate an ethical value, and transpose it into a moral maximum. The Kantian model stipulate such value, namely human dignity, which is transposed into the moral principle as a form of the second formulation of the categorical imperative, which pretends the treating of a human being as a purpose in itself, and never as a means. The fulfilment of this imperative requires the individual's ability to rationalize their behaviour in such way that their own moral norm can stand as a moral maximum for others (Sandu, 2017).

Even if it is often mentioned in the official act of the European Union, the European social model is not crystalized, and rather represents a sum of principles and common idea of the systems of social protection from the Union able to offer a unitary answer to the problem of irregularities to economic and/ or social problems, a set of principles, interests, standards and qualitative services necessary to ensure a decent living for the European citizens, being based on solidarity and social responsibility (Frunză, 2011, p. 90).

The contemporary global interdependence imposes the necessity of social workers to review their knowledge and social practices through the international events and perspectives in order to feel more equipped in making a certain activity which, in its turn, will have intercultural dimensions, if we take into account the intensification of the migratory torrents characterized at the present stage as a significant growth of the cultural heterogeneity. In such conditions, the assurance of a good communication and of a non-conflictual contact involves the understanding and mutual acceptance of the values shared by every population, ethnicity, professional group, etc.

Sandu (2013) mentioned the efficient intervention as having two dimensions, one on the individual as a system that interacts in a given social field, and a second one on the social environment as a system that conditions and channels the possible interactions at the level of the given social field. The first dimension is constituted by counselling, and the second one by advocacy.

Social workers should recognize and respect the ethnical and cultural diversity of their society where they practice taking into consideration individual, familial, group and community differences (Buzducea, 2009, p. 205). In Bulgaru's opinion, our cultural uniqueness derives from the belonging to multiple cultures – associated to those two sexes, to certain occupations, clubs or organizations, some geographic zones, communities, some ethnicities and religions, etc. the members of a group in general follow common rules of behaviour of participating and/or belonging to a group. However, each member of the group presents many qualities and behaviours that differentiate him/ her from others, being generated by the socioeconomic statute, education, family past, etc. (2009, p.10).

In the current stage, the economic crisis the Republic of Moldova is facing contributes to the development of social services which are not only tools of combating the poverty and social maintenance, but as well as an additional source of jobs. They could considerably ameliorate the negative impact of the economic crisis and can generate the welfare and economic growth in communities (Onofrei, 2013, p. 26). At the moment, the society registered significant differences between social groups, lack of social equity and equality, and as consequence, a social justice based on group or personal interests. Social workers have the obligation to confront the social conditions that contribute to the social exclusion, stigmatization and subduing, and to improve the development of an inclusive society (Buzducea, 2009, p. 209).

THE *SOFT LAWS* OF ASSURING THE RESPECT OF SOCIAL VALUES

Social workers should know that there is no book or guidelines that would help them find the answer to the complex sets of causes and effects of the potential conflicts generated by different cultural, ethnical and religious traditions of the groups, when they are applied to certain beneficiaries and in certain moments of life. "Social workers can do this by bowing their ear to ideas, learning theories of research". All these offer the possibility of an appreciation and clear cultural agreement (Littlechild, 2012, p. 62).

Social workers are checking the equality of chances regarding the access of persons assisted to information, services, resources and from their worth in the process of making decisions. They consider that the different forms of social justice as: poverty, unemployment, discrimination, exclusion, etc. The social worker should plead for the change of policies and legislation in order to improve the social conditions and to promote social justice, to support the creation of opportunities for disadvantaged people, to promote the general welfare of the society at the global and local level. Social workers have the obligation to confront the social conditions that contributes to the social exclusion, stigmatization or subduing in order to develop an inclusive society (IFSW & IASSW, 2004, art.4.2, 3.4.5; NASW, 2008, art.6.01).

Rossiter (2005) mentioned that „In recent years, I believe that the experience of asymmetry between expectations of practitioners and the possibilities of practice has become more intense, as social work struggles to conceptualize how to bring practice into social movements. In this hope for practice as justice, the responsibility of social work is shifted from change at the more discreet levels of individuals, families, groups, communities, to the social determinants that produce private troubles".

According to Sandu and Unguru on a study made in 2012, regarding the supervision of social work practice in North-Eastern Romanian rural areas, the authors mention that: "we believe that the low professional prestige of the community social worker negatively interferes with the quality of their work and thus allow us to make the following recommendation, especially towards the Social Work College, but also towards other professional associations: to develop and implement national programs regarding the awareness of the place and role of the social worker in the community, which directly relates to increasing the dignity and professional prestige of the social worker" (p. 390).

The general report published by the European Commission presents the main initiatives and achievements of the UE for the last year – 2016, according to Chapter 7, *A space of the justice of the fundamental rights of women based on mutual reciprocity,* in 2016, the union of security gave an urgent and firm answer to terrorism and progresses were registered regarding the citizens; rights and some aspects linked to the internal market of the civil legal act.

In May 2016, the Commission published the Report 2015 regarding the application of the Book of fundamental right of the UE, underlying the way in which these fundamental laws were taken into account, and its legislative activity.

The report was focused on the "first annual colloquium regarding the fundamental rights, with the topic "Tolerance and respect: prevention and combating the anti-Semitism and Islamophoby in Europe". The colloquium's result was a list of concrete actions in the domains such as combating the racism, xenophobia, the discourses of inciting to hate, as well as other domains, among which promoting the tolerance, diversity and non-discrimination.

The second colloquium regarding the fundamental rights was focused on the topic “the media pluralism and democracy”; it determined the Commission to define the subsequent action aiming for protecting mass media of political pressure and guaranteeing the financial independence of it, journalists protection that are confronting threats and discourses incited with hatred, as well as monitoring the freedom of expression in member-states.

The Commission began the implementation of the list of actions meant to promote the equality of lesbian, gay, bisexuals, transgender and intersex persons, including some activities in areas such as non-discrimination, education, health, crimes motivated by hate and discourses incited by hate.

The report of 2016 regarding Roma people signalized the existence of some serious jams, such as residential and educational segregation and forced evictions of the Roma people.

About 80 million people from EU have a certain degree of handicap. The approval of the European act regarding the accessibility that began to be disputed in the Parliament and Council in 2016, would improve the accessibility of some useful products and services such as phones, transportation or bank services.

In order to help people with handicap to travel more easily between the member states, the European Union launched the initiative “the European framework for disability”. The Framework will offer equal access to certain specific benefits, especially in the cultural domains, spending the free time, sport, transport, on the base of a system of mutual recognition (C. E., 2017).

FUTURE RESEARCH DIRECTIONS

The research on social justice in social work we have conducted is limited to the preliminary aspects, the general topic being a broad one, which can be studied from ethical, social and legal aspects. At the moment, there can be conducted studies on the fundamental values of the contemporary world, due to the crisis of ethical values which give in to the material values worldwide; each individual’s equal chances in relation to equity and equality of chances as fundamental principles of social co-existence. Another field that could be subject to further analysis is the study of social European policies in promoting and supporting the social behaviour based on universal values; Social justice between theory and practice in different countries. From a legal point of view, social justice can be studied as a value which contributes to ensuring the compliance to the human rights; the legal and *quasi legal* framework of approaching the social justice; and the divergences between the legal regulations and the practice of non-discrimination in the national space.

CONCLUSION

We could conclude the importance of the state's intervention through the authorities of public administration, with attributions in social work and civil society in elaborating and promoting policies of social and non-discriminatory support to the people. The analysis of the EU report for 2016 in the social domain has shown the tendency of treating unceasingly the respect for the human being, the assurance of chances, the simplification of the procedures of claiming the fundamental rights, fact which contributes to ensuring the social justice.

REFERENCES

Ahmadi, N. N. (2003). Globalisation of consciousness and new challenges for international social work. *International Journal of Social Work Welfare*, *12*, 14-23.

Borţun, D. (2010). *Responsabilitatea socială corporativă* [Corporative social responsibility]. Bucureşti: SNSPA.

British Association of Social Workers (BASW). (2012). *Code of Ethics*. Retrieved July 13, 2017, from http://www.basw.co.uk/codeofethics/

Bulgaru, M. (2012). Asistenţa socială în contextul globalizării [Social assistance in the context of globalization]. *Studia Universitatis Moldaviae. Seria Ştiinţe Sociale*, *8*(58), 5-11.

Bulgaru, M. (2013). Deontologia asistenţei sociale [Deontology of social work]. *Studia Universitatis Moldavie Seria Ştiinţe Sociale*, *8*(68), 3-15.

Business Integrity. (2013). Justiţia socială [Social justice]. *Jurnal de cercetare anticoruptie*, *65*. Retrieved May 25, 2017, from http://www.businessintegrity.ro/content/justi%C5%A3ia-social%C4%83

Buzducea, D. (2009). *Sisteme moderne de asistenţă socială. Tendinţe globale şi practici locale* [Modern systems of social work. Global tendencies and local practices]. Iaşi: Editura Polirom.

Buzducea, D., Rujoiu, V. & Lazăr, F. (2011). *International Social Work: A Supplement of Social Work Review*. Bucureşti: Editura Universităţii din Bucureşti.

Campanini, A. (2013). *International perspective in Social Work – A new challenge?* Retrieved May 25, 2017, from http://scienzepolitiche.unical.it/bacheca/archivio/materiale/1862/Social%20Work%20in%20a%20globalizing%20world%20(University%20of%20Calabria,%20May%2026%20-%2031%202013)/INTERNATIONAL%20CAMPANINI%20International%20perspective%20in%20sw%20[modalit%C3%A0%20compatibilit%C3%A0].pdf

Clark, C. (2000). *Social Work Ethics*. London: Palgrave.

Cojocaru, S. (2005). *Metode Apreciative în Asistența Socială. Ancheta, Supervizarea și Managementul de Caz* [Appreciative Methods in Social Work. Inquiery, Supervision and Case Management]. Iasi: Polirom Publishing.

Comisia Europeana (C.E.). (2017). *Raport general - Activitățile Uniunii Europene. Raportul general publicat de Comisia Europeană prezintă principalele inițiative și realizări ale UE din anul precedent. UE în 2016*. Retrieved May 25, 2017, from https://europa.eu/european-union/documents-publications/reports-booklets/general-report_ro

Frunză, A. (2016). *Către o nouă expertiză etică - deconstruind valorile etice* [Towards a new ethical expertise - deconstructing ethical values]. Iasi, Romania: Lumen Publishing.

Frunză, S. (2011). *Comunicarea etică și responsabilitatea socială* [Ethical Communication and Social Responsibility]. Bucharest: Tritonic Publishing.

IFSW & IASSW. (2004). *Ethics in social work. Declaration of principles*. Retrieved May 25, 2017, from http://ethics.iit.edu/ecodes/node/3934

InfoEuropa. (2012). *O soluţie pentru criza valorilor: mai multă Europă: Declaraţia Preşedintelui APCE cu ocazia Zilei Europei* [A solution for the values crisis: more Europe: Declaration of the RACE President on Europe Day]. Retrieved July 13, 2017, from http://www.infoeuropa.md/evenimente-europene-in-moldova/o-solutie-pentru-criza-valorilor-mai-multa-europa-declaratia-presedintelui-apce-cu-ocazia-zilei-europei

Larkin, H. (2006). Social Work as an Integral Profession. *Journal of Integral Theory and Practice*, *1*(2). Retrieved May 25, 2017, from https://www.researchgate.net/publication/251743486_Social_Work_as_an_Integral_Profession

Littlechild, B. (2012). Values and cultural issues in social work. *ERIS Web Journal*, *1*, 62-76. Retrieved May 25, 2017, from http://periodika.osu.cz/eris/dok/2012-01/07_values_and_cultural_issues_in_sw.pdf

Miftode, V. (2011). *Tratat de asistenta Sociala. Protectia populatiilor specifice si automarginalizate* [Social Work Treaty. Protection of specific and self-marginalized populations]. Iasi: Lumen Publishing.

Nash, M. (1998). *People, policies and practice: Social work education in Aotearoa New Zealand 1949-1995* (PhD thesis). Massey University.

National Association of Social Workers (NASW). (2008). *Code of Ethics*. Retrieved May 25, 2017, from http://www.socialworkers.org/pubs/code/code.asp

Nemţoi, G., & Ignătescu, C. (2014). National Citizenship as Representative of European Citizenship. *Procedia Social and Behavioral Sciences, 149*, 653-658. Retrieved May 25, 2017, from http://www.sciencedirect.com/science/article /pii/S1877042814049568

O'Brien, M. (2013). Social work registration and professionalism: Social justice and poverty – fellow travellers or discarded passengers? *Aotearoanew Zealand Social Work Issue, 25*(3), 50-59. Retrieved May 25, 2017, from http://anzasw.nz/wp-content/uploads/Social-Work-Review-Issue-25-Number-3-Aticles-OBrien.pdf

Onofrei, A. (2013). Modernization of social services in the Republic of Moldova – key factor to an effective system of social work. *Studia Universitatis Moldavie. Seria Ştiinţe Sociale, 8*(68), 2013, 26-29.

Qreferat. (2006). Standarde profesionale în domeniul asistenţei sociale. *Chişinău*, pp. 7-15. Retrieved May 25, 2017, from http://www.qreferat.com/referate/psihologie/Standardele-profesionale-in-do258.php

Rossiter, A. (2005). *Discourse Analysis in Critical Social Work: From Apology to Question*. Retrieved May 25, 2017, from http://www1.uwindsor.ca/criticalsocialwork/discourse-analysis-in-critical-social-work-from-apology-to-question

Sandu, A. (2013). *Asistenţa socială aplicată. Tehnici de cercetare şi modele de intervenţie* [Applied Social Work. Research techniques and intervention patterns]. Iasi, Romania: Lumen Publishing.

Sandu, A. (2016). From distributive to procedural justice. Justice as a constitutive value of public administration. *Annals of "Ştefan cel Mare" University of Suceava Philosophy, Social and Human Disciplines Series, 1,* 43-58. Retrieved from http://www.apshus.usv.ro/arhiva/2016I. pdf#page=45

Sandu, A. (2017). *O etică centrată pe valori în sfera publică* [An ethics centered on values in the public sphere]. Iasi: Lumen Publishing.

Sandu, A., & Unguru, E. (2013). Supervision of social work practice in North-Eastern Romanian rural areas. *Procedia: Social and Behavioral Sciences*, *82*, 386–391. doi:10.1016/j.sbspro.2013.06.280

Staniforth, B. (2010). *Past, present and future perspectives on the role of counselling in social work in Aotearoa New Zealand* (PhD thesis). Massey University.

The Official Monitor of Romania. (2008). *Codul deontologic al profesiei de asistent social* [The deontological code of the profession of social worker of Romania]. Code nr.1/2008. The Official Monitor of Romania. Part I, nr.173 din 06.03.2008. Retrieved May 25, 2017, from http://www.carp-omenia.ro/wp-content/uploads/2015/07/cod_deontologic_as.pdf

Section 2

Applied Ethics in Social Work Practice

Chapter 6
Strengths-Based Social Work:
Issues, Controversies, and Ethical Considerations

Sana Loue
Case Western Reserve University School of Medicine, USA

ABSTRACT

The strengths-based approach to the provision of social work services is said to rest on a respect for the worth and dignity of every individual and a concern that every individual be able to fulfill his or her potential. The strengths perspective transforms the role of the social worker role from that of an authority to that of a collaborator and seeks to facilitate client identification of internal and external strengths and resources and delineation of goals. Numerous criticisms have been raised about the approach, which has not been standardized in practice and has not been systematically evaluated through rigorous research to ascertain the effects of the approach or its acceptability to clients. As a consequence, numerous ethical issues are raised, including questions relating to client self-determination and informed consent. Additional research is needed to further evaluate the value of this perspective to client growth and development.

INTRODUCTION

The Social Work Dictionary defines the "strengths perspective" as an "orientation in social work and other professional practices that emphasizes the client's resources, capabilities, support systems, and motivations to meet challenges and overcome adversity. This approach does not ignore the existence of social problems, individual

DOI: 10.4018/978-1-5225-3090-9.ch006

disease, or family dysfunction; it emphasizes the client's assets that re used to achieve and maintain individual and social well-being" (Barker, 2003, p. 420). Strengths-based social work has been said to rest "on helping to discover and embellish, explore and exploit clients' strength and resources in the service of assisting them to achieve their goals, realize their dreams, and shed the irons of their own inhibitions and misgivings, and society's denunciation" (Saleebey, 2006, p. 1).

As such, it is claimed by its proponents to represent a sharp departure from social work's focus on the diagnosis of pathology, the identification of individuals' and families' deficiencies, and the imposition of the social worker's interventions that may or may not be relevant in the context of clients' lives (Rapp et al., 2005; Saleebey, 2002; Weick et al., 1989). It is said to both flow from and reflect social work's most deeply held values (Weick et al., 1989). It has been asserted that the purpose of social work and the values upon which the practice rests is "to release human power in individuals for personal fulfillment and social good, and to release social power for the creation of the kinds of society, social institutions, and social policy which make self-realization most possible for all men [and women]. Two values which are primary in such purposes are respect for the worth and dignity of every individual and concern that he [or she] have the opportunity to realize his [or her] potential as an individually-fulfilled socially contributive person" (Smalley, 1967, p. 1).

To the best of this writer's knowledge, there has been no published commentary on ethical issues that may arise with social work practice that is premised on a strengths perspective. This chapter first presents an overview of the strengths approach, including points of disagreement between proponents of the perspective and those who have expressed concerns regarding its use. The practice of strengths-based social work is then examined with reference to various provisions of several ethical codes that guide social work practice. The chapter concludes with strong recommendations for both the conduct of methodologically rigorous research to assess the actual effects of a strengths-based approach and the inclusion of specific disclosures to the client as part of the informed consent process.

BACKGROUND

Strengths-based social work practice comprises six specific features:

- Goal orientation
- Systematic assessment of strengths
- Perceptions of the individual's environment as resource-laden
- Explicit methods that rely on client strengths for the attainment of goals

- Hope-inducing relationship and
- Provision of meaningful choices and client authority to choose (rapp et al., 2005).

Each of these features is explored in greater detail below. In the context of this discussion, the strengths-based approach as compared to what has been referred to as the traditional social work approach.

Goal Orientation

The characterization of the strengths-based approach as goal-oriented initially may appear surprising because even problem-focused approaches have included a capacity building component (McMillen et al., 2004). It is the nature of the goal orientation and the foundation on which it rests that is believed to distinguish the goal orientation of strengths-based social work practice from other approaches.

Social work's earliest goals included a focus on the elimination of poverty, which was variously attributed to drunkenness, intemperance, ignorance, and a lack of moral will, all believed to represent moral deficiencies (Axinn and Levin, 1975). Accordingly, appropriate persuasion and influence were to be utilized to combat these perceived moral weaknesses and ultimately lead to the goal of eliminating both individual and societal poverty. The Charity Organization Societies of the early 1900s investigated those applying for assistance in order to identify individual and family deficiencies and eliminate those who were undeserving from further consideration. Individuals found to be inefficient, stupid, ignorant, shiftless, and/or immoral were viewed as more likely to become permanently dependent on assistance and/or perpetually impoverished (McClain, 1907).

Mary Richmond (1917) has been credited with helping to move social work from a focus on individual moral failings to a consideration of the larger social context in which individuals and families function (Blundo, 2001; McMillen et al., 2004; Weick et al., 1989). Her perspective, which she termed "social diagnosis," represented an "attempt to arrive at as exact a definition as possible of the social situation and personality of a given client. The gathering of evidence, or investigation, begins the process, the critical examination and comparison of evidence follows, and last come its interpretation and the definition of social difficulty. Where one word must describe the whole process, diagnosis is a better word than investigation, though in strict use the former belongs to the end of the process" (Richmond, 1917, p. 62). Although Richmond advocated for the use of an evidence-based method that encompassed an examination of both internal psychological factors and external social issues, she continued to emphasize the role of individual behavior as a causative factor (McMillen et al., 2004).

The social work profession continued to emphasize human frailty and weakness as a critical variable well into the 1960s, but with somewhat of a shift (McMillen et al., 2004; Weick et al., 1989). Individual weakness was no longer viewed as a moral failing but, with the profession's developing interest in psychopathology and psychoanalysis, it was now seen to result from underlying psychopathology (Blundo, 2001; McMillen et al., 2004; Weick et al., 1989). The goal of intervention thus was transformed from efforts to rectify a moral failing into attempts to define and treat an individual's underlying problem, which was often framed in terms of psychopathology.

An alternative approach to social work casework, known as functionalism, developed during the 1930s (McMillen et al., 2004). Although this perspective provided a growth-oriented view of development, it, like the diagnostic perspective, retained a focus on client "problems." By the late 1950s, it was clear that social work comprised two dominant perspectives: one that viewed difficulties as the result of individual psychopathology and the second that attributed difficulties to issues related to social functioning (Boehm, 1959). The two approaches shared a common characteristic: a focus on identifying problems and the concomitant goal of problem-solving through a reduction of "the effects of symptoms and the negative personal and social consequences of actions, emotions, thoughts, or relationships" (Saleebey, 1996. p. 298).

In contrast to this emphasis on defining and solving problems as the goal, efforts from a strength-based perspective are directed towards the identification of client strengths and resources, possibilities and commitments; moving forward with one's life; the affirmation and development of values and commitments; and the construction and discovery of "membership in or as a community" (Saleebey, 1996, p. 298). The approach does not ignore the client's problems and challenges, but seeks to address them with a greater awareness and appreciation of client knowledge, abilities, and internal and external resources that may be leveraged in that effort.

Disagreement appears to exist among writers with respect to the inclusion of greater client empowerment as an explicit goal of the strengths-based approach. While some have claimed that the strengths-based approach is specifically intended to facilitate an enhancement of client empowerment (George, 2012; Greene et al., 2005; McMillen, et al. 2004), others have drawn critical distinctions between a strengths-based approach and an empowerment model. It has been argued, for example, that an empowerment model presumes that clients are powerless and in need of a greater sense of empowerment, whereas a strengths-based approach rests on the assumption that clients are resilient, possess important strengths, and have significant capacities (Guo and Tsui, 2010).

Systematic Assessment of Strengths

The strengths-based perspective is premised on the understanding that individuals are better able to function and grow when they identify, recognize, and utilize their internal resources and those available to them in their environments (Graybeal, 2001; Guo and Tsui, 2010). Individuals' ability to recognize and utilize their strengths will ultimately enhance their resilience, thereby facilitating their ability to address the numerous challenges that are often a part of life and to cope with and surmount periods of adversity (Garmezy, 1994; Norman, 2000).

An assessment using the strengths-based approach as a foundation requires a broadened and more reflective approach than is often seen in social work practice, particularly in the context of agency-based practice (Graybeal, 2001; Guo and Tsui, 2010). An expanded assessment will encompass the biological, psychological, sociocultural, and spiritual dimensions of a client's experience (Graybeal, 2001). The assessment does not ignore the client's problems or challenges, but views them in a larger context. Additionally, "[h]aving assessed the damage, the social worker needs to ensure that diagnosis does not become a cornerstone of identity" (Saleebey, 1996, p. 303). Accordingly, the social worker must be careful to distinguish between the client's identity, attributes, and behaviors (Graybeal, 2001) and help the client similarly make and understand the significance and implications of these distinctions.

The ROPES (Resources, Opportunities, Possibilities, Exceptions, and Solutions) model serves as one example of a strengths-based assessment (Graybeal, 2001). As an example, the domain of Resources permits the identification of strengths in the personal, family, social environment, organizational, and community contexts. "Exceptions" focuses on the identification of time periods and circumstances in which the identified problem or difficulty was absent and the mechanisms that the individual or family has used to survive and flourish (Graybeal, 2001).

As an example, consider a situation involving a client who has been experiencing auditory hallucinations, disordered speech and thought, and a panoply of behaviors generally associated with a diagnosis of schizophrenia. In working with this client from a strengths perspective, the social worker might engage with the client conversationally to identify with the client what he believes are his strengths and potentially available internal and external resources. The symptoms of his illness are not ignored, but they are not given undue emphasis in the client's efforts to move forward. Rather, they become one ingredient in a larger picture of the client's life.

Consider this same client. All too often, those around the client eradicate his human-ness and he becomes, rather than an individual suffering from the unwelcome symptoms of schizophrenia, a "schizophrenic." Often, characteristics associated with schizophrenia in the popular press, such as extreme and sudden violence towards others, are attributed to the client, even when there is no indication that he has engaged in such behaviors or displayed any proclivity towards them. As one writer has noted, "Labels have the power not only to explain, but to confine and constrict, to objectify the client in ways that reduce the meaningful facts of their lives to secondary trivia" (Graybeal, 2001, p. 237).

The client's integration of the "schizophrenic" label into his identity is but one example of the iatrogenic effect of professional services, i.e., "the treatment causes an unintended adverse reaction" (Greene, Lee, and Hoffpauir, 2005, p. 270), which may exacerbate the client's original difficulties and ability to move forward with his or her life. A social worker using a strengths-based approach would be mindful of the impact of language, monitor his or her own use of language, and refrain from equating the client's diagnosis with the client's identity.

Another example of a strengths-based assessment is one that this author has utilized with many of her clients to help both her and the client to better understand their growth and circumstances. The client is asked to use a sheet of paper and write a single letter of the alphabet on each separate line, from A to Z. On each line, the client is to write one word beginning with that letter that he or she believes describes who they are or how they behave.

As an example, the client might write "stubborn" for the letter "S." At each session with the social worker, the client chooses two or three of his or her words to explore during the course of that session. The client discusses with the social worker-therapist the events or circumstances that, in the client's perspective, explain the origin of his or her attribute or behavior and how he or she has exhibited or utilized that quality or behavior. Through this ongoing process, the client is able to reframe and integrate an alternative understanding of him- or herself, ultimately coming to identify and recognize their strengths, how they have utilized them in the past, and how they can serve them as they move forward with their lives. The process also provides the social worker with considerable insight into the client's self-understanding and the course of his or her life. The client may come to see that what is possibly regarded as stubbornness and what may have been referred to as stubbornness by those around him. may also constitute determination and perseverance, qualities that have helped him or her survive traumatic experiences of childhood abuse and neglect.

Either of these approaches to assessment would likely encounter the criticisms that have been leveled against a strengths-based approach in general. It has been claimed that a strengths-based approach represents yet another form of positive thinking, is merely an effort to reconceptualize individuals' misery and suffering, wrongly denies that some individuals are manipulative and destructive ("Pollyannaism"), and ignores and diminishes clients' real-life problems (Saleebey, 1996). Such criticisms have been countered by the observation that "there is nothing in the strengths approach that mandates the discounting of problems in life that people bring to us [social workers]" (Saleebey, 1997, p. 238).

Perception of the Individual's Environment as Resource-Laden

The strengths-based approach views the individual's environment broadly to encompass elements of his or her culture, such as stories and narratives; family stories, including those of survival; networks of individuals who have undergone similar experiences and that may be supportive such as survivors' networks (George, 2012; Saleebey, 1996); and informal helping networks (Brun and Rapp, 2001). An inventory of available resources might also include contacts and networks developed through the client's community involvement, including his or her place of worship and family rituals (Graybeal, 2001). The identification of environmental resources that match client strengths and desires is deemed critical to the client's attainment of his or her goals (Rapp, Saleebey, and Sullivan, 2005).

The emphasis on "local circuits of cooperation and systems of connectedness" (Jordan, 2008, p. 444) has been criticized due to its shift from a focus on governmental responsibility to civil society to address and correct systemic deficiencies (Gray, 2011). Concerns have also been raised about the strengths-based perspective's "overly optimistic claims about the strength of social capital, community, and community development" and its over-alignment with "contemporary neoliberal norms of self-help and self-responsibility" (Gray, 2011, p. 10).

Explicit Methods That Rely on Client Strengths for the Attainment of Goals

According to one proponent of the strengths-based approach, common sense and tacit knowing are to be prioritized above scientific knowledge (Saleebey, 2002). Yet another writer has advanced a constructivist approach that recognizes how reality is negotiated through human language and interaction and that utilizes client narrative to both engage the client and facilitate client transformation (Greene et al., 2005). Social workers are advised to "dialogue with clients conversationally rather than interviewing them, keeping their conversations focused as much as possible on client strengths, competencies, assets, and resources" (Greene et al., 2005, p. 268). Social workers are urged to use language of collaboration, ownership, possibilities, solutions, elaboration, and clarification to assist the client in his or her efforts to identify strengths, assets, and resources (Greene et al., 2005). Through these mechanisms, it is believed that the client will develop a greater sense of agency, reframe experiences so as to accept more positive interpretations of events and actions they previously defined as negative, identify their strengths, and recognize how they might utilize these strengths to help them overcome their difficulties.

Poetry therapy has been suggested as a potential method that is congruent with a strengths-based approach (Furman et al., 2002). Poetry therapy, which is one form of bibliotherapy, involves the structured reading and writing of poetry to achieve delineated therapeutic goals (Lerner, 1981). The use of poetry may facilitate clients' ability to develop alternative metaphors for their lives (Furman et al., 2002), in much the same way as a narrative approach may promote their recognition and development of alternative narratives.

Despite the identification of such methods for the delivery of a strengths-based approach, the extant literature lacks extensive discussion relating to the application of a strengths-based approach in the moment and throughout the course of the social worker-client relationship. Additionally, at least one writer has observed that "there is a clear lack of support for the claimed success of these strengths-based approaches" (Grayson, 2011, p. 10). Indeed, relatively few published studies focused on the effectiveness of a strengths-based approach have been conducted with methodological rigor, e.g., controlling for confounding factors, comparing the strengths-based approach to another approach with a control group, utilizing an adequate sample size to permit detection of a statistically significant effect, to name but a few aspects that demand additional consideration. Qualitative studies of strengths-based approaches have similarly lacked the methodological rigor expected of qualitative research (Rapp et al., 2005; Staudt, Howard, and Drake, 2001. Cf. Allison et al., 2003).

Hope-Inducing Relationship

Relationships are central to the strengths-based perspective and are considered to be its moral bulwark (Goldstein, 2002; Gray, 2011). The relationship between the client and the social worker has been characterized as accepting, purposeful, and empathetic (Rapp et al., 2005). The social worker is to guide the client towards the identification of his or her strengths, possibilities, and opportunities, and the enhancement of his or her confidence by inspiring, questioning, and encouraging the client (Gray, 2011; Rapp et al., 2005). The strengths-based approach is premised on the idea that this interaction will foster trust in the relationship and facilitate the development of client feelings of hope (Brun and Rapp, 2001; Early and GlenMaye, 2000; Rapp et al., 2005).

Provision of Meaningful Choices and Client Authority to Choose

Various authors have suggested that the transformation of the social worker-client relationship from that of an unequal dyad to one of equals undertaking a collaborative partnership both fosters client hope and facilitates the client's identification of strengths, possibilities, and opportunities (Chapin and Cox, 2002; Greene et al., 2005; Guo and Tsui, 2010; Weick et al., 1989). Problems are not ignored during this collaborative process, but neither are they accorded pre-eminence. The social worker and the client work collaboratively to explore various strategies and courses of action, with the client retaining the authority and agency, in most cases, to define and redefine his or her goals and to select from among the identified strategies and courses of action (Early and GlenMaye, 2000). (The exception would be in situations in which client possibilities and potential courses of action may be constrained due to a court order, conditions of probation, and other legally-imposed limitations and considerations.) The role of the social worker is changed from that of an expert to one of facilitator or translator (Guo and Tsui, 2010; Weick et al., 1989).

The reformulation of the social worker role to be an equal collaborative partner with the client instead of an authority has been criticized for its failure to recognize the power disparity and asymmetry that are part of the social worker-client relationship due to the very nature and existence of the relationship (Cowger, 1998; Guo and Tsui, 2010). A client in the context of social work practice is, all too frequently, not a client voluntarily, but instead has presented for services in response to a court order, a condition of probation, or a situation that has come to the attention of a social service agency, e.g., due to abuse or neglect or a need for health care.

Case Example: The Therapeutic Farm Community - An Integrative, Strengths-Based Approach to Mental Health Treatment

There are various configurations of therapeutic farm communities for the provision of services to mentally ill adults in both the United States and Europe, not all of which are premised on a strengths-based perspective (Loue, 2016). It is beyond the scope of this chapter to present even all of those that do rest on such a foundation. This portion of the chapter describes one therapeutic farm community in the United States and one in Ireland that explicitly rest on a strengths perspective.

CooperRiis Healing Community (CooperRiis)

CooperRiis Healing Community (CooperRiis) was established in 2003 as a private, not-for-profit organization through the efforts of Don and Lisbeth Riis Cooper. The farm, located in Mill Spring, North Carolina, consists of 95 acres and includes two administration buildings; three lodges, each of which houses 12 residents; several houses for staff who live on-site; vegetable gardens; farm animals, including horses, goats, rabbits, and chickens; cats and dogs; a labyrinth; a pond; tennis courts; and numerous nature trails. An urban alternative to the farm is available to residents and is housed in a building in Asheville, North Carolina. The building, known as 85Z, offers essentially the same services as the farm, with the exception of activities involving the animals.

CooperRiis has explicitly adopted a strength perspective, although not naming it as such. CooperRiis describes itself as "a place of integration and recovery of wholeness, a place where isolation is replaced by relationship, and where the mind, body and spirit are nurtured within nature" (CooperRiis Healing Community, 2014a, p. 1). Its approach is clearly reflected in its mission statement: "Our mission is to help individuals whose lives are impeded by mental health challenges or emotional distress to develop their capacities for creativity, wholeness, relationship, and optimal health so that they may achieve their highest levels of fulfillment and functioning and respond productively to their future challenges and opportunities for growth" (CooperRiis Healing Community, 2014a, p. 1). Additionally, staff members are expected to provide and foster

- "A culture of emotional and physical safety;
- A personal life of meaning, belonging, hope and purpose;
- An atmosphere of kindness, respect, and open and authentic communication;
- Each individual's ideas, contributions, and service to the work and the social life of the community;
- Interactions that facilitate comfort and ease within the cooperriis environment; and
- Relationships that are founded on empathy and mutuality" (cooperriis, 2014a, p. 2).

At entry into CooperRiis, each resident is asked to compose a Dream Statement, setting forth their hopes and wishes for their future. The development of each resident's Recovery Plan is aligned with both the goals identified in their Dream Statement and with the holistic richness of the therapeutic community. Recovery is viewed as a nonlinear process that progresses through three phases. Programming is designed to facilitate individuals' development in seven distinct domains through each of the three phases of recovery. These seven domains include community and connectedness, spirituality, physical wellness, emotional and psychological health, purpose and productivity, empowerment and independence, and the domain of intellectual functions, learning, and creativity. Available services include individual and group therapy, medication optimization, recovery planning and coordination, psychoeducation, substance abuse support, wellness planning and education, physical health support strategies, family education and support, arts and recreational activities, and scheduling coordination. The specific services available to each individual often depend upon the individual level of need.

CooperRiis evaluates its programming and approach on an ongoing basis. Residents are asked at least once each year to provide feedback with regard to whether their participation in the social, recreational and therapeutic life of CooperRiis is welcomed and appreciated; whether they feel believed in; whether they feel that their input makes a difference; and whether they are empowered and encouraged to assert themselves and plan for the future, while also being encouraged to feel empathetic for others and supportive of them to do the same (CooperRiis Healing Community, 2014b). CooperRiis has also conducted methodologically rigorous research to evaluate the effectiveness of its intervention approach. While not examining the strengths perspective specifically, the research to date indicates that its integrative model focused on the seven domains and provision of individualized recovery supports facilitates both individuals' recovery from the effects of severe mental illness and promotes their continued growth and functioning (Snyder, Young, and Schactman, 2015; Young, Schactman, and Snyder, 2014; Young, Snyder, and Schactman, 2015).

Slí Eile

Slí Eile is located in Burton Park in the village of Churchtown, Ireland, approximately a one hour drive from the larger city of Cork. Slí Eile was established by Joan Hamilton only a few years ago, through her efforts to identify an appropriate and effective intervention to aid her daughter in her struggle to recover from her mental illness. The 50 acre farm and farmhouse are rented from the farm's owner and an additional 90 acres are reserved for forestry. Slí Eile also has a bungalow in the nearby town of Charleville, a portion of which has been transformed into a bakery. The bakery and the farm provide Slí Eile residents with opportunities to develop and improve necessary socialization and occupational skills to successfully interact with co-residents and the world outside of Slí Eile.

The enunciated goal of Slí Eile "is to provide a safe environment conducive to recovery" (Sapouna, 2007, p. 6). Notably, Slí Eile staff do not utilize diagnostic labels or categories for the residents; the focus remains on individuals' behaviors and the development of residents' abilities to interact meaningfully with others and to set and achieve their goals.

Slí Eile does not provide direct care services. Instead, residents obtain mental health services from their mental health team that was in place prior to their residence at Slí Eile and attend clinical appointments with support from Slí Eile staff. The perspective of the therapeutic community is premised on William Glasser's Choice Theory and Reality Therapy (William Glasser Institute, 2010a, b). Choice theory theorizes that humans choose most of their behaviors and that genes drive humans' efforts to fulfill their five basic needs of survival, love and belonging, power, freedom, and fun (William Glasser Institute, 2010a). Staff and residents are encouraged to practice the Seven Caring Behaviors (listening, encouraging, negotiating, supporting, trusting, affirming, respecting) and refrain from engaging in the Seven Deadly Behaviors (blaming, complaining, criticizing, bribing, threatening, punishing, nagging) of Glasser's Choice Theory (William Glasser Institute, 2010a).

According to Glasser, reality therapy derives from choice theory. Reality therapy urges individuals to focus on the present rather than the past; avoid discussing symptoms and complaints; focus on what can be accomplished through thinking and acting; refrain from criticizing, blaming, or complaining; be nonjudgmental and noncoercive, avoid allowing excuses to interfere with their ability to make connections, attend to specifics, and develop specific, achievable plans with appropriate follow-through (Turnage, Jacinto, and Kirven, 2003; William Glasser Institute, 2010a, b). Like a strengths-based perspective, reality therapy focuses on the positive and on the formulation of specific, achievable goals. Unlike a strengths perspective, it dissuades discussion of symptoms, even though symptoms may represent one of the challenges that impede client growth and that must be addressed in order to accomplish one's identified goals.

Slí Eile conceptualizes of recovery as progressing through four phases. During each phase, individuals, referred to as tenants, are tasked with the responsibility of evaluating their own behavior, the consequences of their behavior, and alternative approaches to dealing with various situations that may arise. At each stage of recovery, individuals assume increasing responsibility, e.g., self-administration of their medications as prescribed at stage 2; development of educational, employment, and living goals at stage 3. Unfortunately, Slí Eile has conducted minimal research to evaluate the effectiveness of its approach.

ETHICAL CONSIDERATIONS AND STRENGTHS-BASED SOCIAL WORK

Client Decision-Making/Self-Determination

Client self-determination constitutes a primary ethical responsibility owed by the social worker to the client. The *Code of Ethics* of the National Association of Social Workers in the United States provides: "Social workers respect and promote the right of clients to self-determination and assist clients in their efforts to identify and clarify their goals. Social workers may limit clients' right to self-determination when, in the social workers' professional judgment, clients' actions or potential actions pose a serious, foreseeable, and imminent risk to themselves or others" (National Association of Social Workers, 2008, 1.02).

This ethical precept derives from the broader ethical perspective of respect for persons, which encompasses the concept of client autonomy. The extant literature relating to the strengths-based approach appears at first reading to consider client decisionmaking paramount in its implementation. Closer inspection, however, raises questions regarding the extent to which this actually occurs.

Clients who present for social work services, whether voluntarily or involuntarily, are often vulnerable, whether due to the occurrence of a major life event, a change in their circumstances, and/or legal difficulties. It is somewhat disingenuous to assert that the social worker-client relationship is transformed from one of authority to one of true collaboration and equality merely because the social worker is to focus with the client on the identification of the client's strengths and how best to utilize them. A discussion that is characterized by a collaborative exchange of ideas and information cannot be equated with a collaborative relationship, even when these discussions occur over a period of time. The exchange of financial consideration in the form of payment to the social worker or to his or her agency, and/or the existence of probation requirements or court order, negate a true collaborative relationship. The social worker is still seen as an authority, someone who possesses the specific skills and knowledge that are needed to facilitate the achievement of a specific outcome (Gambrill, 2001). The extent to which the social worker's values affect the client's perceptions and understandings of his or her situation through this process has generally not been the focus of systematic inquiry.

Issues Related to Informed Consent

Like client self-determination, the requirement of informed consent also derives from the ethical principle of respect for persons. Valid informed consent requires that a client be provided with the information necessary to allow him or her to make an informed choice, that the information that is provided be made available in an understandable format that the client actually understands, that the client have the capacity to make an informed decision, and that whatever decision is made is done so voluntarily.

Codes of ethics governing social work practice make clear that the provision of treatment to a client is to be conditioned upon the receipt of valid informed consent. The *Code of Ethics* of the (U.S.) National Association of Social Workers provides: "Social workers should provide services to clients only in the context of a professional relationship based, when appropriate, on valid informed consent. Social workers should use clear and understandable language to inform clients of the purpose of the services, risks related to the services, limits to services because of the requirements of a third-party payer, relevant costs, reasonable alternatives, clients' right to refuse or withdraw consent, and the time frame covered by the consent. Social workers should provide clients with an opportunity to ask questions" (National Association of Social Workers, 2008, 1.03).

A similar requirement is enunciated in the *Code of Ethics* of the Clinical Social Work Association. That *Code* states in pertinent part: "Clinical social work treatment takes place within a context of informed consent. This requires that the client(s) be informed of the extent and nature of the services being offered as well as the mutual limits, rights, opportunities, and obligations associated with the provision of and payment for those services regardless of whether the services are mandated or voluntary or delivered in person or via electronic media (such as computer, telephone (including land line or smart phone), telehealth media devices, television or radio). In order for the consent to be valid, the client(s) must be informed in a manner that is clear to them, must choose freely and without undue influence, and must have the capacity to make an informed choice" (Clinical Social Work Association, 2016).

As indicated earlier, there is a striking lack of rigorous research relating to the effectiveness of a strengths-based approach. Indeed, a major proponent of the strengths perspective has claimed that common sense and tacit knowing are to be prioritized above scientific knowledge (Saleebey, 2002). The absence of a body of research that tests this approach against the more traditional, problem-focused approach calls into question the extent to which a client can make an *informed* decision regarding his or her wish to proceed along this path. Evaluations of the effectiveness and the risks and benefits of utilizing a strength perspective have not been conducted; as a result, it is possible to advise the client of risks and benefits of the approach only from an almost purely theoretical vantage point. Because of the paucity of research, a social worker cannot represent to the client that focusing on the identification of his or her strengths may be superior to focusing more directly on his or her problems. As one writer noted, "If there are no means by which to tell what is accurate and what is not, if all methods are equally effective, the vacuum is filled by an elite who are powerful enough to say what is and what is not. The "many ways of knowing" rhetoric prevents the critical appraisal of practice-related claims and protects social work from making its work and its consequences transparent" (Gambrill, 2001, p. 169).

Indeed, the sincerity of social workers and the social work profession in general has been questioned due to the lack of attention to research and its findings. The same writer has asserted, "I see a deep thread of insincerity in our profession. Many are insincere in their efforts to help clients if, by sincere, we mean caring enough to draw on practice-related research findings, carefully evaluate the effects of services, and involve clients as informed participants" (Gambrill, 2001, p. 172). In the case of strengths-based social work, the research must first exist in order to draw on its findings.

SOLUTIONS AND RECOMMENDATIONS

The benefits ascribed to the utilization of a strengths perspective in social work practice are often presumed to exist. However, this assumption is clearly misplaced in view of the dearth of methodologically rigorous research deigned specifically to evaluate the effects of this approach. As a result, both social workers and the clients who receive their services maintain a false sense of knowing, the social worker with respect to the actual effectiveness of the approach that he or she is employing, and the client with respect to the risks, benefits, feasibility, and acceptability of this approach in his or her specific situation. Accordingly, there is a need for additional research, described further below. In addition, clients should be advised as part of the informed consent process that the social worker will be utilizing this approach, that there is no research to demonstrate that it is either more or less effective than any other approach in helping the client to identify and accomplish his or her objectives, and that the risks and benefits of the approach are largely unknown. The provision of this information is no different, for example, than advising a client that the social worker approaches the conduct of therapy from a Jungian perspective or uses techniques from Gestalt therapy, or recommends a cognitive behavioral approach.

FUTURE RESEARCH DIRECTIONS

Various authors have offered suggestions for how to reframe questions and language so as to approach clients from a strengths perspective (Graybeal, 2001; Greene et al., 2005; Saleebey, 1996). Greene and colleagues (2005), for example, have stressed the importance of utilizing language of collaboration, ownership, possibilities, solutions, elaboration, and clarification. Graybeal (2001), who developed the ROPES assessment strategy noted earlier in this chapter, has identified questions that may be asked of clients to facilitate a strengths approach. "S," representing "Solutions," encompasses the following questions:

- "What's working now?
- What are your successes?
- What are you doing that you would like to continue doing?
- What if a miracle happened?
- What can you do now to create a piece of the miracle?" (Graybeal, 2001, p. 237).

This focus on language suggests the possibility of designing a research protocol that would first manualize a strengths approach and then test the approach in an intervention trial. The intervention arm that utilizes the manualized strengths approach could potentially consist of various agencies and the comparison group that receives the standard problem-focused approach could include different agencies whose populations client populations present with similar issues. Clearly, informed consent would be needed from the participating agencies, social workers, and clients. An adequate sample size of agencies in each arm of the intervention trial and of clients across the agencies in each intervention arm would permit adjustment for at least major confounding variables and for comparison between the two approaches. An obvious difficulty would be to account for the multiple factors that could modify and/or confound the effect of the strengths based intervention or the problem-focused approach.

Methodologically rigorous qualitative research is also needed. Although some qualitative research has been conducted in an effort to ascertain client perspectives about the approach (e.g., Brun and Rapp, 2001), the research is less than optimal in that it has focused on specific populations, the sample sizes have been small, and the research has largely been confined to a single evaluation point in time. A study that follows clients longitudinally to understand their perceptions of the strengths approach and to document their adoption, or lack thereof, of strength-based strategies over time would be a contribution to the field.

Such research designs address questions related to the effects of the strength-based approach. Additional research is needed to answer questions raised in the ethical context. What, if anything, are clients told about the strengths-based approach when it is being used? What do they understand about it? Are there potential risks that have not been identified and, if so, how can they best be addressed? Are there benefits that can be documented that have not heretofore been recognized?

CONCLUSION

The strengths-based approach to social work services promises to facilitate client identification of strengths and resources that can be used to assist the client in his or her development and growth. Whether this promise is actually fulfilled remains an open question due to the absence of a systematic delivery of the approach and the paucity of methodologically rigorous research that has evaluated its effectiveness. As a consequence, ethical questions exist regarding the extent to which client consent for the delivery of social work services utilizing this approach can be said to be informed, even if the services provided to a particular client prove to be beneficial. Additional research is needed to evaluate the effects of this approach and its acceptability to clients.

REFERENCES

Allison, S., Stacey, K., Dadds, V., Roeger, L., Wood, A., & Martin, G. (2003). What the family brings: Gathering evidence for strengths-based work. *Journal of Family Therapy*, *25*(3), 263–284. doi:10.1111/1467-6427.00248

Axinn, J., & Levin, H. (1975). *Social welfare: A history of the American response to need*. New York: Harper & Row.

Barker, R. L. (2003). *The social work dictionary* (5th ed.). Washington, DC: NASW Press.

Blundo, R. (2001). Learning strengths-based practice: Challenging our personal and professional frames. *Families in Society*, *82*(3), 296–304. doi:10.1606/1044-3894.192

Boehm, W. W. (1959). *The social casework method in social work education. A project report of the curriculum study* (Vol. 10). New York: Council on Social Work Education.

Brun, C., & Rapp, R. C. (2001). Strengths-based case management: Individuals' perspective on strengths and the case manager relationship. *Social Work*, *46*(3), 278–288.

Chapin, R., & Cox, E. O. (2002). Changing the paradigm. *Journal of Gerontological Social Work*, *36*(3-4), 165–179. doi:10.1300/J083v36n03_13

Clinical Social Work Association. (2016). *Code of ethics*. Retrieved from http://www.clinicalsocialworkassociation.org/CSWA-Ethics

CooperRiis Healing Community. (2014a). *Board operating principles*. Mill Spring, NC: Author.

CooperRiis Healing Community. (2014b). *Manual of policies, programs, procedures and practices*. Mill Spring, NC: Author.

Cowger, C. D. (1998). Clientilism and clientification: Impediments to strengths based social work practice. *Journal of Sociology and Social Welfare*, *25*(1), 25–37.

Early, T. J., & GlenMaye, L. F. (2000). Valuing families: Social work practice with families from a strength perspective. *Social Work*, *45*(2), 118–130. doi:10.1093/sw/45.2.118 PMID:10710985

Furman, R., Downey, E. P., Jackson, R. L., & Bender, K. (2002). Poetry therapy as a tool for strengths-based practice. *Administration in Social Work*, *3*(2), 146–157.

Garmezy, N. (1994). Reflections and commentary on risk, resilience, and development. In R. J. Haggerty, L. R. Sherrod, N. Garmezy, & M. Rutter (Eds.), *Stress, risk, and resilience in children and adolescents: Processes, mechanisms, and interventions* (pp. 1–18). Cambridge, UK: Cambridge University Press.

George, M. (2012). Migration traumatic experiences and refugee distress: Implications for social work practice. *Clinical Social Work*, *40*(4), 429–437. doi:10.1007/s10615-012-0397-y

Gray, M. (2011). Back to basics: A critique of the strengths perspective in social work. *Families in Society*, *92*(1), 5–11. doi:10.1606/1044-3894.4054

Graybeal, C. (2001). Strengths-based social work assessment: Transforming the dominant paradigm. *Families in Society*, *82*(3), 233–242. doi:10.1606/1044-3894.236

Greene, G. J., Lee, M. Y., & Hoffpauir, S. (2005). The languages of empowerment and strengths in clinical social work: A constructivist perspective. *Families in Society*, *86*(2), 267–277. doi:10.1606/1044-3894.2465

Guo, W., & Tsui, M. (2010). From resilience to resistance: A reconstruction of the strength perspective in social work practice. *International Social Work*, *53*(2), 233–245. doi:10.1177/0020872809355391

Jordan, B. (2008). Social work and world poverty. *International Social Work*, *51*(4), 440–452. doi:10.1177/0020872808090238

Lerner, A. (1981). Poetry therapy. In R. Corsini (Ed.), *Handbook of innovative psychotherapies* (pp. 138–152). New York: John Wiley and Sons.

Loue, S. (2016). Therapeutic farms in Europe and the U.S.: Recovery from mental illness. New York: Springer Science+Business. doi:10.1007/978-3-319-13539-7

McClain, W. H. (1907). Relations existing between defective characteristics and dependence. *Proceedings of the National Conference of Charities and Correction*, 347-354.

McMillen, J. C., Morris, L., & Sheraden, M. (2004). Ending social work's grudge match: Problems versus strengths. *Muskie School of Public Service*, 5. Retrieved from http://digitalcommons.usm.maine.edu/muskie/5

National Association of Social Workers. (2008). *Code of ethics*. Retrieved from https://www.socialworkers.org/pubs/code/code.asp?print=1&print=1&pr

Norman, E. (2000). *Resiliency enhancement: Putting the strengths perspective into social work practice*. New York: Columbia University Press. doi:10.7312/norm11800

Rapp, C. A., Saleebey, D., & Sullivan, W. P. (2005). The future of strengths-based social work. *Administration in Social Work*, *6*(1), 79–90.

Richmond, M. (1917). *Social diagnosis*. New York: Sage.

Saleebey, D. (1996). The strengths perspective in social work practice: Extensions and cautions. *Social Work*, *41*(3), 296–305. PMID:8936085

Saleebey, D. (1997). The strengths perspective: Possibilities and problems. In D. Saleebey (Ed.), *The strengths perspective in social work practice* (2nd ed.; pp. 231–248). New York: Longman.

Saleebey, D. (2002). *The strengths perspective in social work practice* (3rd ed.). New York: Longman.

Saleebey, D. (2006). Power in the people: Introduction. In D. Saleebey (Ed.), *The strengths perspective in social work practice* (4th ed.; pp. 1–24). Boston: Allyn & Bacon.

Sapouna, L. (2007, May). *Progress report on the Slí Eile housing project*. Cork, Ireland: Department of Applied Social Studies, University College Cork.

Smalley, R. E. (1967). *Theory for social work practice*. New York: Columbia University Press.

Snyder, M., Schactman, L., & Young, S. (2015). Rates and correlations of change in three dimensions of recovery within a recovery model oriented therapeutic community. *The Psychiatric Quarterly*, *86*(1), 123–136. doi:10.1007/s11126-014-9318-2 PMID:25294276

Staudt, M., Howard, M. O., & Drake, B. (2001). The operationalization, implementation and effectiveness of the strengths perspective: A review of empirical studies. *Journal of Social Service Research*, *27*(3), 1–21. doi:10.1300/J079v27n03_01

Turnage, B. F., Jacinto, G. A., & Kirven, J. (2003). Reality therapy, domestic violence survivors, and self-forgiveness. *International Journal of Reality Therapy*, *22*(2), 24–27.

Weick, A., Rapp, C., Sullivan, W. P., & Kisthardt, W. (1989). A strengths perspective for social work practice. *Social Work*, *34*(4), 350–354. doi:10.1093/sw/34.4.350

William Glasser Institute. (2010a). *Choice theory*. Retrieved from http://www.wglasser.com/the-glasser-approach/choice-theory

William Glasser Institute. (2010b). *Reality therapy*. Retrieved 16 July 2015 from http://www.wglasser.com/the-glasser-approach/reality-therapy

Young, S., Schactman, L., & Snyder, M. (2014). Early report on the effectiveness of a recovery model oriented therapeutic community for individuals with complex and persistent recovery challenges. *The Psychiatric Quarterly*, *85*(3), 329–343. doi:10.1007/s11126-014-9292-8 PMID:24615555

Young, S., Snyder, M., & Schactman, L. (2015). Early recovery from psychotic spectrum disorder within a therapeutic community: Significance and effects. *Psychosis*, *7*(1/2), 37–47. doi:10.1080/17522439.2014.926387

Chapter 7
Ethical Dilemmas in Social Work Practice:
Case of Botswana

Tumani Malinga
University of Illinois at Urbana-Champaign, USA

Poloko Nuggert Ntshwarang
University of KwaZulu Natal, South Africa

Masego Lecha
Ministry of Local Government, Botswana

ABSTRACT

Ethical dilemmas are conflicts that arise when two or more ethical principles clash. As social work practitioners often grapple with ethical dilemmas in their practice, it is important and informative to explore how they address them, especially in different cultural contexts. Drawing on data from a qualitative exploratory study of social work practitioners in different settings in Botswana, this chapter identifies and discusses several ethical dilemmas that social work practitioners in Botswana come across in their practice in both government and non-governmental organizations and how they address them. The chapter also examines the struggles practitioners deal with such as ethical stress, as they try to address and deal the ethical dilemmas. The chapter brings forth recommendations that social work ethics should be part of the educational curriculum and the importance of practitioners' self-awareness.

DOI: 10.4018/978-1-5225-3090-9.ch007

INTRODUCTION

Throughout the world, social work practitioners are expected to conform to social work ethics and principles and to uphold the ethical standards of social work practice. Ethical standards are critical in research, education and practice (Congress & McAuliffe, 2006). These standards include responsibility to society at large; clients; colleagues; ethical responsibility in practice settings; and responsibility as professionals as well as to the profession (Congress, 2000; NASW 1996). Ethics are critical in fields such as social work to ensure that practitioners maintain some professional conduct. It is critical to abide by the set professional conduct of ethics and values to ensure legitimacy and credibility of the profession (Banks, 2008). However, the extent to which social workers uphold the code of ethics in practice depends on the nature of their work environments, and the uniqueness of the country's legal requirements. Furthermore, it depends on clients' culture, as well as social workers' own individual values and backgrounds. Because of all these interactions, social work practitioners are confronted with ethical issues that often lead to ethical dilemmas.

Ethical issues are challenging situations that are connected to rights, responsibilities, and obligations that are founded within moral and value based foundations (McAuliffe, 2005). Ethical dilemmas are complex and difficult circumstances where social work practitioners should make decisions pertaining to issues that conflict with ethical principles, agency procedures, laws of the country or directives that may create disagreements and/or are likely to be unaccepted by the receiving party (Kadushin & Egan, 2001; McAuliffe, 2005). An ethical dilemma arises where values or ethical principles are placed in conflict with one another and resolution at either pole of the dilemma is unsatisfactory, leading to outcomes that one would not seek in an ideal world (Banks, 2001; McAuliffe, 2005). Ethical dilemmas are due to the clash of multiple ethical principles such as challenging injustice; helping people in need; respect for the dignity and worth of a person, and recognizing the importance of human relations (NASW, 1996). They can also be propelled by the clash between workplace or organization's expectations and professional values (McAuliffe, 2005). In some instances, ethical dilemmas relate to boundary issues where social work practitioners experience struggles or possible conflicts between their professional duties and their various personal relationships (Congress & McAuliffe, 2006; Reamer, 2003). Other challenges creating ethical dilemmas relate to issues of confidentiality, cultural competence, and competence in the field of practice (Congress, 2000). Streets (2008) argues that clients' culture, religion, and spirituality are critical in social work profession, and that once these clashes with the values of the profession, then ethical dilemmas are created, hampering social work practice in service delivery and impacting on the wellbeing and identity of clients and the integrity of the social work profession.

Like other Sub-Saharan African countries, social work practitioners in Botswana are faced with several challenges such as shortage of staff, shortage of office space, poor salaries and work conditions, and burnout which in general terms worsens ethical dilemmas, as well as lack of professionalism in practice. Some authors such as Congress and McAuliffe (2006) and Reamer (2003) attest that ethical dilemmas obstruct the social worker's ability to make professional discretion and judgment about clients' situations. For example, if social work practitioners experiencing ethical dilemmas do not get adequate supervision and social support networks, they are likely to experience occupational stress, workplace burnout, as well as emotional and psychological distress (Congress & McAuliffe, 2006; McAuliffe, 2005). The situation among social work practitioners in Botswana is worsened by the lack of a professional social work body at a national level to guide them. All practitioners are mainly guided and controlled by the varying employer's conditions of service. As such, this chapter seeks to examine ethical dilemmas that social work practitioners in Botswana experience, and the impact of ethical dilemmas on service provision and how they are resolved.

BACKGROUND

Botswana experienced rapid social and economic development since its independence in 1966. Before independence, the citizens of Botswana relied on self-sufficient agricultural economies and the traditional welfare system where there was communal spirit and collective participation (Nthomang, 2007). After independence however, there was a shift to cash based economies as traditional structures were eroded by modernization and rural-urban migration (Seleka, et al., 2007). These social changes had adverse implications on family welfare. Poverty became prevalent in many households (O'laughlin, 1998). The government therefore, introduced more formalized services and more families sort formal social protection measures for 'relief' (Seleka, et al., 2007). Such services were provided by social workers and the need for social workers grew in the country.

Even though the social welfare function was evident in Botswana since 1946, it was not clear how they operated as they were a unit in the then Department of Education. However, after independence and social changes impacting on the family, the importance of the social welfare function became evident, as it was introduced in the Ministry of Health – (Directorate of Public Service Management (DPSM, 2000)). It was later transferred to the then Ministry of Local Government, Lands and Housing (MLGLH) in 1995 for better coordination as there were challenges that practitioners had in reference to which ethics to adhere to, those of nurses or teachers, at the expense of social work ethical principles (DPSM, 2000).

Because of the nomadic history of the Social Work profession in Botswana, professional ethical principles had been blurred. The blurriness can be explained by practitioners working under the supervision of non-social work professionals who do not fully understand the roles, principles, and ethics of social work. Social work practitioners are involved in direct work with clients and need to have proper organizational structures to support, enhance, and strengthen the direct functions (Hoffmann, 1967). As a result, there is a need for social work supervision from professionals who have social work training to ensure that needs of direct practitioners are met.

Social work training in Botswana, could also contribute to this blurriness, as it is informed by western world Universities' curriculum content. The emphasis is to train practitioners in emerging knowledge, technology, skills, and techniques to develop their potential in practice. Even though the training tries to align the curriculum to national needs and to also address the lack of "relevance" and "appropriateness" of Social Work curriculum in Africa as was alluded to by Hutton (1992); Osei-Hwedie (2000); and Mwansa (2011), it is still a challenge as most of the literature used is from western countries based on their experiences, values, ethics, and laws. In addition, social work professionals in Botswana do not have a professional body that guides and help them uphold the standards of the profession.

As a result, social work practitioners in Botswana are faced with several challenges emanating from human service settings that are stifled with limited resources such as shortage of staff, shortage of office space and supervisors who do not fully understand the social work mandate. Therefore, social work practitioners are constantly faced with ethical dilemmas. In as much as they attempt to address ethical dilemmas by adhering to professional ethics, bearing in mind the requirements of international professional standards, they still should adhere to their organizational code of conduct, which might conflict with NASW code of conduct.

Even though Botswana National Social Work Association (BOSWA) was formed, it is still at infancy stage and does not have a code of conduct. However, there was a blink of hope as in October 18, 2016, the Assistant minister of Local Government and Rural Development reported that the ministry has drafted an ethical code of conduct for social work professionals that would ultimately be presented to cabinet for approval (Motsamai, 2016). Despite lack of professional code of conduct to guide social work practitioners' conduct in Botswana, they attempt to abide by the NASW code of ethics.

METHODS

Qualitative research employing in-depth interviews was conducted with social work practitioners in Botswana to achieve a depth of understanding of ethical dilemmas they face in practice. Qualitative research enables the researchers to examine how people make sense of their settings and experiences through roles, identities, and why people act as they do (Kalof, Dan & Dietz, 2008). Secondly, it allows the research problem to be investigated and be reported considering the complex and multiple contexts in which it occurs (Rubin & Babbie, 1993).

Ten social work practitioners were purposively selected from practitioners who had been practicing for five years or more in government agencies, and Non-Governmental Organizations (NGO) and who interact with clients on regular basis. Purposive sampling allowed the researchers to select participants that are satisfactory to the research needs (Neuman, 2007) and knowledgeable about the phenomenon investigated (Engel, & Schuitt, 2013). The authors deliberately sampled 10 practitioners who had been practicing for five years or more, as they believed this group of practitioners are well established in the profession and have experience on dealing with challenges that come along with their practice. While a small sample is needed to facilitate in-depth understanding of research phenomenon in qualitative studies (Hesse-Biber, 2006, p. 19; Maxwell, 2013), it is important to note that the sample size in the study should be determined by data saturation (Bowen, 2008; Brod, Tesler, & Christiansen, 2009; Fusch & Ness, 2015). As was argued by Fusch and Ness (2015, p. 1409) selecting a sample that '*has the best opportunity for the researcher to reach data saturation*' can be beneficial than relying on a bigger sample size. For this study, data was collected up to the point of saturation because the authors did not see any reason to increase the sample by the 10th participant as common themes were already identified. Data saturation was shown by data duplication denoted by lack of additional information during data collection and no need for further coding (Bowen, 2008; Brod, Tesler, & Christiansen, 2009; Fusch & Ness, 2015).

To ensure data saturation, the authors constructed a saturation grid whereby the main themes were listed on the vertical and interview responses on the horizontal (Brod, Tesler, & Christiansen, 2009). The saturation grid was filled in as data collection continued between the two authors. The two authors did coding, and this is one recommendation made by Brod and colleagues to help in reaching saturation. It became obvious as the interviews progressed that no new data was emerging as was shown in the saturation grid. The third author examined the saturation grid and the developed codes. After discussion, the authors agreed that saturation had been reached, as there was correspondence between the codes and the grid. Asking probing questions allowed participants to explain their points, and the use of the same structured interview tool among all participants facilitated data saturation (Fusch & Ness, 2015). Additionally, in qualitative research the richness and thickness of data prevail over sample size as it also helps the researchers to decide the point of data saturation during data collection (Burmeister, & Aitken, 2012; Dibley, 2011).

In analyzing the data, the three authors independently read the transcripts to solicit ideas of developing categories. Allowing categories to come from data, and not from preconceived ideas informed by a theory allowed the authors to fully engage with the data and be open to innovative ideas that are prompted through reading the transcripts. Miles and Huberman's (1994) framework of qualitative data analysis, thematic analysis, was used. Thematic analysis focuses on identifiable themes and patterns of living and/or behavior. Steps followed include data reduction, data display, and conclusion drawing and verification.

RESULTS

The data for this chapter was collected between May and August 2016, and analysis was done from September until December 2016. The results indicate that social work practitioners in Botswana experience various ethical dilemmas because of the nature of their jobs, the culture of the agency they work in, client's culture and expectations as well as their competency and personal values as practitioners. The ethical dilemmas obstruct the social worker's ability to make professional discretion and judgment about clients' situations. However, use of different strategies to address the ethical dilemmas was reported. Such strategies include having team meetings to discuss cases, consultation with supervisor or other social workers with more experience in practice, and reading social work journal articles.

Organizations That Employ Social Work Practitioners in Botswana

Social Work practitioners in Botswana work in diverse settings, such as the government and NGOs. Below is an overview of settings that social work practitioners are found.

Government

The government of Botswana is the major employer of social work practitioners. The Department of Social Protection (DSP), under the Ministry of Local Government and Rural Development has the mandate to coordinate, monitor and evaluate social protection programmes and projects delivery to improve the quality of lives of Batswana (Government of Botswana, 2010). DSP was initially called Department of Social Services (DSS) and changed its name to DSP in 2014. As outlined in the Social Development Policy Framework for Botswana: Phase I - Situation Analysis, DSP has nine divisions, namely;

Departmental Management: Responsible for human resource issues, budgeting, and general administration.

Community Development: Responsible for the Remote Area Development Programme (RADP) and overseeing Village Development Committees (VDC).

Specialized Services: Responsible for clinical social work. Practitioners are deployed in health centers.

Probation and After Care: Responsible for the rehabilitation of juvenile offenders at the Ikago School of Industries.

Family Welfare Services: Addresses psychosocial issues and complex social cases such as adoption, marital cases, and suicides to mention a few.

Child Protection Services: Coordinating policy and programmes for Orphans and Vulnerable Children (OVC), as well as child protection generally.

Elderly and Benefits Services: Co-ordinates payment of old age and war veterans' pensions; support to destitute in cash and in kind, as well as the CHBC programme.

Home Economics Programme: Responsible for early childhood care and education. It also provides training in a range of food, nutrition, textile production and handicrafts activities, and co- ordinates local authority projects aimed at the rehabilitation of destitute by building their income generation capacity.

Information, Research and Public Relations: Enhance the monitoring and evaluation of state social protection programmes, among other functions (Government of Botswana, 2010).

Even though DPS in within the Ministry of Local Government and Rural Development, it also deploys social work practitioners to the Ministry of Health. Some practitioners are also found in the Ministry of Youth, Sports, and Culture, the army and police departments where they provide a variety of services to individuals, families, and communities.

Non-Governmental Organizations (NGOs)

Botswana has a large and growing NGO sectors that are anchored in the development of the nation and guided by the principles of democracy, social justice, good governance and sustainable development (Government of Botswana, 2001). Majority of NGO sectors found in Botswana today are a result of post-independence development and their formation was based on community needs. Their focus is on national development, education, gender empowerment, environment, and health.

Botswana Council of Non-Governmental Organizations (BOCONGO) is the national umbrella body for non-governmental organizations in Botswana and promotes and coordinates NGOs and builds capacity among its more than eighty (80) members, which include networks and individual bodies. It was due to the realization by NGOs themselves that their development efforts were uncoordinated and fragmented that BOCONGO was formed and officially registered in 1995 with the registrar of Societies (Government of Botswana, 2001).

The mandate of BOCONGO is to co-ordinate the NGO movement in Botswana and to facilitate the establishment of an enabling environment for NGO work. The Council is also responsible for networking, capacity building, and the mobilization of resources for NGO sector. Since then both the government and the Council has endeavored to strengthen the relationship, partnership and to create an enabling environment between NGOs and the government for equal participation in development. Among key organizations in BOCONGO are the Botswana Network of AIDS Service Organizations (BONASO), the Botswana Family Welfare Association (BFWA), the Women's NGO Coalition and Youth Health Organization (Government of Botswana, 2001). NGOs sustainability has mainly depended on donor funding over the last three decades. International NGOs and governments from developed nations have been supporting indigenous NGOs work in different areas of social welfare, poverty alleviation, disability, HIV and AIDS, environmental management, training and development of Small, Medium and Micro Enterprises among others (Government of Botswana, 2001). Support has often taken the form of funds, personnel, equipment, and technical assistance.

Study Participants

Participants were derived from government agencies and NGOs. A sample of ten social work practitioners participated in the study. A broad range of participants were selected from different work places and with longer work experience to help answer the research questions. Participants reported that they had been practicing for about 5 to 17 years. Majority of study participants had graduated with a four years' bachelor's degree in social work from the University of Botswana (UB) and some graduated from universities in the neighboring South Africa. Participants also had on the job training through short courses organized by DSP and NGOs. They hold different job positions and perform roles such as provision of psycho social support, resource mobilization, advocacy, child and family welfare, child protection, community development, providing education to clients, and supervision of junior officers and social work students.

Ethical Dilemmas

Participants reported that in their line of work, some ethical principles and values that guide them include confidentiality, being non-judgmental, recognition of clients' uniqueness, and respect for clients. They also reported that these ethics are significant in their professional practice as they help guide practice and enhance service quality. They indicated that through adhering to these ethics and values, it helps provides integrity to the profession. As illustrated by the International Federation of Social Workers (IFSW) and International Association of Schools of Social Work (IASSW), 'Ethical awareness is a fundamental part of the professional practice of social workers' (IFSW & IASSW, 2004). By adhering and being guided by ethical principles, this upholds the professional standards and clients feel that they are given the respect and dignity they deserve. Despite the acknowledgement that ethics are critical in social work practice, practitioners will continue to be challenged in their practice due to the uniqueness of where they practice and the culture of their clients. However, they should uphold human rights, dignity, and social justice (Congress & McAuliffe, 2006; IFSW, & IASSW, 2004).

Even though practitioners alluded to the significance of adhering to ethical principles and values, they reported that due to the nature of their jobs and agency, client culture, and interactions with politicians, they face some ethical dilemmas. Ethical dilemmas that practitioners face are due to challenges that practitioners face when trying to balance loyalties to the profession and fulfilling their roles in their different organizations (Banks, 1998). Banks pointed out that this is exacerbated by the complex practicing environments which include changing organizational policies and procedures, coupled with diverse social workers' role and limited resources (Banks, 1998). Below is a discussion of where practitioners face ethical dilemmas.

Ethical Dilemmas Due to Nature of Job

Social work practitioners indicated that they have diverse roles and responsibilities, and attend to diverse cases, which include abuse, domestic violence, mental health issues, foster care and adoption, family and child welfare, among others. In addition, some alluded that beside case work, they do administrative work. One disheartening example that was alluded to is an encounter where social work practitioners have cases of children who are maltreated in their families. Even though they have ethical responsibilities to serve the best interest of the children, by ensuring their safety, for example removing them from unsafe environments and placing them in places of safety, practitioners report that this is a challenge, as they are limited places of safety where children can be placed. This was illustrated by one practitioner who said:

It is hard practicing here. Children are always in danger in their families, but if I remove them, where do I place them. There are no places of safety as the few we have in the country are always fully occupied. So, if I remove the child, where do I take them, to my place or what? It's a tight call for us (Social worker #7, May-August, 2016).

Because of this limitation in the system, practitioners report that they feel they do not do justice to the integrity of the profession. Even though they have the commitment to the clients, limited resources in their organizations inhibits what they can and cannot do for the clients. Encountered with such client cases and limited resources frustrates practitioners as it limits them in promoting quality standards of practice, as stipulated in the Code of ethics of the National Association of Social Workers (NASW, 1996). Limited resources and competing roles that practitioners face is a challenge that was also acknowledged by the IFSW and IASSW (2004). That being the case, the attempt by practitioners to fulfil the beneficence and least harm to clients is heavily challenged.

Ethical Dilemmas Due to Nature of the Organization

Even though DSP is the major employer of social work practitioners, some practitioners are deployed in other organizations where they reported challenges with supervision. They reported that they are supervised and evaluated by professionals who are not social work professionals and do not understand social work ethical principles and responsibilities. That being the case, they receive unfair supervision and evaluation. Due to lack of proper professionals who share the same professional values and beliefs, they report that their professional growth is restricted as they do not receive proper mentoring. As illustrated by Brill (2001), practicing in complicated environments creates ethical dilemmas, hence the need to have models to address these.

Furthermore, practitioners report that being deployed in organizations that do not understand and appreciate the social welfare function curtails their efforts to advocate for resources that can help service clients better, such as office space, and transportation to make follow ups and do home visits. This therefore inhibits them in practicing at their level best, as a result jeopardizing quality of services clients receive.

Ethical Dilemmas Due to Clients' Culture and Values

Even though the social work profession adheres to the ethical principle of autonomy and freedom, including right to self-determination, practitioners reported that in most cases they struggle with clients who expect practitioners to make decisions for them. When clients do not get decisions from practitioners, they feel that the practitioner is not supportive. In addition, clients' cultural belief hampers service delivery. Practitioners reported that clients resist treatment in hospitals, and report that they will consult traditional doctors. An example of such an incident was reported in a study in Botswana where one participant reported that:

Men are brave and strong. We believe in our tradition/culture. It is not easy for us to go and consult the doctor. Men believe in herbs.... (WHO, 2006, p. 42).

Working with such clients therefore, becomes a challenge as there is clash between professional ethics and clients' values. In other cases, practitioners reported that they are faced with challenges of pregnant minors, and parents of the minor are not always willing to report the matter to the authorities, as they claim that the issues will be addressed in the traditional setup, amongst families involved. Practitioners therefore report that they are torn between trying to be accommodating and sensitive to clients' culture while also serving the best interest of the children. This was captured by one practitioner dealing with issues of child welfare when she said:

Parents want the responsible father to pay for impregnating their daughter. Parents argue that if the man is reported, then he would likely go to prison, and then who will provide for the child? (Social worker #5, May-August 2016).

The clash between client's culture and the law inhibits quality service provision to vulnerable populations. Traditionally, it was always accepted that in cases of pregnancy, involving a minor and caring for a minor, the father's family took full responsibility in the upkeep of both the child and the mother.

Lack of Regulatory Local Bodies

The social work profession in Botswana does not have a regulatory body that oversees and guides the practitioners. As such, practitioners adhere to organizational conditions of services at the expense of social work professional conduct. One participant narrated that a challenge for social work practitioners is lack of a professional association, like other professions that have regulatory bodies such as teaching and nursing. She said:

Social work is not licensed as a professional entity and this undermines uniform standards of practice to realize ethical principles and values and keep the integrity of the profession (Social worker #4, May-August, 2016).

Having established regulatory body like professional association or a council enhances the credibility of the profession as it stipulates the code of ethics and values that professionals should adhere to. Banks (1998) illustrated that code of ethics is linked with the status of social work profession and helps guide practitioners and protect clients. Professional bodies help establish professional code of conduct, ethics, and standards that all members must adhere to, and keep professionals accountable, and improve service delivery (Banks, 1998). A code of ethics is a public declaration which stipulates values of the profession, principles, that members of a profession have relevant skills, do not discriminate clients, do not use their knowledge for inhumane purposes, amongst other (Banks, 1998). Functions of code of ethics are summarized by Banks (1998, p. 221) as follows:

1. Guidance to practitioners about how to act.
2. Protection of users from maltreatment or abuse.
3. Contribution to the professional status of an occupation.
4. Establishment and maintenance of professional identity.

Due to lack of such a code in Botswana, social work practitioners rely on codes of practice from countries in the west, which in most cases do not align with the laws of the country, the policies and procedures of the organizations, and the culture of clients. This therefore, inhibits practitioners to have 'the spirit and standard of ethical reflection' (Rice, 1975, p. 381). However, social work practitioners in Botswana are mainly guided by employers' conditions of services, and they continue to do their best in practice despite the limited resources they face in practice. They use codes of ethics as frameworks to provide guidance and to help make practice decisions, but not that code of ethics is the blue print of achieving agency goals. Even though the code of ethics should not be a blue print in practice, Banks (1998) argues that practitioners should be careful and not let professional code of ethics to be overridden by agency and government codes of practice which have rules on what is expected of practitioners.

Political Influence

Social work practitioners stated that another challenge they face is working with politicians. They stated that politicians have no understanding of the social welfare function, and as a result, they use their positions to intimidate practitioners to perform their will against practitioners' professional ethical standards, which is violation with agency procedures and against professional conduct. This fulfillment of politicians' agenda is done at the expense of the professional integrity. They reported that this political influence hampers their service provision which is already challenged by the limited resources they grapple with. This challenge faced by practitioners was also alluded to by Mwansa, Malinga-Musamba, Ntshwarang, and Maripe (2012) in their tracer study report where they followed social work practitioners' post-graduation. It was noted that the pressure from political figures adversely affect practitioners professional and ethical performance.

Besides ethical dilemmas that social work practitioners encounter, they also reported that they face challenges such as poor working conditions where they have limited office space, no computers and internet, no transport to follow up on clients; high burn out due to heavy caseloads; staff welfare issues not catered for resulting in stress; and lack of specialization (Mwansa, Malinga-Musamba, Ntshwarang, & Maripe, 2012).

Impact of Ethical Dilemmas on Service Provision

The results of this study indicate that social work practitioners are continuously overwhelmed in their practice. Since they experience ethical problems, this can result in what Corley, Minick, Elswick, and Jacobs (2005) referred to as ethical stress. Ethical stress is occupational stress due to the emotional, physical, and psychosocial consequences of moral distress (Corley, Minick, Elswick, & Jacobs, 2005). Practitioners in this study reported that they have interpersonal conflict and get frustrated in their practice. Due to the frustrations and interpersonal conflicts that practitioners' experience there is diminished quality of service provision. They reported that whenever there are ethical dilemmas, clients become angry and this hampers the helping relationship. This is mainly because in most cases, clients expect practitioners to make decisions for them, and once they learn that practitioners can only guide them, they feel they have been let down. This can result in early termination of the helping relationship by the clients who feel they are not getting what they want.

Additionally, clashes between the legal policies, organizational policies and procedures, professional values, and clients' values had been reported to impact service delivery. Clients might feel disrespected if they are told that in some cases, legal policies should take precedence over personal and cultural values. Further, practitioners reported that some ethical issues they face are due to limited organizational resources and non-supportive work environment. This leads to frustration and moral distress. As a result, this impact on practitioners' interactions with clients and the quality of service they give to them.

Strategies to Address Ethical Dilemmas

Social work practitioners alluded to several strategies that they use to address ethical dilemmas. The strategies were not aligned to any ethical dilemma that practitioners mentioned but were discussed in general terms. These include team meetings to discuss cases; consultation with supervisor or other social workers with more experience in practice; reading social work journal articles; and having discussions with multidisciplinary team members, and holding educational activities to educate stakeholders, other team players, and clients about social work practice and their roles and responsibilities. For example, most participants talked about consulting their supervisors and colleagues about the ethical dilemmas that they encounter. One of the social work practitioners said the following about consulting colleagues when faced with an ethical dilemma:

In our department, we share personal limitations through case conferencing with colleagues. We have this every week (Social worker #2, May-August, 2016).

Case conferencing permits social work practitioner's opportunities to report how they handled difficult cases and highlight their limitations and strengths. This allows the practitioners to work as a team in making ethical decisions that does not violate professional conduct and agency regulations. The use of inappropriate methods that do not conform to social work profession is rendered a violation of professional ethics (Daley & Hickman, 2011). Therefore, case conference and supervision help the practitioners to use ethical methods in practice. Consultation with colleagues and supervisors is critical because it gives practitioners an opportunity to reflect on their agreements with the clients and further review implications of decisions as colleagues bring up questions and ideas that were previously not considered prior to their interaction with the supervisor or colleagues (Congress, 2000) and it helps practitioners to avoid more ethical problems (Daley & Hickman, 2011). Chenoweth and McAuliffe (2005) also support having a support network where ethical issues can be discussed and taking time to reflect with colleagues. Relying on the advice from colleagues and supervisors has been deemed effective in practice (Howard, McMillen, & Pollio, 2003).

Further, social work practitioners, especially those who work in multidisciplinary settings such as in hospitals, police departments, and NGOs, noted that they hold interdisciplinary meetings to share experiences and educate others about ethical conduct. For example, one of the hospital social workers lamented:

We convene meetings with stakeholders and colleagues to discuss the best measures to execute and share experiences (Social worker #6, May-August, 2016).

The above quote indicates that interdisciplinary team meetings gives social work practitioners opportunities to come up with new and best practice interventions to resolve some of the ethical dilemmas they might have. In Botswana generally, some stakeholders are not familiar with the mandate of social workers, therefore interdisciplinary meetings help social workers to educate other officers on ethical principles especially in situations where the client receive services from the social work practitioners and other key personnel from a different agency. For example, one practitioner from DSP said:

We attempt to educate other officers on confidentiality and care of orphans and vulnerable children and we also educate our clients about shared confidentiality (Social worker #9, May-August, 2016).

Furthermore, the interdisciplinary meetings strategy enables practitioners to do their work professionally, reduces the burden experienced when one encounters difficult clients and enhances objectivity in handling of cases (Csikai, 2004). However, Csikai (2004, p. 75) highlights that it is important to have one member of the team who is knowledgeable and competent with basic ethical principles and models of ethical decision-making because that will facilitate ethical decision-making.

Educating clients about the practitioner's role in the helping relationship was another way that practitioners decrease ethical dilemmas in practice. Practitioners indicated that during counseling sessions, they educate clients about making decisions, shared confidentiality, and best interest of the child among others. This was summed up by one practitioner who said:

We continuously address ethical dilemmas during counseling where we educate clients when there are confusions brought by cultural values of our clients versus organizational values (Social worker #5, May-August, 2016).

This emphasizes the need to educate non-social work practitioners and clients about services that social workers provide and the context in which they are offered so that they understand some of the ethical principles and values involved in social work service provision.

In addition to educating clients about social work practitioners' roles and responsibilities, practitioners reported that they dialogue with clients about their culture and values. Considering and discussing clients' cultural values is important because it helps to minimize and to avoid ethical dilemmas. Moreover, it aids the practitioner to be culturally sensitive when working with clients by enhancing the use of culturally sensitive methods and trying to accommodate some of the client's culture in the helping process. Integration of culturally sensitive approaches allows social work practitioners to adopt ethical practices that are in line with the individual and community norms and hence yields effective results (Daley & Hickman, 2011).

A few social work practitioners mentioned that they attempt to resolve ethical dilemmas by resolving personal limitations through reading of social work journal articles. Reading of social work journal articles help practitioners to learn best practices and innovative ideas on how they can resolve ethical dilemmas that are similar to their situations. As was argued by Cournoyer, and Powers (2002) and Howard, McMillen, and Pollio (2003), relying on scientific evidence increases the effectiveness and enriches the credibility of the profession. It is important to note that only a few practitioners reported consulting current literature to guide their practice mainly because there are limited resources such as lack of computers, internet unavailability, especially in rural areas where resources such as electricity and office space are scarce.

The NASW (1996) code of ethics also allows leeway for social workers to make different decisions when faced with a client in different circumstances. Therefore, in trying to address ethical dilemmas that practitioners face, there is no one right strategy. Different practice organizations, cases, and circumstances might present with ethical dilemmas that might require diverse ways to address. Also, in addressing ethical dilemmas, practitioners should be aware of client's culture and ensure that ethics followed are culturally responsive (Lovat & Gray, 2008). As such, it should be noted that the following recommendation are suggestions on what practitioners might consider doing to address ethical dilemmas.

SOLUTIONS AND RECOMMENDATIONS

Social work practitioners in Botswana are charged with diverse roles and responsibilities with limited resources. In their attempt to perform to their level best, they are continuously exposed to ethical dilemmas. As a result, they need to be supported to reduce on the job stress by continuous education to impart them with new skills that can help deal with some of the challenges. For this to happen, social work professionals should establish social work council which will set laws regarding how practitioners should get continuous education to keep them relevant in practice.

In addition, practitioners need to be aware of ethics and arrange their priority listing of ethical dilemmas based on their own values (Harrington & Dolgoff, 2008). The list will help in making decisions when faced with ethical dilemmas. In as much as it is important that practitioners are guided by code of ethics or conditions of services, most important is that practitioners should know and be able to apply relevant laws and regulations of the country they operate from (Corey, Corey & Callanan, 2003). Further, Congress (1999) argue that there is need to scrutinize professional, client, societal, and agency values, bearing in mind laws, code of ethics where available, and the client situation, and evaluate who is likely to benefit or likely to be harmed. Congress (1999) discusses a five-step decision making ETHIC model for identifying and resolving ethical issues and dilemmas. The model is as follows:

- *E*xamine relevant personal, societal, agency, client and professional values;
- *T*hink about what ethical standard of the relevant Code of Ethics applies to the situation, as well as about relevant laws and case decisions;
- *H*ypothesize about possible consequences of different decisions;
- *I*dentify who will benefit and who will be harmed in view of social workers' commitment to the most vulnerable; and
- *C*onsult with supervisor and colleagues about the most ethical choice (Congress, 1999).

Even though this model can prove to be beneficial to practitioners, they also should depend on agency policy, research evidence, and be aware that ethical decision making is subjective and is dependent on the context and situation in which it occurs (Chenoweth & McAuliffe, 2005). Self-awareness is also critical for social work practitioners. This is critical in ethical decision making as decisions made might be influenced by practitioners' personal values, consequently, if they are aware of their own values, it can help to not be biased in practice (Osmo & Landau, 2001). For practitioners to benefit from this model therefore, continuous education can include content related to ethics, relevant laws, regulations, and policies of country they operate in, cultural competence, as well as relevant research findings that can inform social work practice, and learn new skills to keep them current with available new research findings outlining new techniques on how to deal with ethical dilemmas.

Furthermore, besides focusing on continuous education for practitioners, social work ethics should be part of the curriculum (McAuliffe & Ferman (2002). Even though there is no one approach that had been established on how ethics can be taught, Hugman (2005) states that there is need for understanding ethics as a way of thinking and acting, as well as learning to think ethically as one reflects on their practice. Harrington and Dolgoff (2005) also note that social work education should be involved in ensuring that students are aware of ethical dilemmas they are likely to encounter in practice, and steps they can take in addressing them. It is critical that social work educators make social work students and practitioners aware of the relevance of scientific findings in enhancing professional practice through providing knowledge and skills in selecting, evaluating, and applying the evidence in their practice (Howard, McMillen, & Pollio, 2003). As such, this will help practitioners to meet ethical obligation as they apply evaluation and research evidence in their practice (NASW, 1996), and reduce practice pressure that they continue to be exposed to (Cournoyer & Powers, 2002).

Moreover, Gray and Gibbons (2007) argue that social work educators should strengthen field education placements for students as it offers experience that will help students grow professionally and help produce morally serious professionals who are committed to ethical practice. Students in field placement should continuously reflect on their ethical preference and choice of action they choose (Mattison, 2000). Reflective learning should focus on student values and commitments, to allow them to discover themselves before they start practicing (Gray & Gibbons, 2007). When a foundation is set during early training, it will likely continue when individuals are in practice, as they continuously reflect to better serve their clients.

These study findings can help develop future research by informing the development of a survey that can help conduct research that can demonstrate the prevalence of ethical dilemmas that social work practitioners in Botswana deal with. This can be combined with having focused group discussions in different organizations. Such future research can provide insights and understanding on the ethical dilemmas that social work practitioners come across in their different settings. The research should also focus on the process of addressing ethical dilemmas by examining factors that facilitate resolution of ethical dilemmas as well as those that makes it difficult for social workers to resolve them. Research that considers both negative and positive aspects of resolving ethical dilemmas has the potential to prompt social work practitioners to be culturally sensitive in decision making and to promote the dignity of their clients. Such research should be conducted nationally, taking into consideration the country's specific legal policies and law, and diverse client's culture. As was argued by Osei-Hwedie (1993, p. 22) that:

The outcome should reflect local inputs and processes.

Such kind of research can be informative for social work educators as they design and strengthen their curriculum, as it will be context based and students can conceptualize ethical issues in real world settings. With context based research on social work ethical principles and ethical dilemmas, development of relevant and culturally appropriate models to inform practice can be achieved. This had been referred to as culturally relevant social work education and practice (Gray, Coates, & Bird, 2008).

CONCLUSION

The findings of this qualitative study indicated the different ethical dilemmas experienced by social work practitioners working in both public and private organizations in Botswana, their impact on service provision as well as strategies used to address the dilemmas. Ethical dilemmas are influenced by political factors, organizational culture, and the nature of the job as well as the unavailability of professional bodies to monitor professional conduct. The strategies noted to address ethical dilemmas are many and they include case conferencing; consultation with supervisor or other social workers with more experience in practice; reading relevant social work journal literature; having discussions with multidisciplinary team members, and holding educational activities to educate stakeholders, other team players, and clients about social work practice and their roles and responsibilities.

REFERENCES

Banks, S. (1998). Professional ethics in social work—What future? *The British Journal of Social Work*, *28*(2), 213-231. https://doi.org/10.1093/oxfordjournals.bjsw.a011324

Banks, S. (2001). *Ethics and values in social work*. Hampshire, UK: Palgrave.

Banks, S. (2008). Critical commentary: Social work ethics. *British Journal of Social Work, 38*(6), 1238-1249. https://doi.org/10.1093/bjsw/bcn099

Bowen, G. N. (2008). Naturalistic inquiry and the saturation concept: A research note. *Qualitative Research*, *8*(1), 137–152. doi:10.1177/1468794107085301

Brill, C. K. (2001). Looking at the social work profession through the eye of the NASW Code of Ethics. *Research on Social Work Practice*, *11*(2), 223–234. doi:10.1177/104973150101100209

Brod, M., Tesler, L. E., & Christensen, T. L. (2009). Qualitative research and content validity: Developing best practices based on science and experience. *Quality of Life Research: An International Journal of Quality of Life Aspects of Treatment, Care and Rehabilitation*, *18*(9), 1263–1278. doi:10.1007/s11136-009-9540-9 PMID:19784865

Burmeister, E., & Aitken, L. M. (2012). Sample size: How many is enough? *Australian Critical Care*, *25*(4), 271–274. doi:10.1016/j.aucc.2012.07.002 PMID:22835279

Chenoweth, L., & McAuliffe, D. (2005). *The road to social work and human service practice: An introductory text*. Southbank Victoria: Thomson Learning.

Congress, E., & McAuliffe, D. (2006). Social work ethics: Professional codes in Australia and the United States. *International Social Work*, *49*(2), 151–164. doi:10.1177/0020872806061211

Congress, E. P. (1999). *Social work values and ethics: Identifying and resolving professional dilemmas*. Chicago: Nelson Hall.

Congress, E. P. (2000). What social workers should know about ethics: Understanding and resolving ethical dilemmas. *Administration in Social Work*, *1*(1), 1–25.

Corey, G., Corey, M. S., & Callanan, P. (2003). *Issues and ethics in the helping profession* (6th ed.). Pacific Grove, CA: Brooks/Cole Publishing.

Corley, M. C., Minick, P., Elswick, R. K., & Jacobs, M. (2005). Nurse moral distress and ethical work environment. *Nursing Ethics*, *12*(4), 382–390. doi:10.1191/0969733005ne809oa PMID:16045246

Cournoyer, B. R., & Powers, G. T. (2002). Evidence-based social work: The quiet revolution continues. In A. R. Roberts & G. Greene (Eds.), *Social workers' desk reference* (pp. 798–807). New York: Oxford University Press.

Csikai, E. L. (2004). Social workers participation in the resolution of ethical dilemmas in hospice care. *Health & Social Work*, *29*(1), 67–76. doi:10.1093/hsw/29.1.67 PMID:15024920

Daley, M. R., & Hickman, S. (2011). Dual relations and beyond: Understanding and addressing ethical challenges for rural social work. *Journal of Social Work Values and Ethics*, *8*(1), 99–108.

Dibley, L. (2011). Analyzing narrative data using McCormacks lenses. *Nurse Researcher*, *18*(3), 13–19. doi:10.7748/nr2011.04.18.3.13.c8458 PMID:21560921

DPSM. (2000). *Management Services Review Report on the Organizational Review of the Social Welfare Function of the ministry of Local Government Lands and Housing* (Approved by Cabinet). Gaborone, Botswana: Directorate of Public Service Management.

Engel, R. J., & Schuitt, R. K. (2013). *The Practice of Research in Social Work*. Sage Publications.

Fusch, P. I., & Ness, L. R. (2015). Are we there yet? Data saturation in qualitative research. *Qualitative Report*, *20*(9), 1408–1416.

Government of Botswana. (2001). *National Policy for Non-governmental Organizations.* Gaborone, Botswana: Ministry of Labour and Home Affairs. Retrieved from http://www.icnl.org/research/journal/vol3iss3/2-01.pdf

Government of Botswana. (2010). *A Social Development Policy Framework for Botswana Phase I: Situation Analysis.* Gaborone, Botswana: Ministry of Local Government. Retrieved from https://www.uea.ac.uk/documents/439774/4406128/Botswana+SD+policy+phase+I+report+26+May+10.pdf/211a67cb-3773-4822-8034-4b98e9c2bef7

Gray, M., Coates, J., & Bird, M. Y. (2008). Introduction. In M. Gray, J. Coates, & M. Y. Bird (Eds.), *Indigenous Social Work Around the World: Towards Culturally Relevant Education and Practice* (pp. 1–12). Aldershot, UK: Ashgate Publishing.

Gray, M., & Gibbons, J. (2007). There are no answers, only choices: Teaching ethical decision making in social work. *Australian Social Work, 60*(2), 222–238. doi:10.1080/03124070701323840

Harrington, D., & Dolgoff, R. (2008). Hierarchies of ethical principles for ethical decision making in social work. *Ethics and Social Welfare, 2*(2), 183–196. doi:10.1080/17496530802117680

Hesse-Biber, S. N. (2006). The practice of feminist in-depth interviewing. In S. H. Hesse-Biber & P. L. Leavy (Eds.), *The Practice of Qualitative Interviewing* (pp. 111–148). London: Sage Publishing.

Hoffmann, W. (1967). Social Work Supervision. In B. McKendrick (Ed.), *Introduction to Social Work in South Africa* (pp. 206–248). Pinetown, South Africa: Owen Burgess Publishers.

Howard, M. O., McMillen, C. J., & Pollio, D. E. (2003). Teaching evidence-based practice: Toward a new paradigm for social work education. *Research on Social Work Practice, 13*(2), 234-259. DOI: 10.1177/1049731502250404

Hugman, R. (2005). Exploring the Paradox of Teaching Ethics for Social Work Practice. *Social Work Education, 24*(5), 535–545. doi:10.1080/02615470500132772

Hutton, M. (1992). *Social Work: An extension of community.* Gaborone, Botswana: University of Botswana.

IFSW & IASSW. (2004). *Ethics in social work, statement of principles.* Retrieved from https://www.iassw-aiets.org/wp-content/uploads/2015/10/Ethics-in-Social-Work-Statement-IFSW-IASSW-2004.pdf

Kadushin, G., & Egan, M. (2001). Ethical dilemmas in home health care: A social work perspective. *Health & Social Work, 26*(3), 136-149. https://doi.org/10.1093/hsw/26.3.136

Kalof, L., Dan, A., & Dietz, T. (2008). *Essentials of Social Research.* New York, NY: Open University Press.

Lovat, T., & Gray, M. (2008). Towards a proportionist social work ethics: A Habermasian perspective. *British Journal of Social Work, 38*(6), 1100-1114. https://doi.org/10.1093/bjsw/bcl396

Mattison, M. (2000). Ethical decision making: The person in the process. *Social Work, 45*(3), 201-212. https://doi.org/10.1093/sw/45.3.201

Maxwell, J. A. (2013). *Qualitative research design: An interactive approach (3rd ed.).* London: Sage Publication.

McAuliffe, D. (2005). I'm still standing: Impacts and consequences of ethical dilemmas for social workers in direct practice. *Journal of Social Work Values and Ethics*, *2*(1), 1–10.

McAuliffe, D., & Ferman, T. (2002). *Meeting the Challenges of Designing Ethics Education for Social Work.* Melbourne: RMIT, Faculty of Education, Language & Community Services.

Miles, M. B., & Huberman, A. M. (1994). *Qualitative data analysis: An expanded sourcebook.* Thousand Oaks, UK: Sage Publication.

Motsamai, M. (2016). Code of conduct for social workers in offing. *Botswana - Daily News*. Retrieved June 18, 2017, from http://www.dailynews.gov.bw/mobile/news-details.php?nid=31693&flag=

Mwansa, L.-K. (2011). Social work education in Africa: Whence and whither. *Social work education, 30*(1), 4–16. doi:10.1080/02615471003753148

Mwansa, L.-K. J., Malinga-Musamba, T., Ntshwarang, P. N., & Maripe, K. (2012). *Report on the tracer study project: University of Botswana 1998-2008 social work graduates (1998-2008)* (Unpublished report). Gaborone, Botswana: Office of Research and Development, University of Botswana.

NASW. (1996). *Code of ethics - Approved by the 1996 NASW Delegate Assembly and revised by the 2008 NASW Delegate Assembly.* Retrieved July 2, 2017, from http://www. naswdc. org/pubs/code/code

Neuman, W. L. (2007). *Basics of Social Research: Quantitative and Qualitative Approaches*. Boston: Allyn and Bacon Publishing.

Nthomang, K. (2007). *Provisions of services and poverty reduction: The case of Botswana. Geneva: UNRISD.* Retrieved October 15, 2013 from http://www.unrisd.org/8025 6B3C005BCCF9/(httpAuxPages)/B8AFAF7E9C8AEB33C1257AF6003 05225/$file/Botswana%20Nthomang%20web.pdf

Olaughlin, B. (1998). Missing men? The debate over rural poverty and women-headed households in Southern Africa. *The Journal of Peasant Studies*, *25*(2), 1–48. doi:10.1080/03066159808438665

Osei-Hwedie, K. (1993). The challenge of social work in Africa: Starting the indigenisation process. *Journal of Social Development in Africa*, *8*(1), 19–30.

Osei-Hwedie, K. (2000). Culture as a Tool for Social Work Practice. *Social Work Africa*, *1*(1), 11–18.

Osmo, R., & Landau, R. (2001). The need for explicit argumentation in ethical decision-making in social work. *Social Work Education*, *20*(4), 483–492. doi:10.1080/02615470120064723

Reamer, F. G. (2003). Boundary Issues in Social Work: Managing dual relationships. *Social Work, 48*(1), 121-133. https://doi.org/10.1093/sw/48.1.121

Rice, D. (1975). The Code: A voice for approval. *Social Work Today*, *18*, 381–382.

Rubin, A., & Babbie, E. (2014). *Research Methods for Social Work*. Pacific Grove, CA: Brooks Cole.

Seleka, T., Siphambe, H., Ntseane, D., Mbere, N., Kerapeletswe, C., & Sharp, C. (2007). Social Safety Nets in Botswana: Administration, Targeting and Sustainability. Gaborone, Botswana: Lightbooks - Lentswe La Lesedi (PTY).

Streets, F. J. (2008). Religion and Social Work: Dilemmas and Challenges in Practice. *Journal of Jewish Communal Service*, *83*(2/3), 170.

WHO. (2006). *From Access Adherence: The challenges of antiretroviral treatment, studies from Botswana, Tanzania and Uganda.* Geneva, Switzerland: World Health Organization. Retrieved from http://apps.who.int/medicinedocs/pdf/s13400e/s13400e.pdf

Chapter 8
Ethical Dilemmas That Turkish Social Workers Encounter and Factors That Influence Their Decisions in Case of Ethical Dilemmas

Oğuzhan Zengin
Çankırı Karatekin University, Turkey

ABSTRACT

The purpose of this study is to present the ethical dilemmas that social workers in various institutions in Turkey encounter as well as the factors that influence their decisions in case of ethical dilemmas. 234 social workers participated in the research. Statistical analyses were performed in the SPSS program and p<0.05 was considered statistically significant. Three out of four social workers who participated in the research (76.5%) indicated having experienced ethical dilemmas in their practices. When we look at the causes behind the emergence of ethical dilemmas, clients' request or need for service conflicting with legislative regulations comes to the fore among the responses given (77.6%). More than half of the social workers who participated in the research (54.1%) stated that they decide primarily according to the principle of client's best interest in case of an ethical dilemma. Social workers often encounter ethical dilemmas due to legal and institutional causes and in case of an ethical dilemma, they usually make a decision in favor of the client.

DOI: 10.4018/978-1-5225-3090-9.ch008

INTRODUCTION

Ethics has been among the most fundamental concepts to which social work referred as it historically developed with a philantropic motivation and went on to being professionalized. The concept of occupational ethics which provides a kind of roadmap regarding attitudes and behaviors towards persons and institutions that members of various professions work with in practice, is called social work ethics in the discipline of social work and it guides social workers in the services to be provided to clients, relationships to be established with clients and in professional decisions to be taken by social workers. On the other hand, ethics is the body of ideal attitudes and behaviors and in some cases it is not possible to act in line with ethical principles. Especially ethical dilemmas due to macro structures may tend to leave social workers in a tight spot in terms of making a professional decision. The aim of this study was therefore determined as presenting the ethical dilemmas that social workers working in various institutions in Turkey encounter and the factors that influence their decisions in case of ethical dilemmas.

DEVELOPMENT OF SOCIAL WORK ETHICS

Abraham Flexner's 1915 report questioned whether social work was a profession since it had no code of ethics and following this, Mary Richmond who was a social work pioneer authored the first draft of code of ethics (Congress and McAuliffe, 2006). Around the same time, Australian authors Mary Van Kleeck and Graham R. Taylor pointed out that the profession of social work should have definite and agreed ethical principles and specified the general principles fit to shape the ethical principles as 'practical activities and methods that can be tested with their results, appropriate standards for the effectiveness of social workers, social workers' attention and functions regarding professional development, channeling personal attention into public welfare and offering appropriate services' (Özateş, 2010, p. 95). The American Association of Social Workers developed a code of ethics for social work in 1960 and with this work, it has become the first professional social work organization to develop and accept code of ethics (Congress, 1999). Biestek's (1961) seven part classification regarding social work ethics constitutes another cornerstone. This classification is as follows:

1. Unconditional acceptance of the client as an individual,
2. A non-judgmental approach to the client,
3. Individualization of the client,
4. Purposeful expression of feelings,

5. Controlled emotional involvement,
6. Confidentiality,
7. Clients' right to self-determination.

In the 2004 publication "Ethics in Social Work, Statement of Principles" of the International Federation of Social Workers, fundamental values of social work are defined as believing that every individual has worth and dignity, commitment to equality and anti-discrimination, accepting that people have a right to self-determination and confidentiality in their relationships with social workers. In addition to this, social workers have an ethical responsibility to clients, colleagues and members of other professions; practice settings, the social work profession and society in general (IFSW, 2004). These ethical responsibilities are as follows:

1. Social workers' ethical responsibilities to clients,
2. Social workers' ethical responsibilities to colleagues,
3. Social workers' ethical responsibilities in practice settings,
4. Social workers' ethical responsibilities as professionals,
5. Social workers' ethical responsibilities to the social work profession,
6. Social workers' ethical responsibilities to the broader society (NASW, 1999).

ETHICAL DILEMMAS IN SOCIAL WORK

Ethical dilemma is the situation where one makes a choice between two unwanted options concerning human welfare (Banks, 1995 In a broader sense, an ethical dilemma can also be defined as a member of the profession being torn between two ethically inappropriate options in his/her professional work. Ethical dilemmas may also be the case in social work profession. The International Federation of Social Workers (IFSW) classified possible ethical dilemma fields in social work practice into four groups (IFSW, 2005). These four groups are as follows:

1. Loyalty of social workers is usually in the middle of ethical dilemmas in social work practice.
2. Social workers function both as a helper and a controller.
3. The conflict between the duty of social workers to protect the interests of the people, with whom they work and societal demands for efficiency and utility.
4. Resources in society are limited.

Reamer (1982) addresses the ethical dilemmas that social workers may experience with their colleagues and managers in two categories. The first category involves exposing the questionable practices of colleagues and can also be defined as "whistle-blowing". The second category involves a social worker deciding to infringe an institutional arrangement or an administrative policy in favor of a client, colleague or herself/himself. Whistle-blowing should meet these three criteria: 1) the act of notifying powerful actors of wrongful practices in an organization, 2) an act motivated by the desire to prevent unnecessary harm to others and 3) the action of an employee or former employee who has privileged access to information (Greene and Latting, 2004). (Whistle-blowing in social work is usually considered a type of advocacy and it is compatible with the fundamental ethical principles of social work profession. It explicitly encourages social workers to disclose their colleagues' or organizational practices' acts that violate human rights and are unethical (NASW, 1999).

The Swedish Association for Social Work (2006: 6) points out the 11 cases of ethical dilemma that social workers may encounter as follows:

- Care, support and assistance versus control and demands.
- The risk of a—seemingly necessary—caring attitude leading to the loss of a person's own power of initiative and sense of dignity.
- Respect for a person's right to self-determination and freedoms versus the risk of one's efforts leading to the stigmatization of that person and their wounded self-esteem.
- Difficulties in treating clients with respect and of creating a positive relationship in a job that has unavoidable elements of demand and control.
- Maintaining democratic values such as individual freedoms and equal opportunities for both sexes versus showing admiration for persons and groups who do not uphold these values.
- The conflict between, on the one hand, defending/protecting certain clients and, on the other, taking into consideration the interests of those closely related and others.
- The right of the child to advantageous living conditions versus the right of the parents to exert their parentage and live their family lives on their own terms.
- Prioritizing time and resources between different client categories with different needs.
- Carrying out measures deemed necessary and proper versus demands for economic stringency.
- Maintaining loyalty with the work and the organisation, even when one finds policy and working conditions to be contrary to well-founded practice and the best interests of the client, and perhaps also to juridical norms for the work.
- Conflicts of loyalty between defending the client's best interests and support and defence of a colleague.

Ethical dilemmas may also be about the integration with social policies or about the autonomy from those policies. Professional autonomy is the professionals' power to form their own opinions and judgments based on their ethical values and expertise. However, autonomy of the social workers is more limited in comparison to that of other professionals like lawyers and doctors. This is because social work is usually practiced in bureaucratic organizations in hierarchical structures with specific rules. These structures and laws are not established in accordance with social work values nor do social workers have the power to change these circumstances. Professional autonomy may come to rescue in cases where social workers think social policies and institutional arrangements have an adverse impact on human rights or welfare (Banks, 1995).

Due to the causes mentioned above, social workers often encounter ethical dilemmas and have a hard time making decisions throughout the practices they perform aimed at problem areas (Çifçi & Gönen, 2011, p. 153). The decisions that social workers are to make in such situations are influenced by their thoughts, stances, personal values and feelings as much as the legal processes (Banks & Williams, 2005). Although institutional instructions and policies, legal status and requirements and professional ethical codes are stipulated by institutions, laws and practice standards, social workers can nevertheless view these guiding sources from a moral perspective (McAuliffe, 2005).

METHODOLOGY

The purpose of this study is to analyse the ethical dilemmas that social workers in various institutions in Turkey encounter as well as the factors that influence their decisions in case of ethical dilemmas. The questionnaire prepared by the researcher in accordance with the purpose of this research was shared via Turkish Association of Social Workers' mail group. Approximately two thousand social workers work throughout Turkey (Topuz & Öz, 2012) and 234 of them thus participated in the research. The inclusion criterion of the study has been set as having been worked in a social service institution as a social worker for at least a year.

Methodological orientation of the study is descriptive research based on quantitative research design. Statistical analyses were performed in the SPSS program and $p<0.05$ was considered statistically significant. Categorical variables obtained in the study are expressed in frequences and percentage values.

FINDINGS

Findings obtained from the research are grounded on sociodemographic characteristics of the participants, status of experiencing ethical dilemmas, causes of experiencing ethical dilemmas and factors influencing the decision in case of ethical dilemma. 52% of the 234 participants are female and 48% are male. The mean age of the participants is found to be 30 whereas the mean of working time is 6 years. Table 1 provides information regarding the social workers' status of experiencing ethical dilemmas.

As can be seen in Table 1, the participants were asked if they encountered ethical dilemmas in the decision-making process of their practices and three out of four social workers (76.5%) indicated experiencing ethical dilemmas in their practices. Accordingly, we may assume that a considerable portion of social workers are obliged to cope with and make a professional decision at the end of complex situations where two options are in contradiction yet both options are important in view of ethical principles. The relationships between the sociodemographic variables and the status of experiencing ethical dilemmas were not statistically significant. Table 2 provides information on causes of the ethical dilemmas experienced by the social workers.

Table 1. Status of experiencing ethical dilemmas

Experiencing Ethical Dilemmas	*n*	%
Yes	179	76.5
No	55	23.5
Total	234	100

*Table 2. Causes of experiencing ethical dilemmas**

Causes of Ethical Dilemmas		*n*	%
Client's request/need for service conflicting with legislation	*Yes*	139	77.6
	No	40	22.4
Wants and expectations of managers conflicting with professional requirements	*Yes*	98	54.7
	No	81	45.3
Client's request/need conflicting with institutional policy	*Yes*	85	47.4
	No	94	52.6
Client's request/need conflicting with professional requirements	*Yes*	72	40.2
	No	107	59.8

*Participants selected more than one answer in this question.

According to the findings presented in Table 2, three out of four (77.6%) social workers attribute the emergence of ethical dilemmas they encounter to the conflict between clients' requests and legislative regulations. This situation needs to be addressed together with several developments in Turkey. According to Buğra (2008), state's role in society has started to change and social state mechanisms that provide security to individuals have started to fall short as a result of Turkey's transition to market economy after 1980. Thus, it can be argued that legislative regulations in the social work realm in Turkey are not designed in consideration of comprehensively including clients' needs and that this situation causes social workers to often experience ethical dilemmas.

More than half of the participants think that managers' requests are not in accord with professional requirements. This situation can be explained by the fact that the managers of public social service institutions are appointed by the present political power in the country and the managers in question function almost as representative of the political power. For instance, prior to local elections, the managers of these institutions sometimes demand social workers to increase social welfare in certain regions to win the regional votes in the election or to let a client benefit from social welfare although s/he is not entitled to it but solely because s/he is pro political power.

The conflict between clients' needs and institutional policy leads social workers to think whether institutional policies that shape the services provided to clients are comprehensive enough. This ethical dilemma was experienced by the author of this section as he worked as a social worker in a public hospital. An old patient whose treatment was over and had to be discharged from the hospital exemplifies this dilemma. The patient needed to be discharged due to hospital's policy so he doesn't occupy a bed, however the patient lacked any accommodation facilities. The hospital management asked for the social worker's help in this case but the social worker experienced a great ethical dilemma when he conducted some interviews and consequently learned that the patient had been thrown out of a nursing home due to his alcoholism yet it was the only social work institution in the city that could accommodate him and he had no relatives that could help.

On the other hand, sometimes clients too come up with demands that might contradict ethical principles. This is another issue which social workers often encounter in the field and one that needs to be properly emphasized. Table 3 shows information concerning how social workers decide when they encounter such ethical dilemmas.

More than half of the social workers who participated in the research (54.1%) stated that they decide primarily according to the principle of client's best interest in case of an ethical dilemma. Other factors that influence social workers' decision in case of ethical dilemmas are regulations/legal requirements (34.6%) and institutional policy/managers' opinion (11.1%). When these findings are examined, it is observed that almost half the social workers who work in the field strive not to act in contrary

Table 3. Factors influencing decision-making in cases of ethical dilemma

Factors Influencing Decision-Making in Case of Ethical Dilemmas		*n*	%
Best interest of the client	*Yes*	97	54.1
	No	82	45.9
Regulations/legal requirements	*Yes*	62	34.6
	No	117	65.4
Institutional policy/managers' opinion	*Yes*	20	11.1
	No	159	88.9

to legislation and not to contradict with their administrators and in case of ethical dilemmas, they make decisions in consideration of such worries. This situation can also be viewed as the self-preservation reflex of the considerable portion of social workers who struggle to protect themselves in the institutions they are employed. After all, violating legislative regulations or contradicting with the administrator, albeit in favor of clients, may lead to consequences such as disciplinary proceeding, hindering the chance of promotion or even worse, dismissal for social workers. However the findings also suggest that, in case of ethical dilemmas, more than half the social workers draw on their own professional knowledge strive to pick the best solution for clients rather than succumbing to neither legislative requirements nor administrators' opinions.

DISCUSSION

Laws and agency policies are often involved in complex cases, and social workers are often legally obligated to take a particular course of action (Allen, 2012). This situation, it is also encountered in this study as an ethical dilemma situation. When we look at the causes behind the emergence of ethical dilemmas, clients' request or need for service conflicting with legislative regulations comes to the fore among the responses given (77.6%). Based on this result, it may be speculated that legislative regulations hence the provided opportunities are not effective and comprehensive enough to satisfy clients' needs. 54.7% of the social workers point to the incompatibility that emerges between their managers' expectations and requirements of the profession as another important cause of ethical dilemma. Conrad (1988) states that the most intense ethical dilemmas are about confidentiality in the intervention phase of the planned change process. Whereas according to a study that McAuliffe (2005) conducted with 30 social workers in Australia, the most serious ethical dilemmas that social workers experience are those between organizational and professional values. According to the study in question, ethical dilemmas cause burnout, stress, depression, anxiety, short temper, isolation, paranoia and reluctance in social workers whereas it also causes a decrease in their tolerance towards clients and colleagues.

A widely used strategy is to avoid difficult situations and difficult users of social work services by referring them to colleagues or other services and to follow the professional duty or virtue of caring for oneself in order to be able to provide appropriate services in the long run (Maiss, 2010, p. 40). Ethical decision-making that is based on rules, organizational influences, or legal obligations that guide ethical analysis may also result in a practitioner's favoring different priorities a bias which can lead to different courses of action for ethical resolution. Reliance on rules, obligations, or agency policy reflects an ethical-decision-making style that attempts to resolve ethical dilemmas through the use of technical skills rather than through reasoned ethical inquiry (Joseph, 1991). This tendency of social workers to protect themselves is among the findings of this study. Almost half of social workers (45.7%) stated that they decide primarily according to regulations/legal requirements and institutional policy/managers' opinion in case of an ethical dilemma. On the other hand, other factor that influence social workers' decision in case of ethical dilemmas is the principle of client's best interest (54.1%). Holland and Kilpatrick (1991, p. 138-140) conducted a qualitative research with 27 social workers about ethical dilemmas. The researchers have come to three important conclusions in this study. First of these conclusions is that in case of ethical dilemmas, social workers resort to their internal judgment mechanisms rather than external components like institutional policies and legal regulations. Secondly, it is indicated that social worker's former experiences, level of professional development, role in the workplace, organizational culture and similar characteristics have an impact on making decision in case of ethical dilemmas. The third conclusion the researchers draw is that knowledge and skills are not adequate in case of ethical dilemmas and ethical decision making in such a case requires a careful thinking process on the issues of responsibility and value. In another study, Dolgoff and Skolnik (1996) gave 147 social workers seven different stories involving ethical dilemmas about right to self-determination, confidentiality, responsibility to clients, voluntary consent and authenticity and studied how they made decisions in cases of ethical dilemmas. Findings obtained from this study revealed that social workers made decisions in accordance with their practice-based knowledge driven by their personal values, in case of ethical dilemmas.

CONCLUSION

The most important result obtained from the study is that social workers are experiencing ethical dilemmas because social protection which is an essential feature of the concept of social state is inadequate in Turkey. Social policy of Turkey has a residual social welfare approach just like Mediterranean-type welfare regimes. When viewed from the residual perspective, there are two natural ways to meet the needs of individuals. These are family and market economy. Sometimes when these institutions do not fulfil their functions, family life cracks and depression emerges or sometimes individuals fail to use the normal ways due to reasons like old age or illness. According to the residual view, social welfare institutions become functional when normal institutions like family and market fall short (Karataş, 1999, p. 35). Whereas the existing services are limited. This leads social workers to work with clients who don't meet many of the social work criteria and cause them to face an ethical dilemma. In addition to this, sometimes it may be the case that executives of publicly owned social work institutions in Turkey act in line with political concerns since they are assigned by the political power, therefore wants and expectations of these executives may conflict with professional requirements. In that case, ethical practices of social workers are usually decontextualized as their ability to act on given structures is not recognized (Banks, 2008). According to the research findings, more than half of the social workers make decisions in the client's best interest in case of ethical dilemmas despite all the challenges in the present structure. This is promising in terms of ethical principles and show us that social workers have critical thinking tendencies and it will enable us to view clients as citizens with equal rights instead of individuals simply in need of therapy.

REFERENCES

Allen, K. (2012). What is an ethical dilemma? *The New Social Worker, 19*(2), 6–7.

Banks, S. (1995). *Ethics and values in social work.* London: Macmillan. doi:10.1007/978-1-349-24145-3

Banks, S. (2008). Critical commentary: Social work ethics. *British Journal of Social Work, 38*(6), 1238–1249. doi:10.1093/bjsw/bcn099

Banks, S., & Williams, R. (2005). Accounting for ethical difficulties in social welfare work: Issues, problems and dilemmas. *British Journal of Social Work, 35*(7), 1005–1022. doi:10.1093/bjsw/bch199

Biestek, F. (1961). *The casework relationship.* London: George Allen and Unwin.

Buğra, A. (2008). *Kapitalizm, yoksulluk ve Türkiye'de sosyal politika*. İstanbul: İletişim Yayınları.

Çifçi, G. E., & Gönen, E. (2011). Sosyal hizmet uygulamalarinda etik karar verme süreci. *Toplum ve Sosyal Hizmet Dergisi, 22*(2), 149–160.

Congress, E. (1999). *Social work values and ethics: Identifying and resolving professional dilemmas*. Belmont, CA: Wadsworth Publishing.

Congress, E., & McAuliffe, D. (2006). Social work ethics - Professional codes in Australia and the United States. *International Social Work, 49*(2), 151–164. doi:10.1177/0020872806061211

Conrad, A. P. (1988). Ethical considerations in the psychosocial process. *Social Casework, 69*(10), 603–610.

Dolgoff, R., & Skolnik, L. R. (1996). Ethical decision making in social work with groups: An empirical study. *Social Work with Groups, 19*(2), 49–65. doi:10.1300/J009v19n02_05

Greene, A. D., & Latting, J. K. (2004). Whistle blowing as a form of advocacy: Guidelines for the practitioner and organization. *Social Work, 49*(2), 219–230. doi:10.1093/sw/49.2.219 PMID:15124962

IFSW. (2005). *Ethics in social work, statement of principles*. Retrieved from http://www.ifsw.org/en/f38000032.html

Joseph, M. V. (1991). Standing for values and ethical action: Teaching social work ethics. *Journal of Teaching in Social Work, 5*(2), 95–109. doi:10.1300/J067v05n02_09

Karataş, K. (1999). Sosyal refah: Kavramsal boyutu, gelişimi ve nitelikleri. In N. Koşar & V. Duyan (Ed.), Prof. Dr. Sema Kut'a armağan: Yaşam boyu sosyal hizmet (pp. 33-43). Ankara: Hacettepe Üniversitesi Sosyal Hizmetler Yüksekokulu Yayını No: 004.

Maiss, M. (2010). Ethical learning and ethical deliberation in social work. In D. Zarvisek, B. Rommelspacher, & S. Staub-Bernasconi (Eds.), *Ethical dilemmas in social work* (pp. 39–61). Ljubljana: University of Ljubljana.

McAuliffe, D. (2005). I'm still standing: Impacts and consequences of ethical dilemmas for social workers in direct practice. *Journal of Social Work Values and Ethics, 2*(1), 1–10.

NASW. (1999). *Code of Ethics*. Washington, DC: National Association of Social Workers. Retrieved from http://www.socialworkers.org/pubs/code/default.asp

Özateş, S. Ö. (2010). Sosyal hizmet etiğinin felsefi temelleri. *Toplum ve Sosyal Hizmet Dergisi*, *21*(1), 85–97.

Reamer, F. G. (1982). *Ethical dilemmas in social service*. New York: Columbia University Press.

Swedish Code of Ethics. (2006). Retrieved October 15, 2017, from http://cdn.ifsw.org/assets/Socialt_arbete_etik_08_Engelsk_LR.pdf

Topuz, S., & Öz, M. (2012). Türkiye'de sosyal hizmet eğitimi veren yükseköğretim kurumları, mezunların istihdam durumları ve öngörüler. In V. Işıkhan, T. Tuncay & E. Erbay (Ed.), 50. yılında Türkiye'de sosyal hizmet eğitimi: Sorunlar, öncelikler ve hedefler (pp. 239-246). Ankara: Sosyal Hizmet Araştırma ve Geliştirme Derneği Yayını.

Chapter 9
Values-Based Social Work: Case Study on the Particularities of Probation in Romania

Antonio Sandu
Stefan cel Mare University of Suceava, Romania

ABSTRACT

The purpose of the research is to identify the ethical and axiological perspectives that underlie the process of social construction of the probation practice, and also aim at the ways in which the theoretical perspectives that underlie practice become constituents of the discourse of probation counsellors. The probation practice in Romania derived from social work practice with deviant groups. In the probation practice a large amount of case management instruments are still connected with social work practices. The results lead to the construction of a model of probation that integrates restorative elements with the restitutive ones, but also with elements of utilitarian justice, or centred on humanistic values. The ethical values identified as being constitutive for this model are co-responsibility, dignity and justice.

INTRODUCTION

Restorative practices are aimed at restoring the social equilibrium that has been disturbed by interactions with deviant social environments and even criminality. Taking responsibility cannot be an imposed practice, but rather should be based on an independent decision made by both the subjects involved and a support - based community. Relevant institutions able to implement restorative practices (justice) are also responsible for the social construction of autonomy and responsibility.

DOI: 10.4018/978-1-5225-3090-9.ch009

Responsibility refers to knowingly acting, with competence, maturity, training and in conditions of freedom, and then recognizing the acts and assuming their consequences. Liability, as a form of responsibility from a historical perspective, transforms itself depending on who acquires the mantle of responsibility. The rights holder is subject to the prejudice of responsibility, and is owner of the right to repair. Modern meanings of responsibility derive from the concept of "duty", and perceive otherness as complementary rather than oppositional. The concept of "autonomy" has several meanings, depending on how different ethical theories relate to notions of subjectivity or objectivity.

Autonomy, as a form of self-determination, describes an individual who can enact their own choices, either for the overall conduct of life, or for a situation where he/she has to make a decision. Autonomy as authenticity describes the individual's ability to be consistent with their own ethical decisions and thus their capacity for agency as a social actor. Relational Autonomy implies that an ethical decision is the result of the socialization and internalization of the moral norms of the community in which the individual operates. Social acceptability and social control are essential for managing relational autonomy. The individual is autonomous, meaning he/she is self-managing their own lives and decisions within the framework of social constructs, and internalizing them. Self-determination is understood as self - management in the context of a social interaction of which the individual is a part. Autonomy manifests itself within social interaction as a measure of this.

Theoretical paradigms pertaining to the functioning of probation are not found in social practice in their pure form; the function of *Probation Services* is thus based on elements from several theoretical models: *retributive justice, utilitarian justice, justice oriented towards human rights* and *restorative justice* (Sandu, 2016b). A sociological analysis of the social construction of the profession of probation counsellor therefore arises out of a process of theoretical breeding (Cojocaru, 2010), generating a regional theory with enough explanatory power to describe and explain the local context in which probation works, such as that existing in the N-E region of Romania.

BACKGROUND

The purpose of this chapter is to explore the ideological and axiological perspectives that underlie the social construction of probation practice. The research focuses on the Probation Services in N-E Romania, and aims to identify ways in which the theoretical-ideological perspectives that underlie the practice become constituents of the discourse of probation counsellors.

This research on probation is thus grounded on the practice of social work as the probation practice in Romania derives from social work practice with deviant groups. Within the probation service, many case management instruments continue to be aligned with social work practices.

Paradigms of Justice

Punishment is the reaction of a society to the devious behaviour of its members, and includes both formal and informal sanctions. Beyond its retributive nature, the concept of sanction also implies a series of educational and restorative dimensions (Szabo, 2010a). In general, the Romanian legal literature emphasizes the retributive aspect, considering punishment to be *"the only criminal sanction designed to ensure the re-establishment of order violated by the commitment of a crime"* (Mitrache, 1994). This opinion reflects a powerful retributive current in Romanian society, one that is deeply favourable towards custodial measures. The public discourse records strong accents of discrimination towards the persons that have committed crimes, including after their release.

Regarding the role of sanctioning actions, four theoretical models were selected from the scientific literature (Groza, 2006) to elucidate an understanding of the ideological, axiological and ethical dimensions of the functioning of Probation Services.

Retributive justice (Von Hirsh, 1976) represents the classic paradigm of punishment and is based on reciprocity. The declared purpose of punishment is the retribution of the perpetrator for the act committed (Carroll et al., 1987; Keijser, Van Der Leeden & Jackson, 2002; McFatter, 1978; McFatter, 1982). Retributive justice is considered a form of justice distribution (Sandu & Damian, 2012). The customization of the punishment relates to the social cost of the crime, the (socially constructed) gravity (Sandu & Unguru, 2014) of the act and the circumstances surrounding the crime committed (Ashwoorth, 1989; Hudson, 1996). The theory of retributive justice is based on ethical distributive models (Rawls, 2012). Justice as equity is transposed (Sandu, 2015), in this line of thinking, as fair punishment for the deed. The exclusive focus on punishment within the model of retributive justice has been criticized (Szabo, 2010b) for its failure to emphasize the educational function and socially therapeutic value of punishment (Groza, 2006).

Utilitarian justice, according to which the purpose of applying the sanction is to prevent new crimes being committed, is based on the concepts of deterrence, rehabilitation and the incapacity of the person to commit new crimes. Unlike retributive justice, which is oriented towards the past, the paradigm of utilitarian justice – consequentialist – is oriented towards the future (Duff, 2001).

Justice oriented towards human rights (humanistic values) is based on the idea that society is co-responsible for disrupting social relationships through the criminal act (Sandu & Damian, 2012). Justice that is oriented towards humanist values, specifically human rights (Groza, 2006), implies a synthesis between the retributive principle of proportionality and the utilitarian principle of rehabilitating the criminal, taking into account elements pertaining to the personality of the criminal. The state is obliged to contribute to the criminal's rehabilitation, thus it has not only the right to punish but also several obligations related to the nature of the punishment and the limitations of its execution (Sandu & Unguru, 2014). The state has the power to withdraw a series of rights from the convicted person, along with an obligation to protect the person from inhuman and degrading treatments (Groza, 2006). The punishment cannot be greater than the risk the society is facing, including that faced by the victim (Hudson, 1996; Groza, 2006; Sandu & Unguru, 2014).

Restorative justice is based on the idea that the role of punishment is to facilitate rehabilitation, thus rendering the state co-responsible. Restorative justice is therefore based on reaffirming the consensus of values shared with the community through a process that is at least bilateral (offender-victim based), if not trilateral (offender-victim-community based). The purpose of restorative justice is thus to *de-crime the punishment* (Johnstone, 2011).

Restorative justice arose by questioning the sufficiency, and even the necessity, of punishment as it is defined in modern criminal systems aimed at re-establishing justice after a criminal act was committed. Alternatives to punishment, based on retributive theories, have gradually been constituted into a new ideological and instrumental paradigm termed *restorative justice* (Bazemore, 1998; Bazemore & Umbreit, 2001; Braithwaite, 1989; 1998; 1999; 2002; 2003; Braithwaite, 1998). Implementing restorative justice is achieved by emphasizing the social dimensions of criminal responsibility (Daly, 2000; Johnstone & Van Ness, 2006).

In practice, however, it is believed that elements of restorative justice coexist with those of retributive justice and those of justice centred on human rights.

Thus, theories of restorative justice emphasize the *social construction of autonomy and responsibility* of the offender when interacting with the victim, or even with other persons towards which he or she played the role of victim, throughout the course of his/her personal history. The re-establishment of social *justice* is desirable, in terms of providing equal opportunities to access the resources necessary for pursuing one's own welfare, and in *compensating the advantages obtained* from *the illegitimate access* to resources (Bazemore, 1998).

The Romanian Context of the Social Construction of Probation

The fundamentals of probation in modern Romania – despite certain practices of workplace parole and execution of punishment that existed in communist criminal legislation – emerged in the private sector in 1997, primarily through pilot programs of restorative justice run by NGOs. The N-E area of Romania has benefited from such programs ever since they were established, and many of the probation counsellors are still in the system and taking advantage of the experience. Along with penal reform in 2014 – achieved by changing the Penal Codes and the Codes of Penal Procedure which came, with changes, from the communist era– the Probation Services, public since 2000 (GO no.92/2000), have gained a decisive role in managing non-custodial punishments.

METHODOLOGY

This chapter was written within the framework of a wider research perspective whose purpose is to highlight the *social construction* of probation in the N-E area of Romania and in the Republic of Moldova. For this specific chapter, only the data collected from Romanian institutions was selected and focuses on the ethical dimensions of the social construction of the profession of probation counsellor.

For Romanian data collection, the research team conducted 13 semi-structured individual interviews and a focus-group. Amongst the respondents, 12 were probation counsellors working in Probation Services in the N-E area of Romania and 5 were representatives of other professions involved in implementing non-custodial punishments: forensic doctors, social workers, psychologists. At least two of the probation counsellors participating in the research had experience in the field that extended beyond 15 years, and thus have worked in the probation system ever since its establishment in Romania. The data were collected from November 2015 through to November 2016.

The thematic axes of individual and group interviews focused on the institutionalization of probation in Romania, the models of practice and the ideological and axiological foundations on which the practice was developed. In this paper, only the ethical dimensions of probation practice were analysed – as practice derives from the social services provided for deviant groups.

Data collection and interpretation was conducted using *Grounded Theory* (GT) (Goulding, 1999; Corbin & Strauss, 2008; Creswell, 2007). This comprised an inductive process involving the systematic generation of concepts and conceptual categories at an increasing level of generalization. It aimed to capture the interpretative power of the *regional theory* (Corbin & Strauss, 2008; Sandu, 2010) and compare it to existing theories in the field, such as the theory of retributive justice and the theory of restorative justice, two theoretical models that underlie the functioning of Probation Services.

Data coding was carried out in two stages: initial coding and selective/focused coding (Adam, 2009). The research team identified a series of themes and meaningful categories through a process of focused coding. Data categorization to generate the theory was then achieved by dividing the data into categories and bringing together initial categories which were semantically adjacent. Open coding in the first stage then continued with the process of axial coding (Corbin & Strauss, 2008), where the thematic axes produced a series of theoretical explanatory constructs in the form of an instrumental model that facilitates an understanding of the social construction of probation.

DATA ANALYSIS

Open Coding Stage

During the process of data collection, the researchers simultaneously analysed the data by repeatedly reading the discourse of interviewees. This stage was aimed at identifying keywords that particularize the discourse around probation practice. Furthermore, the repetition of the keywords was taken into consideration when analysing the importance given by respondents to the concepts they discuss. At this stage, an initial connection was identified between key concepts, and significant fragments of the interviewees' discourse were then identified and extracted for further analysis. To illustrate the open coding process, a short example of coding will be provided by selecting keywords and highlighting the central concepts that were of interest to the respondents.

Following this stage, an initial series of thematic categories was established: *Job description of probation counsellor, Professional socialization, Self-perception of probation counsellors as professionals, Professional identity of probation counsellors, Perception of other professionals related to probation counsellors, The experience of beneficiaries (people under supervision), The change of attitude towards the society and normativity of the beneficiaries, Critical experience in the exercise of profession, Professional success and appreciation (Good professional), Professional dilemmas, The center and periphery: probation counsellor and supervised person relationship, Case management between supervision and counselling, Professional expectations regarding the development of the profession, Public expectations regarding the development of probation, Romanian specificity of the practice of probation.* Each

Table 1. Open coding process – working examples

Keywords	Name of Initially Proposed Category	In Vivo Text	Memos
Mentality, respect, power of decision, *performs his community service*	*The center and periphery: relationship between the probation counsellor and supervised person*	*"This is the **mentality** of those that, more or less, know what probation is. ... Only that who undergoes such an experience can understand our role. Only the one who comes here, can understand that it depends on my **decision** that he can continue his profession in the country or abroad, it depends on him to go to prison or not, if he doesn't **respect** the measures, that I have to check the good or the bad will. It depends on me that **he performs his community service** in a certain institution, that in a certain institution he might feel good, and in another one, he might not."* (IRO11)	The respondent emphasizes the role of the counsellor in the trajectory of recovery of the perpetrator, as well as the fact that the professionalism of the counsellor depends on the personal and social development and, ultimately, on the reintegration of the offender.
Community, resource, confidence, involvement, development, building his image	*The change of attitude towards society and normativity of the beneficiaries*	*"If you, as individual, haven't managed to have a place of your own, comfortable, balanced, where all your neighbours, relatives, the people in your **community** would see you as a **resource**, it is clear that somewhere, someone failed. ... I believe that the **community** the offender comes from, also did something wrong, it either didn't grant him enough **confidence**, or enough opportunities, or his family didn't **involve** enough in his **development** as an individual. But I believe that the individual should also make an effort in **building his image**."* (IRO11)	In the respondent's opinion, the responsibility of the individual towards his social image, the effort towards its social integration. This effort leads to a change in the community's attitude towards the individual, and is key in the process of resocialization necessary for the reintegration into society of the supervisee.

of these thematic categories was then reanalysed from the perspective of ethical values involved in probation practice.

Selective Coding Stage

The findings were collated into categories whose structure was based on the constitutive and operational values of probation practice. From these initially identified categories (the open coding stage), the discourse that referred to the ethical values of probation practice was identified and extracted. From this selection, a new series of categories emerged. These new categories were more focused on the ethical approach of the practice, concentrating on both the discourse and its interpretation. The categories emerging in the selective coding stage were: “Constitutive values”, “Operational value of practice. Retributive justice vs. restorative justice”, “Trust as constructive value of the relationship between the probation counsellor – the person supervised”, “From social responsibility to responsible society”, “The moral dimension of the probation practice”, “The role of the probation counsellor in the social construction of the autonomy of the supervised person”, “Role of the probation counsellor in the social construction of the supervised person’s responsibility”, “Why are criminals punished?”, “Victim-offender mediation – constitutive element of the paradigm of restorative justice”, “The functional paradigm of the profession (restorative justice) & justice centred on human rights (retributive justice)”.

To facilitate understanding, interpretation of the categories involved retaining in-vivo fragments from the respondents’ discourse, along with analytical comments made by the researchers. The comments were transposed into the current text from their initial open stage format where they were formulated as memos.

Category 1: Constitutive Values

The respondents emphasized the discursive parallelism between the probation counsellors and other professional categories involved in the act of justice: the prosecutors. Discussion about a prosecutor’s way of thinking referred to retributive discursive accents. The respondents contrast these with a discourse where the accent is on reintegration, suspending any reference to punishment, whereby the offender is exclusively placed under the responsibility of a judge. In the opinion of the research team, such a discourse highlights a series of constitutive values that make necessary the emergence of a profession or, more generally, of a social institution, specific to probation and centred on reintegration. The social reintegration of the offender thus represents the social action generated by the adherence of the professional body to the constitutive values of the profession, values that outline the need for the reintegration of people who have committed crimes.

The constitutive values of probation practice arise from the philosophy of humanism where the focus is on the (moral) values of the individual rather than his/her actions. *Retribution* and *recovery* are therefore core values that define two types of professional discourse seen as moral markers within society: social control and repression of illegitimate practices – considered by respondents as specific to the prosecutor – and care towards an individual who is deserving of dignity and, in general, of humanistic values that extend beyond a responsibility for his/her actions. This is a discourse that is specific to the welfare professions, including that of probation.

One of the discursive strategies specific to probation thus derives from humanism where the principal value is the separation between the negative value of the antisocial action and the unconditionally positive value of the offender as a human being. There is therefore a difference between the personality of the offender and the actions that occur at a certain juncture in their lives. Trust in the unconditional positive value of the perpetrators as human beings is doubled by trust in their capacity to adopt socially desirable behaviour, to become morally *good*.

The respondents expressed the view that the individualization of the punishment should be based on the social danger of the act, and not social resentment towards the perpetrator or his deed. The punishment must therefore be humanized by finding alternatives to imprisonment.

They committed a crime, but the punishment must be applied, from my point of view, according to the level of the social danger he has committed.... They must somehow be individualized, not everyone must be condemned, you must be very careful.... Indeed, it is true that you have committed a crime, you have to pay, but somehow you can pay not necessarily by losing your liberty, but by other means and ways, and that is what we are here for. (IRO04)

The social reintegration of people who have committed crimes answers to a central constitutive value of probation, shared with other welfare professions, namely *the responsibility of society* towards its members. This responsibility emanates from the social consciousness – latent or manifested – of society regarding the actions of its members and transcends the individual responsibility of each for his/her own deeds. However, individual responsibility is not ignored, on the contrary its construction represents one of the operational values of the practice of probation, a sense of personal responsibility for acts being one of the objectives of the probation practice. Accountability, however, cannot be substituted by punishing the offender, this being the judge's responsibility (IRO09).

Responsibility – for the Other – as a constitutive value of probation, lies in two directions: *the responsibility towards the individual* – the perpetrator – and the *responsibility towards society* – as a responsibility towards the *non-presence*. The idea of responsibility towards the *non-presence* stems from the ideas of Karl Otto Apel (1989; 1992; 1993; 1999) who argued that, in post-industrial societies, the (individual or collective) capacity for producing harm goes beyond the limits of immediate space and time, which is why responsibility must be extended towards abstract entities not located in space and time. The counsellor thus construes *responsibility* as a value existing at the level of society, and pointing to a significant individual Other – *the perpetrator* – and the collective – *the community* -within a social and professional practice. This alludes to *the social reintegration* of the perpetrator, in other words the social construction of responsibility. However, a significant Other of the trinomial *perpetrator – victim – society*, the victim, although a key element of the discourse on probation globally, is excluded from the major concerns of Romanian probation due to the specific nature of its legislation.

A purpose of punishment is that of "*protecting the community from the person who have committed a crime* " (IRO09). This respondent believed that a feature of developed societies lies in their emphasis on the interests of the community rather than on the punitive and retributive traditional system. It is therefore the role of the community to (re)establish the equilibrium *vis-a vis* society-victim-criminal. The essence of restorative justice is represented by following this balance exactly. The community is, on the one hand, interested in the existence of homeodynamics whilst, on the other, society is the agent morally responsible for both the offender – by offering illegitimate opportunities that were possible due to a certain level of passivity in the educational system – and the victim – whose prejudice, although caused by the perpetrator, is possibly due to the passivity of the community.

Any trend, and I here refer to the developed societies, has this triad criminal-victim and community very well managed, meaning that the legal system is more focused on the community, rather than on the institutional criminal system. The re-establishment of the balance between the 3 starts obviously from the community, and the relationship victim-community, victim-criminal, criminal-community, this means that the community has the primary responsibility for restoring this balance. (IRO01)

The relationship between the *social image* and *perceived place of the individual in the community* is thus brought to the fore. Positioning the individual in the community – his/her social panorama (Derks, 2005) – and the way in which they are seen by the community, is a possible predictor of prosocial/antisocial behaviour. However, responsibility cannot be viewed as exclusively individual. The co-responsibility of the community for the antisocial behaviour of the individual is indicated. For example, a lack of sufficient, legitimate and accessible opportunities, of public trust and the favouring of the social construction of trust in the individual, family involvement in the individual's socialization (Sandu, 2014) and the construction of attachment (Garhart & Mooney, 2009), may all be causes of anti-social behaviour.

Category 2: Operational Value of Practice - Retributive Justice vs. Restorative Justice

From a social perspective, the retributive discourse is clearly present in the approach of probation, where retribution compensates social balance via the feeling of the existence of coercion, the antisocial deed thus generating the need for retribution. The punishment is personalized by limiting certain rights, limitations made necessary by the act committed, and coercion therefore becomes necessary for both the society and the individual. Society then ensures the individual tries to re-establish the balance by paying damages through community service. A retributive discourse associated with a restorative one, in the form of restoration – restoring the social balance to that prior to committing the crime – is not possible, in one respondent's opinion, outside retribution.

Punishment itself is limiting certain rights. If you committed a crime, they must limit you some rights. (IRO11)

Another perspective that was offered reflected on the meaning of retribution. Punishment should, from this standpoint, be reframed as a positive element, a life experience. Such an approach should result in elimination of the stigmatization. Thus, no matter how serious the deed or how great the consequences, the deed itself is eliminated and thus the punishment should itself be limited. This includes the stigmatization generated by imprisonment which, in most cases, extends beyond the time spent serving the penalty.

Yes, I agree that those who make mistakes should pay, but this should also be offered a positive connotation, I mean you did something wrong, you pay for what you did, but that doesn't mean you are stigmatized for the rest of your life. From this side of the punishment, you must also see something positive. (IRO06)

Restorative and retributive justices are correlated according to the nature of the damage caused by committing the crime. Specific *retributive* discourse is encapsulated in the phrase "you must pay", followed by an argument for the necessity of this payment, through the damage created and the suffering caused to the victim. Retribution itself is a part of restoration – of the social balance that existed prior to the crime being committed.

The nature of the deed matters very much, because if something was done against a person, it brought a touch on life, or upon a good, a right that a person once had, I consider that it is necessary that the punishment would somehow reflect. (IRO11)

Category 3: Trust as a Constructive Value of the Relationship Between the Probation Counsellor and the Person Supervised

A very important ethical value in the practice of probation is *sincerity. Sincerity* is viewed by one respondent as correlating with other operational values such as *dignity, professional integrity* and *consequence.* Establishing a relationship with the beneficiary is greatly facilitated by the existence of certain personality traits held by the counsellor and is consonant with the values mentioned. A simple adherence to the idea of professional integration, of sincerity or consistency, is insufficient. This must be internalized by the probation counsellor to the level of behavioural constants.

To establish the relationship of trust, it means to be honest.... To keep the direction, the backbone. (IRO06)

The confidence – of the counsellor in the supervisee – should be based on frequent checks of those stated by the beneficiary, either through direct observation, for example unannounced visits to their house, or by requesting the relevant data from other state institutions. Empowering the supervisee, considered part of the counsellor – beneficiary relationship of trust, is accompanied by checking both statements and the supervisee's actions.

Trust is also important, but this trust is also somehow checked, by working with the collaborating institutions, because we will not rely solely on trust in the relationship with the beneficiary, because then it would no longer be a professional relationship.... So we empower him, but we also draw the attention that what he communicates to us can be checked, and it is our duty to check. (IRO09)

Mutual trust between the counsellor and the supervised person is considered extremely important, especially if it is based on mutual respect.

Extremely important. It is basically based on respect. (IRO10)

Category 4: From Social Responsibility to Responsible Society

Responsibility, as a value of practice, is enacted in three ways: the responsibility of the probation counsellor *towards the supervised person and towards the society*, the responsibility of the society *towards the victim and the perpetrator,* and, not least, the responsibility of the *perpetrator for his/her own acts* and their consequences. The responsibility of the counsellor is thus directed towards avoiding the recidivism of the perpetrator, and assuring their social reintegration. To facilitate this, the counsellor should mobilize the normative and educational resources available in the community. The location of the counsellor's responsibility as an operational value of practice situates probation within the field of social welfare practices, a particular form of social work. The community is therefore made responsible for creating and maintaining legitimate opportunities for the reintegration and social functioning of the perpetrator. This call to the community's responsibility is relevant to the probation practice in the context of *rehabilitation based on the community*

(Cojocaru, 2003). The responsibility of the offender requires active engagement in the process of social reintegration by mobilizing their inner resources as well as those connected to their own social and family context – their contextual resources.

The responsibility of the probation counsellor is to find those levers and mobilize the internal community resources, educational or legal, at a given point, in order for the perpetrator to avoid committing new crimes and reintegrate in the community... the community has the role of helping him in the process of integration and keeping these reintegration prerogatives optimal in the community...the offender has the responsibility to engage, as well as he can, in this process of reintegration, to mobilize his inner, contextual or family resources for a good integration in the community. (IRO01)

Society therefore operates repressively, rejecting those who have committed a crime by refusing their right to education, work and social development. Moreover, society does not prepare those individuals for an autonomous, culturally rich life. The construction of the cultural autonomy of the supervisee is an integral part of any social intervention carried out by the probation counsellor, compensating elements of *rehabilitation based on the community* (Cojocaru, 2003) in situations where this is impossible or very poor. (IRO08)

Thus, society is responsible for the antisocial conduct of some perpetrators because it cannot provide the elements of an autonomous life for such individuals, consequently they fail in constructing their capacity as moral agents and as responsible social actors. The failure of socialization places the individual in a situation of conflict with the law, for which he/she is incorrectly considered to be solely responsible. The respondent recounts a situation from his own professional practice where, when asking a supervised person to become employed, he receives a negative answer *"but why should I work?"* (IRO08) This rejection of pro-active and pro-social conduct is viewed deviant anticipatory socializing, a consequence of the failure to socially legitimize of desirable behaviours.

When the society, family...doesn't teach you the elementary stuff, you automatically get to come into conflict with the law. Because look, we say there are no vacancies, but there are jobs, I know jobs, and I told someone "look, come and work", and he answered, "but why should I work?" (IRO08)

The respondent above suggests that Romanian society has an extremely high rate of voluntary unemployment, associated with a lack of motivation to search for a job. In the absence of legitimate sources for procuring the necessary resources to satisfy individuals' needs and the refusal of under-paid work, easily accessible on the labour market, individuals resort to illegitimate methods of accessing resources, including committing antisocial acts.

I watched a show saying that in Romania, there are 5 million adults that don't even seek for a working place, not that they are unemployed seeking for a working place, but they actually are not interested in getting a job. (IRO08)

The respondent perceives Romanian society as *handicapped* with regard to displaying prosocial behaviour and social solidarity. A series of crimes are committed – in the respondent's view – daily, from accepting undeclared work through to not declaring income to avoid taxes. The social legitimacy of such behaviour, in the sense that it is assumed to be illegitimate, creates difficulties in working with the people convicted for such acts, which are seen as commonplace at the level of society. Thus, society promotes a range of illegal behaviours – considered light crimes, but still crimes – which means the value of honest, moral behaviour is lacking in society.

Our society is a handicapped society, or wishes to be a handicapped one, especially for the person not to handle it. ... They don't know how to handle things, they don't assume their behaviour, they find ways to live as easy as possible, not necessarily by being honest. (IRO08)

Comparisons with the actions of others reduces moral guilt. The respondent emphasizes the importance of groups to which an offender belongs in socializing the crime. Encouragement within these groups of antisocial behaviours leads to their legitimacy in the conscience of the offender. Moreover, when a certain antisocial behaviour is not considered reprehensible by the collective mind but is instead appreciated, it reinforces this behaviour and makes it particularly difficult to re-socialize people according to morally and socially accepted norms.

Man denies his own behaviour, he considers that what he does is not as bad compared to what others did. The moment you make such a comparison, you minimize the responsibility. (IRO08)

The respondent brings to the discussion the issue of imitation as a source of antisocial behaviour; if others have committed criminal acts, it is legitimate for the individual to commit them also. Another justification for criminal behaviour is founded on the perception of corruption at the level of society and the state which, in the opinion of many perpetrators, justifies antisocial behaviour. Such justification, as acts of *resistance* towards the state's corruption, can be located in the mentality adopted from communist times, when anti-communist resistance, although a crime, was considered a legitimate act of political resistance. A series of acts, considered anti-social by the communist regime, were indeed acts of anti-communist dissidence and represented a political challenge to the regime. The communist state was perceived to be the real enemy of individual liberty which, in the eyes of many, legitimated many anti-social actions, especially those of petty corruption. In the immediate post-communist period, the common attitude amongst people was that the *Romanian figures it out*, meaning that the individual could bypass the rigors of an arbitrary and morally illegitimate legislation. The perpetuation of such a mentality justifies, in the eyes of many offenders, acts of corruption; the enemy no longer being the communist state but the corrupt state, illegitimately governed although democratically chosen. The respondent thus argues that *admitting the guilt* and *accepting* it are the necessary premises for changing behaviour. Admitting the deed must be genuine, accompanied by an awareness of guilt that is not just expressed to avoid incarceration. (IRO08)

Category 5: The Moral Dimensions of Probation Practice

The respondents draw a distinction between professional ethics, seen as having a strong normative component, and moral ethics which represent the personal, human side of the probation counsellor. Such morality relates to the personality of the professional, and derives from their own perception of fairness. Thus, a moral sense does not necessarily arise from legal obligation, or different types of social control, but from their own moral judgment. The construction of moral judgement is a component of probation practice, whose purpose is to ensure fair social conduct is internalized by the supervisee and to replace antisocial behaviour with that which is socially accepted and based on new moral beliefs. To construct moral behaviour, it is important for the offender to develop empathy, to place themselves "in the victim's shoes", and to understand the consequences of their acts from the perspective of the victim.

Ethics is moral stripped of any element of spirituality. It is raw, harsh. Ethics means rule. You must keep the rule fair. Morality also involves human attachment, responsibility. But I see it as a moral thing. Because I see moral firstly reported to my own person. Not what means to be fair. I have to be fair. Not because the law imposes it, or because my friends or my mom tells me to. Because I feel that being fair, I am happy, satisfied, and the others are equally satisfied ... We must teach people to put themselves in other people's shoes, maybe then something will change. And then yes, I give it a moral nature. (IRO08)

The moral approach of probation practice is thus in accordance with a humanist vision: beyond the act committed, there is the perpetrator. The emphasis is thus placed on the person, their motivation to change their conduct, their ability to *understand* the meaning and consequences of their actions and the reasons why they were punished. This convinces the offender to change antisocial habits and to leave the criminal entourage.

First of all, we respect the law in force, the terms, the documents to be filed, but this is only a formal side of things, beyond the file that is visible, and is something material and tangible, there is also the person behind the file, which is very important in overcoming successfully the time of supervision and that we must motivate, we must determine to understand why he is with us, what are the ways of overcoming all obstacles that would constitute an opportunity for relapse, so to speak. (IRO09)

Category 6: The Role of the Probation Counsellor in the Social Construction of the Autonomy of the Person Supervised

The term autonomy is understood, in moral terms, as defining a *social commitment*. This form of moral engagement should encompass taking responsibility for respecting social standards, especially laws, while refraining from committing any new crimes.

I would define the moral meaning of the term autonomy as "social commitment". Or as a beneficiary, I should say that "I commit with responsibility to fit the social norms and avoid committing new crimes." (IRO01)

The process of (re)construction of the moral and social autonomy of those supervised involves developing social and communication skills, and of networking and management. Probation should (re)create the structure upon which the supervisee will develop their autonomy by acquiring information, knowledge and skills.

The social role – the development of social communication skills, of networking and management…the social role of probation practice is to create the skeleton on which you, in the future, will add information, knowledge and especially skills on. (IRO08)

The construction of social autonomy and moral agency is carried out simultaneously by empowering the individuals to do *what they have to do*. Those who are supervised should thus find their own inner resources go to institutions where he/she *should* go to, either to serve the measures imposed by the court or to improve social integration. The probation counsellor may carry out his/her advocacy activities in an institution, but only if the individual takes responsibility for a task-centred behaviour. The respondent thus focuses on the imperative *must*, which assumes that moral and social duties are the key to anticipative socializing based on socially accepted values (IRO11).

The construction of autonomy – both relational (Ho, 2008), functional, and in terms of their own moral agency (Bandura, 2002) – allows the perpetrator to develop self-care and self-transformation management. The practice of probation is centred on the supervisee's strengths – the appreciative probation (Sandu & Damian, 2012) – and will mobilize and motivate a person to use their own inner resources in the process of social reintegration. It is noticeable that the respondent includes the practice of probation in the field of welfare related professions, all of which have in common the aim of helping vulnerable persons to (re)construct their autonomy.

The autonomy of the beneficiary is very important, because he will learn alone the methods to help himself, it is like in any welfare process, like in social work, or in other situations in which the person is dependent on aid, and here, self-determination and autonomy are very important for the convicted person. (IRO01)

Probation is perceived as implying the unconditional support of the counsellor for the client in implementing the decision of change. The support and assistance of the counsellor should not, however, act as a substitute for the individual efforts of the supervisee.

First of all, you must work for them to see the supervised persons that they can benefit from our help. I mean I give them help all the time, but somehow they make the decisions themselves, because there's a trap here, if they expect for me to make the decision all the time, they will never be capable of deciding for themselves. (IRO04)

Respondents such as this show reluctance towards the *problem-centred* approach to probation, named by one respondent as *The Norwegian Model*. The problem-centred approach is perceived as inefficient, leading to a negative psychological load on the supervisee, and thus fails to discourage recidivism. In contrast, a focus on the solution, and especially on the previous successful experiences of the supervisee, enables them to identify the cognitive-behavioural experiences that can generate and maintain the process of social reintegration.

In Romania...we focus on the problem, but I believe that worldwide, we highlight the problem and bring it back into discussion. I don't see this as the best approach ... like I said with the Norwegians: to tell someone he is wrong means bringing him a negative vibe. Tell the person: "You made a mistake, ok, let's see what we can do about it, let's do that..." so that the person gets a positive emotion, have a positive thinking.... This must be the practical purpose of any step, that it is an academic, professional process. Here, the convicted persons lack this type of positive thinking, and this is what I think we should focus on, changing the way of thinking. (IRO08)

Category 7: Role of the Probation Counsellor in the Social Construction of the Responsibility of the Supervised Person

The operational value of responsibility the probation counsellors utilise is that of *accepting the consequences* of the acts committed.

In the criminal framework, responsibility is to support every consequence of the act committed. (IRO09)

The probation counsellors are involved in *reshaping the behaviour* of the supervisee, restoring their motivation for social integration.

We help people reshape their behaviour or maintain it, because there are also cases that have an increased motivation from the beginning, now beginning to come for the re-evaluation of the punishment, who don't have the status of convicts, are integrated and have no problem. (IRO04)

The counsellors' trust in the capacity of the supervisees to empower their own conduct is part of the discourse around their practice. Empowerment is a gradual process, a form of social development and socio-therapy (IRO04). The process of accountability is constructive and depends on the personality traits of the supervisee as well as factors within their socio-economic environment.

Empowering the individuals who have committed crimes It is possible. The level of empowerment is different depending on the person, its personality, evolution, life experience, level of preparation, family environment and social, economic and financial condition. But it is possible gradually. I know, there are cases who have a low level that can't get any lower than that, all these factors prevent you, there are people who almost reach a total accountability. (IRO07)

The construction of responsibility is associated with the counsellor's attitude towards suspending any moral judgement regarding the supervisee and their crime (IRO08).

The essential principle adopted by the probation counsellor should be that of *guiding the practice after the rules.* To help construct the autonomy and responsibility of those supervised, counsellors should conduct their professional activity with impartiality and respect for norms whilst also imposing certain moral principles – derived from professional values – that they themselves should adhere to, mentally and emotionally.

First of all, I think a professional is the one who guides by principles and norms. ... we have to be first of all impartial, and take into account our principles, the ones guiding our activity. And this gives us a certain weight, but also a certain responsibility, and if we don't take into account those moral, legal and ethical principles that guide our activity, we can easily fall into less pleasant matters. (IRO11)

Responsibility for the consequences of actions begins with the honest assumption of the deed. This is considered one of the most important objectives of the probation counsellor when working with the supervisee (IRO11)

The supervision process is thus a process of empowering the offender. This empowerment is the objective of counselling actions, including the more restrictive ones carried out by the counsellor. The respondent in the excerpt below emphasizes the need for congruence between the offender's individual actions and those of the community regarding the social integration of the offender.

The very process of supervision is a process of empowerment. Everything that the probation counsellor does is empowering the convicted person to assume and respect, as well as he can, the measures and obligations imposed by the judge, and bring their contribution so that all the actions are congruent towards a better integration in the community. (IRO01)

The probation counsellor uses *symbolic coercion* in the process of empowering the offender, primarily by invoking the possibility of revoking the non-custodial measure and returning the offender to prison.

Well, of course it is possible because you have some levers, meaning you bring him to the attention and ask him: "Do you like freedom? If you don't respect the measures, I will write you an ex oficio report and you will get to jail. You will no longer see your family, contribute to its maintenance and you will lose your job and image in the community." And this is how I make them aware. That's how I say. (IRO04)

The respondents show that the process of empowering those supervised may start by identifying situations in which they were previously responsible – for example, parental responsibility – and transferring successful experiences of taking responsibility to their own process of social reintegration. (IRO05)

One respondent analyses the dynamics of empowerment embedded in the process of probation, particularly in the first counsellor-supervised interaction where the assumption of responsibility for the offender's acts is developed. In the absence of such an assumption, communication between the supervisee and the counsellor lacks authenticity. Taking responsibility for the consequences of their own actions is completed by taking responsibility for the emergence of the process of social reintegration. Ultimately, the success of the counselling process lies in developing the offender's capacity to take responsibility for all aspects of their existence.

Well, responsibility has a very important significance. One of the objectives of our activity, at least at the beginning of the surveillance period, is empowering the individual.... At the end, it would be about the satisfaction, the success of the case, that he would be responsible for any aspect of his life, as much as possible. (IRO07)

Responsibility is correlated with care for the Other, thus locating probation in the domain of ethics of care (Gilligan, 1997; 1982) as well as ethics based on justice, which is expected from a profession that falls within the Criminal Execution System. The paradigm of restorative justice, which forms the basis of Romanian probation *practice* despite the dual normative speech, is ultimately attributable to a postmodern model of society. The postmodern elements targeted by the Romanian restorative probation model are mainly represented by the *dissolution of duty* (Lipovetsky, 1996) and its interpretative drift towards *social responsibility*. The model of duty is synonymous with the idea of *retributive justice* whilst social responsibility invokes a model of restorative justice.

We very easily talk about responsibility. I've said it before, it means to care about yourself and the others. This is how I would see responsibility. The moment you care about yourself, you also adopt that behaviour not to harm the other around you.... To be responsible means to admit, to face and find solutions while it is in your power to fix something, with the risk of being blamed, judged by the others. For me, it doesn't matter only to admit this thing, if you can also fix something, it always matters the most. (IRO08)

Category 8: Why Are Criminals Punished?

The penalty applied represents the individual's responsibility for his actions. However, simple punishment is merely one step towards rehabilitation. Accountability for the actions the individual was punished for, and an awareness of the anti-social nature of their action, is the real educational function of the punishment. The penalty is considered incomplete if recovery is lacking. Crime should not be associated automatically with punishment, but with the recovery of the offender. The role of justice, and of the probation system, is *social therapeutics.*

The purpose of a punishment is the retribution/sentence of a wrong being done. This is half of the problem. The sanctioning is only the responsibility.... It is one thing to sanction, and another one to rehabilitate the person.... So, for me, crime is not only sanction. (IRO08)

One of the respondents argues that the sentence is important in terms of the nature of the punishment. The retributive discourse is obvious. The imperative of the punishment is undeniable, only its repressive force should be graded according to guilt. A *fair trial* is expected from the judge and this allows him/her to give *the right sentence.* The respondent's discourse indicates a modern, objective understanding of the punishment; justice being somehow inherently understood, and existing outside the process of social construction of justice.

Punishment should be given, in the sense that the person must be punished. The instance should take into consideration the level, the intention, the premeditation, in order to give an appropriate sentence. (IRO02)

Many opinions expressed by the respondents emphasize the preventive role of the penalty rather than the retributive one, where the role of the punishment is to deter offenders from committing new crimes (IRO05).

From this perspective, imprisonment is less efficient than non-custodial punishments. The prison is a source of alternative deviant socializing, which is why imprisonment might lead to a greater deviant career due to criminal *experience* being gained through close communication with other criminals. (IRO05)

Another opinion on the purpose of punishment aligns it with the need to protect society. This protective role is strictly correlated with the preventive one and elevated to the level of social justice. Retribution is delegated by the individual to the society, therefore invoking the perspective of a social contract as a foundation for justice. Sanction as public retribution replaces the individual's right to apply retribution, this – based on the social contract – being the state monopoly.

Well, the reason is a natural one: the society punishes the criminals in order to protect itself because no matter what the criminals do, they bring damage to people, directly or indirectly. And then the society must react because through means of justice, each affected person reacts, or at least those who bear the consequences of criminal acts. If they were not sanctioned, it would probably perpetuate and become chaos. (IRO07)

Punishing criminals has, beyond its formal aspect – an offense which automatically entails punishment – a communitarian side. The offense is perceived as a handicap which takes the form of the individual's incapacity to properly see his life. Placing crime within the perspective of the *social handicap*, the respondent effectively invokes society's *responsibility* towards the offender, in the same way that people suffering from different forms of disability require social protection.

Why are the criminals punished If you take this legally, it actually means breaking the law. If you see it from the point of view of the community, it is a handicap of the person to see their own life. (IRO08)

The respondents often underline the educational nature of the punishment. This primarily aims to make the perpetrator aware of the consequences of his/her actions. Education is thus seen in a retributive manner, meaning that the damage inflicted on the society is repaid through the punishment. The punishment is primarily understood as the limitation of certain rights, limitations which must be perceived as such by the perpetrator. The respondents highlight the importance of non-custodial punishments, which grant the perpetrator increased chances of reintegration, limiting the ownership of criminal patterns facilitated by a custodial environment.

The punishment is somehow an example, because any punishment is a limitation of certain rights.... But the community sanctions are more efficient because the person supervised within the community has more possibilities and opportunities of reintegration than in the custodial environment, namely in the penitentiary. Once there, he internalizes more criminal patterns than assimilates educational programs. This is why I consider that the opportunity of non-custodial punishments is a trend that us, the probation officers, support and hope that the system of probation would open up to these opportunities. (IRO01)

The exemplary nature of the punishment is correlated with its awareness. Without awareness, the penalty is not harsh enough to reduce the risk of relapse. One respondent suggests there is no necessary correlation between the punishment and relapse. In contrast to the retributive paradigm, the probation practice is centred on the value of humanism, on discovering the inherent positive elements within each person, and the development of such elements through the social reintegration of the person supervised. The practice of appreciative probation (Sandu & Damian, 2012) – focusing on elements of inherent positivity within each person – represents, for several respondents, the very motivation to practice.

As long as he doesn't realize, the punishment doesn't give an example.... I consider that if you work with a person, any person has something good in him, if you discover it and dig into it, you can help him.... But not all who are punished will never commit crimes again, they will still commit further offenses. (IRO04)

The respondents thus make a distinction between two types of punishment with suspension, specific to the Romanian legislation, which are *delaying the sentence* and *suspending the penalty under supervision.* In the case of delaying the punishment, the respondent (IRO04) states that this relates to the situation of certain convicted persons where, according to the Probation Service, there is a minor risk of relapse. Delaying the sentence is still considered a punishment but is replaced by conditional suspension. In comparison to *suspension under supervision*, the respondent declares difficulty in working with this category of convicts because there are numerous conditions of the suspension that must be monitored. The practice of probation is familiar with the *delay in sentencing* for a period of trial, a situation where, in the absence of a sentence, the presumption of innocence remains in operation. If the *alleged* offender no longer commits crimes during the incarceration and adheres to several specified measures – educational ones, for example – the judge can decide to close the case without ruling on the guilt of the perpetrator. Consequently, the alleged offender does not have a criminal record and is thus not exposed to the risk of stigmatization and social exclusion. This delay in ruling, although present in the Romanian Penal Code, does not appear as such in the respondents' discourses, probably because there is no systematic practice involving such instances. It is interesting that the respondents consider this practice of delaying ruling to be more efficient, and often felt that it should be the only means of delaying the sentence whilst under supervision.

Delaying the sentence is still a punishment, replaced by conditional suspension.... Suspension under supervision, that's where it is very difficult to work. There are convictions that have a lot of obligation which we must monitor, and we are also the ones making approaches, a lot of them. Nowadays, we also collaborate with hospitals and doctors.... As it was before, they had a deadline, and if they wouldn't commit any other crime, they would no longer be convicted, and then it would have only remained the suspension under supervision, that's how I see things. (IRO04)

One respondent explains that the period of incarceration cannot be indefinite because there are difficulties in knowing who, and under what circumstances, determines the ending of supervision. Furthermore, the respondent intimates that delaying the sentence and/or applying the punishment, which would lead to expunging the crime from the record, can be questionable given that certain criminal acts should be publicly known, especially for serious offenses.

Right now we have suspension under supervision, and delay in applying the punishment.... I believe that certain limits should be made in both cases, each with its own advantages and disadvantages. Suspension normally remains in the record for a certain period of time after finishing the supervision, around 3 years. In delaying, it shouldn't appear in the record. It depends in each case. There are crimes that should draw the attention that the person has previously committed a certain type of crime, or serious crimes.... I can't tell I would choose one or the other. (IRO05)

Other respondents consider that delaying the sentencing and/or ruling on the guilt is too risky, preferring instead the suspension of the sentence.

The punishment should be ruled, with suspension on the condition of following a program of probation or sentencing the punishment to be delayed by the judge for an indefinite period of time, and in the case of success with the social reintegration programs, the punishment should no longer be pronounced. I would go with the first variant, the one with suspension for a specified period of time, the other option seems a little too permissive. (IRO06)

Retributivism is questioned regarding the re-socialization and social reintegration of offenders. The educational side of the punishment, foregrounding the process of understanding the social meaning of the crime, should therefore underpin the ruling of the sentences rather than simple punishment/retribution for the crime committed. Eliminating a talionic mentality, and displacing retribution from the meaning of the punishment, can be considered a postmodern element that exists in the discourse of probation practitioners (Worrall & Mawby, 2014). Punishment is no longer an exercise of power (Foucault, 2005), but rather one of the reconstruction of social cohesion through communicative actions. The punishment is thus a consequence of the act, in the sense of inevitably taking responsibility, but the responsibility, once assumed, exhausts the power of the punishment. In such terms, the punishment is no longer a simple consequence of the social contract, where it encapsulates the role of *collective revenge* of the society and the victim for the damage caused, but instead comprises an active contribution by the (co)responsible community to the individual's re-socialization.

I don't agree with this opinion The criminals deserve to be punished for committing a wrong/antisocial act because if we follow retribution, I don't know if we can manage to reintegrate them afterwards in the society. (IRO07)

The educational role of the punishment is seen differently depending on the subjective perception of the individual regarding the nature of the punishment, the crime and even the system of criminal punishments. It is suggested to be a potential and perverse effect of the practice of probation that certain perpetrators, knowing the specifics of the intervention, are encouraged to commit crimes if they consider the non-custodial punishment to be acceptable.

The role of the punishment can't totally be eliminated because I wouldn't totally deny this allegation.... It depends, for example, if it reaches the other members of the society, because the members who are closer to the person punished understand things differently, because they are closer and can talk to him.... And then that's why I say that the role, for example, is different. There are people who have accepted to commit crimes thinking that they would for sure come into probation, and they know what happens here. About 30% agree with it. (IRO07)

The purpose of probation is simultaneously represented as both the social reintegration of the perpetrator and increasing public safety.

Yes, it is one of the purposes of our intervention, until the end of the supervision period. Of course, once the balance is established, this actually means a reintegration of the person, protecting the society against committing new crimes, and then yes, I believe it is correctly said. (IRO07)

The exemplary nature of the punishment should result in the discouragement of criminal behaviour. The perpetrator should know the advantages and disadvantages of committing future crimes. The respondent mentions the existence of a specific technique in probation work which is based on the perpetrator's understanding of the strengths and weaknesses of a certain behaviour, and of the advantages and losses that may emerge from the reiteration of criminal behaviour. This approach seems to be based on theories regarding the rationality of the social actor and the rational behaviour of the social action. Criminal behaviour is not entirely rational. The call to illegitimate opportunities can be an example of the rationality of the deviant social actor, but this cost-benefit analysis is not always involved as many crimes occur due to existing impulses of the moment where no cost-benefit calculation is involved. A cost-benefit calculation seems to be more logically correlated with premeditated behaviour, than, for example, committing antisocial acts negligently. The technique of risk-benefit awareness can, however, be extremely useful in developing habits of reasoning in relation to social behaviour, and of the cost-benefit calculation of any illegitimate opportunities that may arise.

The punishment should determine the person to think what is in his advantage-disadvantage. We have, in probation, not only the technique of highlighting the strengths and weaknesses of committing crimes, of a behaviour. (IRO08)

In the absence of a redefinition of social practices, no significant and lasting behavioural changes, can be conceived. The simple penalty is considered insufficient for correcting the criminal behaviour. Resocialization should be based on education – through explaining and understanding, including experientially, and by involvement in positive, pro-social actions.

It is not enough, it is not enough to see everything as a punishment, it is not enough for the community. (IRO08)

The social role of probation is represented by the recovery of desirable behaviour. Any behavioural changes are believed to be correlated with the supervisee's will to change

For us, probation should recover the human behaviour, it should help recover the positive human behaviour, and in order to do so, it requires time. We work with people's will. We cannot be made responsible for their mistakes. (IRO08)

Restorative justice is perceived as the compensation the offender makes to the victim and society for the prejudice brought by committing the crime. The respondent (below) considers this necessary, especially for the victim. Such compensation leads to awareness of the prejudice, finally leading to the restoration of balance in the community. The purpose of probation is to protect the community by reducing the risk of new crimes, both in terms of the relapse of the offender and of other members of the community. This occurs through processes of social learning regarding criminal behaviour, and by retributive acts personally assumed by the victim or the members of the social network.

It is about the restorative justice. Meaning the restoration through which the offender brings it to the community. My opinion is that this form of restoration towards the victim, either a person or a legal person or institution, must exist. Realize the damage produced. Or, most of the times, the damage produced to others is not realized unless it also reflects on you. ... The final purpose of probation is protecting the community by reducing the risk of committing certain new crimes, in collaboration with the institutions in the community. (IRO08)

One of the answers to the question, "*why are the criminals punished?*" is that there is a clear *tendency to label* (IRO10 within Romanian society.

The exemplary nature of the punishment as an instrument for discouraging criminal behaviour is rejected by the respondent above. Based on pragmatic arguments, this is claimed to be connected to a lack of significant experiences that would otherwise show a correlation between the severity of the punishments applied – to other criminals – and a decrease in the risk of criminality. Instead, the respondent emphasizes the individualization of the punishment with respect to the concrete situation of the criminal, correlated with the responsibility they have for their own actions. The responsibility, however, to be efficient, does not have to have an anticipatory nature (IRO11).

Some respondents questioned whether the reconstruction of the victim-offender-society balance was fundamental to restorative probation. It is difficult to achieve an adequate compensation, therefore, in practice; either the criminal pays a great deal more compensation than the damage produced, or the victim and the society lose, even after the payment of the agreed compensation. Retribution via a prison sentence serves no useful purpose, because restricting the perpetrator's freedom does not compensate the victim or the society. Furthermore, the prison sentence consumes much needed social resources. The retributive paradigm is therefore rejected from two perspectives, that of equity of retribution, namely from the perspective of ensuring justice, and the utilitarian perspective of the futility of the costs of retribution and its lack of justification within society.

It would be the best if it were like that, but most of the times this balance fails.... There are situations in which the offender pays more than the damage produced to the victim, or sometimes the victim and the society remain with such a great damage, that the offender couldn't repay in not even three lives.... And even if he stays in prison for that crime, ok, what do we get from it? Since in all those 5 years, we are also paying for his food. (IRO11)

Category 9: Victim-Offender Mediation – Constitutive Element of the Paradigm of Restorative Justice

Regarding victim-offender mediation, some respondents are unenthusiastic, considering it more effective to carry out a separate intervention with the victim than with the offender.

The situation is a bit more delicate. I would see some interventions, at least at the beginning, to be separate, or I don't know, not even in the end, I wouldn't see them together. I mean it seems quite delicate. And even from case to case, at least in the beginning, I would work separately. (IRO06)

The respondent (above) rejects the utility of programs of reconciliation through mediation between the victim and the offender. Although this practice is often seen as customary in the Probation Services operating in many countries, their success is strictly conditional and based on the availability for change of the two persons.

Implementing certain programs of counselling and mediation victim-offender would lead to the accountability of the perpetrators No. It is a strictly personal answer. Many probation systems, and not only the probation system, but also the system of child protection in the family, approaches that relationship of mediation between the victim and the offender, or that person who was in a conflict. What is essential is not this approach, but both persons' availability to change something. (IRO08)

The respondent thus shows that the simple obligation of the offender to contact the victim, and eventually express his regret, can be made formally without leading to any real transformation. Such solutions, pronounced by judges in different legal systems, are considered insufficient in ensuring the reconstruction of the social balance.

If there is one single constriction for the perpetrator to contact the victim, he might do it strictly formal. So, there are judges in this world that give this type of obligation for mediation and counselling with the victim. (IRO08)

Refusing this restorative practice – based on offender-victim mediation – is considered inappropriate for the Romanian probation system, due to the psychological particularities of the Romanian criminal, the reluctance to use such an approach and the high risk of the victim's re-victimization. From the respondent's experience (IRO08), such practice is very difficult to achieve if based on the agreement of free participation expressed by both parties and the need to involve a genuine dialogue between them.

My opinion is that at least for the Romanian system, offender-victim mediation is not efficient from two points of view. First, the psychology of the Romanian criminal is deeply closed for such approach. Secondly, the victim reliving the trauma will not lead to a positive change of the situation, but will further increase the negative feelings. (IRO08)

The respondent (IRO08) shows that he, as Head of Probation Service, left it to the discretion of the counsellors to create offender-victim reconciliation programs although personally he is against them. Permission granted to the counsellors in his subordination is rather debatable, given that the Romanian legislative framework does not include such practices amongst the duties of its probation counsellors. However, it does not expressly prohibit them adopting a particular practice within a service. This is difficult to accept given the excessive case load, over 230 in some cases, extremely limited time resources and the excessive bureaucratization of the practice (IRO04; IRO06; IRO08; IRO11).

Rejecting offender-victim mediation programs, quasi-unanimous among the respondents, is motivated by pressure from the family and the psychological pressure raised by the re-encounter that weighs both upon the offender and on the victim. The respondent acknowledges the usefulness of such programs, but feels they require special effort and mediation skills that exceed those of the probation counsellor.

The implementation of counselling and offender-victim mediation programs would lead to empowering the offenders I believe it could, but such an approach is very difficult, because most of the times there are certain pressure from outside, from the family.... And I believe such an approach could only be conducted by turning to specialized counselling services, of mediation. Aspects that don't necessarily relate to the specific of our profession. (IRO11)

Category 10: The Functional Paradigm of the Profession (Restorative Justice) and Justice Centred on Human Rights (Retributive Justice)

Most of the respondents view the principle of the universality of negative retribution, in cases of infringement of norms, as axiomatic. The respondents acknowledge that they are very happy when offenders are given a chance to benefit from adequate counselling support and the social welfare services provided by the probation service.

This approach, however, is relatively inadequate, as it would be desirable for probation counsellors to advocate for reducing the level of retribution and humanizing punishment. The custodial punishments should end up being an exception, not a rule, especially if we correlate this information with the fact that the relapse rate for people under probation is ten times smaller than those who have served a custodial punishment. Even if, in principle, non-custodial punishments apply to people on their first offense (people who usually regret their crime), the circumstances that are likely to reduce the risk of relapse such as the role of the probation counsellor, should not be ignored, nor should the effect the custodial stage has on prison inmates constructing a deviant career, an issue which has been widely discussed by the respondents. Consequently, expressing *joy* towards a judge's understanding of the benefit of supervision seems somehow to be the result of a lack of trust in the social acceptability of the profession of counsellor, given its relatively new status

Us, the probation counsellors, are open and overjoyed when the judge offers the supervised person the chance to benefit from the adequate support of the probation counsellor, through counselling and assistance. We are very delighted when the judge understands the benefit of supervision and social work, and we are more thrilled to support their criminogenic needs. (IRO01)

Evident, therefore, is a discourse specific to the retributive paradigm that contains utilitarian-restorative elements, rather than a discourse specific to the paradigm of restorative justice. The punishment is therefore considered an example, by its limitation of certain rights that are the essence of the punishment. One respondent draws attention to the fact that a specific limitation of rights should be felt as such by the offender if its coercive function is to be fulfilled. Communitarian punishments are therefore seen to be efficient, precisely due to the high level of social reintegration of people undergoing such noncustodial punishments. Prison, in contrast, allows the person to internalize certain illegitimate behavioural patterns, to the detriment of any desirable habits transmitted by rehabilitation programs within prisons. The respondent, therefore, is aware of the importance of actively promoting the importance of noncustodial punishments and the role probation services have in this regard.

The existing discriminatory mentality in certain communities can lead to an exaggerated affinity towards retributivism. The idea of systematic retributivism, in a situation of systemic anomie, is seen in society as a substitute for the legal system.

Maybe the lack of justice, the society somehow tries to substitute the system and make justice. It is possible, in some communities, to also be a discriminatory mentality, of labelling. (IRO09)

The respondent (below) argues that it is the responsibility of the probation counsellor to develop and track the recovering process, which consists of executing the noncustodial measures, an approach that is considered useful for the efficient social reintegration of the offender.

But once the judge thought of it that way, it means it is the best for him. We execute, and here we can choose the obligations, I mean they are established by the judge, but we have the role to somehow introduce him to the obligations, or get him out of it, and not necessarily at the time he has to respect. I mean the probation counsellor has his method of customization and working with a person. (IRO09)

SOLUTIONS AND RECOMMENDATIONS: CONSTRUCTING THE MODEL

Based on these thematic axes, the research team aimed to systematize a values-centred model of probation for the N-E area of Romania.

Through axial coding, we merged the existing categories established in the selective coding stage into a more comprehensive and focused representation. Based on the relations between these categories, we formulated a model of value-centred probation specific to the N-E region of Romania.

The model of value-centred probation in N-E. Romania is thus based on a process of theoretical cross-breeding between the paradigm of retributive justice, the paradigm of restorative justice and that of justice centred on human rights. There were very few elements specific to the utilitarian model.

The constitutive values of the Romanian probation model that have been identified are *justice, responsibility* and *dignity*. Each of these values arises from a different ethical construction.

Justice, as retribution, aims to *subjectively* equalize the reports between social actors, and is based on the universality of retribution and its customization according to the prejudice and conditions surrounding the crime committed.

The central theme of the model is the certainty of retribution, which guarantees fairness between individuals and their equality before the law. The prison-centred paradigm is considered an excessive and costly retribution, probation has therefore introduced social models of retribution such as community service, limitation of rights and supervised freedom.

Responsibility towards the individual comes from an awareness of society's co-responsibility towards the offender and the victim. Society has failed to ensure sociability, the legitimate context for interactions between individuals. Society's responsibility generates a model of transmitting responsibility and of accountability. The social integration of the offenders is paramount whilst retribution is not. In this context, the prison-centred paradigm is rejected as not generating responsibility for the offender. Furthermore, incarceration eradicates society's accountability towards the individual, isolating him/her from the rest of the society. In contrast society's responsibility is heightened when trying to recover and reintegrate offenders, reducing the risk of relapse. In this model, *responsibility* substitutes for equality and recovery takes the place of retribution. *Human rights* (the influence of the humanistic paradigm within the model) are specific to N-E Romania and centred on the individual's *dignity* as a human rather than their actions. *Dignity* appears in the discourse of the respondents as ensuring respect for the offenders' rights.

A model centred on human rights thus rejects the prison-centred paradigm (retributive), especially given that this represents the most severe limitation of individuals' rights and involves a large deviation away from respecting the individual's dignity. Punishment should be humanized and exercised strictly within the law, thus protecting the fundamental rights of the convicted person. This model is not entirely favoured by the Romanian normative framework which eliminates victim-offender mediation from the attributions of probation, nor is it entirely favoured by the practice which generally lacks experience of situations involving a delaying of sentence under supervision – although this form is required by the code of criminal procedure. The model does, however, include an important component referring to humanizing the punishments by customizing and correlating them with the offender's personality and the context within which the crime was committed.

Specific to the new model, neither retribution nor reintegration are the most important aspects, instead *trust* is seen as defining the process of probation.

The Romanian model thus represents a combination of three paradigms – retributive justice, restorative justice and justice based on human rights and values – due at least in part to a model of developing probation in Romania based on custodial initiatives (NGO environment), of introducing restorative justice, and the predominance of the welfare specific of practice.

DISCUSSION

To ensure a high degree of credibility regarding data analysis, attention was paid to careful and accurate reporting of the expressions of each respondent, marked in quotes - """" - when they were cited in the text. The large amount of data made it difficult to retain all references to the discourse of the respondents, these being mentioned in the text only when they provided information that supplemented the analysis of the researcher.

The interviews were conducted and analysed – prior to transcription – in Romanian, the language in which the inductive process of data coding was conducted. When

Figure 1. Model of value-centered probation

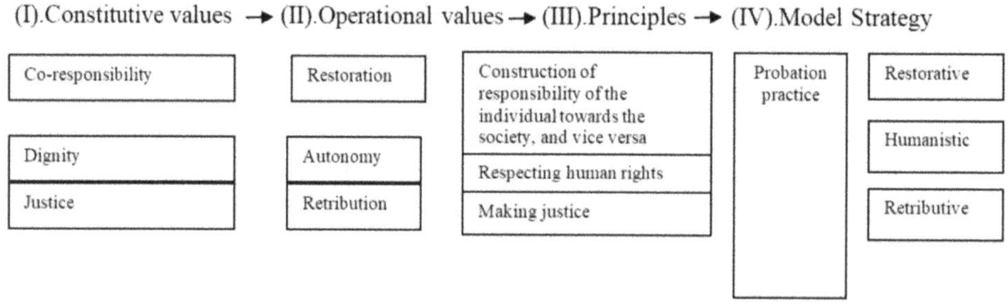

translating into English, we retained a series of extracts – in quotation format – from the discourse of the respondents, taking care that the translation would respect, as far as possible, the stylistic idiosyncrasies of the respondents. Therefore, the reader has access – albeit limited through translation – to the respondent's discourse, allowing him/her to gain a sense of the particularities of it, access which is needed to clarify how language is used in the social construction of reality.

To ensure the veracity of the model and its interpretative fidelity, the model in its nascent form was subjected to a critical review by the participants in the focus group, amongst which were several probation counsellors who acted as respondents in the first set of interviews. In completing the data analysis, the data collected during the focus group was also considered, along with suggestions for interpretation proposed by the participants.

Furthermore, to ensure a greater rigour in the analysis, a process of triangulation between the researchers and the data sources was conducted. Given these methodological precautions for diminishing, as far as possible, the sources of subjectivity in data interpretation, the researchers nevertheless assumed the research to be subjective in nature, appropriate for those wishing to explore the *social construction of a phenomenon* and also the exploratory nature of the research.

The saturation of the model was checked for each category generated. The selection of new respondents ended when new interviews added little in the way of significant data to the thematic axes of the research.

From an ethical perspective, data confidentiality was assured by anonymizing the answers and destroying the initial records upon completion of the research. The consent of the participants was obtained and they were fully informed regarding their right to withdraw from the research at any time. However, the nature of the questions suggested there was no risk for the participants and answering the questions did not generate a high level of discomfort as the interviewees were not part of any recognised category of vulnerable people.

Finally, this analysis was based on a model that identified the axiological and ethical component underlying the functioning of the probation practice, principally by identifying the constitutive values, the operational values, the principles and, finally, the strategy that underlies a social practice (Sandu, 2016a).

DIRECTIONS FOR FUTURE RESEARCH

The Grounded Theory analysis was not meant to provide a valid model, but a credible one that could initiate future investigations in the same area and lead to a quantitative validation of the model. In practice, quantitative research was developed to contribute to the validation of the model and was achieved by sending online questionnaires to probation counsellors. Consequently, a partial validation was achieved and analysis of the data is still in progress, although this extends beyond the topic of this chapter.

CONCLUSION

The model that was identified and analysed in Romanian practice included elements from three existing theoretical models, the constitutive values of each being transformed into operational values within professional practice.

The key value that transpires from the discourse of the respondents is *responsibility*, strongly infused by notions of *trust* and *respect*.

The dominant discourse is predominantly retributive, with most of the respondents arguing that punishment is necessary because anti-social actions should elicit a punitive response from society. Restorative elements, based on human rights, are substituted for retribution when the means of application and the type of applicable sanctions are considered. The social value of responsibility is very important, and is applicable in three situations: the responsibility of the probation counsellor, the responsibility of the society and the construction of responsibility of the offender as a key element of his/her social reintegration.

REFERENCES

Adam, S. (2009, Nov.). Profesia de cadru didactic între reprezentare socială şi vocaţie individuală [The profession of professor between the social representation and the individual vocation]. *Revista de Cercetare în Ştiinţe ale Educaţiei, Sociologia educaţiei.*

Apel, K.-O. (1989). Normative Ethics and Strategical Rationality. The Philosophical Problem of Political Ethics. In R. Schurmann (Ed.), *The Public Realm. Essays on Discursive Types in Political Philosophy* (pp. 107–131). State University of New York Press.

Apel, K.-O. (1992). The Ecological Crisis as a Problem for Discourse Ethics. In A. Ofsti (Ed.), *Ecology and Ethics* (pp. 219–260). Trondheim: Nordland Academy of Arts and Sciences.

Apel, K.-O. (1993). How to Ground a Universalistic Ethics of Co-Responsibility for the Effects of Collective Actions and Activities? *Philosophica, 52*(2), 9–29.

Apel, K.-O. (1999). *The Response of Discourse Ethics to the Moral Challenge of the Human Situation as Such and Especially Today*. Mercier Lectures, Louvain-la-Neuve, March.

Ashwoorth, A. (1989). Criminal Justice and Deserved Sentences. *Criminal Law Review (London, England), 36*, 340–355.

Bandura, A. (2002). Selective Moral Disengagement in the Exercise of Moral Agency. *Journal of Moral Education, 31*(2), 101–119. doi:10.1080/0305724022014322

Bazemore, G. (1998). Restorative justice and earned redemption: Communities, victims, and offender reintegration. *The American Behavioral Scientist, 41*(6), 768–813. doi:10.1177/0002764298041006003

Bazemore, G., & Umbreit, M. (2001). *A comparison of four restorative conferencing models. In Juvenile Justice Bulletin* (pp. 1–19). Washington, DC: U.S. Department of Justice.

Braithwaite, J. (1989). *Crime, shame, and reintegration*. Cambridge, UK: Cambridge University Press. doi:10.1017/CBO9780511804618

Braithwaite, J. (1998). Restorative justice. In M. Tonry (Ed.), *The handbook of crime and punishment* (pp. 323–344). Oxford, UK: Oxford University Press.

Braithwaite, J. (1999). Restorative justice: Assessing optimistic and pessimistic accounts. In M. Tonry (Ed.), *Crime and justice: A review of research* (Vol. 25, pp. 1–127). doi:10.1086/449287

Braithwaite, J. (2002). *Restorative justice and responsive regulation*. New York: Oxford University Press.

Braithwaite, J. (2003). Principles of restorative justice. In A. Von Hirsch, J. V. Roberts, A. Bottoms, K. Roach, & M. Schiff (Eds.), *Restorative justice and criminal justice: Competing or reconcilable paradigms?* (pp. 1–20). Oxford, UK: Hart.

Braithwaite, J., & Strang, H. (2001). Introduction: Restorative justice and civil society. In H. Strang & J. Braithwaite (Eds.), *Restorative justice and civil society* (pp. 1–13). Cambridge, UK: Cambridge University Press.

Braithwaite, V. (1998). The value orientations underlying liberalism conservatism. *Personality and Individual Differences, 25*(3), 575–589. doi:10.1016/S0191-8869(98)00111-1

Carroll, J. S., Perkowitz, W. T., Lurigio, A. J., & Weaver, F. M. (1987). Sentencing goals, causal attributions, ideology, and personality. *Journal of Personality and Social Psychology, 52*(1), 107–118. doi:10.1037/0022-3514.52.1.107 PMID:3820064

Cojocaru, Ş. (2003). Reabilitarea bazată pe comunitate a persoanelor cu dizabilităţi [Community-based rehabilitation of people with disabilities]. *Revista de Cercetare şi Intervenţie Socială*, 2.

Cojocaru, Ş. (2010). *Evaluarea programelor de asistenţă social* [Assessing the social welfare programs]. Iasi, Romania: Polirom Publishing.

Corbin, J. M., & Strauss, A. (2008). *Basics of qualitative research: techniques and procedures for developing Grounded Theory* (3rd ed.). London, UK: Sage Publications Inc. doi:10.4135/9781452230153

Creswell, J. W. (2007). *Qualitative Inquiry and Research Design: Choosing Among Five Traditions* (2nd ed.). Sage Publication, Inc.

Daly, K. (2000). Revisiting the Relationship between Retributive and Restorative Justice. In Restorative Justice: From Philosophy to Practice (pp. 33-54). Aldershot, UK: Dartmouth.

De Keijser, J. W., Van Der Leeden, R., & Jackson, J. L. (2002). From moral theory to penal attitudes and back: A theoretically integrated modelling approach. *Behavioral Sciences & the Law, 20*(4), 317–335. doi:10.1002/bsl.494 PMID:12210971

Derks, L. (2005). *Social Panoramas: Changing the Unconscious Landscape with NLP and Psychotherapy*. Crown House Publishing.

Duff, A. (2001). *Punishment, communication, and community*. Oxford, UK: Oxford University Press.

Foucault, M. (2005). *A supraveghea şi a pedepsi. Naşterea închisorii* [To supervise and to punish. The birth of prison]. Bucharest, Romania: Paralela 45.

Garhart Mooney, C. (2009). *Theories of Attachment: An Introduction to Bowlby, Ainsworth, Gerber, Brazelton, Kennell, and Klaus*. Redleaf Press.

Gilligan, C. (1977). In a Different Voice: Womens Conceptions of Self and of Morality. *Harvard Educational Review, 47*(4), 481–517. doi:10.17763/haer.47.4.g6167429416hg5l0

Gilligan, C. (1982). *In a Different Voice: Psychological Theory and Women's Development*. Cambridge, MA: Harvard University.

Goulding, C. (1999). *Grounded Theory: some reflections on paradigm, procedures and misconceptions.* Working Paper Series. Wolverhampton Business School, Management Research Centre.

Groza, D. (2006). *Drepturile victimei. Recuperarea din uitare* [Victim's rights. Recovery through oblivion]. Iasi, Romania: LUMEN Publishing.

Ho, A. (2008). Relational autonomy or undue pressure? Family's role in medical decision-making. *Scandinavian Journal of Caring Sciences, 22*(1), 128-35. https://doi.org/10.1111/j.1471-6712.2007.00561.x

Hudson, B. (1996). *Understanding Justice: An Introduction to Ideas, Perspectives and Controversies in Modern Penal Theory.* Buckingham, UK: Open University Press.

Johnstone, G. (2011). Restorative Justice: Ideas, Values, Debates. New York: Routledge.

Johnstone, G., & Van Ness, D. (2006). *The Meaning of Restorative Justice. The Handbook on Restorative Justice.* Cullompton: Willan Publishing.

Lipovetsky, G. (1996). Amurgul datoriei: Etica nedureroasă a noilor timpuri democratice [Twilight of duty. The unpainful ethics of new democratic times]. Bucharest, Romania: Babel Publishing.

McFatter, R. M. (1978). Sentencing strategies and justice: Effects of punishment philosophy on sentencing decisions. *Journal of Personality and Social Psychology, 36*(12), 1490–1500. doi:10.1037/0022-3514.36.12.1490

McFatter, R. M. (1982). Purposes of punishment: Effects of utilities of criminal sanctions on perceived appropriateness. *The Journal of Applied Psychology, 67*(3), 255–267. doi:10.1037/0021-9010.67.3.255 PMID:7107551

Mitrache, C. (1994). Drept penal român: partea generală [Romanian Penal Justice: the general part]. Bucharest, Romania: Casa de Editură şi Presă.

Rawls, J. (2012). O teorie a dreptății [A theory of justice]. Iasi, Romania: Alexandu Ioan Cuza University Publishing.

Sandu, A. (2010). Freedom as a hermeneutical pretext. *Revista Românească pentru Educație Multidimensională, 2*(3), 5-24.

Sandu, A. (2014). *Elemente de sociologie. Sociologie generală, juridică şi metodologia cercetării sociale* [Elements of sociology. General and legal sociology, and the methodology of social research]. Bucharest, Romania: Tritonic Publishing.

Sandu, A. (2015). *Etică profesională și transparență în administrația publică* [Professional ethics and transparency in public administration]. Bucharest, Romania: Didactică şi Pedagogică Publishing.

Sandu, A. (2016a). *Social Construction of Reality as communicative Action*. Cambridge Scholars Publishing.

Sandu, A. (2016b). Cadre normativ-instituționale ale construcției sociale a profesiei de consilier de probațiune în zona de Nord-Est a României și în Republica Moldova [Normative-institutional frameworks of the social construction of the probation counseling profession in the North-East of Romania and the Republic of Moldova]. *Sociologie Românească, 14*(1), 23-44.

Sandu, A., & Damian, S. (2012). Applying Appreciative Inquiry Principles in the Restorative Justice Field. *Postmodern Openings, 3*(2), 37–52.

Sandu, A., & Unguru, E. (2014). *Acțiune comunicativă, justiție deliberativă și restaurativă. Perspective socio- juridice asupra medierii și probațiunii* [Communicative action, deliberative and restorative justice. Social-legal perspectives on mediation and probation]. Bucharest, Romania: Tritonic Publishing.

Szabo, A. (2010a). Greşeală, vinovăţie şi pedeapsă: despre reabilitarea persoanelor care au comis infracțiuni [Mistake, guilt and punishment: on rehabilitating the persons who have committed crimes]. In *Asistența socială a grupurilor de risc* [Social care of groups of risk] (pp. 455–482). Iasi, Romania: Polirom Publishing.

Szabo, A. (2010b). From Restorative Justice to Restorative Practices: Applicability in the Field of Social Work. *Revista de Asistenţă Socială, 1*.

Von Hirsh, A. (1976). *Doing Justice: The Choice of Punishment*. New York: Hill and Wang.

Worrall, A., & Mawby, R. C. (2014). Probation worker cultures and relationships with offenders. *Probation Journal, 61*(4), 346 – 357. https://doi.org/10.1177/0264550514548251

Chapter 10
The Limits of Confidentiality and of the Right to Privacy:
A Bioethical Approach of Social Work

Elena Unguru
University of Oradea, Romania

ABSTRACT

Social work acts at within the public and private fields. From an ethical point of view, the first one is governed by the society's right to information and the social worker's obligation for transparency. The second one is the beneficiary's right to private life and the social worker's obligation of confidentiality. The two sets of competing rights and obligations define the dual nature of social work to act both in the public sphere, as well as the private one. Starting from the case of Tarasoff, the American instances stated that the obligation of the therapist to protect the possible victims is a priority to that of confidentiality. The current chapter follows the meaning of this obligation in the practice of social work, as well as the clarification of the importance and limits of applicability of the principle of confidentiality in social work.

INTRODUCTION

The bioethical perspective on social work focuses on the way in which the process of assistance is interfered by a series of particular ethical principles, their reconstruction starting from the particularities of the social intervention. A series of values social work is based on, such as equity, justice, autonomy are found as such in bioethics, since there is a clear connection between social work and the welfare professions in the area of health care. The particularities of the field of social work makes certain

DOI: 10.4018/978-1-5225-3090-9.ch010

central elements in clinical ethics become peripheral, or even questionable in the ethics of social work. The chapter below aims to discuss the limits of applying values: the right to private life, trust and confidentiality in the welfarist area. The frameworks of the discussion consider the inherent limits of confidentiality generated by the controversial Tarasoff case.

BACKGROUND: THEORETICAL PERSPECTIVES ON THE RIGHT TO PRIVATE LIFE, CONFIDENTIALITY AND TRUST

The three values, right to private life, trust and confidentiality are a working triangle in the ethics of helping professions. By customizing the applicability of the values, we can shape a bioethical analysis of social work as social practice.

CONFIDENTIALITY IN SOCIAL WORK

Confidentiality is usually seen as a key principle in the relationship between the social worker and the beneficiary (Collingridge, Miller & Bowles, 2008), since it leads to the construction of a relationship of trust between the two parts. Biestek (1957) considers confidentiality to be an essential principle for any helping profession, including social work. Confidentiality was defined by him as keeping the secret of information regarding the client, that the social worker has obtained during the professional meetings with beneficiaries. Confidentiality was understood as a decisive element in the development of the beneficiary social worker, based on trust (Frunza, 2011).

Confidentiality refers to the information obtained in privileged conversations, and generally refers to the communication that emerges within the counselling dimensions of social practice (Lasky & Riva, 2006). In social work, many of the services are based precisely on communicating the information on the beneficiary (see the situation of social benefits, of the advocacy in favour of the beneficiary or the group of beneficiaries, the need for positive discrimination of different categories of beneficiaries, etc.). In this situation, through the beneficiary's agreement to participate in programs of social intervention, we presume the agreement to disclose information that are strictly necessary for the success of the intervention (Frunza, 2012). It is preferable that on the onset of the intervention, there is a contract of providing social services that would expressly contain informed consent from the beneficiary regarding the intervention and its limitations, implicitly the limitations of confidentiality and the type of information that will be disclosed for developing the intervention.

Respecting confidentiality is, from a (bio)ethics point of view, based on two principles: respect for the autonomy of the beneficiary and fidelity provided to the beneficiary by the social worker. Aside from these principles, the beneficence and the non-maleficence are strictly correlated with respecting confidentiality (Lasky & Riva, 2006).

Beneficence is involved in situations where, for example, by establishing a relationship of trust, it is also created a strong empowerment, leading the beneficiary towards a state of increased autonomy. Positive discrimination also falls under the spectrum of beneficence by creating favourable and customized conditions for vulnerable categories to access certain resource, otherwise difficult to access due to the their type of vulnerability. In this regard, we give the example of positive discrimination in the Rroma community in Romania through access to higher education on publicly funded places, even if the results to the admission exams wouldn't, otherwise, grant them access to such places. The Rroma community is generally vulnerable regarding the access to education, the level of illiteracy among the members of the community being extremely high.

Non-maleficence arises when, by non-disclosing certain information, we avoid placing the beneficiary in a situation of discomfort of potential rejection, marginalization, victimization or discrimination (Lasky & Riva, 2006).

In our opinion, confidentiality also involves respect for the two other principles of bioethics: respect for autonomy, previously discussed, and justice. In case of justice, confidentiality interferes in the social transactions the beneficiary does, without fearing that the privileged information on his private life could be disclosed without his consent.

Confidentiality's starting point is the professional's obligation to respect the right to privacy. This right requires the social worker not to request the beneficiary to include information on his private life in the documents, other than those that are necessary for developing the social intervention (Taubman, 2012; NASW, 2008). A series of authors argue that in practice, there is a confusion between confidentiality and the right to privacy, the latter one being neglected in favour of confidentiality (Collingridge, Miller & Bowles, 2008; Congress & McAuliffe, 2006). Other authors (Gelman, Pollack & Weiner, 1999) consider confidentiality to be an integrated part of the right to private life, subsuming it to the concept of trust. As such, confidentiality is operated in the direct relationship between the social worker and the beneficiary. In our opinion, this approach excludes the obligation of confidentiality from the tasks of the providing organisation, since the relationship between the organisation and the beneficiary is mediated by the social worker as a third party. In practice, the control over respecting the right to private life is mainly done by through the practice of administrative supervision and the control of malpractice.

The ethics code of social workers in the USA (NASW, 2008) contains a series of guidelines that form the standard of "Privacy and confidentiality". This standard refers to ensuring the right to private life through confidentiality, informed consent, regulating the disclosure of information obtained in the relationship between the social worker and the beneficiary (Gelamn, Pollack & Weiner, 1999). Confidentiality can be absolute and relative, Gelman, Pollack and Weiner (1999) showing that in practice, the right to confidentiality is relative, its limits being defined through codes of ethics. The authors criticize the code of ethics of NASW (1996), for the relative lack of clarity compared to the Code of Ethics of the American Psychological Association (APA). The APA code expressly states that no information contained in printed or electronic format is not completely confidential, regardless of the will of the parts (Gelman, Pollack & Weiner, 1999).

In the Jaffee versus Redmond case, the Federal Supreme Court shows that the documents and information held by the social worker in a case in progress, or previously worked, are defended by the law (Federal Rules of Evidence), in the same way as the data obtained by the counselling psychotherapist, the psychiatrist or even the lawyer. In justifying the decision, the Court shows that this level of confidentiality is necessary for establishing trust in the relationship between the two parts (Gelman, Pollack & Weiner, 1999).

Any disclosure of information obtained from a client can be done either based on a legal obligation, or with the beneficiary's consent. The information disclosed must not exceed the necessary limit for the objective of the intervention to be reached. The client must be informed in any situation regarding the social worker's intention to communicate private information to third parties, as well as the reason for which confidentiality is violated. The involvement of third parties from the beneficiary's social network requires a partial disclosure of certain information, and cannot be done without his/her consent. Even the disclosure of information about the beneficiary to a financing third party, or one providing resources, cannot be done without the beneficiary's consent. Confidentiality over the information received from the client must be also kept from colleagues social workers, and the disclosure is only done with his/her consent, in the limits necessary for the social intervention they are about to carry out (Collingridge, Miller & Bowles, 2008).

Congress & McAuliffe (2006) presents a series of obligations that social worker has, in ensuring confidentiality in their relationship with the beneficiary:

- Obtaining informed consent from the client, referring to the use of information collected from them, as well as its disclosure to third parties, including the possibility of disclosure, as well as the accepted limits of disclosure;
- Informing the client on the limits of confidentiality and the circumstances in which the information can be disclosed without consent;

- The beneficiary's consent for recording the meetings between them and the social worker;
- Maintaining anonymity when the information obtained from the beneficiary are used in educational or research purposes;
- The beneficiary's consent for partially violating the confidentiality when the intervention involves counselling with two people or groups;
- Ensuring the preservation of recording and documents in a manner that ensures confidentiality (congress & mcauliffe, 2006).

A serious ethical issue is represented by the personal data protection, and the confidentiality of data between the social worker and the beneficiary in the digital era (Gelman, Pollack & Weiner, 1999). Although the documents can be password-protected, the access to the beneficiary's data can be disclosed through means of different storage media, and their use without consent can influence the quality of the intervention, and sometimes even the beneficiary's quality of life (Congress, 2006). Online and virtual counselling, data storage on different servers that are susceptible of data mining from malevolent third parties involves a special treatment, both by public and private agencies. Rock and Congress (1999) considers that the digital era is, in fact, the end of confidentiality and the right to private life, as it is traditionally defined.

THE RIGHT TO PRIVATE LIFE IN SOCIAL WORK

The idea of private life comes from Habermas' (1991) political and social philosophy. Habermas distinguishes two areas of the individuals' interactions, the public and the private one. In the public area, we have the professional, civic, political, cultural activity, etc. In the private area, there are included activities the individual performs in his own benefit, within the circle of relatives, friends, neighbours, which request the privilege of not being exposed to the interest of the public area. From this point of view, the process of counselling and the different forms of psycho-socio therapy are kept within the private area of life. This approach in the private life is justified by exposing, under confidentiality, the information on private life, to the counsellor. On the other hand, the practice of social work targets the social integration of the beneficiary, aside psycho-social counselling, providing him with a series of benefits (such as minimum guaranteed income[1]) and advocacy social services, the facilitation of access to services meant to place the beneficiary in the public environment. As such, social work is positioned as a service at the intersection between the public and the private area, the beneficiary receiving support both in solving problems related to the private area – for example through family therapies – as well as problems considering his/her integration in the public area and the relationship with different institutions. Given the two areas, the public and the private one, from an ethical point of view, the first one is governed by the society's right to information and the obligation for transparency, and the second one is the beneficiary's right to private life, and the obligation of confidentiality that belongs to the social worker. The two rights and competing obligations define the dual nature of social work to act in both the public and the private area.

Ferdinand Schoeman (1984, p. 2) defines the right to private life as being composed of three domains: the right itself, the owner of the right and the claim of the right; the measure of control the individual exerts over personal information, own intimacy and image; the condition of access limited to the individual, his private life and own identification data (Fuchs, 2011).

Another classification of the types of right to private life is conducted by Ken Gormley (1992, p. 1337):

- Private life as an expression of the person and the personality;
- Private life as an expression of the person and the personality;
- The individual's right to control the information on one's self (fuchs, 2011).

The mentioned author considers that the right to private life is a multi-dimensional value. In turn, Daniel Solove (2008) identifies six different definitions to the idea of private life:

- Right to be left alone;
- Right to limit other's access to oneself;
- Right to keep a secret on oneself;
- Control over information regarding oneself;
- Personhood;
- Right to intimacy (Fuchs, 2011).

Compared to the classifications conducted in 2008, in a previous work of Solove (2004), we also identify the right for protection from the Big Brother, the invasive society and the totalitarian control (Fuchs, 2011).

A criticism of the concept of private life, and implicitly of the right to confidentiality is made by Fuchs (2011), starting from the idea that privacy represents a construct belonging to the liberal paradigm, which could be redefined based on other paradigms of the current political philosophy. The current model of understanding the right to private life is based on the idea of social atomism, the individual being the central point of the social construction. An alternative model can be, according to the author (Fuchs, 2001), established starting from the socialist political philosophy as a right of the social communities to be protected of the corporatist intrusion in their own way and lifestyle.

TRUST IN THE RELATIONSHIP BETWEEN THE SOCIAL WORKER AND THE BENEFICIARY

The respect for the right to a private life and confidentiality are considered to be extremely important for establishing a relationship of trust between the social worker and the beneficiary (Biestek, 1957; Gelman, Pollack & Weiner, 1999; Sandu, Cojocaru, Gavrilovici & Oprea, 2013).

The trust of the beneficiary in the professional is the belief of the first one that the latter one will act to maximize the beneficiary's interest, and therefore offer the best form of intervention and the most adequate possible care (Anderson & Dedrick apud Platonova, 2008, p. 699; Cojocaru, Sandu & Oprea, 2013).

Hall et. al. (2001, p. 615) defines trust as "the optimistic acceptance of the vulnerable situation, in which an individual beliefs the other will serve his/her interests". The relationship of trust, as defined by Hall et al. (2001), places the individuals in an imbalance of power, trust being what balances this situation. In social work, trust becomes an instrument of empowerment since the balancing of the relationship of power between the beneficiary and the social subsystems he belong in is the very purpose of the welfare practices.

O'Neill (2001) considers that trust is an instrument used by the professional to manage the relationship with the beneficiary from the perspective of risks associated with the intervention. The current society is defined as a society of risk (Beck, 1992). Within it, the individual has to manage an increased pressure of the risk of dissatisfaction to the different elements of everyday life (Buzducea, 2017). Among the elements of risk, there are pollution, terrorist threats, spectrum of war, especially the nuclear one, food prepared with different preservatives and enhancers, etc. Aside all these stressful elements, we add the risk given by overpopulation, globalization, threats over the workplace given by hyper-technology, stressful and sedentary lifestyles, etc. For all of these, the society must identify solutions for diminishing the perceived risk (Bostan & Grosu, 2015). If in other historical times, the main instrument of annihilating the risk is represented by the religious factor by promising a happy afterlife in exchange for the suffering in this life, the secular society transforming the spiritual counselling into counselling practices in a much wider process of professionalization of charity (Sandu & Caras, 2013). Cojocaru, Sandu and Oprea (2013) emphasize the knowledge of cultural particularities and the beneficiary's social status, which allows the professional to develop an interpersonal relationship with the beneficiary as member of a social relationship which acts in particular, well-determined social contexts (Gavriluţă, 2013).

Pellegrino (1991, p. 75) shows that: "when we need a doctor, lawyer or priest – or social worker, we might say – we have no choice but to trust them". In this context, the social worker's adherence to the bioethical principles of beneficence, non-maleficence, respect for person's autonomy and justice, becomes extremely important (Beauchamp & Childress, 2001). The professional trust is different from the personal one, since the first one refers especially to the professional's competences, and the second one, to his/her benevolence. For the relationship of trust to work, the beneficiary should cumulate, in the person of the social worker, both types of trust: that he has all necessary competences to help him, and that he is willing to do it (Cojocaru, Sandu & Oprea, 2013).

Confidentiality is important for both types of trust of the social worker. Trust is manifested both in the social worker's competences – since the respect for confidentiality is part of the competences that are universally attributed to the professionals in the helping professions – as well as his benevolence. Maintaining confidentiality shows the beneficiary that the professional is unconditionally *on his side*, and valorises him/her. Violating confidentiality distances the beneficiary, since it shows him/her that the professional either doesn't give him/her enough trust, or he manages the case in the interest of a third party.

For example, in a case of family violence, the counsellor working with the violent side could be suspected of carrying out the activity in the victim's interest. In fact, unlike other counselling professions, the social worker is first in the interest of the community affected by any dysfunction at the level of the social microsystems. As such, the limits of confidentiality are much wider for the social worker, rather than for the psychiatrist or the psychologist.

PRESENTING THE TARASOFF CASE

Prosenjit Poddar and Tatiana Tarasoff were colleagues at Berkley University, in California. The two met on New Year's Eve, when Poddar fell in love with Tarasoff, but she couldn't express her feelings, being involved in a relationship. Poddar developed a fixation for his colleague, repeatedly declaring that he intends to kill her. He declared that even in front of the psychiatrist, during counselling sessions. The psychiatrist reported it to the police, the they investigated his intention, releasing him due to the lack of evidence, although the psychiatrist, dr. Lawrence Moore, warned the police over the possible need for hospitalization in the psychiatry ward for Poddar. Dr. Moore's supervisor refused to involuntarily hospitalize Poddar, and instructed the staff to no longer receive him in the clinic. Short after that, taking advance of recently moving in the same apartment with the victim's brother, he kills Tatiana Tarasoff with a knife (Almason, 1997; Ioan & Gavrilovici, 2005; Kachigian & Felthous, 2004).

Tatiana Tarasoff's family sues the University, the policy and the psychiatrist for failing to prevent the victim's assassination, and did not take all necessary measures in this regard, and did not notify the family of the victim on the potential danger their daughter was being exposed to. The Supreme Court of Justice of California institutes, for the psycho-therapists, the obligation to protect other from potential acts of violence their clients are planning to commit.

The American Psychiatric Association involved in the trial, showing that it is not a psychiatrist's competence to determine the future potentially risky behaviours of patients, and the express obligation for them to determine such possible behaviours exceeds the psychiatric professional standards, therefore the obligation is inapplicable, the risk having to be determined accurately (Kachigian & Felthous, 2004).

We note that such an obligation, applicable to professionals in social services, is all the more inoperative since they don't have psychiatric competences. Even though the social worker, or any other kind of professional counsellor would consider that the beneficiary indicates an increased risk of violence, he/she would not be able to request the involuntary hospitalization only based on the beneficiary's verbal conduct, in lack of psychiatric or criminal history.

The Legal and Normative Implications of the Tarasoff Case

In the McIntosh versus Milano Superior Court of Law, Legal Division, in New Jersey statuated that the obligation to protect the potential victims cannot be limited to the information collected by the counsellor exclusively from the verbal statements of the presumed perpetrator (Kachigian & Felthous, 2004). In turn, the California Supreme Court, starting from the Thomson v. County Alameda, shows that in moving the obligation of protecting possible victims is important to determine the danger's level of importance of the person attending counselling, over other people or the public safety in general. The court rules that the institutions and professionals that work with people who can become aggressive, representing public danger, should have necessary psychiatric training in order to determine the predictable threat.

In the case of Hutchinson v. Patel, Louisiana Supreme Court shows that there is a double obligation of the therapist, to foresee the client's potential of commiting acts of violence, as well as to inform the authorities/presumed victim (Almason, 1997). The first obligation is challenged by the American Association of Psychiatry, meaning that the Court obliges the psychiatrist to appreciate the danger, which exceeds his competences (Kachigian & Felthous, 2004).

The Hedlund court shows that the obligation of informing the potential victims resides not in the therapist's duty to foresee the possible future behaviours, but in the very process of diagnosis, which must include the risk for violent behaviour of the subject and the potential people to whom this behaviour might act upon (Almason, 1997).

The above mentioned cases show that in the counselling professions, the obligation of confidentiality is removed from the obligation to protect the potential victims, and even the society itself from dangers which may arise from the assisted persons.

The Limits of Confidentiality vs. the Limits of the Obligation of Protection

Vitteli (2014), starting from the Tarasoff case, shows that the Court declared the therapist's obligation to protect the potential victims as being prioritary to that of confidentiality. The Tarasoff Law (Lake, 1994) shows that there is a positive obligation of the therapist, and basically of any counsellor, including the social worker, but according to certain researchers, and even the lawyer (Deck, 2016) – to inform the alleged victim of the danger he/she might be facing, or the public authorities of the imminent danger represented by the counselee. A problem connected to the strict obligation to protect the presumed victims, is of determining the gravity of the danger he is in. Vitteli (2014) shows that there are different levels of danger imagined by the client as a perpetrator when he confesses his intention to do harm. But when facing the intention to commit a violent, but un-lethal crime, is the obligation of protecting the victim still valid?

The Duty to Warn and the Duty to Protect in Social Work

In social work, the issue of protecting potential victims, and even protecting the beneficiary against self-victimisation has become an ethical obligation, as a consequence of the Tarasoff case.

The decision in the Tarasoff case raises a series of difficulties in interpreting the importance of confidentiality in the relationship between the client and the social worker. The obligation to alert occurs in the case of the social worker as a duty to explicitly notice the alleged victim that he is in potential danger of violence, and comes to complete the obligation to protect, which requests the social worker to determine the potential risk of the client and adopt a reasonable behaviour that would reduce this risk. Based on the estimated risk, we can reach the obligation to inform the authorities of it (Harvard Mental Health Letter, 2008, January).

Confidentiality vs. Duty to Warn the Persons Infected With HIV/AIDS, in Social Work

In the situation of social workers, the obligation to protect and warn extends to the cases of intervention on people with psychiatric issues, or other social situations that may endanger the population's state of well-being, the public health or the beneficiary's own condition. The social worker working with people infected with HIV confront with an ethical dilemma regarding the obligation to inform versus that of confidentiality, when he/she must make the decision of informing the relatives of the infected person, but also people from his/her social network who could be vulnerable to getting infested with HIV, in case the beneficiary decides to have unprotected sexual contact, without previously informing them of his/her medical condition. If he/she violates the confidentiality, the client is facing major risks of discrimination and social exclusion, due to the prejudices in certain social and cultural environments regarding the carriers of HIV.

For example, in Romania, despite the education on tolerance and acceptance of people with HIV, they are still discriminates based on fearing that the infestation may occur in ways other than the known ones, or simply based on sexual orientation or the state of handicap (Copoeru, et. al., 2013). On the other hand, if the social worker doesn't take measures of informing the social network on the state of health, and the beneficiary doesn't understand the risks his behaviour might have, other infestations may occur, that the social worker can be partially responsible for, too (Granich, 2012). Regarding those mentioned, Stanard and Hazler (1995) quote a case in which a patient infested with HIV tells the counsellor that although he has knowledge of the diagnosis, he continues to have unprotected sexual relationships with both his wife, and other people that are unaware of his diagnosis. The duty to warn doesn't directly derive from the situation mentioned in Tarasoff's case, and the right to violate the confidentiality on the beneficiary's health condition differs from one national legislation to the other.

Confidentiality vs. Duty to Inform, in Social Work, of the Victims of Domestic Violence

Connected to this, the social workers can find out either from the beneficiary himself, or from other people, confidential data on the abusive behaviour of a parent towards his child. The legitimate question the social worker asks himself is: when should he approach child protection through withdrawing them from the family, and when to alert the authorities for bad treatment in minors, especially when there are no evidences of violence other than the children's testimonies? In Romania, there is a special phone number the children can use to report situations of violence in the family. The simple obligation of protecting the victims requires the establishment of certain investigation and taking mesures which can lead to children's institutionalisation and even decay from parental rights, but this measure can not be only based exclusively on minors' statement who claim that they fear of becoming victims, or even of parents who show that they occasionally apply corrections to children, although they are not profoundly harmful. One of the ethical issues raised by the Tarasoff case is to estimate the limits of the presumed danger, from which it is necessary to announce the authorities, and the process of taking emergency protection measures.

The domestic violence is rarely associated with other crimes, such as hitting, bodily harm, but can reach even more serious crimes, such as death-causing hits, murder or manslaughter. The reaction of social work to the risk of domestic violence is different from one society to the other, going from immediate measures of protection, especially in the case of children in societies such as Norway (Sandu, 2016), reaching relative tolerance, motivated by the cultural and spiritual tradition of the country (Litvinova, 2017). In fact, the majority of measures of protection of the victims of domestic violence, or violence against children, are taken based on the duty to protect and only involves the confidentiality of the protected location where the victims are.

Informed Consent in Social Work and the Limits of Confidentiality

In a study elaborated by Givelber and his collaborators (1984) starting from Tarasoff case shows that 90% of the respondents would inform the victim regarding the risk of violence he is facing. Other researchers obtain much lower results, only 71% in case of the study conducted by Jagim and collaborators (1978). Of the responding counsellors, 88% would report the cases with risk of suicide to both the relatives, and the authorities (Pope et al., 1988), and 46% would report the cases of child abuse.

In accordance with the American standards of practice of social work, when the social intervention involves sequences of counselling, the informed consent becomes mandatory. In the process of obtaining informed consent, the client must be made aware and accept that the information he is transmitting remain confidential as long it doesn't involve committing past or future crimes. The client must accept that the information regarding his intention to commit crimes, especially with violence, can be the object of the duty to warn and the duty to protect the potential victims, the social worker has (Taubman, 2012).

Reamer (1998) identifies four necessary conditions for the involuntary disclosure to be necessary and able to be performed by the social worker: the certainty of the client's violent behaviour, and the real threat towards a different person; that the violence would be predictable; the person should be identifiable, the violent act should be assumed to be immediate.

FUTURE RESEARCH DIRECTIONS

As the knowledge-based society and the informational society evolve, the right to a private life becomes more and more important, drawing research to identify the social construction of the idea of private life. In this regard, we consider useful the studies that will emphasize on the confidentiality of digital data. The deprivation of social life will more and more launch, in the public domain, the elements considered as belonging to the private life. The research regarding the even more transparent limit that separates the right to private life from the obligation of transparency will be necessary in order to reposition the practice of social work on the coordinates that are adequate for the digitization of social services.

Regarding the limits of confidentiality in social work, research based on alternative models of confidentiality will rather impose, based on the communities' right to self-determination and responsibility towards the non-presence (Sandu. 2017; Terec-Vlad, 2016).

A series of important research will have to consider the particularities of confidentiality in social work, in the context in which the welfare practices depart from the area of counselling practices. The social intervention is considering the practices of advocacy and the construction of public policies (Murdach, 2011) for people and disadvantaged groups that would replace the classic social casework.

At the moment, the welfare practices are rather based on strengths-based approach, reason for which the inter-institutional cooperation makes the limits of confidentiality become unclear. Last but not least, the studies in the field should aim the very idea of social construction of trust, the confidentiality and right to private life. The analysis of the values should be subsumed to the interest of the beneficiary, but also of the person's dignity.

CONCLUSION

The right to privacy, confidentiality and trust are the three axiological dimensions strictly correlated to contemporary social work. These values come from the modern idea of social practice focused on the individual and his rights. This approach underlies a bioethics model which can be correlated with Beauchamp & Childress' principiism (2001). Along with the Tarasoff case, the society is aware of the limits of the right to confidentiality that cannot prevail the right to life of a third person, or a different major public interest (public health).

ACKNOWLEDGMENT

Article elaborated within the doctoral studies, with the title: "The Social Construction of Supervision in Social Work. Research in Institutions of Child Protection in the N.-E. area of Romania", the Doctoral School of Sociology, University of Oradea.

REFERENCES

Allen, A. (1997). Genetic Privacy: Emerging Concepts and Values. In M. Rothstein (Ed.), *Genetic Secrets: Protecting Privacy and Confidentiality in the Genetic Era* (pp. 31–59). New Haven, CT: Yale University Press.

Allen, A. (2016). Privacy and Medicine. In E. N. Zalta (Ed.), *The Stanford Encyclopedia of Philosophy*. Retrieved May 16, 2017, from https://plato.stanford.edu/archives/win2016/entries/privacy-medicine/

Almason, A. L. (1997). Personal Liability Implications of the Duty to Warn Are Hard Pills to Swallow: From Tarasoff To Hutchinson v. Patel and Beyond. *The Journal of Contemporary Health Law and Policy*, *13*(2), 471–486. PMID:9212527

American Medical Association. (1994). *Code of medical ethics (Report, Council on ethical and Judicial Affairs)*. Chicago: Author.

Anderson, L., & Dedrick, R. (1990). Development of the trust in physician scale: A measure to assess interpersonal trust in patient-physician relationships. *Psychological Reports*, *67*, 1091–1100. PMID:2084735

Atar, B., Saroiu, S., & Koutsky, L. A. (2002). Obtaining Sensitive Data through the Web: An Example of Design and Methods. *Epidemiology (Cambridge, Mass.)*, *13*(6), 640–645. doi:10.1097/00001648-200211000-00007 PMID:12410004

Beauchamp, T. L., & Childress, J. F. (2001). *Principles of Biomedical Ethics* (5th ed.). New York: Oxford University Press.

Beck, U. (1992). *The Risk Society Risk Society: Towards a New Modernity* (1st ed.). SAGE Publications Ltd.

Biestek, F. (1957). *The casework relationship*. Chicago: Layola University.

Bok, S. (1982). *Secrets: On the Ethics of Concealment and Revelation*. New York: Pantheon Books.

Bostan, I., & Grosu, V. (2015). The Health Risk Management and its Legal Impact. *Revista Romana de Bioetica, 13*(1), 37–43.

Buzducea, D. (2017). *Risc si societate* [Risk and society]. Bucharest, Romania: Tritonic.

Cojocaru, D., Sandu, A., & Oprea, L. (2013). Încrederea în relaţia medic-pacient [Trust in the doctor-patient relationship]. In *Relaţia medic-pacient* [The relationship between the doctor and the patient] (pp. 95–123). Iasi, Romania: Polirom Publishing.

Collingridge, M., Miller, S., & Bowles, W. (2008). Privacy and confidentiality in social work. *Australian Social Work, 54*(2), 3–13. doi:10.1080/03124070108414319

Congress, E. (2000). What Social Workers Should Know About Ethics: Understanding and Resolving Practice Dilemmas. *Administration in Social Work, 1*(1), 1–26.

Congress, E., & McAuliffe, D. (2006). Professional codes in Australia and the United States. *Social Work Ethics, 49*(2), 151–164. DOI:10.1177/0020872806061211

Copoeru, I., Moldovan, S., Agheorghiesei, D. T., Ciuhodaru, T., Seghedin, E., & Iorga, M. (2013). The Inter-Agency Cooperation in Healthcare and Social Services for Substance Misuse and Addiction in Romania: A Case Study. *Revista de Asistenţă Socială, 2*, 125–133.

Deck, P. (2016). Ethics—law and social work: Reconciling conflicting ethical obligations between two seemingly opposing disciplines to create a collaborative law practice. *Western New England Law Review, 38*(2), 261–283.

Fennig, S., Secker, A., Levkovitz, Y., Barak, V., Benyakar, M., Farina, J., & Fennig, S. et al. (2004). Are psychotherapists consistent in their ethical attitude to patient confidentiality? *The Israel Journal of Psychiatry and Related Sciences, 41*(2), 82–89. PMID:15478453

Frunză, M. (2012). *Expertiza etică şi acţiune socială* [Ethics expertise and social action]. Bucharest, Romania: Tritonic.

Frunză, S. (2011). Ethical responsibility and social responsibility of organizations involved in the public health system. *Revista de Cercetare şi Intervenţie Socială, 32,* 155-171.

Gavriluţă, C. (2013). Ethical perspectives in sociological research of medical environment and people with vulnerabilities. *Revista Romana de Bioetica, 10*(4), 115–128.

Gelman, S. R., Pollack, D., & Weiner, A. (1999). Confidentiality of social work records in the computer age. *Social Work*, *44*(3), 243–252. doi:10.1093/sw/44.3.243 PMID:10348697

Givelber, D., Bowers, W., & Blitch, D. (1984). Tarasoff, myth and reality: An empirical study of private law in action. *Wisconsin Law Review*, *18*, 443–497. PMID:11653756

Gormley, K. (1992). One hundred years of privacy. *Wisconsin Law Review*, *5*, 1335–1441.

Granich, S. (2012). *Duty to Warn, Duty to Protect*. Retrieved June 15, 2017 from http://www.socialworker.com/feature-articles/ethics-articles/Duty_to_Warn%2C_Duty_to_Protect/

Habermas, J. (1991). *The Structural Transformation of the Public Sphere: An Inquiry into a Category of Bourgeois Society*. MIT Press.

Hall, M., Dugan, E., Zheng, B., & Mishra, A. K. (2001). Trust in phyicians and medical institutions: What is it, can it be measured, and does it matter? *The Milbank Quarterly*, *79*(4), 613–639. doi:10.1111/1468-0009.00223 PMID:11789119

Ioan, B., & Gavrilovici, C. (2005). *Secretul profesional nu poate fi pus inaintea protectiei unui om* [The professional secret cannot be placed before the human protection]. Retrieved June 15, 2017 from adevarul.ro/sanatate/medicina/secretul-profesional-nu-pus-protectiei-unui-om-1_50ad2bad7c42d5a663900bf6/index.html

Jaffee v. Redmond, 116 S. Ct. 1923 (1996).

Jagim, R. D., Wittman, W. D., & Noll, J. O. (1978). Mental health professionals attitude towards confidentialitz, privilege, and third party disclosure. *Professional Psychology*, *9*(3), 458–466. doi:10.1037/0735-7028.9.3.458 PMID:11662548

Kachigian, C., & Felthous, A. R. (2004). Court Responses to Tarasoff Statutes. *The Journal of the American Academy of Psychiatry and the Law*, *32*(3), 263–273. Retrieved from http://jaapl.org/content/jaapl/32/3/263.full.pdf PMID:15515914

Kenny, D. (1982). Confidentiality: The Confusion Continues. *Journal of Medical Ethics*, *8*(1), 5–8. doi:10.1136/jme.8.1.9 PMID:7069738

Lake, P. F. (1994). Revisiting Tarasoff. *Alb. L. Rev.*, *58*, 97, 98.

Lasky, G. B., & Riva, M. T. (2006). Confidentiality and privileged communication in group psychotherapy. *International Journal of Group Psychotherapy*, *56*(4), 455–476. doi:10.1521/ijgp.2006.56.4.455 PMID:17040183

Litvinova, D. (2017). Bill Decriminalizing Domestic Violence Passes First Reading in Russian Parliament. *The Moscow Time*. Retrieved June 15, 2017 from https://themoscowtimes.com/articles/bill-decriminalizing-domestic-violence-passes-first-reading-in-russian-parliament-56783

McIntosh v. Milano, 403 A.2d 500 (N.J. Super. Ct. Law Div.1979)

McLeod, C. (2015). Trust. In E. N. Zalta (ed.), *The Stanford Encyclopedia of Philosophy*. Retrieved May 16, 2017, from https://plato.stanford.edu/archives/fall2015/entries/trust/

Murdach, A. D. (2011). Is social work a human rights profession? *Social Work, 56*(3), 281–293. doi:10.1093/sw/56.3.281 PMID:21848092

NASW. (2008). *Code of Ethics*. Retrieved May 13, 2017, from: http://www.socialworkers.org/pubs/code/code.asp

National Association of Social Workers. (1996). *Code of Ethics*. Washington, DC: NASW Press.

O'Neill, O. (2002). *Autonomy and Trust in Bioethic*. Cambridge, UK: Cambridge University Press. doi:10.1017/CBO9780511606250

Pellegrino, E. (1991). Trust and Distrust in Professional Ethics. In E. D. Pellegrino, R. Weatch, & J. Lagan (Eds.), *Ethics, Trust and the Professions*. Washington, DC: Georgetown UP.

Platonova, E. A., Kennedy, K. N., & Schewchuck, R. M. (2008). Understand patient satisfaction, trust, and loyalty to primary care physicians. *Medical Care Research and Review, 65*(6), 696–712. doi:10.1177/1077558708322863 PMID:18723450

Pope, K. S., Tabechnik, B. G., & Keith-Spiegel, P. (1988). Good and poor practices in psychotherapy. National survey of belief of psychotherapy. *Professional Psychology, Research and Practice, 19*(5), 547–552. doi:10.1037/0735-7028.19.5.547

Reamer, F. (1998). *Ethical strandards in social work: A critical review of the NASW code of ethics*. Washington, DC: NASW Press.

Sandu, A. (2016). Social Protection of Abused Children: A Socio-legal and Ethical Analysis. In Multidimensional Education and Professional Development. Ethical Values (pp. 461-466). Editografica.

Sandu, A. (2017). *O etică centrată pe valori în sfera publică* [A values-centred ethics in the public area]. Iasi, Romania: LUMEN Publishing.

Sandu, A., & Caras, A. (2013). Deconstruction of charity. Postmodern ethical approaches. *Journal for the Study of Religions and Ideologies, 12*(36), 72–99.

Sandu, A., Cojocaru, D., Gavrilovici, C., & Oprea, L. (2013). Trust: An Ethical Dimension of Healthcare in Chronic Disorders. *Revista Romana de Bioetica, 11*(1), 190–205.

Schoeman, F. D. (1984). Privacy: philosophical dimensions of the literature. In F. D. Schoeman (Ed.), *Philosophical Dimensions of Privacy* (pp. 1–33). Cambridge, MA: Cambridge University Press. doi:10.1017/CBO9780511625138.002

Sharpe, V. A. (2005). Perspective: Privacy and Security for Electronic Health Records. *The Hastings Center Report, 35*(6), 18. doi:10.2307/3528564 PMID:16396204

Solove, D. (2004). *The digital person: Technology and Privacy in the Information Age*. New York: University Press.

Solove, D. J. (2008). *Understanding Privacy*. Cambridge, MA: Harvard University Press.

Tarasoff v. Regents of the University of California, 551 P.2d 334 (Cal. 1974)

Tarasoff v. Regents of University of California. (n.d.). Retrieved June 15, 2017 from http://www.casebriefs.com/blog/law/torts/torts-keyed-to-dobbs/the-duty-to-protect-from-third-persons/tarasoff-v-regents-of-university-of-california/2/

Taubman, S. (2012). *Dangerousness to Self and Others in Social Work Practice. School of Social Welfare Field Preparation Panel*. University of California. Retrieved June 15, 2017 from http://socialwelfare.berkeley.edu/sites/default/files/docs/Handouts__Dangerousness_to_Self_and_Others_in_Social_Work_Practice.pdf

Terec-Vlad, L. (2016). The Principle of Responsibility towards the Human Non-Presence or the NonHuman Presence. *Postmodern Openings, 7*(2), 79–89. doi:10.18662/po/2016.0702.06

Thomson v. County of Alameda, 614 P.2d 728 (Cal. 1980)

Vitelli, R. (2014). Revisiting Tarasoff. Should therapists breach confidentiality over a patient's violent threat? *Psychology Today*. Retrieved June 15, 2017 from https://www.psychologytoday.com/blog/media-spotlight/201407/revisiting-tarasoff

ENDNOTE

1 In Romania, the minimum guaranteed income is a social aid offered by the Romanian state to people who doesn't have a different source of income. This can be provided through the Service of Community Social Work. The beneficiaries of minimum guaranteed income have no other obligation than to perform a number of community service hours.

KEY TERMS AND DEFINITIONS

Confidentiality: Acording to Stanford Encyclopedia of Philosophy the concept of *confidentiality* has the following defining aspects: "Confidentiality is defined as restricting information to persons belonging to a set of specifically authorized recipients (Allen, 1997; Kenny, 1982). Confidentiality can be achieved through professional silence and secure data management (Atar, Saroiu & Koutsky, 2002; Sharpe, 2005). Hence Sissela Bok characterized confidentiality as referring "to the boundaries surrounding shared secrets and to the process of guarding these boundaries" (Bok, 1982, p. 119)" (Allen, 2016).

Trust: According to Stanford Encyclopaedia of Philosophy, the concept of *trust* has the following defining aspects: "Plausible, again, only if the conditions required for trust, exist (e.g. optimism about one another's ability). Knowing what these conditions are requires understanding the nature of trust. Well-grounded, only if the trustee is trustworthy, which makes the nature of trustworthiness important in determining when trust is warranted. Justified, sometimes when the trustee is not in fact trustworthy, which suggests that the epistemology of trust is relevant. Justified, often because some value will emerge from the trust or because it is valuable in and of itself. Thus, the value of trust is important. Plausible, only when it is possible for one to develop trust, given one's circumstances and the sort of mental attitude trust is. For example, trust may not be the sort of attitude that one can will oneself to have without any evidence of a person's trustworthiness" (McLeod, 2015).

Section 3

Ethics Expertise in Social Work Organisations

Chapter 11
Supervision of Ethics in Social Work Practice:
A Reconstruction of Ethics Expertise

Ana Frunza
LUMEN Research Center in Social and Humanistic Sciences, Romania

Antonio Sandu
Stefan cel Mare University of Suceava, Romania

ABSTRACT

The chapter aims at arguing the necessity and academic functioning of the supervision of ethics – as a model embodied in ethical expertise. Starting with 2012, the model of ethics expertise in the social welfare practice – the supervision of ethics – was continuously developed. Based on the previous approaches of supervision of ethics, the process is understood as having the following main functions: the Gatekeeping in construction of ethics policies, the mediation in achieving a reflective balance in the organization, the administrative and deliberative function, the construction of ethical climate in organizations and monitoring of ethical conformity and counselling of ethics, ethical advising and support. This model brings together practices from all other forms of ethics expertise, additionally exercising its gatekeeper role in the transfer of political theories on public good through the implementing programs and practices thereof, and making the professional values compatible with the organisational ones.

DOI: 10.4018/978-1-5225-3090-9.ch011

INTRODUCTION

We aim to bring into focus the necessity and the academic function of the supervision of ethics – as a model embodied in ethical expertise. Starting with 2012, the model of ethics expertise in the social welfare practice – the supervision of ethics – was continually developed. Based on the previous approaches of the supervision of ethics, the process is understood to have the following main functions: the function of ethics policies gatekeeping; the mediation function in achieving a reflective balance in the organisation on the interests of each party involved; the function of ethics construction in organisations; the function of ethical conformity monitoring; the function of ethical auditing; the function of the counselling of ethics, support and consultancy; the function of administration and deliberation.

The paper intends to bring about the reconstruction of ethical expertise by discussing the new model functions as a suitable model of aknowledge-based society. We will initiate its reconstruction by differentiating the ethical values of an organisation into the constitutive ethical values and the operational values. The constitutive values are correlated with the organisation's mission, while the operational values are correlated with the policies of the organisation, its products and services.

BACKGROUND: GROUNDS OF ETHICS EXPERTISE

The literature on ethics expertise starts by defining it consistently from an epistemological and pragmatic point of view. Since there is only a small amount of developed scientific literature on the ethics expertise in the area of social work (Reamer, 1987; 2001; 2012; Sandu & Caras (Frunză), 2014), an attempt to reconstruct it can be based on the ethics expertise in medical practice (Iltis & Sheehan, 2016; Rasmussen, 2005; Rasmussen, 2016; (Frunză, 2011) Schicktanz et al. (2012); Singer, 1972; Weinstein, 1994,).

The ethics expert is defined as being the person who has the capacity to decide between what is right or wrong in a specific field and, for such a decision to be made, this person must also be familiar with the concepts and moral arguments and also devote time to gathering information regarding the moral philosophy and reflect upon the moral concepts. These actions could lead to grounded conclusions on an ethical issue, stronger than that of a person who is not familiar with the moral concepts or who does not spend enough time studying and understanding them (Singer, 1972, pp. 116-117).

Recent opinion on ethics expertise (Iltis & Sheehan, 2016) refers to the ethics expert as being the one who knows what needs to be done. This knowledge of *what needs to be done* must include both the "common truth" on the moral values and means through which we can access this truth, as well as an ethics theory and sufficient expertise in a field, necessary for a fundamental ethical practice. A series of criticisms on the idea of ethics expertise (Iltis & Sheehan, 2016) even considers that a consultant on (clinical) ethics should not be called an ethics expert. This is because, in order to be an ethics expert, there should be adequate means of discovering the moral truth and a theoretical knowledge of it. This theoretical expertise is not directly connected to the area of professional practice and, as such, an *ethics counsellor* is not, and cannot be, an ethics expert. In turn, we distinguish between the (meta-) ethical reflection on the professional practice and the ethical reflection of the professional in excercising its practice. In the first case, we have a (meta-) ethical reflection on the convergence between a particular ethical system – for example, the ethics of social work – and the general framework of the ethical reflection (Bubnys, 2014).

The capacity to reflect from a meta-ethical position constitutes the nature of ethics expertise. The professional, in a particular field, reflects upon the ethical nature of his own practice, of the constitutive and operational values which determined the emergence of a social practice, including a profession. This reflection cannot be independent from the general knowledge of ethics, therefore the professional requires general ethical frameworks of norms and principles to guide his professional life and, in certain cases, of counselling and ethics supervision. However, due to the regulations existing in more and more states and the fields of activity, the professionals with little or no training in ethics, after completing a short period of training in the area of professional deonthology, become counsellors of ethics. This is the example of Romania where, according to the code of conduct of public servants – many of the social workers in this country work as civil servants – it is required that *a person in the human resources department* – therefore with no previous training in the field of ethics – can receive the additional attribution of an *ethics counsellor.* Although in practice these people benefitted from training programmes in ethics, these certainly would not be able to provide them with the competences of an ethics expert, and it is very unlikely to provide them with the competences of an ethics counsellor. We state this precisely because the lack of training in ethics makes them unable to understand the particular dimensions of an ethical dilemma and be able to establish, for example, the convergence between the ethical values and the principles of practice, etc. However, they can fulfil the role of ethics counsellor when, for example, it refers to the situation of avoiding malpractice, that a professional may establish by violating confidentiality, through discriminating behaviours, etc. In order to know these aspects and offer guidance in similar situations, a wide knowledge is not required on the ethical nature of the phenomenon of, for example, discrimination or corruption. From this perspective we join the criticism formulated by authors such as Iltis & Sheehan (2016), George

J. Agich (2009) and Ana S. Iltis, Lisa M. Rasmussen (2016). The ethics counsellors should not be legitimately called ethics experts, as long as – we add – they do not have training in theoretical ethics, along with experience in the professional area – of social work, in our case. This is one of the reasons for which we considered that the professional status of the ethics expertise should be developed as a *supervision of ethics*, that would include the counselling side, but go beyond it through its capacity to participate in the construction of ethics policies, in the evaluation of the organisational ethical climate and, not least, through the role of gatekeeping in the construction of policies and organisational programmes.

On the contrary, the question arises whether a person with a thorough training in theoretical ethics, but without professional knowledge, can understand the nature of the ethical dilemmas the practitioners face (Congress, 2000, pp. 1-26). In the absence of a profound understanding of the specifics of practice from a certain profession, the theoretical ethicist can only formulate the meta-ethical reflections on the adequacy of a situation by using different theoretical models existing in the area of ethics, but cannot be fully involved in solving the ethical issue or overcoming the ethical dilemmas[1] specific for social work. The ethics expertise, unlike the simple counselling of ethics, has an inter- and trans-disciplinary nature, the supervisor of ethics requiring theoretical and practical training both in the professional and in the ethical area. The MA programmes in applied ethics and ethical consultancy would be a potential specialisation of professionals in different fields – including social work –also following professional MA programmes in social work may train the theoretical ethicist in the field of the ethics of social services.

In our opinion, we see the ethics expert as being the person capable of offering consultancy so that a person or group of persons would guide the action based on the ethical standards proposed by the expert and his recommendations. The expert in ethics can or can not be a moral person, namely he can apply or not his own knowledge in the current activity. The overlap between the ethics expert who knows what should be done, and the moral person, comes from the Kantian assumption of good faith. The practice of current ethics expertise is based on the professional judgment of the expert, and not his moral conscience.

As such, the ethics expertise is particularly manifested by its consultative practice, by establishing a relationship between the expert in ethics and the professional who requires ethical guidance.

Of course, in the literature there are opposing opinions that challenge the ethics counsellor's quality of expertise in ethics. This objection is based on the idea that the moral judgment is not always rational and the moral decision takes into account other factors, such as the context of moral action, the agent's preferences, his norms and values. In this situation, the intervention of a third party is required to balance the decision – in this case, the ethics counsellor. In Rasmussen's opinion, the ethics counsellor is not an expert in ethics, but only an expert in certain dimensions of a particular ethical phenomenon (Rasmussen, 2016). This approach resonates with the definition given by Richard Zaner (2004) who considers that the ethics counsellor has "expert knowledge on the ethical phenomena". The distinction between the ethics counsellor and the ethics expert is based on their role in making ethical decisions. The dichotomy is based on the distinction between rational and irrational in the ethical decision and the assumption of the exclusively rational nature of the ethics expertise. At the same time, the ethics counsellor is also supposed to base his work on other dimensions of the ethical decision.

However, the expertise is based on knowledge, inclusively of the irrational aspects which determine the moral behaviour, as such, the expert ethics counsellor reasons upon the causes and consequences of the action, without ignoring the final knowledge of the moral truth. The ethics expertise itself is questioned starting from its performative nature. The ethics expertise is divided by the scientific literature into epistemic ethics expertise and performative ethics expertise. If the epistemic ethics expertise is characterised as cognitive ability, which involves theoretical knowledge of the field, the performative expertise implies the possibility to excel in a field (Weinstein, 1994, pp. 61-75).

Weinstein (1994) goes from the importance of the one who "knows what needs to be done" (the epistemic expertise) to that of "the one who does" (the pragmatic expertise) – ethics put into action. The epistemic expertise is defined by that individual who is capable of making judgments with ethical justification (Weinstein, 1994, pp. 61-62).

We support the idea that, according to its areas of manifestation, the ethics expertise is defined by a series of models, among which are the counselling of ethics, ethics audits, developing codes of ethics and the activity of the ethics committees, but also the ethical decision models (Caras (Frunza), Sandu, 2014).

Schicktanz, Schweda & Wynne (2012, pp. 129-139) address the ethics expertise starting from its public understanding. In order to understand the ethics expertise at the level of public understanding, we support the necessity for a transfer from the moral values and the moral behaviour of the individual, to the capacity of having a meta-ethical reflection on their own expertise. In the end, these moral capacities and ethical reflection will be able to be transferred within the field of ethics, which, in fact, means the professionalisation of the ethics expertise (Frunza, 2011, pp. 14-16). The ethics expert should have extensive knowledge of moral philosophy, his role being that of gatekeeper and guide, but also of ethics counsellor of a professional whose preparation does not necessarily involve an ethical training.

HOW TO ACHIEVE A PRAGMATIC ETHICS EXPERTISE: CONSTRUCTING THE ORGANISATION'S ETHICS POLICIES

The most well-known areas of ethical regulation of the professional activity are represented by the professions involving health, education, media, administration and law. We make a distinction between the general ethical reflections on the legal, administrative, political, welfare, evaluative professions, etc. – formulated in a meta-ethical manner, especially by the ethics experts, and the ethical reflection on the nature of their own practice – carried out by the professional. In the first case, that of ethics expertise, it is thought to be the convergence between a particular ethical system and the frameworks of the ethical reflection, under the spectrum of the moral casuistry. In the second case, the professional reflects upon the ethical nature of their own practices, of the constitutive and operational values which determined the emergence of a social practice, including a profession. Finally, there is the moral competence of the professional, who acts in accordance with the ethical standards – internalised – but also with his own moral conscience. This reflection can not be independent from the general knowledge of ethics and, therefore, the professional requires general ethical frameworks of norms and principles that would guide his professional life and in certain cases of counselling and ethical supervision (Loue, 2013). As such, the professional's moral reflection targets his own conduct, inside the norms generated by the operational values of the profession, while the ethics expert also considers the operational values, reflecting upon the particular cases, when offering ethical consultancy, as well as upon the constitutive values, when in a process of the supervision of ethics, proposes policies (of ethics) that would be even more suitable to the practice of the values which led to the emergence of the profession (Sandu, 2017).

Professional practice focuses on issues such as the ethical values of a profession and the standards of good practice, namely the minimal limits of acceptability of practice. We see the professional practice as being divided into two sides, an affirmative one that would describe the professional excellence, which is in direct connection to the practices of ensuring the quality and an interdictive one, minimalist, which guides the professional on the unacceptable situations. The final one is closer to the legal regulations since it introduces the limits of the professional's actions and specifies the sanctions for breaching those limits when they are not legally sanctioned. The mentioned author draws attention to a potential risk of the excess of ethics, which transforms the professional interdictive ethics into repressive action with the potential for abuse. Unlike the legal side, which is universal, applying to all citizens of a certain state, the professional ethical normativeness regulates the activity of certain particular categories of members of society. In practice, in order to have a greater power of regulation, the ethical normativeness is an integral part of certain normative acts with legal power. This is also the case of the code of ethics of public servants (Sandu, 2016).

Most of the time, in applied ethics, we discuss the ethical principles which must be respected by the professional. The bioethics principium is precisely such an approach that targets the construction of a minimalist framework which would guide practice. Behind the ethical principles, less obvious than these, there are the ethical values that govern the principle (Sandu, 2017). Kluckhohn and Strodtbeck (1961) consider that the values are complex and patterned principles, resulting from the interaction between three analytically distinct elements of the evaluative process: the cognitive, the emotional and the directive elements. These give order and direction to the constant flow of human acts and thoughts as they relate to the solution of common human issues. Many of the definitions of the values, such as the ones offered by Kluckhohn and Strodtbeck (1961), consider them as being highly complex principles. Other approaches (Baron & Spranca, 1997) consider that the values are deontological rules and prescriptions refering to action or inaction. The overlap between values, principles and prescriptions is, in our opinion, confusing, especially when united in a principle where there are two or more distinct values. It is the case of the Code of Conduct of the public servant in Romania – many social workers in this country also have the status of public servant – where honesty and fairness are reunited in a principle of good faith.

The overlap between values and principles has, in our opinion, a metaphysical origin. The principle, in the metaphysical sense, has a commanding and primordial character. We support a pragmatic distinction between value and principle, at least at an ethical level. The value has an immaterial and inoperable character and, in general, constitutes the answer to the question: *What do we do a certain action for?* In Kantian terms, value represents the purpose of the action, but also its establishment. The principle operationalises the value in the area of social action, being included in the area of means (Sandu, 2017). If we consider the value of human dignity and the principle of defending human dignity, we notice that the value subsists the failure of defending it. The dignity of the human being subsists to its lack of protection, which may appear, for example, due to the incapacity of a political-administrative system to protect it. An example might be the fact that human dignity remains a valid value, despite its violation in the anti-humanist actions supported by the totalitarian regimes. The principle of defending human dignity raises instrumental questions, *How can the human being's dignity be defended?* and, of a structural-operational nature, *Which are the components of the human being carrying dignity, that need to be defended?* The answer to these questions can generate debates refering to the violation, or not, of human dignity in different specific situations.

We formulate the point of view according to which each constitutive or operational value can be associated with an affirmative and a negative principle, which would lead to the correct realisation of that value. Any value can only be accomplished through respecting certain affirmative and negative or interdictive principles, which only together ensure its observance. Taking justice as an example of a value, this transposes into social reality through accomplishing justice and excluding injustice. The Kantian categorical imperative, through its two formulations, accomplishes this complementariness between affirmative-negative in the foundation of ethics.

The USA Social Workers' Code of Ethics (NASW) presents each value followed by the principle which is meant to transpose it into the practice of social workers.

The value of social justice *corresponds to:* "Ethical Principle: Social workers challenge social injustice. Social workers pursue social change, particularly with and on behalf of vulnerable and oppressed individuals and groups of people. Social workers' social change efforts are focused primarily on issues of poverty, unemployment, discrimination and other forms of social injustice. These activities seek to promote sensitivity to and knowledge about oppression and cultural and ethnic diversity. Social workers strive to ensure access to needed information, services and resources; equality of opportunity; and meaningful participation in decision making for all people (NASW, 2008)".

The construction of the policies of organisational ethics should start from defining the (ethical) mission of the organisation. Within the ethical mission, the ethical constitutive values are integrated – those values whose implementation led to the necessity of the emergence and functioning of the organisation. Precisely these are the values that will most influence the interaction between the organisation and its audiences. Aside from the constitutive values, the organisation defines – at the level of ethics policy, explicit or implicit – a series of operational ethical values, based on which they organise their current activities.

Based on the constitutive values, the organisation assumes its goals, its members being open to putting these values into practice. These values come to define the mission of the organization, although it rarely appears as such in the programme of missions. For example, an organization in the area of protecting people with disabilities, will rarely formulate as such the value of *human dignity* in its documents, although its establishment is precisely for the benefit of people with disabilities and the promotion of respect for the dignity of this category of persons and is the reason for which the organisation was established and functions. What is more, the organisation becomes capable of assuming the specific objectives derived from the constitutive ethical values, becoming operational by their integration at the level of organisational culture. The establishment of the constitutive values is highlighted at the level of results and deliverables. In our example, the protection of the dignity of people with disabilities may have, among the results, the establishment of certain protected workshops, or the provision of occasional help. In the first case, the employment in protected workshops comes to promote the dignity of this category of people by including them in an active social life, and to create the feeling of social utility in the consciousness of those people. In turn, the solution of granting financial help also promotes these people's dignity, since the help received from public funds can enable them to live in more decent conditions. Such interventions allow the avoidance of the exposure to situations that might damage their dignity, such as begging or illicit access to resources.

The postmodern organisation, especially that which is active in the field of increasing the subjective welfare, renounces the ideal of axiological and ethical neutrality, assuming the implementation of certain values, not only at the level of the outcomes – the fulfilment of the constitutive values – but also its effective functioning. By establishing certain operational values, the organisation will be capable of orienting its effective practice starting from them. Based on these operational values, the organisation will be guided, from the example above, to establish the type of service that will benefit the people targeted. If the respect for the beneficiaries' autonomy is an operational value important for the organisation, it will probably be oriented towards certain protected workshops. While, if the value of solidarity prevails among the operational values, offering help will be the most adequate solution since the funds necessary for the subventions come from redistributing the added value created at a social level. This redistribution of the added value operationalises the social solidarity, since the society therefore manifests its moral responsibility towards its members who belong to certain disadvantaged categories. The society is jointly solid, practically included in the amount of taxes and duties owed to the state. The choice of applicable operational values represents a process of ethical decision, the implementation of which the organisation can benefit from the support of the ethics expert, through a process which we call 'supervision of ethics' (Frunza, 2016). The ethics expert, with the role of supervisor of ethics, basically assumes a role of gatekeeper (Frunza, 2016) in the construction of the programmes of the organisation in accordance with its own ethics policy.

The same ethical operational values guide the reports of the organisation within the internal environments.

Beyond the minimal ethical practices, such as avoiding and sanctioning corruption, promoting equity in establishing salary rights and other benefits, an equal and non-discriminatory treatment, we discuss the management of ethics policies. Ethics becomes an engine of organisational development (Tosatia, Lawthongb, Suwanmonkhab, 2015), and a guide to good practices in the organisation. At this level, the ethics expert becomes supervisor of the professional practice (O'Donoghue, Yuh Ju & Tsui, 2017). The term supervision does not involve control over practice, but guidance in implementing the ethical values, simultaneously with the counselling of ethics offered to professionals in a decision-making situation with ethical implications.

The process of adopting the operational ethical values occurs through negotiation between the members of the organisation, but also through its representatives and different stakeholders in order to obtain internal consensus on the types of values and their hierarchy in the organisational practice.

The policies of ethics and ethical know-how are part of the intellectual capital of the organisation. The ethics management of the organisation includes the construction and implementation of its ethics policies, in accordance with the instruments for implementing organisational ethics: codes of ethics, training of ethics and the function of the ethics committee in the organisation. The ethics expert can play the role of ethics manager in the organisation, a situation in which he fulfils the above-mentioned attributes refering to the ethics policies. Also, the ethics expert can be a counsellor and/or supervisor of ethics. The supervision of ethics targets a complex relationship between the people in charge of the ethics management in the organisation and its members. The supervision of ethics targets is a first step in the consultancy provided to the organisation in the construction of the ethics policies. This consultancy can directly address the ethics managers, when the ethics policies are developed institutionally and imposed on its members by internal normative documents. When the process of the construction of ethics policies is based on a consensual strategy in the form of deliberate democracy, the supervision of ethics offered at this level addresses both the organisation's members and stakeholders.

In the process of implementing the ethics policies, the ethics expert has a series of attributions generated by its expertise, but also his quality of a neutral third party who can function as a mediator between the organisation's management and its members. In implementing the ethics policies inside the organisation, the counsellorr addresses the individual social actor – a member of the organisation – in his role of moral agent, who is offered support in approaching the ethical dilemmas derived from his professional practice. However, when the ethical dilemma targets the very relationship between the professional and the beneficiary, solving it requires both ethical and professional competences and not simple ethical general issues, therefore, we see the need for ethics supervision. This should be provided by an ethics expert with training in applied ethics, but also competences specific for social work. In this case, the ethics supervisor can be capable of identifying the best solutions of professional practice, in accordance with the values and moral principles agreed by the organisation and the beneficiary.

Another attribution of the ethics expert in his quality of supervisor of ethics is represented by his involvement in the functioning of the ethics committees. We are not referring here to the committees of professional deontology, developed within the professional organisations of social workers, whose main role is to construct deontological codes that would provide minimal ethical standards – whose lack of compliance constitutes malpractice – and the sanctioning of the situations of malpractice denounced to the professional organisation. We refer to the ethics committees that should be formed in the organisation of social work, on the model of those functioning in the medical system, for example in the United States or many countries in the European Union (France, Germany). These committees approve the more complicated intervention plans, monitor the compliance to the patient's rights and the correct use of ethical instruments, such as informed consent forms, etc. Another model which could be followed in constituting ethics committees within the organisations of social work is that of research ethics committees, which approve, from an ethical point of view, the research on human subjects. In the practice of social work, seldom being considered as research-action, where the intervention could become harmful in certain circumstances, such ethics committees can prove to be useful in the functioning of the organisation (Caras & Sandu, 2013). Even in the absence of such ethics committees, the ethics expert belongs to the professional committees which approve the intervention plans, where there are any.

Another purpose of the ethics expert, with the role of ethics supervisor, is in the field of the audit of ethics practices within the organisations. The ethics audit is an instrument for evaluating the compliance of ethics in the organisation by highlighting its position over its own standards and expectations. Such an audit involves a complex and comprehensive evaluation of the policies of the procedures, products and services for highlighting their consistency with the (ethical) values and the mission of the organisation. The ethics audit allows identifying and solving the issues referring to the organisational ethical culture (Sandu, 2016). Any problems that may arise in implementing the ethics policies will also be highlighted following their case and formulating possible solutions for improving or solving them (Hofmann, 2006).

Constitutive and Operational Ethical Values in the Organisation

In the following, we will synthesise some constitutive and operational values which – in our opinion – sanction the welfare practice. This does not mean that the other values present in different ethical codes are less important for the professionals.

Public good is the central purpose of the policy and the development and existence of the state. The idea of *"public good"* knows an evolution over time, towards the concept of "public interest", as well as towards that of the "quality of life". The operationalisation and measurement of public good and the quality of life makes it possible to create and apply certain instruments of the public decision. Public good represents a constitutive ethical value of any administrative system. The system of social services is, in fact, a part of the kind of value that generates the need for public administration as a social system (Graumann, 2012). In implementing the "quality of life" as public good, the systems of social services operate with a series of other values, among which are *transparency, welfare, equity,* etc., which become such operational values (Sandu, 2017, p. 59).

In implementing the "public good", the state has the role of arbiter between the individuals, in the process of following their own interests, in excercising their own liberty. The state, therefore, gains the role of guarantor of the citizens' freedoms (Crisp, 2015). The welfare obligations of the state derive from the extrinsic value of social solidarity. Redefining the public good in contemporary society is done by including the state's obligation to ensure at least the minimal standards of the quality of life under the circumstances of offering social support to citizens who cannot provide those standards for themselves – therefore prefiguring the idea of a social state (Sandu, 2017, p. 59). In essence, the welfare state is based on redistributing a part of the value existing at the level of society, for the benefit of the groups and categories of vulnerable and/or disadvantaged people. All public policies that develop within a state which aims to be social – for example this is the case of Romania, whose quality of social state is written in the Constitution – must consider promoting justice, social equality, as well as solidarity. Public good transforms into public interest when the *welfare state* gains a central place both in the moral theory, as well as in the public one, centred on establishing the ethical values.

Justice as an ethical value is seen by us as being constitutive for social work. Social work is asked to transpose the ideal of justice accepted by the majority of the community, into practice (Sandu, 2017). In the ethics of interpersonal relationships – Aristotle considers – the individual's character traits are primary, constituting his moral nature, the emphasis being on moral values, especially nobility. On the other hand, in the political ethics, the intellectual virtues should be primary. In the balance between the two aspects of Aristotlian ethics, justice resides at the level of action and moral decision, while "nobility" was separated into two components, "charity" and its correlation, "altruism" in relation to the other (Sandu, 2017). In the area of public action, the virtue of nobility takes the form of integrity, being oriented towards accomplishing justice. Public justice becomes equity. "Charity, which originally characterizes the private conduct under the aspect of justice as redistribution, returns to the public area as solidarity and practice of institutionalised welfare and social work" (Sandu & Caras, 2013). The modern theories on justice understood it as mutual advantage and impartiality. For the sense of mutual advantage discussed by philosophers such as Th. Hobbes, D. Hume, D. Gauthier – "cooperation with others", is seen as of great importance (Iser, 2013). On the other hand, we have a series of theories on "justice as impartiality", among the most significant authors of this theory being John Rawls (2012). Within the theories of justice as impartiality, the emphasis is on "principles". These should be reasonably chosen based on the agreement between the members of the community.

In the sense proposed by Rawls: equity implies an equal distribution of values, either in the sense of goods and services, or the subjective one, of benefit and loss (Rawls, 2012). By equal opportunities, we understand the distribution of social positions based on merit in a society which created the conditions that, regardless of the social class in which the individuals are born, all citizens who have the same talent and same will to use it, and should be able to benefit from equal opportunities to access those positions.

Transparency as an ethical value becomes an administrative principle of good practice, which promotes a series of constitutive values, such as equal chances and opportunities and the respect for the individual's dignity and autonomy in the process of the administrative decision. We make a connection between transparency and public trust, which we qualify as a constitutive value of the functioning of democracy, and implicitly of social services in the democratic systems (Sandu, 2017).

Integrity is considered a condition compulsory for the activity of the social workers. The need for integrity is justified by the need for constructing and maintaining the beneficiaries' trust in the social services. We consider integrity to be an operational value of social services, ensuring that its functioning is legitimate.

In correlation to integrity, there are the values of impartiality and equidistance. Integrity is most often analysed from the negative perspective, the authors of certain codes of ethics, such as that of NASW (National Association of Social Workers) and BASW (British Association of Social Workers), who insist on the need for control overunethical conduct. Within certain affirmative ethics policies, the emphasis is on integrity as a virtue and on promoting integrity and its internalisation.

How the Organisation Develops and Applies Its Ethical Behaviour

Tenbrusel, Smith-Crowe & Umphress (2003) refer to the mechanism necessary for implementing ethics within the organisation, in terms of "ethical infrastructure". The ethical infrastructure consists of formal and informal systems (each of them including components of communication, supervision/surveillance and sanctioning), but also the climate that supports these systems. There are established relationships of interdependence between the formal and informal systems of communication, supervision or surveillance of the ethical or unethical organisational behaviour and the climates that support the establishment of organisational ethics. There are therefore identified three types of favourable climates of those already mentioned, namely, the ethical climate, the climate for respect and the climate for procedural justice. The authors refer to the specific organisational climates which facilitate ethics, respect and procedural justice in the internal and external relationships (Tenbrusel, Smith-Crowe & Umphress, 2003) and not an ethical climate itself, built on certan values, principles, ethical actions of the organisation through its members and the constitutive documents where the mission, vision and purpose of the organisation are stipulated. The organisational climate for ethics is constituted by the shared perceptions of the members of the organisation on the actions, practices, procedures and behaviours which are rewarded, supported and promoted in order to implement the ethics in the organisation (Dickson, Grojean, & Ehrhart, 2001; Schneider, 1990, p. 384; Tenbrusel, Smith-Crowe & Umphress, 2003, p. 294).

The organisational climate in favour of respect sums up the perceptions of the individuals on the way in which they are respected, treated with dignity and have their efforts and pro-organisation actions acknowledged, and the climate for procedural justice which follows those perceptions of the members of the organisation on the way in which the fairness of the procedures, used in making decisions, is respected (Naunabb & Bennett, 2000; Tenbrusel, Smith-Crowe & Umphress, 2003, p. 294).

The specialist knowledge of the ethical principles of the organisation, and also the adherence to these principles, facilitates the ethical action of the organisation. At the same time, by manifesting these principles into practice, the social responsibility of the organisation takes form. Along with its members– as autonomous moral agents, the social responsibility of the organisation outlines its ethical framework and its ethical climate. We consider the ethical climate of the organisation to encompass a series of constitutive and operational ethical values. Unlike Tenbrusel, Smith-Crowe & Umphress (2003), we include values such as respect and procedural justice, along with integrity, as component parts of the organisational ethical climate.

In this chapter, we support the approach of the organisational ethical construction based on identifying and adopting a model of ethics based on the relationship between the constitutive and operational ethical values within the organisation. The ethical principles that underlie the implementation of such values are, in fact, the practical way in which organisational ethics (stipulated in mission statements, vision, organisational code of ethics) is achieved. We take, for example, the value of "credibility" in the organisation – as a constitutive value. This value targets the communication between the organisation and the external environment. For the communication to be credible between it and its target audience, a series of operational values, such as honesty, integrity, loyalty, respect, must be integrated into the organisational culture and put into practice by its members. Credibility can be respected through the honesty of the information circulating in and out of the organisation, but also through their fairness. Integrity can be demonstrated through the agreement between the individual's actions and his own conscience, while loyalty is found in the communicational practice through the stakeholders' real interest towards the organisation – promoting and respecting their rights and interests. When we refer to respect as an operational value, emerging from the value of credibility, we see the organisation as accepting the differences between the individuals they collaborate with, respecting their own values, beliefs and firmly communicating this with members and stakeholders. The operation of respect, both in the internal and external actions, will lead to reciprocity, the organisation receiving respect.

If we see "respect" as a constitutive value, we will notice that it is necessary to adopt and support certain operational values such as: dignity, courtesy, fairness, tolerance and acceptance.

"Responsibility" as a constitutive value requires the organisation to bring into practice values such as excellence – reaching excellence being an attitude integrated in the practice of the organiation, the continual development and improvement of practices and services, as well as perseverance. Showing responsibility as a constitutive value is facilitated by its answer to the actions of the society, but also the impact the organisation has in the community. Therefore, it can become active from the point of view of social responsibility through supporting the community's sustainable development.

In its ethics policy, the organisation may include the value of "justice" – whose operation is manifested through the fair distribution of resources in a community, through the actions of the organisation. Equity, equality, impartiality, transparency, rigour – are operational values which serve the implementation of justice.

THE CODE OF ETHICS IN A SOCIAL WORK ORGANISATION

The first code of professional ethics of the social workers was proposed by Mary Richmond in 1920, under the name *Experimental draft code of ethics for social case workers* (Bulgaru, 2013; Freeman, Engels, & Altekruse, 2004). The first code of ethics adopted by a professional association was that of NASW in 1951. The code of ethics of NASW was adopted in 1975, and modified in 1996 and 2008.

We will continue to analyse the way in which the ethical values are integrated in the codes of ethics of social workers (Congress, 2006, 151-164) in the USA, Great Britain, Australia and Romania. In the Social Workers' Code of Ethics of the USA (NASW, 2008), we notice that there are identified the core values of service: social justice, dignity and the worth of the person, the importance of human relationships, integrity and competence. Each such value corresponds to a principle of practice, meant to lead to implementing the value in the practice of the social workers. The code mentions all these values as being central to the practice. However, if we analyse carefully the principles to be implemented, we notice that some of them are rather formulated in order to answer the questions *what? (what do we do? What should the result of practice be?)* or *why? (what is the purpose of practice?),* leading to the idea of constitutive values, and others seem to be answering the question *how? (how is practice done?),* therefore being operational values. The value *Service* is operational as a principle "*to help* people in need and to address social problems," showing the *what* that is the practice of social work, at a first analysis, as being about a constitutive value. However, *the help* the social workers are providing considers a different value, expressed as *to address social problems*. The same value becomes operational, but in its operating it, it mentions: "Social workers are encouraged *to volunteer* some portion of their professional skills" (NASW, 2008), answering the question *how* the work of the social worker should be done.

The value of *Social Justice*, which, at the level of a principle, corresponds to: "Social workers *challenge social injustice"*, represents a constitutive value, showing what the social workers must do: "Social workers *strive to ensure* access to needed information, services and resources; equality of opportunity; and meaningful participation in decision making for all people" (NASW, 2008).

On the other hand, the value *Dignity and Worth of the Person* is an operational value, since the corresponding principle "Social workers *respect* the inherent dignity and worth of the person" shows how the practice of the social worker should develop.

The value *Importance of Human Relationships* is transposed into the principle: "Social workers understand that relationships between and among people are an important vehicle for change" (NASW, 2008). In its turn, change can not be a purpose in itself, but rather an extrinsic value, whose establishment seems to lead to a different value, such as social justice, responsibility, respect for Otherness.

Integrity is also an operational value, since it is transposed into an *ethical principle:* "Social workers behave in a trustworthy manner" (NASW, 2008).

Competence is also an operational value since it is transposed into the *Ethical Principle:* "Social workers practice within their areas of competence and develop and enhance their professional expertise" (NASW, 2008).

Responsibility, as an operational ethical value is transposed in the NASW code as ethical standards. "These standards concern (1) social workers' ethical responsibilities to clients, (2) social workers' ethical responsibilities to colleagues, (3) social workers' ethical responsibilities in practice settings, (4) social workers' ethical responsibilities as professionals, (5) social workers' responsibilities to the social work profession, and (6) social workers' ethical responsibilities to the broader society" (NASW, 2008).

The practice of social work involves, in the vision of NASW, the existence of the beneficiary's informed consent for any form of intervention. The use of informed consent as an ethical instrument is associated by the authors of the NASW Code of Ethics with the responsibility of the social workers towards the client, along with respect and promoting their self-determination. Here, we identify a different value, namely that of the (moral) autonomy of the beneficiaries, transposed through the right toself-determination, the informed consent being generally an instrument of promoting autonomy.

As such, we add the ethical values of *professional responsibility* and the *autonomy* (as self-determination) of the beneficiaries as other ethical operational values included in the Code of Ethics of social workers in the USA. Along with it, regarding the professional standards, we identify *competence* and *cultural competence, avoiding conflict of interests, confidentiality, the beneficiaries' access to their own files, the social workers' avoiding to engage into intimate relationships with the beneficiaries.* All these standards, in turn, are based on a range of operational values, such as *trust, respect,* etc.

The code of social workers in Great Britain (The Policy, Ethics and Human Rights Committee, 2014) identifies ethical values such as *human rights, social justice* and *integrity.* Of those, we consider the first two as being constitutive values, since they show why the practice of social workers is necessary (Neamtu, 2012), and the last is an operational value guiding the development of good professional practice for an ethical point of view.

In order to put into operation the value *human rights,* the British code identifies a series of principles: "Upholding and promoting human dignity and well-being", "Respecting the right to self-determination", "Promoting the right to participation", "Treating each person as a whole", "Identifying and developing strengths". We observe that, in turn, the principles encode a series of values: dignity, self-determination, right to participate, person as a whole, strengths (The Policy, Ethics and Human Rights Committee, 2014)[2].

The value of *Social Justice* is also put into operation through a series of principles: "Challenging discrimination", "Reconsidering diversity", "Distributing resources", "Challenging unjust policies and practices" and "Working in solidarity". These principles include, in turn, a series of values: equality, equity, (distributive) justice, social solidarity (BASW Code of Ethics, 2010).

The value *Professional integrity* is put into operation with principles such as: "Upholding the values and reputation of the profession", "Being trustworthy", "Maintaining professional boundaries", "Making considered professional judgments", "Being professionally accountable". In these principles we also identify a series of ethical operational values, among which are: responsibility (towards the beneficiary, the profession and the society), balance and trust.

In turn, the Australian social workers' code of ethics refers to "Respect for persons", "Social justice" and "Professional integrity" as core values of welfare practice. These values include a series of other values considered as part of the area of central values – and which we consider to be operational: "inherent dignity, worth and autonomy of every person", "human rights of individuals and groups", "duty of care and duty to avoid doing harm", "individual wellbeing, autonomy, justice and personal/ social responsibility", "respects group identity, interdependence, reciprocity and the collective needs", "justice and social fairness", "expand choice and potential for all persons, with special regard for those who are disadvantaged, vulnerable, oppressed or have exceptional needs". "advocates change to social systems and structures that preserve inequalities and injustice", "honesty, transparency, reliability, empathy, reflective self-awareness, discernment, competence and commitment." (AASW Code of ethics, 2010). Values such as inherent dignity or autonomy could express constitutive values of practice, but the Australian code of ethics connects them in a reverse order.

In Romania, the Deontological Code of the profession of social care is effective, issued by the National College of Social Workers (CNASR, 2008). The code does not define which are the ethical values protected by the social workers in Romania, but only a series of *obligations* for the professionals: "to exercise their profession according to the legal provisions in force", "to promote and respect the values of the profession, the methodology of exercising the profession, as well as guides of good practice in the field", "to constantly improve their professional knowledge" (CNASR, 2008). The principles are rather general, and, although we talk about the values of the profession, the reference to it is vague, and without a practical reference, as long as they are not part of the Code. The Code also involves a series of *principles*, united under the name of "professional independence and responsibility of the social worker", which involves obligations for the social worker: "The social worker must exercise his profession with responsibility", "The professional act of the social worker is excercised necessarily by hand" (CNASR, 2008). The professional obligations are also the object of a different article entitled "obligations towards the beneficiaries".

We notice the prevalence of the term 'obligations', to the detriment of that of values. In our opinion, an approach to ethics focused on values and not obligations, makes the voluntary compliance to the professional ethical principles generated precisely by those values the professionals adhere to, to be more efficient. An ethics exclusively focused on obligations creates a reticence towards the ethical dimension of the profession, which crunches the professional, instead of opening him towards the values that underlie the emergence of social work, precisely those values which determined many professionals to embrace such a career.

COUNSELLING AND EVALUATION PRACTICE OF ETHICS EXPERTISE IN SOCIAL SERVICES

Counselling of Ethics

The role of guiding the members of an organisation in respecting the ethics policies should be fulfilled by an ethics counsellor. The ethics counsellor can be guided by the supervisor of the organisation or the representatives of the human resources department. The counselling of ethics can be identified as a concept in the scientific literature under different names, such as: ethics consultation, ethics advice, ethics consultancy. In this chapter we will refer to the consultation process in the area of ethics as the "counselling of ethics" which we consider the most adequate. Counselling of ethics can be defined as a service provided by a consultant, a team or a committee with the expertise in the field of ethics of the professionals in the organisation which is providing the services, who face ethical difficulties/dilemmas in everyday practice. According to Tomlinson (1999), the core purpose is improving the process and the results in the relationship of the professional with the beneficiaries of the services through the support offered by the counsellor of ethics in identifying, analysing and solving ethical dilemmas.

The counsellors of ethics' main goals are:

- The interpretation of individual cases arising from the perspective of general ethical principles, included in the organisation's Code of Ethics;
- To monitor the application of the code of ethics in order to ensure management control (Sandu, 2012; Sandu, Caras (Frunza), 2014);
- To maximise the benefits and minimise the negative effects on the beneficiaries of services, by adopting certain correct decisions which are sensitive to the individual's needs;
- Facilitating the conflict resolution based on respecting the interests, rights and differences between the individuals and the responsibility of those involved in the process;
- Supporting the institutional efforts to develop policies of organisational ethics, policies of improving the quality and fairly distributing the existing resources – by identifying the ethical issues and promoting the ethical standards (Fletcher & Siegler, 1996, p. 125; Tomlinson, 1999).

We make the distinction between ethical counselling and the counselling of ethics. Counselling as a process should be based per se on a series of ethical values such as human dignity, autonomy, beneficence, justice, etc., and therefore any counselling process should implicitly be ethical. Counselling of ethics expressly targets the issues or ethical dilemmas, aiming at facilitating the professional's ethical decision.

Counselling of ethics, as well as social counselling, addresses the vulnerabilities of a cognitive nature in particular, trying to obtain an effective output by reconstructing the vision over the problem. The ethical expert as a counsellor of ethics is recommended to provide the client with a specific overview on the ethical dilemma he is facing. This approach can be considered to be the epistemic part of the ethical expertise, also having a meta-ethical dimension (Sandu & Caras, 2013).

Ethics Audit and the Ability to Assess the Level of Ethics in the Social Welfare Organisations

The ethics audit is seen as a tool for assessing the level of influence the ethical standards have, at an individual and an organisational level, allowing for systematic evaluation of the performances obtained in the ethics fields (Agheorghiesei, 2011; Sandu, 2012).

Conducting an ethics audit highlights the structure of the system's values which operate effectively within the organisation, both manifested and latent (Agheorghiesei, 2011; Sandu, Caras (Frunza), 2014).

Reamer (2001, pp. 355-366) considers that the ethics audit should consist of two dimensions: *the ethical reflection on the current knowledge of the ethics in the field,* and *the relevance of this knowledge in the daily practice, and identifying the ethical risks and decisions.*

The organisation whose practices are ethics audited, should allocate resources for the reflection on current knowledge, each specialist making a proper inventory of the knowledge in ethics and, later on, after determining the level of knowledge, the organisation should be able to connect this level to the knowledge of daily practice. The ethics auditor identifies the organisation's ability to comply with their ethically acceptable values, providing them with a number of proposals for improving their practice and operation (Sandu, Caras (Frunza), 2014; Caras, 2014).

We further present the necessary stages in accomplishing an ethics audit as exposed by Hofmann (2006) for the healthcare system. In our opinion, this model can easily be implemented by the ethics experts in fields such as public health, social work, organisational development, community ethics audit (Sandu, 2015) etc.

The stages proposed by Hofmann (2016) are:

- (Qualitative) analysis of the documents regarding the (ethical) mission, ethics policies, codes of ethics, available in the organisation etc.;
- (Qualitative) analysis of the content of ethics training;
- Evaluation of the processes in the organisation and the compliance with its ethical standards;
- Interviews and focus-groups with members of the organisation in order to highlight the meanings assigned to the policies and ethical standards in the current activity. The members of the organisation can also be interviewed regarding reporting unethical practices of which they had knowledge over the time spent in the organisation. The adherence of its members to the ethical standards is evaluated, as well as their compliance to them and the identification of practitioners (chateauneuf, ramde & avril, 2016) with organisational ethical values, the identification of ethical issues acknowledged

by the members of the organisation, the analysis of the ethical organisational culture, as well as the agreement between the staff and the ethical values promoted by the organisation;

- The investigation over the organisational structure and the place of theethics management in the institutional structure. The existence of the ethics committees and their role in the organisation, is also considered;
- The analysis of the relationship between the organisation and the external environment. There is an evaluation of the organisation's obligations towards the external environment, the social responsibility etc.

In addition to these directions of the ethics audit, we recommend the audit of ethical communication within the organisation (Sandu, 2015). In our opinion, the elements of the audit of communication are a component part of the ethics audit since the communicative action is an ethical action. We also consider, in achieving an ethics audit of the programmes developed by the organisation, what would at least respect the principles of beneficence, non-harm, respect for the autonomy of the beneficiaries, justice and equity (Beauchamp, Childress, 2009). Aside from these principles, we prefer to audit the programmes of an organisation from the perspective of its social responsibility assumed in implementing the project, non-discrimination and equal treatment, the accessibility of the programme, including for the vulnerable and disadvantaged populations; transparency in selecting the beneficiaries and implementing the project; equal chances and opportunities both for the beneficiaries and the project's staff.

A particular area of the ethics audit is the audit of policies and programmes developed by the organisation and governance (Sandu, 2015). The audit of the governance aims to transpose the general idea of public good, from the level of a concept and programme value, at the level of the programmes aimed at increasing the quality of life (Caras, 2014; Caras (Frunza), Sandu, 2014; Sandu, Caras (Frunza), 2014). The ethical analysis of the governance can be understood as an evaluation of the way in which the managers choose between competing values. The ethical gatekeeping or the option over the constitutive values of policies and social programmes make governance involve a process of making ethical decisions, so that the managers of social services should have enough ethics expertise or benefit from the supervision of an ethics expert, in order to exercise the process of making an ethical decision in good conditions (Sandu, 2015).

Last, but not least, we wish to mention the need for auditing the transparency of decisions and the functioning of public services. The audit of transparency should target the affirmative actions conducted in order to include all stakeholders who wish to participate in the decision-making process, in the decision-making field (Sandu, 2015).

Ethics Committees' Activities and Arguments in Favour of Their Activities

The ethics committees are, both in the medical, research or education area, as well as in other fields, multidisciplinary groups meant to contribute to supporting the ethical behaviour in the presented fields.

The scientific literature assigns, in accordance with the internationally acknowledged practice, a series of roles to the ethics committees:

- Assessment; monitoring and control of the decisions, methodologies and ethical practices;
- Improvement of ethical knowledge within the organisation;
- Promotion of fair policies and procedures in maximising well-being;
- Promotion of the beneficiaries' rights;
- Raising the debate and critical examination of the ethical issues and their consequences that could emerge from the social practice;
- Supervising the formal and substantive conditions of the instruments for ethical compliance – informed consent;
- Checking the content of the informed consent proposal, focusing on the client's full understanding;
- Contribution to the construction of the codes of ethics in accordance with the mission, values and professional standards of practice specific to the organisation (Caras (Frunza), Sandu, 2014; Furlong, 1986; Reamer, 1987).

The different approaches to the ethics committees' activities bring into discussion both the positive and the negative nature of such committees' practices. Verweij, Brom & Huibers (20002) outline the following roles of the ethics committees:

- The motivation of adopting an ethical reflection within the organisation;
- Offering support in making the decision;
- The demystification of ethics – in the sense of bringing ethics to the common understanding of the professionals in their everyday practice;
- Ensuring "comfort" for moral debates – by respecting the opinion of the participants in the debate, encouraging the expression and ensuring the confidentiality of the debate;
- Offering examples of moral deliberation;
- Organising efficiently and effectively the debates and ethical evaluations (verweij, brom & huibers, 2000).

The above-mentioned authors discuss each of these values, also showing the limitations of such an ethics committee in ensuring the debate over the ethical issues in the organisation. Fully assigning the ethics committee the role of facilitator, evaluator, determinant of the ethical reflection in relation to the professional, the last one will be tempted to distance himself from their own responsibility as moral agent.

In a previous paper (Caras (Frunza) & Sandu, 2014) we approached the importance of the need for establishing ethics committees in the area of social services, either at the level of the organisations of social work, or the external ones, prepared to activate in accordance withtheir case law.

Of the theoretical arguments, we support the fact that, through its interventional nature, social work is a form of research action, and thus requires an ethical evaluation of practice. This evaluation will be based on the same ethical criteria of evaluation as in the research on human subjects (Caras & Sandu, 2013).

Of the practical arguments for the need for ethics committees in the social services, we remember:

- To prevent and control malpractice in social services;
- The need for using instruments specific for social work in the case management – informed consent as an ethical instrument (Caras & Sandu, 2013).

IMPROVEMENT OF ETHICS EXPERTISE. THE MODEL OF THE SUPERVISION OF ETHICS

We proposed a model of ethics expertise grounded on Habermas's theory (2000) of communicative action. We started its development from the professional supervision model (Cojocaru, 2005; Kadushin, 1992).

In establishing the model of the supervision of ethics, we started by identifying the main reference points of the social services:

- **Organisation:** It offers social work services;
- **The Professional:** The representative of the organisation and the one who implements the social work practice;
- **The Beneficiary:** The customer of social services.

The supervisor of ethics intervenes as facilitator, with the role of supporting the ethical relationships set up between the organisation, the professionals and the *beneficiaries.*

The supervision of ethics partially complements the functions of ethics committees, ethics audit and counselling of ethics. The supervision of ethics performs these functions by continuing training and monitoring of the professionals whose work involves taking ethical decisions, constantly covering their need for counselling, assessment and support in order to adhere to the ethical norms of their profession (Caras (Frunza) & Sandu, 2014; Sandu & Caras (Frunza), 2014).

We represent graphically the relationship between the organisation, professional and beneficiary, in the context of the supervision of ethics, illustrating the functions the supervision of ethics fulfils in any of the relationships.

We present each party's position in relation to the supervision of ethics. In addition to normalising the practices' complementary functions that are already existing in the system of social services, met by the supervision of ethics, we previously brought into discussion the additional functions of the practice, as innovation elements which can lead to effective development of any viable social system (Caras (Frunza) & Sandu, 2014; Sandu & Caras (Frunza), 2014).

Figure 1. Ethics expertise: Supervision of ethics - roles and relations
Source: Caras (Frunză), A., Sandu, A. (2014). Epistemic and Pragmatic Backgrounds of Supervision of Ethics, Procedia - Social and Behavioral Sciences, 149, 142-151. DOI: https://doi.org/10.1016/j.sbspro.2014.08.178

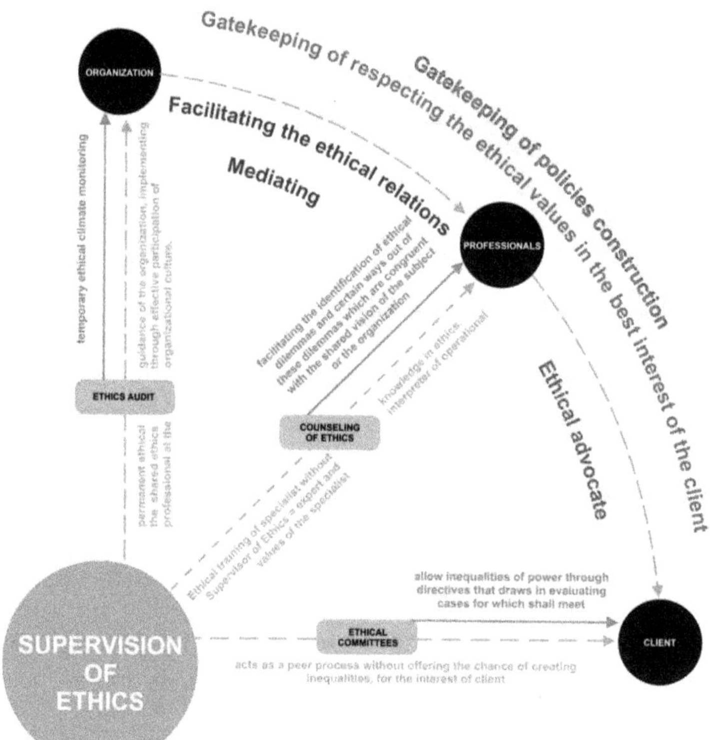

We consider the purpose of the supervision of ethics to be the decrease in inequalities in the relationship of power, by making the values of the people involved to be compatible. If, in certain cases, the ethics committee may allow for inequalities of power through certain directives which shall be met in the ethical evaluation of specific cases, the supervision of ethics acts as a peer process, without allowing the inequalities.

In the relationship *ethics supervisor–organisation,* this has the role of maintaining the balance of power. *The professional* applies the ethics policies as they are set by the *organisation* through a constructive deliberate process, from which he/she may have been excluded. Moral duty is not self-undertaken by a professional, unless he/she adheres to the organisational culture. The supervisor of ethics intervenes in this organisation–professional relationship, by facilitating the deliberation on the contents of ethical practice. The *supervisor of ethics* will inform and advise the *professional* over the ethical values of the organisation and how it is transmitted into practical principles, facilitating the professional adherence to the organisational culture.

The ethics supervisor's duty is to bring into the consciousness of the organisation and the professional the values and principles on which their practice is based, encouraging them to apply these values in the case management (management of the relationship with the beneficiary). This role of the supervisor is equivalent to the mediator, translating the ethical values on which the public and ethical values are based.

The relationship between the professional and the beneficiary is based on the ethical constitutive values of the organisation's practice. The professional's role is to transpose these values into the relationship with each beneficiary.

Taking for example the value of "equity", the professional can develop a personalised service plan, specific for the beneficiary and his needs, which will allow the beneficiary to access those benefits which will cover his needs. In this relationship, the supervisor will be able to fulfil the role of ethics counsellor, assisting the professionals in identifying the best solutions in accordance with the public policies in the field. The role of the ethics supervisor is not transposed with those of the professional supervisor, since the ethical reflections do not target the professional quality, but the ethical value of practice. In the same relationship, between the professional and the beneficiary, the ethics supervisor intervenes as "lawyer" for the beneficiary's rights, bringing these rights into the professional's consciousness and facilitating the ethical deliberation.

The relationship between the organisation and the beneficiaries is mediated by the ethics supervisor who fulfils the role of gatekeeper of the ethics compliance, by contributing to the development of public policies. The ethics supervisor's intervention of gatekeeper is an indirect one. In a situation of choosing between two possible actions, starting from the competing ethical values, the supervisor indicates the possible alternatives in the ethical decision that are in line with its values.

The ethical gatekeeper intervenes when discussing the public policy, the ethics supervisor pointing out the ethical characteristics for each option. To the extent that he participates in proper ethical decisions by facilitating the deliberation on ethical values, transposing the instruments of public policy to the organisation's effective practices, the gatekeeping function becomes instrumental (Caras (Frunza) & Sandu, 2014; Sandu & Caras (Frunza), 2014).

Functions of the Supervision of Ethics

During the construction of the model of ethics supervision, we identified a series of functions whose action improves the practice of ethics of the professionals, and implicitly of the organisation.

Gatekeeping in the Construction of Ethics Policies

The supervision of ethics verifies the convergence of the interpretative agreement on the practical activities with the contents' interpretative agreement on values, and the conduct compatibility between them. The gatekeeping function ensures the shift from the values originated in the political ethics (public good, social justice, etc.) to the constitutive ethical values and, finally, to the operational ones and the practice of the ethical principle (Caras (Frunza) & Sandu, 2014; Sandu, 2014; Sandu & Caras (Frunza), 2014).

The Mediation in Achieving a Reflective Balance in the Organisation

The supervisor of ethics acts within a triadic construct, being the facilitator of communicative action in the relationships between the organisational, professional and clients of services provided by the organisation through the professional.

The Administrative and Deliberative Function

It implies involvement in the ethics committees, making reports and referral activity, sanctioning the non-compliant behaviour of those being supervised. One of the roles of the supervisor of ethics in the relationship between the professional, the organisation and the client is being an ethical lawyer for the client, by participating as a member of the ethics committee. Along with the experts in the complementary fields of social services, the supervisor of ethics as a member of the ethics committee is involved in the administrative deliberative process of ethical acceptability of the services (Caras (Frunza) & Sandu, 2014; Sandu & Caras (Frunza), 2014).

The Construction of an Ethical Climate in the Organisations and the Monitoring of Ethical Conformity

It implies the development of ethical standards and the appropriate context for ethics understanding and its applicability in practice, in accordance with the organisation's needs. The supervisor of ethics should promote the highest possible ethical standards and ethical particularities of professional or institutional practices. The supervisor will also empower the professionals in order to comply with their own professional practice principles and monitor the professional ethical standards of practitioners who operate in areas with explicit ethical impact. The monitoring function could be correlated with the ethics audit, both in terms of the culture of organisational ethics and of compliance.

Counselling of Ethics, Ethical Advice and Support

It implies the ethical training and ethical preparation of the staff, involving the application of ethical standards in the current practice and, in particular, with regard to the counsellors of ethics and the members of the ethics committees (Caras (Frunza) & Sandu, 2014; Sandu & Caras (Frunza), 2014).

FUTURE RESEARCH DIRECTIONS ON ETHICS EXPERTISE IN SOCIAL WORK

It is desirable for the field of ethics expertise to be developed at the level of social services, in favour of the beneficiaries, hence the need for validating ethical consensus and practice of ethical gatekeeping. Starting from the model of implementing an ethics expertise in the medical field, as domain oriented towards the research on human subjects, we support the need for awareness on the development of ethics expertise in the area of social services, whose intervention targets the alteration of the beneficiaries' quality of life and, hence, its need for ethical reflection. We developed a model of ethics expertise in the social welfare practice – the supervision of ethics.

The model of the supervision of ethics is a continual progress. Previous stages of its construction, namely the analysis of supervision as professional practice (Caras & Sandu, 2014a), of deconstruction of ethical values (Caras (Frunza) & Sandu, 2014b; Frunza, 2016), the epistemic and pragmatic documentation of the model of supervision of ethics, was positively received by the scientific community.

The scientific impact is to open a new direction of research in the field of ethics expertise in the sphere of public services and of social work practice. Ethics expertise, including consultancy and counselling of ethics, are better developed in the field of public health and bioethics, in the age of technologies with dangerous potential and of constituting responsibility towards the non-presence. Taking ethics expertise in the field of practices of improving the quality of life can constitute an area of wide interest in the context of the need for redefining social practices as practices that require an ethical opinion.

Possible future research in supporting the development of ethics expertise in the field of social services would focus on the identification of the particularities of institutional ethics management and social construction of ethics, as derived from the constitutive and operational values acknowledged in the organisational culture. A diagnosis of the practices from the field of counselling of ethics in social work public institutions could be followed, so to highlight any faults in the process of disseminating public servants (social workers) with attributions of a counsellor of ethics.

Another future research thematic could be the piloting of the counselling of ethics as a philosophical practice, starting from the previously theorised ethics expertise model (supervision of ethics) meant to facilitate self-responsibility of the professional from the public services, in consent with the social responsibility of the institution.

CONCLUSION

This chapter highlights the construction of a new model of ethics expertise, which is applicable to public administration, especially in social services, starting from the difference between the ethical values on which the organisation bases its practices. In the previous research, and more in-depth in this chapter, we identified two types of ethical values: the constitutive ethical values and the operational ethical values. The constitutive ethical values are those due to which the organisation took shape, being correlated with its mission and vision. The operational values are those around which there are established the best practices of the organisation, being correlated with its policies, services and products. Implementing the organisation's ethics policies – supported in its code of ethics, can be done through the contribution of the next models of manifesting the ethics expertise: the activity of the ethics committees, counselling of ethics, ethics audit and the supervision of ethics.

Being newly introduced as an ethics expertise model, the supervision of ethics is understood as having the following main functions: the ethics policies gatekeeping role in the construction of public policies and their implementation; it verifies the convergence of interpretive agreement of the practical activities with the contents' interpretive agreement on values, and conducts compatibility between them; the mediation function in achieving a reflective balance within the organisation on the interests of each party involved – the supervisor of ethics acts within a triadic construct, being the facilitator of communicative action in relations between the organisation, the professionals and the clients of services provided by the organisation, through the professional.

The function of the ethics construction in organisations - implies the development of ethical standards in accordance with its needs, by promoting the highest possible ethical standards and ethical particularities of professional or institutional practices, in accordance with the ethical vision and mission of the organisation; ethical conformity monitoring ensures the compatibility of procedures with ethical standards; monitoring the professional ethical standards of practitioners who operate in areas with explicit ethical impact, including those working with vulnerable people and groups and contributing to the improvement of the professionals' ethical practices; ethical auditing, both in terms of the culture of organisational ethics and of compliance; counselling of ethics, support and consultancy - it implies the ethical training and ethical preparation of staff involving the application of ethical standards in current practice and, in particular, with regard to ethics counsellors and members of the ethics committees; the administrative and deliberative function implies the involvement in ethics committees, making reports and referral activity and sanctioning the non-compliant behaviour of those being supervised.

ACKNOWLEDGMENT

The model construction process started while attending the doctoral studies and project, and further published in extenso, in Romanian language, in the volume: Frunza, A. (2016). Catre o noua expertiza etica - deconstruind valorile etice, [Towards a new ethics expertise – deconstructing the ethical values]. Iasi, Romania: LUMEN Publishing. Previous publications on the construction of this model were published by the authors Ana Frunza and Antonio Sandu in articles such as:

Caras (Frunză), A., & Sandu, A. (2014). Epistemic and Pragmatic Backgrounds of Supervision of Ethics. *Procedia - Social and Behavioral Sciences*, *149*, 142-151. https://doi.org/10.1016/j.sbspro.2014.08.178

Sandu, A., & Caras (Frunză), A. (2014). Some Considerations on the Construction of Ethics Policies. Shared Ethics and Communicative Action. *Procedia - Social and Behavioral Sciences*, *149*, 846-854. https://doi.org/10.1016/j.sbspro.2014.08.325

Caras (Frunză), A. (2014). Perspectives for Reconstruction of Ethical Expertise. *Postmodern Openings*, *5*(2), 81-96. http://dx.doi.org/10.18662/po/2014.0502.06

REFERENCES

Agheorghesei, D. T. (2011). *Etica în afaceri* [Ethics in business]. Iasi, Romania: Alexandu Ioan Cuza University Publishing.

Agich, G. J. (2009). The Issue of Expertise in Clinical Ethics. *Diametros,* (22), 3–20. Retrieved from: http://www.diametros.iphils.uj.edu.pl/serwis/pdf/diam22agich.PDF?id=8055

Australian Association of Social Workers. (2010). *Code of Ethics.* Retrieved from: https://www.aasw.asn.au/document/item/1201

Baron, J., & Spranca, M. (1997). Protected Values. *Organizational Behavior and Human Decision Processes, 70*(1), 1–16. doi:10.1006/obhd.1997.2690 PMID:9236161

Beauchamp, T., & Childress, J. (2009). Principles of Biomedical Ethics (6th ed.). New York: Oxford University Press.

Bubnys, R. (2014). Reflektavimo kompetencijos struktūra socialinio darbo studentams atliekant praktikas [The Structure of Reflection Competency during Social Work Students' Practices]. *Socialinė teorija, empirija, politika ir praktika, 9*, 50-63.

Bulgaru, M. (2013). Deontologia asistentei sociale [The deontology of social work]. *Studia Universitatis Moldaviae. Seria Științe Sociale, 8*(68), 3-15. Retrieved from: http://studiamsu.eu/wp-content/uploads/01.-p.03-15.pdf

Caras, A. (2014). Perspectives for Reconstruction of Ethical Expertise. *Postmodern Openings, 5*(2), 81–96. doi:10.18662/po/2014.0502.06

Caras, A., & Sandu, A. (2013). Ethical Evaluation of Social Services and the Need for Ethics Committees. *Procedia - Social and Behavioral Sciences, 92,* 142-149. https://doi.org/10.1016/j.sbspro.2013.08.650

Caras, A., & Sandu, A. (2014a). The Role of Supervision in Professional Development of Social Work Specialists. *Journal of Social Work Practice: Psychotherapeutic Approaches in Health, Welfare and the Community, 28*(1), 75–94.

Caras, A., & Sandu, A. (2014b). *Relational Autonomy – Connections Between Moral Agent Theory and Supervision of Ethics.* Presented at the ISUD Tenth World Congress, the Human Being: Its Nature and Functions, Craiova, Romania.

Caras (Frunză), A., & Sandu, A. (2014). Epistemic and Pragmatic Backgrounds of Supervision of Ethics. *Procedia - Social and Behavioral Sciences, 149,* 142-151. https://doi.org/10.1016/j.sbspro.2014.08.178

Chateauneuf, D., Ramde, J., & Avril, A. (2016). Processes Employed by Social Work Practitioners in Child Welfare for Exchanging and Using Knowledge. *Journal of Social Work Practice*, *30*(4), 397–415. doi:10.1080/02650533.2015.1116439

Cojocaru, Ş. (2005). *Metode apreciative în asistenţa socială. Ancheta, supervizarea şi managementul de caz* [Appreciative methods in social work. Inquiry, supervision and case management]. Iaşi: Polirom Publishing.

Colegiul National al Asistentilor Sociali (CNASR). (2008). *Codul deontologic al profesiei de asistent social*. Publicat in Monitorul Oficial al Romaniei, Partea I, Nr. 173/6.III.2008. Retrieved from: http://www.carp-omenia.ro/wp-content/uploads/2015/07/cod_deontologic_as.pdf

Congress, E. (2000). What Social Workers Should Know About Ethics: Understanding and Resolving Practice Dilemmas. *Administration in Social Work*, *1*(1), 1–26.

Congress, E., & McAuliffe, D. (2006). Professional codes in Australia and the United States. *Social Work Ethics*, *49*(2), 151–164. https://doi.org/10.1177/0020872806061211

Crisp, R. (2015). Well-Being. In *The Stanford Encyclopedia of Philosophy*. Retrieved from: http://plato.stanford.edu/archives/ sum2015/entries/well-being/

Dickson, M. W., Smith, D. B., Grojean, M. W., & Ehrhart, M. (2001). An organizational climate regarding ethics: The outcome of leader values and the practices that reflect them. *The Leadership Quarterly*, *12*(2), 197–217. doi:10.1016/S1048-9843(01)00069-8

Fletcher, J. C., & Siegler, M. (1996). What Are the Goals of Ethics Consultation? A Consensus. *The Journal of Clinical Ethics*, *7*(2), 122–126. PMID:8889887

Foot, P. (1978). The problem of abortion and the doctrine of the double effect. In Virtues and Vices and Other Essays in Moral Philosophy (pp. 19-32). Berkeley, CA: University of California Press.

Freeman, S. J., Engels, D. W., & Altekruse, M. K. (2004). Foundations for ethical standards and codes: The role of moral philosophy and theory in ethics. *Counseling and Values*, *48*(3), 163–173. doi:10.1002/j.2161-007X.2004.tb00243.x

Frunză, A. (2016). *Către o nouă expertiză etică. Deconstruind valorile etice* [Towards an ethics expertise. Deconstructing the ethical values]. Iasi, Romania: Editura LUMEN.

Frunză, M. (2011). *Expertiză etică și acțiune socială* [Ethics expertise and social action]. Bucharest: Tritonic Publishing.

Furlong, R. M. (1986). The Social Workers Role on the Institutional Ethics Committee. *Social Work in Health Care, 11*(4), 93–100. doi:10.1300/J010v11n04_08 PMID:3775618

Graumann, S. (2012). Social Services Ethics, Overview. In Encyclopedia of Applied Ethics (2nd ed.; pp. 175–181). Academic Press. doi:10.1016/B978-0-12-373932-2.00398-7

Habermas, J. (2000). *Conştiinţă morală şi acţiune comunicativă* [Moral consciousness and communicative action]. Bucharest, Romania: All Educaţional Publishing.

Hofmann, P. B. (2006). The Value of an Ethics Audit. *Healthcare Executive, 21*(2), 44–45. PMID:17020183

Iltis, A. S., & Sheehan, M. (2016). Expertise, Ethics Expertise, and Clinical Ethics Consultation: Achieving Terminological Clarity. *J Med Philos, 41*(4), 416-433. https://doi.org/10.1093/jmp/jhw014

Iser, M. (2013). Recognition. In *The Stanford Encyclopedia of Philosophy*. Retrieved from: http://plato.stanford.edu/archives/ fall2013/entries/recognition/

Kadushin, A. (1992). *Supervision in Social Work* (3rd ed.). New York: Columbia University Press.

Kluckhohn, F. R., & Strodtbeck, F. L. (1961). *Variations in value orientations.* Evanston, IL: Row, Peterson.

Loue, S. (2013). Social Work, Advocacy, and Ethics: Opportunities and Challenges in Romania. *Procedia: Social and Behavioral Sciences, 92*, 1039–1043. doi:10.1016/j.sbspro.2013.08.796

NASW. (2008). *Code of Ethics.* Retrieved from: http://www.socialworkers.org/pubs/code/code.asp

Naumann, S. E., & Bennett, N. (2000). A case for procedural justice climate: Development and test of a multilevel model. *Academy of Management Journal, 43*(5), 881–889. doi:10.2307/1556416

Neamtu, G. (2012). The specific of professional education in social work adjusted to labour marketplace. *Revista de Cercetare şi Intervenţie Socială, 39,* 39-58.

ODonoghue, K., Yuh Ju, P. W., & Tsui, M. S. (2017). Constructing an evidence-informed social work supervision model. *European Journal of Social Work*, 1–11. doi:10.1080/13691457.2017.1341387

Rasmussen, A. (2005). *In Search of Ethics Expertise in Ethics Expertise. History, Contemporary Perspectives and Applications*. Springer. https://doi.org/10.1007/1-4020-3820-8

Rasmussen, L. M. (2016). Clinical Ethics Consultants are not "Ethics" Experts—but They do Have Expertise. *J Med Philos*, *41*(4), 384-400. https://doi.org/10.1093/jmp/jhw012

Rawls, J. (2012). O teorie a dreptăţii (H. Târnoveanu, Trans.). Iaşi, Romania: Alexandu Ioan Cuza University Publishing.

Reamer, F. (2001). *The Social Work Ethics Audit: A Risk Management Tool*. NASW Press.

Reamer, F. G. (1987). *Ethics Committees in Social Work, Faculty Publications*. Retrieved from: http://works.bepress.com/frederic_reamer/8

Reamer, F. G. (2012). Social Work. In Encyclopedia of Applied Ethics (2nd ed.; pp. 189–197). Academic Press. doi:10.1016/B978-0-12-373932-2.00415-4

Sandu, A. (2012). *Appreciative ethics. A constructionist Version of Ethics*. Lap Lambert Acad. Publ. GmbH & Co. KG.

Sandu, A., & Caras (Frunză), A. (2014). Some Considerations on the Construction of Ethics Policies. Shared Ethics and Communicative Action. *Procedia - Social and Behavioral Sciences, 149*, 846–854. https://doi.org/10.1016/j.sbspro.2014.08.325

Sandu, A. (2015). Etică profesională şi transparenţă în administraţia publică [Professional ethics and transparency and public administration]. Bucharest, Romania: Didactică şi Pedagogică-RA Publishing.

Sandu, A. (2016). *Etică şi practică socială* [Ethics and social practice]. Iasi, Romania: Lumen Publishing.

Sandu, A. (2017). *O etică centrată pe valori în sfera publică* [An ethics centred on values in the public sphere]. Iasi, Romania: Lumen Publishing.

Sandu, A., & Caras, A. (2013). Philosophical Practice and Social Welfare Counselling and Supervision of Ethics. *Journal of the APPA Philosophical Practice*, *8*(3), 1287–1296.

Sandu, A., & Caras, A. (2013a). Deconstruction of charity. Postmodern ethical approaches. *Journal for the Study of Religions and Ideologies*, *12*(36), 72–99.

Schicktanz, S., Schweda, M., & Wynne, B. (2012). The ethics of public understanding of ethics—why and how bioethics expertise should include public and patients voices. *Medicine, Health Care, and Philosophy*, *15*(2), 129–139. doi:10.1007/s11019-011-9321-4 PMID:21448745

Schneider, B. (1990). The climate for service: An application of the climate construct. In B. Schneider (Ed.), *Organizational climate and culture* (pp. 383–412). San Francisco: JosseyBass.

Singer, P. (1972). Moral Experts. *Analysis*, *32*(4), 115–117. doi:10.1093/analys/32.4.115

Tenbrunsel, A. E., Smith-Crowe, K., & Umphress, E. E. (2003). Building Houses on Rocks: The Role of the Ethical Infrastructure in Organizations. *Social Justice Research, 16*(3), 285-307. https://doi.org/10.1023/A:1025992813613

The Policy, Ethics and Human Rights Committee. (2014). *The Code of Ethics for Social Work. Statement of Principles.* Retrieved from: http://cdn.basw.co.uk/upload/basw_95243-9.pdf

Tomlinson, T. (1999). Ethics Consultant: Problem Solver or Spiritual Counselor? *Human Studies*, *22*(1), 43–52. doi:10.1023/A:1005408718236

Tosatia, S., Lawthongb, N., & Suwanmonkhab, S. (2015). Development of an Appreciative Inquiry and Assessment Processes for Students Self-Knowing and Self-Development. *Procedia: Social and Behavioral Sciences*, *191*, 753–758. doi:10.1016/j.sbspro.2015.04.422

Verweij, M., Brom, F. W., & Huibers, A. (2000). Do's and Dont's for Ethics Committees: Practical Lessons Learned in the Netherlands. *HEC Forum, 12,* 344–357. https://doi.org/10.1023/A:1008997605664

Weinstein, B. D. (1994). The possibility of Ethical Expertise. *Theoretical Medicine*, *15*(1), 61–75. doi:10.1007/BF00999220 PMID:8059434

Zaner, R. M. (2004). *Ethics and the Clinical Encounter*. Lima: CSS Publishing.

ENDNOTES

1 By ethical issue we understand a situation that contravenes certain moral norms and needs to be solved. The corruption emerged at the level of an organisation, or discrimination are examples of such ethical issues. The ethical dilemma is the situation of having a choice between two ethically equivalent values. We have an ethical dilemma, originally debated by Foot, P. (1978). The problem of abortion and the doctrine of the double effect. In Virtues and Vices and Other Essays in Moral Philosophy, 19-32. Berkeley and Los Angeles: University of California Press, in the hypothetical situation in which, for example, we have

to chose between saving a person's life, or of three people situated on parallel train lines and a train is rushing towars them without brakes due to a terrorist attack. We can only use a switch that would direct the train towards the line on which there is one person, who would therefore die, thus saving the other three lives, or do nothing, the train continuing its trajectory on the line that would cause the death of the three. In both situations, the value is the same, the human life, and there is no moral criteria to say which life matters most. The choice of saving the life of the three over one is a simple quantitative choice, not based on the moral value of the person or the deed.

2 Starting from the practice focused on strengths, we developed a model of applied ethics called appreciative ethics. For more details, see Sandu, A. (2012). *Appreciative ethics. A constructionist Version of Ethics.* Lap Lambert Acad. Publ. GmbH & Co. KG.

Chapter 12
A Brief Overview of Ethics Audit Practice in Organizations:
Specific Auditing Aspects in Social Work Activity

Daniela-Tatiana Agheorghiesei
Alexandru Ioan Cuza University of Iasi, Romania

ABSTRACT

This theoretical chapter presents the general issue of applying ethics audit to organizations. In the first part of the chapter are presented information about the origin of the term and several definitions of the ethics audit, which have been selected from the literature, the role and advantages of the ethics audit, the main characteristics, the principles, the content and implementing requirements of the ethics auditing process. The results of some research and good practices in the field are also mentioned. The second part of the chapter addresses the issues and particularities of ethics audit in social work field.

INTRODUCTION: FROM AUDIT TO ETHICS AUDIT

More and more intense concerns about ethics management in organizations or in businesses over the last few decades have imposed the ethics audit practice as a tool of preventing possible vulnerabilities in compliance with ethical policies and standards, in addition to the consolidation of trust in stakeholder relations.

DOI: 10.4018/978-1-5225-3090-9.ch012

In this chapter we briefly review the theory of ethics audit practice in organizations, from definitions, principles, advantages and disadvantages to the structure and steps to be followed in conducting the auditing process. Special attention is paid to the importance and role of ethics audit in social assitance/work. We also mention various research in the field and some examples of best practices of ethics audit implemented in companies, institutions of healthcare and social work. Although the focus of our analysis is theoretically and largely descriptive, the chapter brings together most of the well known authors' view on the issue, and offers a wealth of information about what ethics audit is essentially about.

The term of audit has its origins in the Latin word "auditum", with the meaning of listening (https://dexonline.ro/definitie/audit). According to Muel Kaptein (1998), the retired officers of the Roman Army, who revelled in good training, experience and reputation, were chosen as auditors "to listen to soldiers' problems and complaints in order to identify and solve them in time" (Kaptein, 1998, p. 60). "As a way of listening, then investigating and, finally, suggesting solutions, the *audit* allows reasoning a motivated and independent contribution" (Dimitrescu, 1997, p. 32). Likewise, some authors refer to the metaphorical association that Lionel Stoléru, minister for Dialogue during the term of office of François Mitterand, has done between the audit and the inner ear, the latter being "the headquarters of the human body's equilibrium" (Dimitrescu, 1997, p. 32; Ungureanu, 2017). It is stressed that, however, the audit does not have the task of ensuring the equilibrium, but to check whether "the necessary conditions are met to preserve it, to handle the mastery of disorder, the adaptation to changes, to assess the degree of security and the risks". The nature of the audit is financial as it is "attested" as a practice since "year 500 b.ch., in Athens, where 3 councils were responsible for checking the city revenue and expenditures" (Dimitrescu, 1997, p. 32).

In a world that is "not perfect" and where unethical behaviours exist inevitably, the ethics audit is part of the internal control systems required to be set up by organizations "to discourage, prevent and detect unethical actions" (Sears, 1993).

Metaphorically, we appreciate that the ethics audit is the "medical check-up" that every organization, which has assumed its mission in society and is concerned about how it is accomplished along with the expectations of the stakeholders and its reputation, should be performing regularly. The ethics audit "measures its ethical temperature", "identifying the relevant behavioural risk especially that related to the integrity risk of the information" (Ramamoorti & Luke, 2011).

As a first observation, we consider that although ethics audit is gaining higher credibility and acceptance, by being added to the wide variety of methods applied to assessing the organization's performance, whether it be from the public or business sector, in some cases it can only be a panacea. Moreover, in institutions with a high distance power and where abuses may arise, ethics audit can be the „umbrella behind which many managers hide themselves if they want to control employees with an „iron hand". In spite its main role is to detect organizational ethical risks in a timely manner, it can in turn generate also some risks if it is strictly applied as a bureaucratic control method without regard to the "voice and feelings" of employees, available ressources, the specific environment of the organization, the sector of activity, but also the characteristics of the socio-cultural context of each country.

THE PRACTICE AND SPECIFICITY OF ETHICS AUDIT

Definitions

The specialized literature offers a wide range of definitions of ethics audit, which, at the same time, helps to identify its importance and role in organizations.

In his approach to clarifying the terms, John Rosthorn (2000) defines the ethics audit in terms of "Regular, complete and documented measures of compliance with published policies and procedures of the company" (Figure 1, p. 11).

Donald C. Menzel (2007, p. 72), quoting Wiley (1995), considers the ethics audit to be a proactive tool for improvement, the purpose of which is to determine, through the assessments made, what *changes* are required in terms of climate, working environment, codes and consolidating the ethical policies of the organization.

From the perspective of the authors Gael McDonald and André Nijhof (1999), the ethics audit may "identify the factors and pressures that encourage unethical behaviour, or that may act as incentives for unethical behaviour within the organization". Therefore, in the development approach of the ethics program, the audit joins other elements that contribute to the "cultivation of ethical practices" (codes of ethics, ethics trainings and ethics dilemmas awareness programs, communication channels and ethics lines, the existence of the ethics officer, etc.).

Some authors define the ethics audit through the ethical climate assessment (see Menzel, 2007; Boyle, Hermanson, & Wilkins, 2011; Waring and Daugherty, 2004, Sears, 1993). Applying statistical analyses, Waring and Daugherty, 2004) demonstrate the positive correlation between ethical climate and financial or administrative results organizational (costs). Consequently, the ethical climate factors that implicitly can be evaluated in an ethics audit are: the attention paid to ethics by executive and supervising leadership, favourable notice for the delivery of bad news, the efforts to detect violations of ethical standards, the consistency between policies and practices, open discussion regarding the ethics, the freedom to contest the authority, correct handling, penalizing the unethical behaviour, rewarding the ethical behaviour, tracking the reports regarding the ethical concerns (Waring and Daugherty, 2004, p. 38). We can say that this finding is important in the context in which the assessed issues essentially consider how managers apply ethics standards in dealing with employees and set "the tone of ethics" in their organization.

Other definitions of the ethics audit selected from the specialized literature are presented below:

"a systematic evaluation of the program and the organization ethical performance with the intent to determine whether they are effective and involving regular, complete and documented measurement of compliance with the organization declared policies and procedures" (Ferrell, Fraedrich, & Ferrell, 2012, p. 243);

"a means of constantly being in touch with the stakeholders, of knowing and experimenting their needs and expectations, and of improving their own ethical performance in line with these needs" (the judgement of the companies Body Shop or Ben & Jerry's) or "a means of control and, in particular, of feedback (by reviewing the ethics management system and the values program" (Wieland, 2003, p. 244);

"an effective way to ensure that the organization fulfils its mission even in the most demanding times" (Hofmann, 1995);

"...a practical and valuable tool to assess whether the organization is below its own standards and expectations" (Hofmann, 2006), that is, in an unfavourable situation, at risk.

"a process of analysis and dialogue that enables the organization to get suggestions and identify new ways to integrate the social benefits with the economic ones; a basic mechanism for gaining the trust of stakeholders in the organization because this can demonstrate transparently how it fulfils its economic, social and environmental responsibilities" (Garçia-Marza, 2005);

"a proactive tool for building the organizations of integrity (Menzel, 2016, p. 120)"

"describing, analysing and evaluating the relevant aspects of the organization ethics" (Kaptein, 1998, p. 60).

In general terms, we define the ethics audit as being the assessment of the ethical health status in the organization in a specific context.

What the Role of Ethics Audit Within the Organization

From the perspective of Douglas M. Boyle, Dana R. Hermanson and Anne Wilkins (2011), the ethics audit implies "auditing the control environment of an organization", which includes six elements: "the integrity and ethical values; the managerial philosophy and operational style; the organisational structure; the delegation of authority and responsibility; the policies and practices of human resources; the competence of the staff". All these elements require the evaluation of "soft controls", such as ethics, along with the commitment to competence and the operational management style.

An ethics audit can derive as an initiative from the senior management side who is interested in "tracking and improving the ethical performance" of the company. In the United States of America, due to the fact that executives or financial directors can be criminally liable if they consciously cover the irregularities in financial statements (according to Sarbanes-Oxley Act, the managers must prove that their company adopted code of ethics in order to avoid the misconduct and wrongdoing), the ethics audit may be demanded by them "as a tool of improving their confidence in the reporting processes of the company". In companies where an ethics program is implemented, it is the ethics officer who can start an ethics audit in order to "measure the effectiveness" of this program (Ferrell, 2016, p. 17). The ethics audit can be conducted even a formal ethics program doesn't exist in organization. Top-managers (or even shareholders) could decide to have an overview and a deep diagnosis of ethical profile of the organization: the degree with witch the ethical values are embedded within the organization, the way of ethical policies are understood and applied by employees in accordance with the organizational mission, the ethics of decisional process at each managerial level, the norms and behaviours adopted by employees (also by managers) in relation to organizational ethical standards (if these policies already exist), as well as ethical risk areas in the activity and the relationships of the organization. Additionally, the ethics audit provides recommendations and guidelines through which problems can be prevented in the future, the weaknesses can be remedied, but also the methods and tools that can be used in order to strengthen the ethical climate. From this point of view, the ethics audit can support to implement an ethics program if it does not already exist or enhance the existing one.

In companies where the corporate governance policy is not just formal ("window dressing"), but it is intended to be really useful, it is suggested "including the ethics audit in each major policy decision adopted during the year of reporting". This would help increase the reputation of the particular company by providing an overall picture "on its decisions and offer a proactive defence against criticism" (Francis & Armstrong, 2003). This would ensure a good transparency and would avoid the reputational risk.

The Characteristics of an Ethics Audit

The large list of characteristics (selected from the literature) of an ethics audit illustrates the benefits of adopting this tool in managing ethics within organization: it provides an objective and large checklist of organizational "ethics health"; appreciates the real commitment of organization to accomplish its the mission according the needs and expectations of stakeholders and the whole society; assesses the ethics of leadership style, examines the ethics of procurement and investment processes; evaluates the ethics of accounting, financial, marketing, human resource and social responsibility practices of organisation; appreciates the fairness of recruitment, selection, treatment (including working conditions and life-work balance), rewarding and promoting human resources practices; assesses the managerial policies and procedures in supporting the values declaration addressed to its stakeholders and public.

The Advantages of Conducting an Ethics Audit

Among the advantages of the ethics audit there can be listed (Ferrell & Ferrell, 2012, p. 244-245; Menzel, 2007, p. 72): it is possible to identify incorrect actions and behaviours in time, before they become major issues and crises for the organization with extensive consequences, thus helping to minimize or eliminate the costs that may be unforeseen and as a penalty for unethical behaviour; offers a realistic picture of the functioning of the ethics program implemented in the organization (if this already exists); provides a realistic overview of the internal and external impact of the ethical performance of the organization; helps to improve the organizational efficiency and performance by discovering and eliminating the ethical issues, the "bottlenecks" that could affect the employees' productivity, contributing to the increase of the satisfaction degree, of loyalty towards the organization, and reduction of staff fluctuation; helps to protect a good image and good reputation of the organization by identifying on time the risks of ethics and moral weakness and by preventing unethical behaviours, minimizing the negative external impact; increases the interest of investors for the organization, gives them the guarantee that it is worthy to invest and allocate funds to support its activities and operations; improves the relationship with the stakeholders by sending a trusting message from the behalf of the organization that it is permanently concerned with improving its performance, their expectations, and the way they can be met without breaking the morale; highlights the trends, improves the process of organizational learning and the ethical climate, of communication and of working relationships; demonstrates the interest and efforts of the organization to comply with the law, or the progress made when deviations have occurred in the past in this respect; helps proactively to create an integrity system in the organization, starting from an objective reporting.

Principles in Conducting an Ethics Audit

Ronald Jeurissen and Frans van der Putten (Jeurissen & van der Putten, 2007, p. 269) identify several principles in social audit, principles that can be also found in the implementation of an ethics audit: "*integrity*" – stakeholders are provided with all the existing information (or which will be obtained in the future) necessary and relevant to the performance of the organization, so that they can make a decision or have a well-founded and informed choice; "*comparability*" (the results are comparable to previous years' results or other bases); „*inclusion*" (the extent to which the stakeholders are free and have the opportunity to participate in the dialogue needed to substantiate the organizational performance); "*regularity and evolution*" (the audit should be repeated at regular intervals. and the stakeholders' changing expectations should be taken into account); "*organizational integration*" (the audit should be an integral part of the systems and structures of the organization); "*public disclosure*" (the organization must publish its performance in a report accessible to the general public); "*external verification*" (the internal report of the organization is verified by an independent expert); "*continuous improvement*" (recognizing and verifying continuously the steps to improve the performance).

We add that in general an ethics audit needs "the five Ps" of a good merchandising: to be conducted *the right audit* (to be assessed the right issues), at *the right moment*, in *the right place* (organization/department/unit), the *right amount* (of issues and time), the *right quality* of auditing process.

Different Types of Ethics Audit

Several types of ethics audit are presented in the specialized literature (Parsons, 2008, pp. 170-171): *compliance audit* - reflects the extent to which the ethics program of the organization (formulated policies and application methods) respect (comply) with applicable laws and policies and industry-specific rules in which it operates; *cultural audit* (of organizational culture) – represents an examination and diagnosis of organizational culture regarding the way employees perceive, feel and relate to the ethical standards of the organization in which they work; *system audit* – is the audit that includes both the audit of compliance and the cultural audit, and provides a comprehensive view of ethical efforts across all of the organization functions. Linda Klebe Treviño & Katherine Nelson (2011, pp. 194-197) analyse *the audit of ethical culture* as a formal way to change or develop organizational ethics through diagnosis. In the opinion of the mentioned authors, this implies a systematic analysis of both formal organizational systems (organizational structure, reward and advancement criteria) and informal (heroes, daily behaviours supported by stories, rituals and language) that have the role of maintaining ethical culture on its way. The issues to be audited are whether or to what extent: the organization's leaders send a clear message about ethics; they have it on their agenda; ethics is embedded in selection procedures, integrity is highlighted in the new programs' orientation programs or training programs of those already existing; there are formal codes of ethical conduct, and values, are widely distributed to employees, and are supported by other formal systems (performance management, decision-making systems); performance management systems promote ethical conduct, only integrity is promoted, ethical means and goals are taken into account in the performance management system); unethical behaviours are disciplined quickly and justified at all organizational levels; employees at all levels of the organization are encouraged to assume responsibility for their behaviour, they challenge authority when asked to do something wrong, and how; employees are encouraged to report ethics violations, there are confidential communication channels; ethical concerns are incorporated into decision-making processes; managers are oriented towards organizational values within the orientation programs and trained in decision-making ethics; ethical issues are part of planning and policy meetings, and new risk reports; there is a formal committee at the top level of the organization to address these issues.

As the above authors mention, the informal systems can predominate in small organizational entities where formal policies and procedures are often lacking, so their analysis is very important. The issues that can be audited are: role models and heroes of the organization, what values do they represent, what advice the mentors give; the informal socialization processes that exist and the ethical / unethical behaviour rules they promote, and if they are different from those of the subgroups in the organization; organizational rituals and how they promote this ethical / unethical behaviour; who receives promotions - individuals or people who use unethical means to succeed; the message passed by the stories and myths of the organization, if it highlight those who fight for what's right despite pressure or appreciation of compliance, talking about people promoted or dismissed; there is a language for discussing ethical issues, conversations about ethics are daily.

The audit ends with discussing the data obtained through auditing with employees so as to establish a plan to improve the organizational culture, including "complementary changes in formal and informal organizational systems" (Treviño & Nelson, 2011, p. 196).

The ethics audit may be part of a social audit, but th first one is generally limited to assessing the organizational behaviour and performance from the perspective of compliance with legal requirements and ethics standards (usually known as an ethics and compliance audit). However, the social audit has a wider approach and shows the extent to which the organization is able to cope with the all layers of the CSR pyramid proposed by Archie Carroll (Carroll & Buchholtz, 2012): economic, legal, ethical and philanthropic expectations of its stakeholders and the community in general.

A more complex classification of ethics audit is conducted by David Murray (1995, p. 145), that illustrate the main aspects targeted by the auditing process: audit of existing policies and procedures; audit of compliance with company policies and procedures; audit of current performance (external impact); audit of employees' perception; audit of employees' aspirations / concerns; audit of consumer and other stakeholders' perceptions; audit of specific ethical issues / problems; audit of compliance with legal regulations and norms; audit of comparison based on the reference scale, with colleagues or benchmarking.

But we consider that the organizations may choose to audit at a certain point only certain ethical issues, depending on the perceived risks, the objectives pursued, or the resources at their disposal. An ethics audit is not only about the ethical evaluation of the functioning of the organization internal environment. This process must be global, holistic, and take into account all of its operations and its network, i.e. transactions with business partners, suppliers or other categories of stakeholders, which can bring risks to the activity and support of the image of the organization.

One conclusive example is the ethics audit that Apple Company (see Apple Supplier Responsibility 2012 Progress Report, https://www.apple.com/supplier-responsibility/) is implementing annually in order to assess in what manner the code of ethical behaviour is respected by its suppliers. The ethical principles and practices included in the code comprise the following areas: business integrity; information disclosure, protection of the alarmist and anonymous complaints, protection of the intellectual property. By joining the code, the company asks its suppliers to commit to "maintaining the highest standards of ethical behaviour in dealing with their employees, suppliers, and customers."

In order to monitor the compliance with the code of ethical behaviour, Apple company conducts standard audits that "include interviews with employees and contract staff regarding the management procedures". It is also being followed if, through coaching situations, "the management has directed the employees to provide inaccurate information during the audits". Similarly, interviews are conducted with suppliers' senior managers, documents, records, and record keeping processes are analysed. The audit evaluates the supplier's availability to amenably make available the records and information about its management procedures. During the interviews with employees in the auditing process, Apple Company provides them with telephone helpline cards that allow them to offer additional information, and to report, without being afraid of retaliation, if they have suffered negative consequences on them after participating in audit. The audit is conducted annually with suppliers in the four areas of ethics, monitoring the compliance of their practices and management systems with the code of ethical behaviour.

Most concerns that arise when it comes to the conduct of an ethics audit are related to its purpose (what to be improved or the organizational gained after implementing it) and what aspects to be assessed within organization (from compliance and ethics management aspects, system and tools, to values, attitudes and behaviours). Thus, Carole L. Jurkiewicz and Glen M. Vogel (2015, quoted by Menzel, 2016) recommend that the scope of the audit be broad and include three key areas: cultural values (respect, transparency, problem solving - in due time, with respect and openness, by addressing, in regular sessions, the ethical dilemmas arising and the responses to the unethical behaviours that have been reported -, equity, honesty, dignity, discipline), organizational governance (power, responsibility, accountability, relationship and transparency from those who are managing); compliance with the law (non-discriminatory treatment of employees and candidates, adequate financial reporting and internal controls, sensitivity to the environment - ensuring compliance with law and regulations, compliance with codes of ethics of a specific profession or industry).

Brian S. Sears (1993) recommends that auditors evaluate the ethical climate from within and include all functional areas, "to identify all those functions and activities where the ethical implications involve the greatest risk". Among these areas of risk mentioned by the author, the following can be found: adverse publicity, loss of business, legal implications, damage to employees or consumers, disclosure of sensitive information. Sensitive functions to ethics are: "inflated" accounting records, the acquisition process (de ex., consistent gifts, unusual gratuities or favours from suppliers or customers), issues of respect for the environment, security and health, lobbying activities, marketing activities, records concerning the workforce, payments to local and international consultants, sensitive / competitive information, practices in human resources (employment, promotion, dismissal, reward, trade union relations, professional training), product safety.

Constituent Parts of an Ethics Audit According Muel Kaptein (1998)

Muel Kaptein (1998, pp. 60-62) identifies 6 parts of an ethics audit that have the role of describing and improving the moral positioning of the organization: *Quality Monitor* – the application of an instrument in order to monitor the extent to which the organization has a certain number of moral qualities; *Scanning the Measures* – the use of the identification and analysis method of the organizational context from the perspective of the impact on organizational ethics and the ability to prevent and / or combat unethical behaviours and incorrect actions. All policies, the system of procedures, rules and regulations, methods and tools, written codes, manuals, job descriptions with the description of tasks and responsibilities, documents, books and descriptions of the organizational mission are taken into account; *Evaluation of Individual Characteristics and Circumstances* – this assessment appreciates employees' relevant moral characteristics (of the intentions, insights, abilities, skills), as well as, the specific circumstances (disadvantageous personal financial situations, family problems, etc.) in which they act; *Decoding the Dilemmas* – is a method used to give the auditor an overview of the potential dilemmas and conflicts of expectations / interests faced by employees at their workplace. These dilemmas and conflicts can be identified through discussion sessions with employees, and through their analysis, the auditor can create a realistic picture of their real moral expectations; *Behaviour Detection* – is a method similar to a lie detector, highlighting the unethical behaviours of employees and the organization as a whole; *Stakeholders' Reflector* – is a tool that brings to attention the expectations of all stakeholder categories that the organization has and the way it is capable of taking them into consideration and to fulfil their needs and interests.

We can observe that the above approach proposed by Kaptein is in its essence a decisional process pattern useful not only to auditors, but also to managers that could initiate an internal audit ethics when is appropriate and needed in their organization.

Stages and Aspects in the Process of Conducting an Ethics Audit

The conduct of the audit involves the collection of a large and comprehensive amount of information. Obtaining it involves accessing multiple sources and going through several stages (Allen, 1995): making direct, on-site observations within the institution (auditors' visits within the institution); analysis of documents with key information (written and published policies and procedures, financial statements, public relations reports, specialized literature), first inspection manual (acc. Allen, 1995); interviews / discussions with the top-management; structured questionnaires and detailed interviews with internal and external stakeholders (employees, senior management, community representatives, representatives of other professional organizations, etc.); final report (main conclusions and recommendations); designing and implementing educational programs as regards ethical topics; corrective measures – change management (*follow-up*); designing / reviewing the ethics manual (optional).

Aspects That Are Assessed During the Ethics Audit Process: Some Examples and Best Practices

In general, among the aspects that can be assessed and monitored through an ethics audit are found: compliance with the legal regulations; the formal (or the informal) ethics management system performance (mission, values, norms, ethical culture, ethical leadership, communication process and methods, specific ethics policies and procedures, methods and tools); values, policies and procedures that serve the rights, values and interests of stakeholders (employees, clients, investors, suppliers, local and central authorities, community, etc.);; ethics of investments and accounting-financial issues; ethics of marketing practices; ethics of human resource management system; social responsibility programs and reporting (if is the case) – aim, types, allocated resources, reporting system.

The study conducted by Agheorghiesei & all (2013) among the quality managers in Romanian hospitals highlighted that the issues considered important by the respondents in conducting an ethics audit integrated in the accreditation process of the hospital units, "should include primarily the respect of the patients' rights, the good relations of the institutions with its patients and the respect of the moral rights of the employees". Other aspects that worth to be assessed (slightly under-average scores) in the opinion of respondents are "concerning the personnel (ethical training, policies regarding loyalty), policies about the management of the institution (the protection of the institution's assets, the voluntary use of instruments for the implementation and monitoring of ethics, the protection of the environment and aspects related to social responsibility, formulation of the organization mission/ vision), but also concerning different aspects of institutional values (evaluation of the organizational culture), professional principles (compliance with international ethical principles) and medical ethics (ethical policies in medical activity, and the activity of ethical and medical research committees)".

Other research conducted by Min-Hua Wu & all (2011) revealed that the structure of an ethics audit within a hospital could include the following six chapters: medical ethics, policies, regulations and leadership; establishment and functioning of medical ethics committees; establishment and functioning of committees related to ethics research committees; medical ethical education; ethical organizational climate; respecting patients' rights and establishing good hospital-patient relationships.

An example of good practice on a hospital's ethical audit is the one conducted at Chris Hani Baragwanath Hospital in 2001 (Landman, Mouton, & Nevhutalu, 2001). According to the objectives and results of the research report, the audited issues were related to key issues and ethical aspects that "are alive in the minds" of several "actors" of the hospital: the general work environment (buildings / infrastructure, resources, security facility) and the impact of its factors on personal attitudes and personal and interpersonal behaviour of employees; the detailed description of ethical culture - the attitudes, beliefs and predominant values that employees have, and what effect they have on their day-to-day conduct in the hospital. Specific ethical issues related to: leadership, management and communication channels have been analysed; human resources issues, standard of care and lack of ethical conduct; problems and sources of stress for employees; the patient's perspective on the correct operation of the hospital medical service. The audit was carried out on the basis of a complex methodology, applied in several stages - focus group, pilot questionnaire, questionnaire survey (multi-stage stratified sampling, 772 employees and 205 patients).

John Rosthorn (2000) signals metaphorically that the ethics audit is "more than a stakeholder toy", that send the message of the importance of this process for the performance of the organisation that in essence has as the final mission to serve de community. In global affairs, the audit check-list of "ethical" investors includes a wide areas that cross the borders between countries, in order to identify "breaches and vulnerabilities" in conducting the desired operations, to avoid the risks that may be induced by specific factors in certain countries, where legal and ethical standards may not be strictly applied. So, they previously asses: the environmental records, the human rights positioning, working under oppressive regimes, military contracts, nuclear power, tobacco and drugs that establish habits, alcoholic beverages, gambling, pornography, prostitution, animal rights / animal testing, intensive farming, the compliance with marketing codes for pharmaceutical substitutes and milk for babies, high-flow banks in the third world.

Merle Ojasco (2016) highlights, however, that although the ethics audit mainly follows the way in which the ethics management and "the pattern of ethical behaviour" are done, current approaches do not analyse or assess the ethical risk or the managerial risk.

Based on the revision of the specialized literature, the above mentioned author offers an improved model of ethics audit, "in the light of stakeholders' interests" and for "preventing the hypocrisy". Ojasco makes the connection between the social responsibility audit and the ethics audit. In his view, the ethics audit is more comprehensive, broader, including under its umbrella the social audit, which, in turn, includes the compliance audit. The improved model of the ethics audit (author Rihma, 2014, presented by Ojasco, 2016) is centred on the analysis and risk assessment. The carried out activities are: interviews and questionnaire-based study applied among stakeholders, business observation tours, document observation. Based on these evaluations, the feedback is provided to the organization management. The model offered by Ojasco (2016, p. 10) presents relatedly, on the one hand, the inputs - taking into account stakeholders' interests, from which the principles of social responsibility will be formulated, which will be pursued (profitability, ethics and sustainability) and in CSR reporting, and, on the other hand, the output – the transparency is ensured, which will generate a low degree of ethical risk, which will lead to increased stakeholders' confidence and in CSR reporting, and finally to a strategic planning of CSR (see Ojasco, 2016, Fig. 4, p.10).

Analysis Points Before Organizing the Conduct of an Ethics Audit

In general, the ethics audit is conducted by an external auditing team in order to ensure the full objectivity and the competency of the process.

In conducting an ethics audit, it must be taken into account that each organization is unique in many terms (mission, strategic objectives, tactics, resources, field of activity, size, management style, employees' expertise and character, values and organizational culture, specific national cultural environment in which operates, etc.), consequently, each audit process is unique.

"Documents do not tell always the whole truth". Therefore the meetings, interviews and discussions with the all categories of personnel is vital. The auditors must spend time to *listen carefully the voice* and *understand the body language of employees* (especially from the bottom line) it in order to identify the real values (not only the declared ones) shared by employees, the ethical climate that predominates in organization and how it supports the work performance, and the leadership style practiced by their managers. Also, the auditors must assure the confidentiality of all data gathered in the auditing process and to assure the employees that their participation is protected against retaliation.

The ethics audit is an expensive process (Menzel, 2007, pp. 72, 82), both in terms of time and financial ones, that is why an objective substantiation of costs is necessary, as well as, an assessment of the resources available to the organization in order to achieve an equilibrated cost-benefit balance. This is a voluntary process, which is not enforced by law, and therefore it requires the support of top-managers of the organization. Its routing can encounter numerous barriers that need to be eliminated through good information, communication and support from their behalf: employees' fear and anxiety about the need for this audit; the need to obtain exhaustive and comprehensive information through the involvement of all members of the organization; the fear of compromising the confidentiality of the information held by the organization (ibidem, 2007, p. 73).

In addition, this ethics audit requires careful selection of the auditor ensuring the process who needs to have more abilities: specific knowledge of the organization and its environment, aspects of organizational authority and culture, the ability to work at the superior management level of an entity, along with the presidents and executive officers, top managers and other members, strong abilities to connect and facilitate with other people, maximum capacity to maintain credibility in a sensitive political environment, specific skills of project management (Fawcett & Wardman, 2008, p. 132).

Once the decision to conduct an ethics audit process is decided, it should take into account the following aspects, highlighted by David Murray (1995, pp.143-145): scope clarification; type of audit and the addressed aspects; managerial context ; the audit process itself; people who will participate in conducting the audit; data analysis and report implementation; tracking and evaluation.

In Table 1 there are examples of questions that can be included in an audit process (based on Rigg, M. & Allen, M. (1994) cited by Susan Schissler Manning, 2003; and Douglas M. Boyle, Dana R. Hermanson and Anne Wilkins, 2011, p. 6; Waring &Daugherty, 2004).

Source: after Susan Schissler Manning, "Ethical Leadership in Human Services: A Multi-Dimensional Approach, Ed. Allyn and Bacon., 2003, Pearson Education, Inc. A P P E N D I X B. Part 3. The Audit with Questions Only (after Rigg, M.

Table 1. Some aspects and types of questions addressed in an ethics audit

Aspects Addressed in the Ethics Audit	Types of Questions
Questions about the policies regarding the top-manager activity	Does the behaviour of the management team demonstrate the organization strong commitment to ethics? Does the management have a clear mission? Does the management take into account the use of mission as the basis for decision-making? Do all the members of the management team know the contents of the mission statement? Does the management team know its responsibilities accurately? If there are family or business relationships in the organization, are there clear policies for addressing these issues? Does the policy management team have clear policies to manage all categories of conflicts of interest? Is there a document with the formulation of values and / or a code of ethics/a code of conduct?; Is this document known to all people in the organization? Is it regularly communicated to employees and other stakeholders? Do managers insist that employees comply with the formulated laws and policies? Do managers represent a good example for employees so that the laws and policies to be applied at the workplace? Are there clear policies regarding the dismissal of people who are repeatedly missing from formal meetings or who fail to fulfil their responsibilities properly? Is free expression of ideas encouraged? Does the management team regularly evaluate its performance?
Questions about the policies regarding the employees' activity	Do the employment policies reflect the diversity of employees? Is there an official anti-discrimination policy? If there are family or business relationships in the organization, are there clear policies for addressing these issues? Do staff policies ensure the correctness to all employees? Are there staff policies regarding the health care and support in case of employees' illness, sick leave or support in case of relatives' illness? Are there clear policies for staff assessment? Are there policies to reward the clear performance? Does the reward program reflect management's commitment to ethics? Do employees have the opportunity to participate in training programs and development opportunities required for their workplace performance? Were there opportunities for employees to participate in ethics awareness programs, other than those specific to the integration of new employees? Does the organization have confidential bodies to which the employees may address if they want to report the unethical behaviours they face within the organization? Can the employees report the unethical behaviours they have observed in the organization, without being afraid of retaliation? Are there clear policies and procedures for penalizing unethical behaviours? do they quickly and effectively penalize those who do not follow the code of ethics? Are there safe, healthy and comfortable working conditions for employees? Do the employees' personal values coincide with those of the department and organization?.

continued on following page

Table 1. Continued

Aspects Addressed in the Ethics Audit	Types of Questions
Questions about the policies regarding the customers	Are there policies aimed at confidentiality of information targeting the customers? Are there policies that seek to gain consensus from customers' side when their data is given to external bodies? Do customers have access to their data records, can they make changes and corrections to them? Are there policies that penalize the social and sexual relationships between clients and staff? Are clients treated with dignity and respect? Is there sufficient information available to customers to evaluate and choose the appropriate services? Are customers fully and honestly informed of alternative services that can be made available to them? Are there appropriate policies and procedures for customers who are dissatisfied with the offered services? Are the services offered without discrimination? Is the organization program accessible to customers in terms of location, timetable, facilities?

& Allen, M. (1994). The ethics audit checklist. In Conducting an ethics audit: A checklist for nonprofits (pp. 53–59). Colorado Association for Nonprofit Organizations (CANPO))"; and Douglas M. Boyle, Dana R. Hermanson, & Anne Wilkins (2011), p. 6; Waring &Daugherty, 2004.

When and How an Ethics Audit Should Be Conducted

Carrying out an ethics audit is expensive because it involves a broad and consistent range of resources (human, financial, informational, time). Generally, an ethics audit should be conducted every 3-5 years, but with the condition that the organization make constant monitoring of ethics and managerial policies and procedures, and to observe closely the behaviour of staff and the all activities.

The ethics audit must be focused on the specifics of each organization, depending on its size, the industry in which it conducts the activity, the corporate culture, the identified risks and the legal environment in which it operates (Ferrell, Fraedrich,& Ferrell, 2012, p. 216).

In Eric Krell's approach (2010), the steps for effectively conducting process of an ethics audit include: starting with a detailed grounding (the more detailed the policies and procedures, the better a better comparison can be made between the current behaviour of employees and standard, as defined therein); the development of metrics ("tangible ethical measures are put into practice" - the ethics objectives of the annual performance system, the reward-ethical behaviour relationship); setting up a transfunctional team (professional human resources, ethics and compliance manager, internal auditor, legal manager); effective auditing (avoiding disruptions in activity that can occur by implementing the audit, combining efforts with other evaluation teams, scheduling interviews with employees, obtaining information to be evaluated, and any process that will not require observation in the organization); correlation with other aspects (identifying other opportunities for improvement and sharing with colleagues, such as the impact of ethics in sales on recognition in financial reporting); consistent response and communication (application of disciplinary measures in case of violation of ethical standards in line with policies, procedures and codes of ethics; introduction of ethics lessons learned through communication and training programs):

Ferrell, Fraedrich &Ferrell (2012) suggest six steps that need to be followed for the effective conduct of an audit: *Getting the total support from the top management and / or the board of directors of the company; Appointing a committee or a team to monitor the audit process* (ideally it would be the financial audit committee of the board of directors, but in most cases these are the ethics managers or officers who are in charge with the conduct of the audit); the committee has the mission of recruiting employees inside the company, or external consultants to conduct the audit process and report its results; *Establishing the scope of the audit* – of the key issues to be assessed and the risk areas (these also depend on the type of business, the risks faced by the organization, and the "opportunities available to manage ethics"); *Examining organization's mission, values, objectives and policies*. At this stage, the formal documents are analysed, which show the commitment of the organization to the sum of ethical, legal and social responsibilities, as well as less formal documents (marketing materials, labour force policies, policies and standards of ethics for suppliers and sellers. The stage has the aim of establishing the "ethical priorities and their articulation in a set of parameters or performance indicators, which are to be assessed objectively and quantitatively"; *Identifying the tools and methods needed to measure the progress of the organization and collecting and analysing relevant information* (the analysis of some internal and external documents, formal discussions with stakeholders in order to identify how they perceive the company, confirmation with the accounting records of the company). Similarly, it is useful to analyse how other organizations, from the same field, work on the issue; *Calling an external party to analyse the results of the conducted analysis.*

Boyle, Hermanson, & Wilkins (2011) suggest that the first step should be that of *educating* the managers (but also the board of directors and the audit committee) regarding the value of an ethics audit, in order to obtain their support. The second step would be to talk to these parties in order to identify the optimal ethical values, which are desirable in that organization. The third step, in the view of the particular authors, is the identification and evaluation of the risks that arise from non-compliance with the respective ethical values. The fourth step involves an action plan of the ethics audit using a risk-based approach. Step five requires structured interviews at the entity level or opinion polls conducted through the entire organization in order to verify whether the values of organization set by senior management are in line with those of the employees' vision, at all organizational levels. Step Six involves reporting the results to authorized parties and the last step implementing and monitoring an action plan in areas where improvements are needed.

THE ROLE OF ETHICS AUDIT IN SOCIAL ASSITANCE/WORK

The values and ethics are essential elements in the practice of social assistance (Akhtar, 2012, p. 14). In social assistance, the professional "is constantly involved in judgments in which the conflicting values must be weighed carefully" and faces a number of different situations, sometimes contradictory or questionable, in which he/she has to make decisions" (Beckett, Maynard, &Jordan, 2017). Social assistants have a "complex liability" generated by the fact that "in any given situation… they have a range of responsibilities that can collide simultaneously (Akhtar, 2012, p. 17). The particularity of social assistants' work consists in the fact that they are working with a special category of service users, with special needs, sometimes with limited legal capacity, however the result of work must be beneficial for them and for the community in general. Values can be competing, in conflict, even though those are provided by law for these users, which, due to problems and vulnerabilities (sometimes people with mental disabilities) that they have, they may end up not accepting the aid for their own benefit, they can hurt themselves or even others. These values are the right to personal freedom, the right of the general public to protection, the right, under certain circumstances, to be protected from oneself (Akhtar, 2012, p. 17). Some values and principles stipulated by law may not be easy to assure in practice due to the way the government policies are applied at local or national level (for instance, the priorities depending on available funds), or the way they come into conflict with the principles of professional ethics. The tension in the work of the social assistants is the result of the conflict that can be manifested by the clash of personal values with professional values, the values of the agency in which they work and the values of society, influenced, in turn, by other cultural values, the values of other agencies, the values of other professions (doctors, lawyers, teachers) and the personal values of others (see figure 1.2., authors Beckett, Maynard, &Jordan, 2017).

The ethics audit should ensure that social work professionals promote ethical values specific to the profession and organization in which they work, and know to correctly identify and solve the ethical dilemmas in everyday work.

The value matrix offered by Farrukh Nahid Akhtar (2012, p. 17), which has in its core the values, groups four aspects to which the professional in social work must adhere in social work activity: professional codes of practice (promoting professional values towards vulnerable people, and ways of dealing with them), laws and policies (the social worker must understand the system of benefits in which the service is delivered, must reflect and decide who is entitled to it; moreover, the "social workers employed by municipalities, government agencies, public organizations may be in conflict with norms, laws and regulations", which they may consider to be "unfair", according to Guttmann, 2013, p. 160), the reflective practice and the anti-discriminatory practice (reflection and critical analysis of the situation involving ethical issues).

These elements are, in our opinion, the main milestones that must guide the ethics audit process of how to take into account the ethical values that support the whole activity and behaviour of the social worker: what are the personal and professional values shared by the social worker? are these in conflict? how does he/she make a decision in case of a conflict of ethical values? which is the level of commitment and responsibility towards the client? to what level does the social worker share personal values with the social service user? what is the reflection process and what are the steps taken to solve an ethical dilemma in his/her work? how does he/she decide on what social services one can benefit from? how does the social worker react when he/she observes that his/her colleagues are providing an incompetent service, for various reasons (mental illness, inappropriate behaviour)? what does the social worker do if he/she notices fraud actions or conflicts of interest? to what extent is the activity of the social assistant negatively influenced by ideologies and politics? how does the social worker position himself/herself towards the mission, the reputation, the code of ethics and the regulations of the agency he/she works in? do the values of his/her profession reflect his/her behaviour from his private life?

In the domain of social assistance, Frederic G. Reamer (2013, p. 213) suggests the ethics audit in order to provide the social workers with a "practical framework" on which to "critically examine and analyse the ways in which a wide range of critical issues are addressed". Moreover, it is considered the most effective way to avoid complaints and processes related to ethics. Opportunities that are made available to social workers through ethics audit are numerous: they can identify specific ethical issues in their work with the target client, the type of treatment, the design of the program, the staff; to analyse and review ethics policies and procedures; to design an appropriate strategy to review procedures, so as to prevent potential complaints and lawsuits; to monitor the implementation of a quality strategy.

In the view of this author, the ethics audit is mainly addressed in terms of risk.

Based on specialized literature, Reamer (2000) identifies two significant aspects, which constitute the foundation of an ethics audit: the extent to which social workers have the essential knowledge, i.e. they are familiar with the ethical risks known in practice, based on empirical data that synthesizes the complaints and processes that have taken place against the social workers, and findings and dispositions of ethics committees and bodies; and the current procedures and protocols of the agency for managing ethical issues, dilemmas and decisions. The risk management - that is "assessing the extent to which agencies and social assistants have procedures to identify risks and to prevent the complaints and ethics-related disputes", it is a fundamental function of the ethics audit.

The author enumerates and describes in detail 15 areas to be assessed from the risk perspective in an ethics audit, in the practice of social assistance. The audit should analyse the existence and adequacy of policies and procedures application for each of these aspects, the extent to which they generate risks in the work of the social assistant and the degree of the risk (Table 2).

Also, Reamer lists 10 key steps in implementing an ethics audit in social assistance agencies: appointing a chairperson of the ethics audit committee among the agency staff, who will demonstrate an interest in the agency's ethics policies, practices and procedures; using as a guide a list of major risks to be investigated by the audit committee in order to identify the ethical issues on which the analysis should focus; establishing, by the audit committee, the type of data required to implement the ethics audit (for instance, the source of data could be document analysis with customer rights and the informed consent, interviews, surveys based on questionnaires among staff, the analysis of legal regulations in the field, discussions with lawyers, records with customer data ...); assessing the level of risk associated with each aspect identified in the stage of data collection and analysis, at policy and procedure level; establishing, at the end of the audit, the assertive steps to ensure the constructive use of the findings, emerged from the implemented process; setting priorities in addressing the areas of concern, depending on the degree of risk assessed and the available resources; identifying measures to address problems in the identified areas; appointing responsible persons concerned with problem solving, setting tasks and deadlines; identifying mechanisms for monitoring tasks and implementing them; documenting the conduct of the ethics audit process (which may be useful in the case of a complaint or trial, a guarantee that efforts have been made to address the ethical issues by the social agency).

Based on the Social Work Ethics Audit risk management tool proposed by Reamer (2001), McAuliffe (2005) conducted a research ("a pilot ethics test") in eleven social work government and non-government agencies "with a health focus" (hospitals, community health service, community-based women's health service, counselling agencies, disability support service community, small volunteer-based service community for adoptions) to determine whether ethics audit is applicable "to human services in the Australian context". The study was conducted under the consideration that the ethics audit could be "an adjunct" to the quality assurance and accreditation processes.

Table 2. Areas to be assessed in the ethics audit in the work of the social assistant – approach by Frederic G. Reamer (2000)

Areas to be Assessed in the Ethics Audit	Aspects / Policies and Practices to Avoid the Risk
Customer Rights	The existence of confidentiality and privacy policies; providing the information; informed consent; access to services; access to recorded data; service plans; alternative options for services and references; the right to refuse the services provided by the agency; the conditions for terminating the services provided; procedures regarding the complaints.
Confidentiality and privacy	Adequacy of policies and procedures used by social workers in requesting personal information belonging to clients; Disclosure of confidential information that / about: protects the customers from self-harm or third parties from damage that can be induced by customers; the treatment for alcohol consumption or substance abuse; deceased clients; are offered to parents or guardians; mass-media representatives, legal authorities; service protection agencies; other social service agencies; are shared between family counsellors, couples, groups, marriages.
Informed consent	The documents and procedures regarding the disclosure of confidential information, receiving schedule, service delivery, video and audio recordings. The conditions in which informed consent is offered and obtained to the customer – lack of coercion and unwanted influence, the mental capacity of the client at the time of signing and his / her consent to specific procedures and actions, informing the clients of their rights to refuse the signature, the layout of sufficient information for making the decision, valid consent forms and procedures.
Service delivery	Policies and procedures for social workers to provide customer service only within the limits of education, professional training, licensing, certification, received consultancy, supervised experience, other professional experience
Border issues and the conflict of interest	The existence of clear criteria that help the social workers to maintain adequate collaboration limits with current and former clients in terms of sexual relations, friendships, meetings in public places, physical contact, receiving gifts, avoiding conflicts of financial interests, providing services for two or more people who are in relationships with each other (family, couple), participation in customers' social or life events, the trade of goods and services with customers, the self-disclosure of information to customers.
Defamation of the character	The policies and procedures demonstrating that social workers have training, which ensures that in the documentation used and the communication about the clients and employees he/she avoids using the language that could lead to the defamation of the character.
Supervision	The policies and procedures to ensuring that the social assistants have documentation regarding the nature of their supervising activity realized to the client (providing the necessary information to supervisees in order to obtain the informed consent, identifying and resolving the customer-related errors, protecting the third parties, detection and termination of negligent or prolonged treatment plans for a particular client, regular meetings with supervisees, analysis and approval of supervisee's records, decisions and actions, adequate coverage in the absence of the supervisee).

continued on following page

Table 2. Continued

Areas to be Assessed in the Ethics Audit	Aspects / Policies and Practices to Avoid the Risk
Professional training	Policies and procedures demonstrating that social assistants have had access to training programs on ethics topics (relevant practical skills, professional ethics and liability, legal regulations).
Consultation	The existence of appropriate procedures to receive and use third-party consultancy with specialized expertise (colleagues, members of other professional alliances).
Customer recommendation	Policies and procedures showing that clients are advised to well-known colleagues and credibility practitioners, when social workers do not have adequate expertise and time to respond appropriately to the client's need.
Fraud	The existence and implementation of policies and procedures that help to avoid the fraud (avoiding employees' falsification of records, clinical diagnosis, exaggerated to obtain payments from third parties, payments from third parties for services that have not been provided).
Termination of service	The criteria and procedures for avoiding spontaneous abandonment of the agency by the social worker without recommending the client to a practitioner; leaving a vulnerable client by the assistant, who has not paid a residual balance; the lack of social assistance in emergency situations or the lack of adequate training of the client to react in such situations.
Impairment of the practitioner	The extent to which social assistance practitioners understand the nature and possible causes of professional impairment (offering poor quality services, failure to meet professional responsibilities as a result of substance abuse or mental illness, involvement in sexual relations with clients, etc.), are alert when they recognize the signs and have procedures to identify and resolve this situation.

Source: elaborated after Frederic G. Reamer, *The Social Work Ethics Audit: A Risk-Management Strategy*, Social Work, Vol. 45, No. 4 (July 2000), pp. 355-366, Oxford University Press, http://www.jstor.org/stable/23718779

Besides the conclusion of the study on the importance and usefulness of ethics audit, it is worth noting that the methodology and the ethics auditing process must be adapted according to the context and specificity of every institution, field of activity and country.

INSTEAD OF CONCLUSION

The rich literature on ethics audit topic demonstrates that it has already earned his right place in the panoply of managerial assessing methods. The ethics audit practice is increasingly adopted in the management of organizations that want to manage the weak points and vulnerabilities accurately in due time, and identify the risks that could negatively affect their activity and outcomes. It is the signal that managers give to their stakeholders as they care about their interests and expectations in terms of ethics and responsibility. It is a preventive but also a corrective treatment. However there is no recipe. Implementing an audit process is costly and can also have negative effects (such as fear and frustration on the part of employees). In social care, ethics audit is a "support stick" for social workers who often face complex situations and ethical dilemmas in providing service to clients with special needs. Through ethics auditing, it is possible to discover on time what does not work well and what can be improved in activity. However, taking into account the specificity of the activity, it is necessary to adopt public policies that promote uniformly this practice and legitimize the spending of resources for this purpose. Moreover, it is necessary to train internal and external auditors to fully understand how the particularities of providing social assistance services in the interest of the individual and society. Managers have the key-mission to build an authentic ethical culture based on ethical leadership, the ground on which ethics audits to be regularly applied in order to improve organizational activity and quality of service, consistent with the increasingly challenging environment and the demanding requirements of the stakeholders. Overall, ensuring a high quality service in every organization can be guaranteed by an ethics audit as it alerts early on the neuralgic points in carrying out the activities. From this point of view, the ethics audit, if properly and rigorously conducted, can become a reliable „partner" in the process of quality assurance and institutional accreditation.

REFERENCES

Agheorghiesei, D. T., Iliescu, L., Gavrilovici, C., & Oprea, L. (2013). What is to be expected from an ethics audit integrated within the accreditation process of hospitals from Romania? *Iranian Journal of Public Health*, *42*(7), 737–747. PMID:24427752

Agheorghiesei (Corodeanu), D.T. (2013). Etica în Administrația Publică. Ed. Tritonic. București.

Akhtar, F. N. (2012). *Mastering Social Work Values and Ethics*. Jessica Kingsley Publishers.

Allen, M.B. (1995). The ethics audit. *Nonprofit World*, *13*(A6), 51.

Beckett, C., Maynard, A., & Jordan, P. (2017). Values and Ethics in Social Work. *Sage*.

Boyle, D. M., Hermanson, D. R., & Wilkins, A. (2011). *Ethics Audits: Implications for Internal Auditors Internal Auditing*. ProQuest Central.

Carroll, A., & Buchholtz, A. K. (2012). Business & society: ethics, sustainability, and stakeholder management. South-Western Cengage Learning.

Dimitrescu, F. (1997). *Dicţionar de cuvinte recente*. Audit. LOGOS SRL.

Fawcett, G., & Wardman, M. (2008). Ethical governance in local government in England: A regulator's view. In Ethics and integrity of governance: perspectives across frontiers. Edward Elgar. doi:10.4337/9781848441378.00018

Ferrell, O. C. (2016). A Framework for Understanding Organisational Ethics. In P. E. Peterson & O. C. Ferrell (Eds.), *Business Ethics: New Challenges for Business Schools and Corporate Leaders: New Challenges for Business Schools and Corporate Leaders*. London: Routledge.

Ferrell, O. C., Fraedrich, J., & Ferrell, L. (2012). *Business Ethics: Ethical Decision Making & Cases*. South-Western Publishing. SUA.

Francis, R., & Armstrong, A. (2003). Ethics as a risk management strategy: The Australian experience. *Journal of Business Ethics*, *45*(4), 375–385. doi:10.1023/A:1024163831371

Garçia-Marza, D. (2005). Trust and Dialogue: Theoretical Approaches to Ethics Auditing. *Journal of Business Ethics*, *57*(3), 209–219. doi:10.1007/s10551-004-8202-7

Guttmann, D. (2013). *Ethics in Social Work: A Context of Caring*. Routledge.

Hofmann, P. (1995). Performing an ethics audit. *Healthcare Executive Journal*, *10*(6).

Hofmann, P. (2006). The Value of an Ethics Audit. *Healthcare Executive Journal*, *21*(2).

Hofmann, P. B. (2012). *Fear of Conflict: Management and Ethical Costs. Healthcare Executive, 27, 1*. ProQuest Central.

Jeurissen, R., & van der Putten, F. P. (2007). Ethics in international business. In Ethics in business. Van Gorcum.

Kaptein, M. (1998). *Ethics Management: Auditing and Developing the Ethical Content of Organizations*. Dordrecht: Kluwer. doi:10.1007/978-94-011-4978-5

Krell, E. (2010). How to Conduct an Ethics Audit, An ethics audit can reveal gaps in your ethics policies and practices. *HR Magazine*. Available at https://www.shrm.org/hr-today/news/hr-magazine/pages/0410agenda_social.aspx

Landman, W. A., Mouton, J., & Nevhutalu, K. H. (2001). *Chris Hani Baragwanath Hospital Ethics Audit*. Research Report No. 2. Available at https://www.tei.org.za/phocadownloadpap/Research_Reports/CHBHFinalReport.pdf

McAuliffe, D. (2005, December). Putting ethics on the organisational agenda: The social work ethics audit on trial. *Australian Social Work*, *58*(4), 357–369. doi:10.1111/j.1447-0748.2005.00232.x

McAuliffe, D. (n.d.). *Social Work Ethics Audits: A New Tool for Ethical Practice*. Retrieved from http://citeseerx.ist.psu.edu/viewdoc/download?doi=10.1.1.202.1345&rep=rep1&type=pdf

McDonald, G., & Nijhof, A. (1999). Beyond codes of ethics: an ntegrated framework for stimulating morally responsible behaviour in organisations. *Leadership and Organization Development Journal*, *20*(3), 133-146. Available from Deakin Research Online: http://hdl.handle.net/10536/DRO/DU:30024095

McDonald, G. M. (2009). An anthology of codes of ethics. *European Business Review*, *21*(4), 344–372. doi:10.1108/09555340910970445

Menzel, D. C. (2007). *Ethics management for public administrators: building organizations of integrity*. Armonk, NY: M.E. Sharpe.

Menzel, D. C. (2016). *Ethics Management for Public and Nonprofit Managers: Leading and Building Organizations of Integrity*. Routledge.

Murray, D. J. (1995). *Ethics in organisations*. London: Kogan Page.

Ojasoo, M. (2016). CSR Reporting, stakeholder engagement and preventing hypocrisy through ethics audit. *Journal of Global Entrepreneurship Research*, *6*(1), 14. doi:10.1186/s40497-016-0056-9

Ramamoorti, S., & Luke, E.R. (2011, Aug. 1). The corporate ethics audit: to prevent and detect management fraud, internal auditors must have a sound understanding of human behavior. *Internal Auditor*.

Reamer, F. G. (2000). The Social Work Ethics Audit: A Risk-Management Strategy. Social Work, 45(4), 355–366. Available at http://www.jstor.org/stable/23718779

Reamer, F. G. (2013). *Social Work Values and Ethics*. Columbia University Press.

Rosthorn, J. (2000). Business Ethics Auditing – More Than a Stakeholders Toy. *Journal of Business Ethics*, *27*(1/2), 9–19. doi:10.1023/A:1006414502730

Sears, B. P. (1993). *Auditing business ethics. The Internal Auditor, 50(3),* 38. ProQuest Central.

Treviño, L. K., & Nelson, K. A. (2011). *Managing business ethics: Straight talk about how to do it right*. Wiley.

Ungureanu, S. Autoritatea Națională de Management al Calității în Sănătate (ANMCS). (2017). *Managementul riscului clinic componentă esențială a siguranței pacientului în unitățile sanitare. Auditul Clinic*. Available at www.sanatateromania.ro

Waring, C. G., & Daugherty, C. A. (2004). Auditing Ethics-Make Them an Offer They Can't Refuse Waring. *The Journal of Government Financial Management*, *53*(1), 34. ProQuest Central.

Wieland, J. (2003). Standards and audits for ethics management systems: the European perspective: with 4 tables. Springer. doi:10.1007/978-3-662-05107-8

Wu, M.-H., Liao, C.-H., Chiu, W.-T., Lin, C.-Y., & Yang, C.-M. (2011). Can we accredit hospital ethics? A tentative proposal. *Journal of Medical Ethics*, *37*(8), 493-7.

Chapter 13
The Assurance of the Quality of Social Services Through Supervision or Accreditation and Possible Ethical Dilemmas:
The Case of the Republic of Moldova

Svetlana Haraz
Free International University of Moldova (ULIM), Moldova

Teodor Vicol
National Council of Accreditation of the Provider of Social Services, Moldova

ABSTRACT

The profession of social work promotes the social change, the resolution or diminution of social problems and contribution to the development of social autonomy of the individual in order to increase his/her welfare. One of the most efficient ways of professional improvement of social workers is represented by implementing a complex process of supervision which involve the analysis and observance of the whole activity of social work. In this context, the accreditation of the providers of social services is the identification of their capacity to provide qualitative social services to people and to increase the responsibility for respecting the minimal standards of quality, regardless the type of property, legal form of organization and administrative subordination. In this work, we will present the experience of the Republic of Moldova in the development of the mechanism of supervision in the context of social services integrated and the process of accreditation of the providers of social services.

DOI: 10.4018/978-1-5225-3090-9.ch013

INTRODUCTION

The profession of social work promotes the social change, the resolution or diminishing of social problems and contribution to the development of social autonomy of the individual in order to increase his/her welfare. Based on the theories of social work and the knowledge of social systems, the activity of social workers is focusing on the continuous interaction between the individual's social system and the general social systems in order to facilitate the planned social changes.

One of the most efficient ways of professional improvement of social workers is represented by implementing a complex process of supervision which involves the analysis and observance of the whole activity of social work.

The supervision should support the social workers in order to build productive professional relations, to develop good practices and to exercise the professional thinking and the discretion in taking decisions. For a good and efficient supervision, it is necessary to have a combination of the systemic and complex approach of the professional skills, with the process of supervision and continuous interviewing according to the individual needs of the specialist and, to the profession requirements.

In this context, the accreditation of the providers of social services is the identification of their capacity to provide qualitative social services, and to increase the responsibility for respecting the minimal standards of quality, regardless of the type of property, legal form of organization and administrative subordination.

It is important to be understood that the accreditation of the providers of social services contributes to increasing the efficiency and improvement of the quality of social services, as well as to defend the rights and interests of the beneficiaries of the given services.

Respectively, the complex approach by accreditation and continuous supervision ensures the quality of social services and the efficiency of functioning of the integrated systems of social services.

BACKGROUND

Modern practices of providing qualitative social services play an important role in providing some qualitative services. The social field is the domain where the "human being" is both the object of research actions, and the object of assistance, he/she is the beneficiary of services, as well as the "indicator" of quality of the social services, of the specialists' performance. The feed-back received from the beneficiaries of different social services has an undeniable value in the process of quality assuring.

The issue of ethics in the field of supervision is discussed by many authors and presents an increased interest for the researchers of the domain, as well as for the practitioners that apply the results of the epistemological pursuit. That is why we will refer to the works of Bogo and McKnight (2005), Harkness and Poertner (1989) and Tsui (1997) who established, in their investigations, that the previous reviews of supervision research have noted the dearth of studies, the limited knowledge that they provide for practice and the need for a clear research agenda, for social work supervision reviewed twenty-six studies to determine whether supervision assisted clients. They found that the majority was focused on the supervisor and supervisee dyad, and none was focused on client outcomes. To remedy this deficit, proposed that the research agenda should concern the contribution that supervision makes to client outcomes.

We can conclude that the supervision problematic is in a tight relation with the professional ethics, being indispensable in the professional activity and providing qualitative services. The process of supervision shares such values as responsibility, respect for autonomy, justice, diversity, equity, as well as all other values proper to the social work domain.

MAIN FOCUS OF THE CHAPTER

The goal of the chapter: we will present the issue of ethics in the activity of supervision of the professionals from the social domain by analysing the data gathered in the process of evaluation of providers of social services in order to accredit them.

The research was developed in the Republic of Moldova, but we will make a correlation with the data presented in works internationally. We analysed the scientific literature on the subject “Ethics in supervision in the social domain”.

The objectives of the research: to clarify the issue of ethics in supervision in the context of the procedure of accreditation of the providers of social services; to analyse available information on ethical dilemmas in supervision, at international level.

Methods, procedures and techniques of research: we used the inductive strategy specific to the qualitative research and the methods: (i) *proper observation* of the present phenomena (facts were observed and registered without selection or suppositions), (ii) *documents' analysis* (content analysis, generalizations derived inductively as relations between facts using such technics as conversation, synthesis, conclusions); (iii) mini-surveys (questionnaire, presenting data in numerical and percentage value, structured and arranged in tables and figures).

Issues in Supervision Process

According to Sandu (2015, p. 14), the favourite area of the contemporary deontology is the professional one. In the professional field, there are some minimalistic standards that derive rationally from the status and role of the professional in a certain domain.

In the same work, the author refers to the significance of the term *ethical axiology,* which, according to the mentioned authors (Sandu & Caras (Frunză), 2014; Caras, Sandu, 2014), generally means the world of moral values, and in the context of professional ethics – the constitutive ethical values of the given profession. In the practice of regulating the standards of ethics, the (operational) value, simultaneously with the principle that includes it, being followed by an explanation of its social applicability.

The supervision within the social framework is correlated to the activity of the social worker. He/she is supervised, i.e. accompanied in his/her activity on the case, in the activity of analysing and identifying the ways of action – the most beneficial for the client of social services. Cojocaru St. (2005) considers that there are some confusing situations regarding the supervising of social service or social program. According to the most part of specialized literature, the supervision / supervising is an activity of transferring of knowledge, skills, attitudes from an experienced person – the person resource – to another person with less experience. The whole activity involves theoretical and practical knowledge regarding the client and the social system. Kadushin and Harkness (2002) present the functions of the supervising process. Thus, they underline the fact that in the first issues of the specialized literature related to the given subject, the supervision has two basic functions: *administrative* (function that assures the activities accomplished according to the values, procedures and policies of the organizations, maintaining the organizational control) and *educative* (transmitting knowledge related to the skills of social work from an experienced person to another one, less experienced). The authors recognize these functions that the supervising social worker should apply in his/her activity, but they consider that these two functions don't give a complete definition of the concept of "supervision" in the given context; thus, they mention and emphasize the importance of the third function, namely that of *support.* According to this function, the supervisor has the responsibility to morally support the social worker; he/she should help the social worker in case of discouragement and dissatisfaction with the job, giving him/her the feeling of belonging to the organization and the feeling of safety in realizing the activity in order to achieve high performances (Holunga, 2013).

The efficiency of functioning of the integrated system of social services depends on the level of professional performances of the providers of social services. These involves the implementation of the culture of professional supervision and evaluation of the performances for the employees of the system of social work, organized by the types of services, areas of responsibilities and levels of competence.

The professional supervision is an important component of the system of social work, additionally being involved the Territorial Structure of Social Work (TSSW) – supervisor – supervised employee. The improvement of the professional performances of the social workers has a direct influence on the situation of the beneficiaries and contributes to the increase of the quality of provided services.

The concept of supervision is relatively new for the system of social work of the Republic of Moldova, and its implementation is based on the following documents: The mechanism of supervising in social work, approved by the Order of MPSFC nr.99, 31.12.2008, the Guide of implementation of the mechanism of supervising in social work, approved by the Oder MMPSF 5 nr.15, 10.11.2009.

The Goal of the professional supervision consists of improving the quality of social services provided to the beneficiaries by assuring the opportunities of professional and personal growth of the employed staff, acknowledgement of the roles and responsibilities, as by contributing to the organizational development or service development (Rîjicova & Grigoraş, 2017).

The studies regarding the supervision are mainly focused on defining what supervision is (Tsui, 2008), what are the tasks of the supervisors (Kadushin, 1992), and what are the functions of supervision (Hawkins and Shohet, 1989). These studies are very often concentrated on the experience of the professional qualified personnel, and, as usually, they don't explore the impact of the intervention of supervising (inclusively the costs and benefits), consequently it is difficult to know if a certain type of intervention of supervising is more efficient than another. In this context, some researchers carried out a practical survey regarding the best practices in the field of supervision. They present a series of findings regarding the application of supervision in social work and provision of social services that result in the following scheme:

The identified areas are in a tight connection and determine the performing of supervision, as the impact of supervision, and finally the benefits directly felt by the client.

Social work supervision is a process through which an organization provides support and guidance to social workers. Supervision should be made up of a variety of components. Godden Joe (2012) supports the following definition of supervision: "Supervision must enable and support workers to build effective professional relationships, develop good practice, and exercise both professional judgment and discretion in decision-making. For supervision to be effective, it needs to combine a performance management approach with a dynamic, empowering and enabling supervisory relationship. Supervision should improve the quality of practice, support the development of integrated working and ensure continuing professional

Figure 1. Interconnection of the supervision areas
Source: (Lambley & Marrable, 2013).

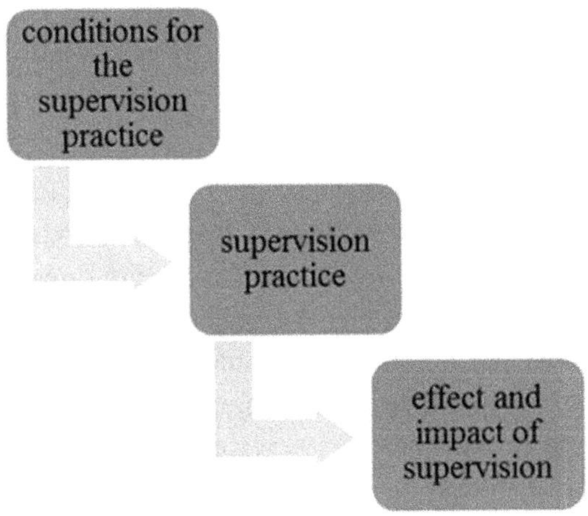

development. Supervision should contribute to the development of a learning culture by promoting an approach that develops the confidence and competence of managers in their supervision skills. It is therefore at the core of individual and group continuing professional development".

The analysis of the studies on supervision and the procedure / license of the providers of social services allows us to *establish* the following observations:

- The quality of social services depends mainly on the professional training of the social worker or of the other professional that provides social services;
- The professional qualification of the social worker or other professional of the social domain depends on the initial training, continuous development and professional supervision;
- The accreditation/license of the provider of social services is tightly related to the quality of professional training of the social worker/professional of the social domain;
- The accreditation/license of the providers of social services and the supervision of the professional require clear regulations and efficient methodology with applicable tools.

Assurance of the Quality of Social Services by Supervision and Accreditation and Possible Ethical Dilemmas

Frequently cited aspects related to care quality include the accessibility to services, responsibility, attitudes and behaviour of the staff, the continuity of the workers in the care process, the fluid communication of changes in the care process, the flexibility of the service in emergency cases, unexpected changes in the private life, the dignity, reliability and capacity of reaction of the workers from the care domain, as well as the competences, knowledge and the trust of the staff. The identification of the indicators of good quality in social work of any of those three groups represents a complex task.

First of all, the services are described as "performances", in such a way that their products are intangible and cannot be measured, counted, tested or checked so easy; they are rather "experimental" merchandise that require direct contact in order to establish some of its most valuable characteristics.

Secondly, the services of social work are intensive regarding the labour forces, fact that could lead to a high degree of heterogeneity of the services.

As a result, the performance of the services could vary significantly from a producer to another, from the producer to the customer (Malley & Fernández, 2010).

The European Union supports every citizen, mainly the disadvantaged one that could count on the qualitative social services as:

- Education and care for young children;
- Long-time care for elder people;
- Long-time care for people with disabilities;
- Social work (social work or benefits);
- Social living places;
- Training and services for integrating in the labour market.

Qualitative social services represent an intelligent and sustainable investment. As the Social Investments Package (SIP) specifies, they:

- Help to avoid personal crises;
- Make the inactive people to become active;
- Allow people to face their personal challenges.

Social Services are the subject of an intensive demand for quality and effectiveness. All the European Member States have embarked in a so-called process of modernization of their social services. The common challenge in this process is to tackle the tensions between universality, quality and financial sustainability. In many member states of the European Union, social services are currently undergoing transformation as a consequence of political, economic and social redirection. As result of the modernization of the social sector, the social service sector is developing into a more open and competitive market. This will have consequences for the quality approaches that will be applied:

- Quality approaches should facilitate a process on self-evaluation on performance against criteria;
- Quality approaches should also encourage the quality development with service providers;
- Certification of quality and accreditation of services could be used to assure the quality of the service provider and eliminate bad services in the market.

A major pre-condition for quality of social sector is access to these services, which means that the services are affordable, available, and accessible.

Therefore the quality of services should be a question of combining choice of the individual user, availability and affordability of services with some basic quality guarantees.

The quality management approaches can be presented in two groups: international concepts and local Member State initiatives (Quality of Social Services in Europe, 2014). Both groups are used in the European Member States: International concepts are implemented in the social service sector at national level and also locally, quality approaches have been developed and implemented. Most of the local quality initiatives in the European Member State in the social service sector have been inspired by and based on the international concepts. There are a large variety of different quality approaches that can be applied in social services. In order to create an overview of this complex topic, a limited number of approaches will be analysed and described. A most important criterion for selection was that the quality approach could be applied in all types of social services at national and international level.

The overall quality of life of the person served or client satisfaction, as well as the capacity of the services to respond objectively to users, are considered as a key outcome in evaluating and monitoring social services.

Figure 2. Common quality framework for social services of general interest
Source:(Van Beek, 2010)

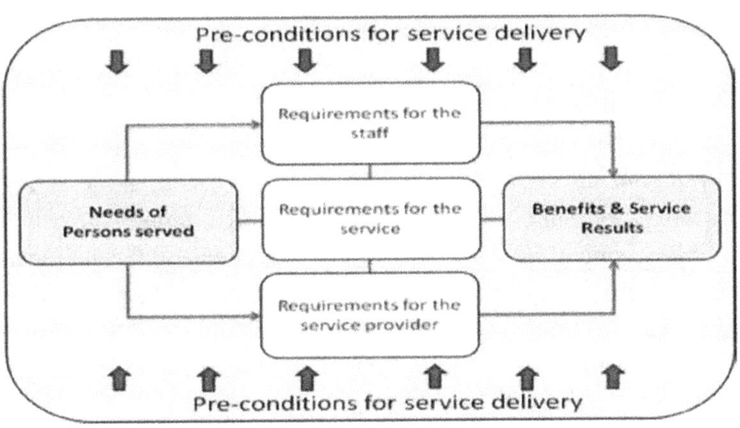

The relationship between the domains and the principles for quality is characterised as interdependent and should not be viewed or evaluated isolated from the framework. The figure illustrates a process that links the needs of persons served to those who have responsibilities in providing the service to the person (service providers and staff) and characteristics of the provided service itself, with the aim of creating appropriate outcomes and benefits for the person served. The needs of the persons served in the provision of services are reflected in the principles: *Rights* and *Participation*. The shared responsibilities of the regulators of Social Services of General Interest (SSGI) for creating and facilitating a context in which the quality services can be delivered, being expressed by the blue arrows: the preconditions for service delivery.

In case of the Republic of Moldova, which tends towards the European vector of development, the sphere of social services is in the developmental stage. In the last 10 years, new services were developed, the programs of social work were implemented having as goal the adaptation of the issues related to the integration of disadvantaged groups to the international standards, the Law regarding the accreditation of the providers of social services was adopted. Beginning with 2008, a new "philosophy" was adopted in providing services that involved the reorganization of the system of social work, assuring the decentralization and unitary approach of the social problems, as well as the assurance of the quality of providing social services by elaborating minimal standards for every provided social service (Decision of the Government of the Republic of Moldova nr. 1512, 2008).

Referring to the *assurance of quality by accrediting the social services,* we will thoroughly analyse some models at the national and international levels.

Accreditation of Providers of Social Services in the Republic of Moldova

In the *Republic of Moldova,* there are a series of normative acts that specifically stipulate the elaboration and implementation of the mechanism of accreditation and assessment of the social services' providers since 2007. We will enumerate only some acts of major strategic importance in the reform of the system of social protection and social assistance:

1. *"The national strategy and Plan of actions regarding the reform of the residential system of child's care for 2007-2012" approved by the Decision of the Government No.784, 09.07.2007.* The goal of the national strategy regarding the reform of the residential system of child's care for 2007-2012 represents the assurance and respecting of the child's rights to grow up in the familial environment (Decision of the Government Nr. 784: 2007);

2. *National Strategy of Development for 2008-2011 approved by the Law No. 295, 21.12.2007.* The basic objective of the Strategy is creating conditions to improve life quality by consolidating the ground for a robust, durable and inclusive economic increase (Law Nr. 295: 2007);
3. *National program regarding the creation of tan integrated system of social services for 2008-2012* provides a comprehensive policy regarding the support of the people in difficulty by providing efficient and highly qualitative social services. These services have as goal to offer support to persons on short or long period of time in order to satisfy their social needs, to reduce the social exclusion and to improve the life quality (Decision of the Government nr. 1512: 2008). (National program, 2008-2012);
4. *Law of social work no. 547-XV, 25.12.2003* has the goal of determining the principles and objectives of social work, the establishment of law to social work, provisions and services of social work, their beneficiaries, as well as the requirements towards the staff of the social care system (Law nr 547-XV, 2003);
5. *Law no. 123, 8.06.2010 regarding the social services* establishes the general framework of creation and functioning of the integrated system of social services, determining the tasks and responsibilities of the authorities of central and local public administration, of other legal and physical persons habilitated to assure and provide social services as protection of rights of the beneficiaries of social services. Social services represent an ensemble of measures and activities developed to satisfy the social needs of persons/families in order to overtake some difficult situations, to prevent the marginalization and social exclusion (Law no. 123, 2010).
6. *Law no. 129, 08.06.2012 regarding the accreditation of the providers of social services* establishes the framework regarding the creation and functioning of the national system of accreditation of the providers of social services, as well as the basic principles, general criteria, *modus operandi* and conditions of accreditation of the providers of social services (Law no. 129, 2012).

Accreditation

The procedure by which the National Council of Accreditation of the Providers of Social Services will officially evaluate the functional, organizational and administrative capacity of the providers to provide social services according to the legislation and minimal standards of quality.

The accreditation of social services providers is based on the following principles:

- Assurance of the quality of social services, which involve the certification of respecting the criteria, indicators and standards of quality established for the accessible, flexible and adjusted social services, or that involve the continuous evaluation of social services by the state authorities and providers taking into account a set of principles, indicators and standards of quality.

- Equality on rights of the social services providers, that include the assurance of the rights of all providers of social services, regardless of the type of property and legal form of organization, in conditions of equal and non-discriminatory treatment.
- Priority of the public interest that involves the fact that in accomplishing the functional attributions of the representatives of national system of accreditation, the public interest is above the personal interest.
- Confidentiality, presupposes not disclosing the information obtained in exercising the function and not using it in personal interest.
- Multidisciplinary representation that supposes the involvement of a professional team and the cooperation of all interested parties at all stages of the process of accreditation in order to ensure the quality of the provided social services.
- Transparency of the adopted decisions that involve the assurance of the visibility of decisions and results of the accreditation process by their periodic and adequate communication.
- Participation of the beneficiary that presupposes the active implication of the beneficiaries of social services and, in case, of their families in the decisional process and in that of providing social services.

According to the Decision of the Government no. 95, 07.02.2014, art. 29, the criteria of evaluation are appreciated on the base of the self-evaluation sheet, general and for every type of service, with the score from 0 to 3 points for every criterion.

The points of evaluation are summed, determining the percentage of the conformity of the social service with the minimal standards of quality.

In order to determine which is the percentage of the conformity of the service, the offered points for every criterion is calculated by the formula shown in Figure 3, where:

Figure 3. Formula of determination the percentage of service conformity

$$C.s. = \frac{100\%}{Nr.t.p.p.} * Nr.p.a.$$

- **C.s.:** The conformity of the service with the minimal standards of quality;
- **Nr.t.p.p.:** Total number of possible points (differs from service to service);
- **Nr.p.a.:** Number of points accumulated in evaluation.
- **For example:** "After analysing the sheet of specific evaluation of the Service, we determined that the provider *accumulated 139 of 147 points = 94.55%* of conformity".

Thus, having the results after the counting and according to the provisions of the articles 31-35 of the Decision of the Government no. 95, 07.02.2014 for the approval of the regulation regarding the procedure of accreditation of the social services providers, the necessary decision will be taken.

The decision of accreditation, temporary accreditation, initial accreditation, recall of the certificate, suspension of the certificate and the non-accreditation of the providers of social services is taken by the Council (CNAPSS) on the base of the report and recommendations of the group of experts, as well as according to the sheet of self-evaluation presented to the Council by the provider.

The council has the right to take the decisions shown in Figure 4.

Decisions taken by the Council until the present moment – 215 decisions.

At the present moment, in the Republic of Moldova, there are 19 social services that have approved the Regulation-framework and the minimal standards of quality. 78 providers of social services from the Republic of Moldova were accredited:

1. Social services evaluated and accredited – 177;
2. Accredited services – 132 services;

Figure 4. The decisions of the council

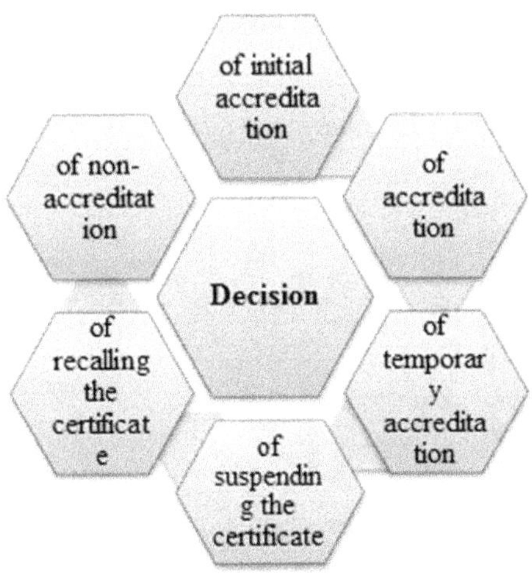

3. Services accredited initially – 7 services;
4. Services accredited temporary – 18 services;
5. Non-accredited services – 17 services

Accreditation of the Providers in Romania: General Legislative Framework

- *Law nr. 292/2011,* Law of social work, with subsequent modifications (Law no. 292, 2011);
- *Law nr. 197/2012* regarding the assurance of quality in the domain of social services, with subsequent modifications (Law no. 197, 2012);
- *D.G. no. 118/2014* for the approval of the Methodological norms of application of the provisions of the Law nr. 197/2012 regarding the assurance of quality in the domain of social services, with subsequent modifications, annexes 1-30 (D.G. no. 118, 2014);
- *D.G. no. 867/2015* for the approval of the Nomenclature of social services, as well as of the regulations-frameworks of organizing and functioning of social services, with modifications and annotations (D.G. no. 867/2015).

According to the provisions of the art.0, paragraph (3) of the Law no. 197/2012 regarding the assurance of quality in the domain of social services *accreditation* is done at the request of the provider, and only if on the date of request submission, he/she has the social services (established already) or undertakes that in 3 years from the date of receiving the certificate of accreditation, will establish and provide social services.

Regarding the employment of social workers, according to the provisions of the art. 40 of the Law of social work, the providers of social services employ social workers in their own structures, or in their lack, they could purchase the given services

Figure 5. Social service providers subject to accreditation

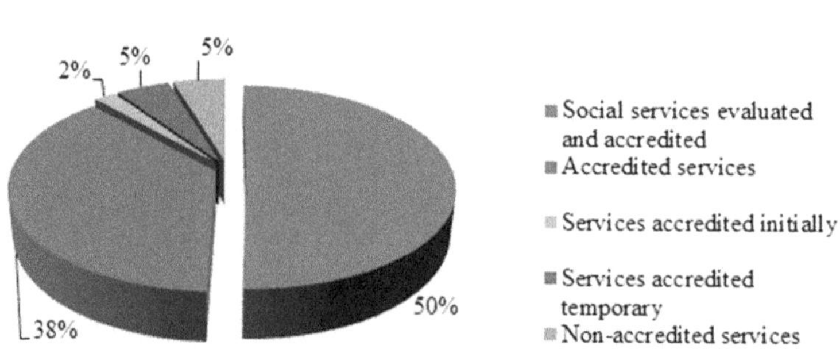

**For a more accurate representation see the electronic version.*

provided by the social workers registered with individual offices or professional civil societies of social work.

In the situation, when due to objective reasons, the providers of social services could not employ social workers or purchase their services, they could employ social workers for the activities of identification and, depending on case, evaluation of the needs of the persons that require social services (Accreditation of the social services providers, 2014).

Accreditation of the Providers of Social Services in Bulgaria

The legislative system of Bulgaria establishes the order of registering of social services and the order of license for provision of services to children and services of training. The first regimen is instituted for different types of social services offered to adults and doesn't provide some criteria, standards or requirements. The second regimen was established by the State Agency for Children Protection that elaborated a set of Instructions (guideline) regarding the criteria and standards of social services for children. The control of respecting these instructions is made by the Department of monitoring the children's rights of the State Agency for the Child Protection.

The license for provision of social services to children is granted by the president of the State Agency for Child Protection at the suggestion of special commission formed by representatives of the Ministry of Labor and Social Policy, Ministry of Education and Science, Ministry of Health, Ministry of Internal Affairs, Ministry of Justice, State Agency for Child Protection and the Agency of Social Work. The license is issued for a period of 3 years and is personalized, i.e. it cannot be transmitted to other organization.

In general, we can affirm that introducing the regimen of accreditation, license and registering is useful because such organizations as ours, that is working with beneficiaries from the socially vulnerable layers of people and organizes trainings for specialists that work with such groups of beneficiaries, is always under control, fact which increases the transparency of their activity (Stokic & Bajec, 2014).

The Impact of the Accreditation Mechanism Upon the Beneficiaries and Providers of Social Services

In order to guarantee the quality of the provided social services and to respect the rights of the beneficiaries, the Ministry of Labor, Social and Family Protection promoted the Law regarding the accreditation of the providers of social services according to the recommendations of international structures.

In this context, the implementation of the accreditation mechanism in the Republic of Moldova contributes to the efficiency and considerable improvement of the quality of social services by their assessment according to the minimal standards of quality and other normative acts of the given domain.

The implementation of the mechanism of accreditation of the providers of social services will have the following impact:

1. Respect of the rights and interests of the beneficiaries with the application of techniques of expressing the beneficiaries' opinion on agreeing to the international recommendations and standards in the process of social services' evaluation;
2. Assurance of the beneficiaries' access of the social services in equal and non-discriminating conditions;
3. Assurance of quality and increase of the efficiency of social services according to the minimal standards of quality;
4. Promotion of loyal competitiveness and transparency between providers of social services;
5. Promotion of the process of reorganization of the residential system of care of children and adults;
6. Improvement of the quality of children's care in the residential system, as the consequence of evaluating the services provided to them, according to the minimal standards of respective qualities;
7. Assurance of the sustainability of qualitative social services;
8. Development of the social services avoiding the duplication, overlapping or gaps in their provision;
9. Consolidation and increase of professionalism of the human resources engaged in the system of social services;
10. Avoidance of the conflicts of interest in providing social services, monitoring their provision in order to avoid their providing for a long period of time to the same person;
11. Increase of the potential and responsibility of the social services providers in giving qualitative social services according to the minimal standards of quality.

ETHICAL DILEMMAS IN THE PROCESS OF ACCREDITATION OF THE PROVIDERS OF SOCIAL SERVICES: MICRO-RESEARCH

During our research, we carried out a micro-research as well, by applying a questionnaire in order to establish and analyse some ethical dilemmas of the providers of social services in their professional activity, as well as those experienced in the period of accreditation.

The questionnaire statements:

1. Are you familiar with the procedure of supervision and would you apply it as supervisor? Have you been supervised?
2. Which are the ethical dilemmas that you meet in your professional activity?
3. How do you solve the ethical issues that you meet in your professional activity?

Sampling: the selected people represent 28 providers of social services from different institutions.

We present the description of the sample according to the variables of sex, profession / professional training and the experience in the field: from 28 questioned subjects, men constitute 30% and women – 70% (Figure 6):

The variable "experience in the field" was important in separating it from the duration of the course of work, to crystalize the data offered for processing.

The sample presented different data regarding the experience in work (Figure 7):

- Over 10 years and more – 10 subjects (36%);
- 8 - 10 years – 5 subjects (18%);
- 5 years - 4 subjects (14%);
- 3 years- 3 subjects (11%);
- 2 years – 6 subjects (21%).

Figure 6. Distribution by sex variable

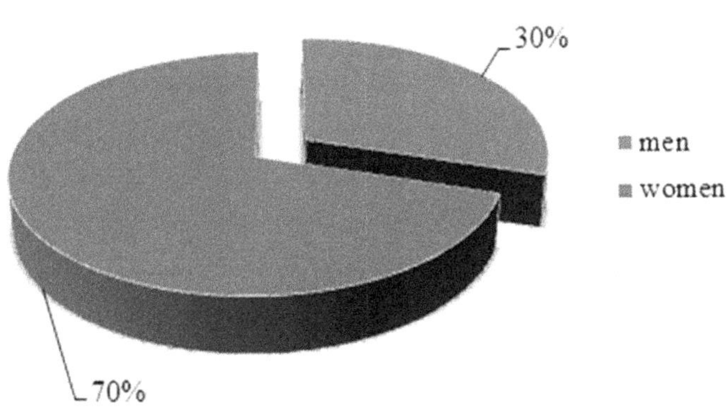

**For a more accurate representation see the electronic version.*

Figure 7. Experience in the field (accreditation and management)

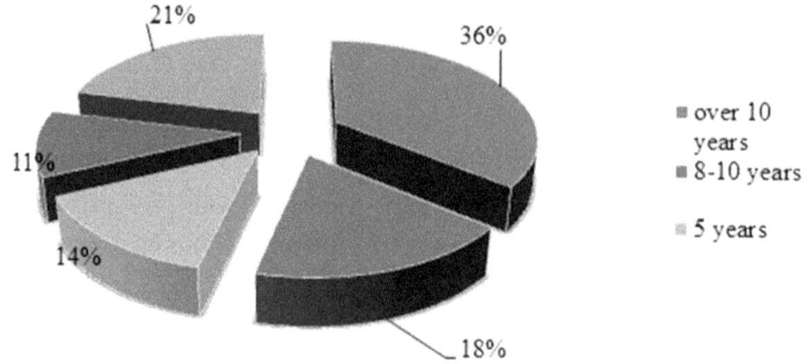

**For a more accurate representation see the electronic version.*

The following variable refers to the profession / professional training of the participants, the results offering us an image of a well-trained group in different domains: (Figure 8)

- Lawyer – 3 subjects (11%);
- Manager – 6 subjects (21%);
- Psychologist - 5 subjects (18%);
- Social worker- 11 subjects (39%);
- Teacher/university lecturer– 3 subjects (8%).

1. Are you familiar with the procedure of supervision and would you apply it as supervisor? Have you been supervised?

Figure 8. Profession/ professional training of the participants
Note: the professional training of the participants doesn't correspond exactly to the field of their professional activity, or only to the main activity according to the professional training.

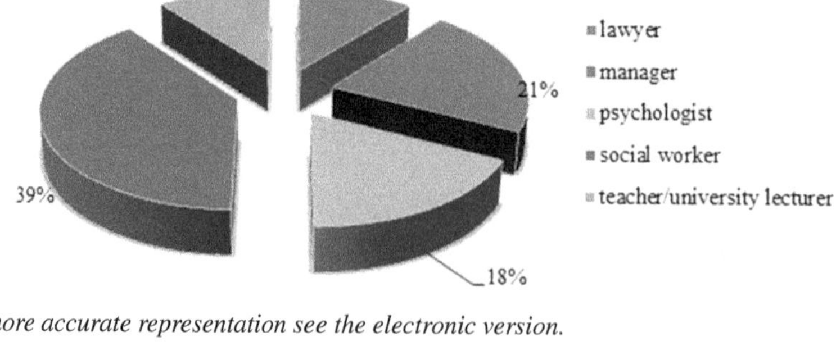

**For a more accurate representation see the electronic version.*

Figure 9. Knowing the procedure of supervision
Observations on the conversations with the participants:

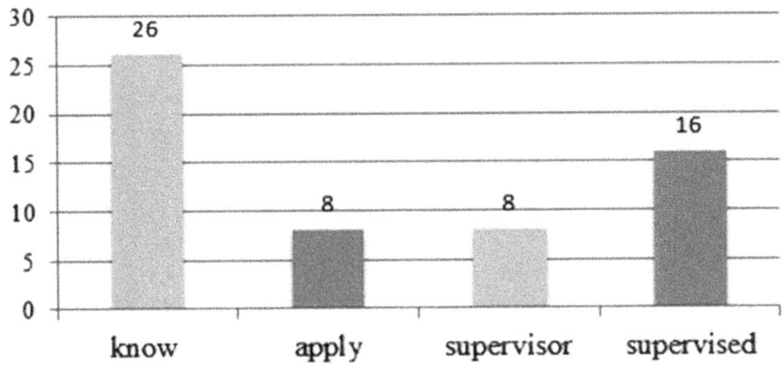

- Participants to the survey have little experience in the field of social supervision, they are rather acquainted theoretically, from the methodological point of view, but less practically.
- Participants assume that the supervision in the social field is an evaluation, a "control performed by the superiors";
- Supervision is a formality, but it is supposed to be a real support for specialists, but for this the mechanism and procedure of supervision should be applied very well;
- Participants state that the procedure of accreditation cannot be applied without previous supervision, in order to respect all exigencies and requirements of accreditation.

2. Which are the ethical dilemmas that you meet in your professional activity?

Observations on the conversation with the participants:

- Ethical dilemmas are as a satellite of the professional activity in the social field. Customers are a section of population, with different social issues, respectively a social worker, a specialist is obliged to work with any category or group of population. In real life, the values and principles of social work are difficult to respect;
- The ethical problem would be equal with a conflict between the client and the specialist, between the manager and the subordinate in most frequent cases.

3. How do you solve the ethical issues you meet in your professional activity?

Figure 10. Frequent ethical dilemmas

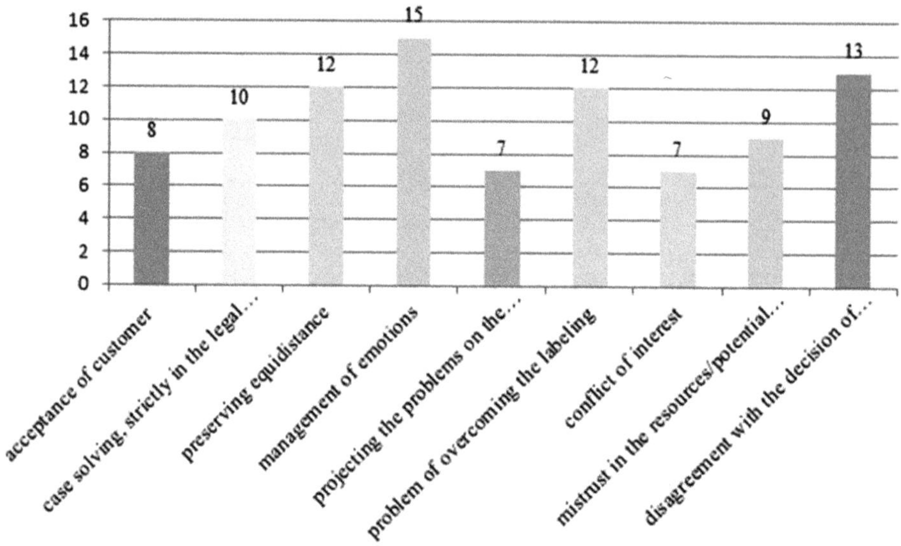

Table 1. According to the respondent, the ethical dilemmas are different, the ones frequently met in the professional activity being:

• Accepting the client	8
• Case solving strictly within the legal framework	10
• Preserving equidistance	12
• Management of emotions	15
• Projecting own problems on the client	7
• Difficulty in overcoming the labelling	12
• Conflict of interests	7
• Mistrust in resources/potential of the client	9
• Disagreement with the decision of the manager in the case management.	13

Observations on the conversations with the participants:

- Participants have confirmed the necessity of supervision for the specialists, in order to avoid professional errors, professional burnout and solving the ethical dilemmas.
- Participants admit that in the majority of cases, they react non-constructively (emotional experience, quarrels, avoidance, ignorance);

Figure 11. Ways of solving the ethical dilemmas

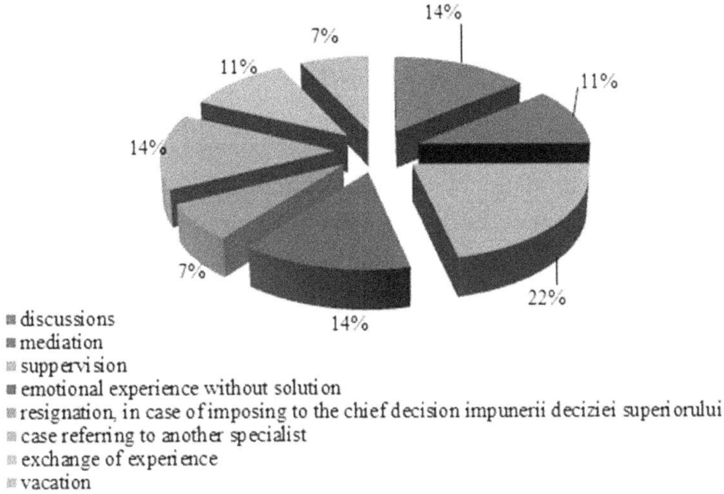

**For a more accurate representation see the electronic version.*

- Participants present different situations that would reflect an ethical issue, but don't register these situations/problems/dilemmas;
- Participants admit that the ethical dilemmas are "solved" by the superior's decision;
- Participants express their opinion on the need for a structure authorized by a specialist, competent in solving the ethical problems.

FUTURE RESEARCH DIRECTIONS

The supervisor is the person who possesses vast and different theoretical concepts, and also practical experience (Haynes, Corey, Moulton, 2003) he can use in improving the social workers' skills from various areas, covered by the social system (Frunză, 2017).

The practice of the social workers regarding the services offered to the beneficiaries is influenced by the relationship with the supervisor directly. The benefits of a compatible relationship are found in the quality of provided services, as well as in the organization's results. The perception of specialists on supervision properly indicates the situation of the process running in the studied organization. The training and professional formation of the specialists is directly related to the qualitative results of working with the beneficiaries of social work, that is why the supervision of the professional activity represents a need of priority that should be satisfied (Frunză, 2017).

In the context of the general process of reformation of the systems of social work and of health protection, one of the most important prerogatives of the states in the field of social work is the reformation and streamlining of the social services developed nationally. This involves the increase of access and quality assurance, efficiency of the provided social services.

The improvement of services quality after the supervision process is a positive effect of the modernization process of the system of providing services, a tight link between the respect of some qualitative standards in training of the specialists, and in providing services, in order to respect the professional deontology and preventing the professional burnout.

CONCLUSION

Our article is not only an attempt to research and analyse the issue of ethics in social work, aspect proven to be of major interest for the researchers internationally, but less applied by the practitioners.

In the process of accreditation of the providers of social services, we have identified several ethical issues, of lack of compliance with the deontological code in the professional activity. The situations described by the specialists have awaken our interest in order to clarify and research this aspect: the ethical dilemmas emerged within the process of providing social services. Applying a set of question to a sample of 28 specialists, we concluded the following:

- Supervision in social work is reduced to an experience exchange between colleagues, being similar to a report on the difficulties encountered;
- Supervision is rather conducted based on experience, and not on methodical-practical training in the field;
- Within the sessions of supervision, the ethical dilemmas are not being analysed, but only the difficulties in achieving the task proposed;
- The ethical dilemmas are a hidden phenomenon, unrecognized and rarely presented for analysis and solutions;
- The specialists who have participated in a mini-survey express the belief that the ethical dilemmas only exist in the client-specialist relationship (e.g. When the social worker refuses to work with certain categories of population), or between the superior and the subordinate in most cases.

General conclusion: the issue of professional ethics is acute in the Republic of Moldova, and requires a prompt, qualified and professional intervention. The experience of the colleagues in Romania and the United States is an opportunity to develop the service of supervision in social work in the Republic of Moldova, therefore ensuring the quality of the services provided by the specialists, of an indisputable professionalism.

REFERENCES

Accreditation of the social services providers. (n.d.). Retrieved from http://www.mmuncii.ro/j33/index.php/ro/comunicare/intrebari-frecvente/3575-2014-acreditarefss?highlight=WyJhY3JlZGl0YXJlIl0=

Bogo, M., & McKnight, K. (2005). Clinical supervision in social work. *The Clinical Supervisor, 24*(1/2), 49–67.

Caras, A., & Sandu, A. (2014). The Role of Supervision in Professional Development of Social Work Specialists. *Journal of Social Work Practice: Psychotherapeutic Approaches in Health, Welfare and the Community, 28*(1), 75-94. https://doi.org/10.1080/02650533.2012.763024

Cojocaru, S. (2005). *Metode Apreciative in Asistenta Sociala – Ancheta, Supervizarea si Managementul de Caz* [Appreciative Methods in Social Work – Inquiry, Supervision and Case Management]. Iasi, Romania: Polirom Publishing.

Decision of the Government no. 118, 11.03.2014, for the approval of the Methodological norms of application of the provisions of the Law nr. 197/2012 regarding the assurance of quality in the domain of social services, with subsequent modifications, annexes 1-30. (2014). *Official Monitor of Romania, Part I, 172*.

Decision of the Government no. 1512, 31.12.2008 for the approval of the National Program for the Establishment of the Integrated System of Social Services for 2008-2012. (2009). *Official Monitor of the Republic of Moldova, 7-9*.

Decision of the Government no. 95, 07.02.2014 for the approval of the Regulation regarding the procedure of accreditation of the social services providers.

Decision of the Government no.867, 10. 2015, for the approval of the Nomenclature of social services, as well as of the regulations-frameworks of organizing and functioning of social services, with modifications and annotations. (2015). *Official Monitor of Romania, Part I, 834*.

Decision of the Government of the Republic of Moldova nr. 1512, 31.12.2008 for the approval of the National program regarding the creation of tan integrated system of social services for 2008-2012. (2009). *Official Monitor of the Republic of Moldova, 7-9*.

Decision of the Government of The Republic of Moldova nr. 784, 09.07.2007 for the approval of the National strategy and Plan of actions regarding the reform of the residential system of child's care for 2007-2012. (2007). *Official Monitor of the Republic of Moldova, 103-106*, 832.

Frunză, A. (2017). *Supervizarea şi dezvoltarea profesională a asistenţilor sociali* [Supervision and professional development of social workers]. Iaşi, Romania: Lumen Publishing.

Godden, J. (2012). *BASW/CoSW England research on supervision in social work, with particular reference to supervision practice in multi disciplinary teams*. Retrieved from http://cdn.basw.co.uk/upload/basw_13955-1.pdf

Harkness, D., & Poertner, J. (1989). Research and social work supervision: A conceptual review. *Social Work, 34*(2), 115–119.

Hawkins, P., & Shohet, R. (1989). *Supervision in the Helping Professions. An individual, group and organizational approach*. Milton Keynes, UK: Open University Press.

Haynes, R., Corey, G., & Moulton, P. (2003). *Clinical Supervision in the Helping Professions: A Practical Guide*. Pacific Grove, CA: Brookes/Cole.

Holunga, L. (2013). *Evaluation and supervision of the social services*. Alba Iulia: POSDRU.

Kadushin, A. (1992). *Supervision in Social Work* (3rd ed.). New York: Columbia University Press.

Kadushin, A., & Harkness, D. (2002). *Supervision in Social Work* (4th ed.). New York: Columbia University Press.

Lambley, S., & Marrable, T. (2013). *Practice enquiry into supervision in a variety of adult care settings where there are health and social care practitioners working together*. Social Care Institute for Excellence.

Law nr. 129, 08.06.2012 regarding the accreditation of the providers of social services. (2012). *Official Monitor of the Republic of Moldova, 181-184*.

Law nr. 197, 01.11.2012 regarding the assurance of quality in the domain of social services. Text actualized according to the modifying normative acts. (2013). *Official Monitor of Romania, Part I*.

Law of social work nr. 292, 20.12.2011, with subsequent modifications. (2013). *Official Monitor of Romania, 905.*

Law of social work nr 547-XV, 25.12.2003. (2004). *Official Monitor of the Republic of Moldova, 42-44.*

Law of the Republic of Moldova Law Nr. 295, 21.12.2007 for the approval of National Strategy of Development for 2008-2011. (2008). Official Monitor of the Republic of Moldova, 18-20.

Law regarding the social services nr. 123, 8.06.2010. (2010). *Official Monitor of the Republic of Moldova, 155-158.*

Malley, J., & Fernández, J.-L. (2010). Measuring quality in social care services: Theory and practice. *Annals of Public and Cooperative Economics, 81*(4), 559–582. doi:10.1111/j.1467-8292.2010.00422.x

Quality of Social Services in Europe. (n.d.). Retrieved from http://www.epr.eu/images/EPR/documents/policy_documents/2014policypapers/Quality_of_Social_ServicesinEurope.pdf

Rîjicova, S., & Grigoraş, S. (2017). *Mecanismul de supervizare profesională în asistența socială. Ghid de implementare practică* [The mechanism of professional supervising in social work. Guide for practical implementation]. Retrieved from http://www.mmpsf.gov.md/sites/default/files/document/attachments/usaid_2_ghid_supervizare_rom.pdf

Sandu, A., & Caras (Frunză), A. (2014). Some Considerations on the Construction of Ethics Policies. Shared Ethics and Communicative Action. *Procedia: Social and Behavioral Sciences, 149*, 846–854. doi:10.1016/j.sbspro.2014.08.325

Sandu, A. (2015). *Etică profesională şi transparență în administrația publică.* Bucharest, Romania: Editura Didactică şi Pedagogică.

Stokic, P. L., & Bajec, J. (2014). European Social Policy Network (ESPN). Thematic Report on Social Investment Serbia 2015. European Union.

Tsui, M. S. (2008). Adventures in re-searching the features of social work supervision in Hong Kong. *Qualitative Social Work: Research and Practice*, 7(3), 349–362. doi:10.1177/1473325008093706

Van Beek, G. (2010). *Common Quality Framework for Social Services of General Interest.* Brussels: Prometheus.

Chapter 14
Contribution of Social Learning in Counterproductive Work Behaviors

Naman Sharma
Amity University, India

ABSTRACT

Unethical employee behaviors pose a grave challenge for organizations today. Research has established that every year organizations lose millions of their dollars along with their valuable reputation due to immoral conduct of their employees. Practitioners and researchers in the past have undertook such instances very seriously and analyzed various antecedents to these employee behaviors. While various personality and attitude related variables have been held responsible for counterproductive work behaviors, the role of social learning was often overlooked in this pursuit. Current chapter address this gap and presents a logical framework for establishing social learning as potential antecedent of employee deviance in organizations.

INTRODUCTION

A new employee being mocked by the senior executives in the company; a lecturer picking up a personal phone call during the lecture; a clerk with holding an arrear bill of employees for no legitimate reason; manager downloading videos/playing games on the company's internet network; a worker sabotaging the equipment because he didn't get the salary raise as expected. All these above unethical incidents and practices are only but few examples of Counterproductive Work Behaviors (CWB) also sometimes known as workplace/employee deviance.

DOI: 10.4018/978-1-5225-3090-9.ch014

You are free to make choices but you are not free to choose the consequences. (Unknown)

The above vignette suggests that many of times employees due to various reasons including frustration, negligence, work overload and stress make wrong choices at work and get engaged in the unethical behaviors such as mentioned earlier in the text only to later on finding themselves pay for it either in form of social humiliation or sometimes through losing their jobs as well as reputation in society at large. It is important to notice here that everybody believes that nobody forces an employee to deviates from the set rules and regulations of the organization and ultimately it is the free will of an employee to participate or not to participate in such acts. Despite this well established notion discussed above, there are observations from time to time that suggest that a person is often influenced by his surroundings while indulging in deviant behaviors. The impact of these behaviors become all more important in social work organizations as it directly impacts the life of people who are already at a disadvantageous state of life. This chapter will attempt to add momentum to this notion by focusing on concepts related to Counterproductive Work Behaviors (CWB) and its dynamics with social interactions covered under the widely researched Social Learning Theory (SLT).

BACKGROUND

It would be an untrue statement to say that CWB is a newer term to organizations or researchers. Many leading sociologists and criminologists over the past century had attempted to undertake studies on this subject. However' some of the most concrete researches in this field have surfaced only in past few decades (Fox & Spector, 2005; Sackett & DeVore, 2001).

Researches concerning counterproductive behaviors at work draw inspiration from various schools of thoughts. These schools include organizational behavior, vocational psychology, behavioral business ethics etc. bringing in their own understanding of the subject leading to usage of their own unique terms/vocabulary to define such acts. These terms include deviance, unethical behavior, incivility and counterproductive work behavior etc. In this course of definitions, the most comprehensive definition on the subject that surfaced is perhaps this one:

Employee Deviance is a voluntary behavior that violates significant organizational norms and in so doing threatens the well-being of an organization, its members or both (Robinson & Bennett, 1995).

This definition specifically focused on two distinct aspects related to deviant behavior which are: a) these behaviors exhibited by the employees are voluntary in nature either due to the lack of motivation to follow norms or presence of motivation to break them and b) these behaviors violate the said organizational norms instead of any societal norms or moral standards (Robinson & Bennett, 1995).

Researchers from time to time have also tried to classify these deviant behaviors. The first comprehensive attempt to build a framework was taken by Hollinger and Clark (1982) segregating these acts into two categories named production deviance and property deviance. This framework however, found to account mainly for deviant acts directed against the organization and lacked the perspective on deviant acts of interpersonal nature such as aggression and harassment (Robinson & Bennett, 1995). Building on this premise later Robinson & Bennett (1995) and their follow up study (2000) used multidimensional scaling techniques to develop a typology of deviant workplace behavior. This taxonomy developed during their research suggested that deviant behaviors at workplace vary along two dimensions i.e. minor versus serious and organizational versus interpersonal. On the basis of these two dimensions, employee deviance is further categorized into four quadrants namely production deviance, property deviance, political deviance and personal aggression respectively (See Figure 1). These four kinds of employee deviance are then broadly categorized into two types of employee deviance namely organizational deviance (those deviant acts that are directed against the organizations) and interpersonal deviance (those deviant acts that are directed against co-workers). Production deviance and property deviance comes under the banner of organizational deviance while political deviance and personal aggression covers the latter (Robinson & Bennett, 1995; Bennett & Robinson, 2000).

Quadrant 1 represents a minor but organizationally harmful deviant acts that are termed as production deviance (Robinson & Bennett, 1995). Hollinger & Clark (1982) defined production deviance as:

Violations of the boundaries of workplace norms delineating the minimum quantity and quality of output and effort expected from employees. (Hollinger & Clark, 1982)

Being late to work, soldiering (deliberate reduction one's individual performance), cyber loafing (spending work time on internet doing personal work), absenteeism, social loafing, leaving early and taking excessive breaks etc. are few acts of production deviance (Robinson & Bennett, 1995; Wren & Bedeian, 2009).

The next quadrant comprises of property deviance which according to above discussed typology is considered as a serious kind of organizational deviance. It consists of behaviors such as sabotaging equipment, theft from workplace, fiddling,

Figure 1. Robinson and Bennett's Conceptualization of Deviance (1995); Bennett and Robinson (2000)

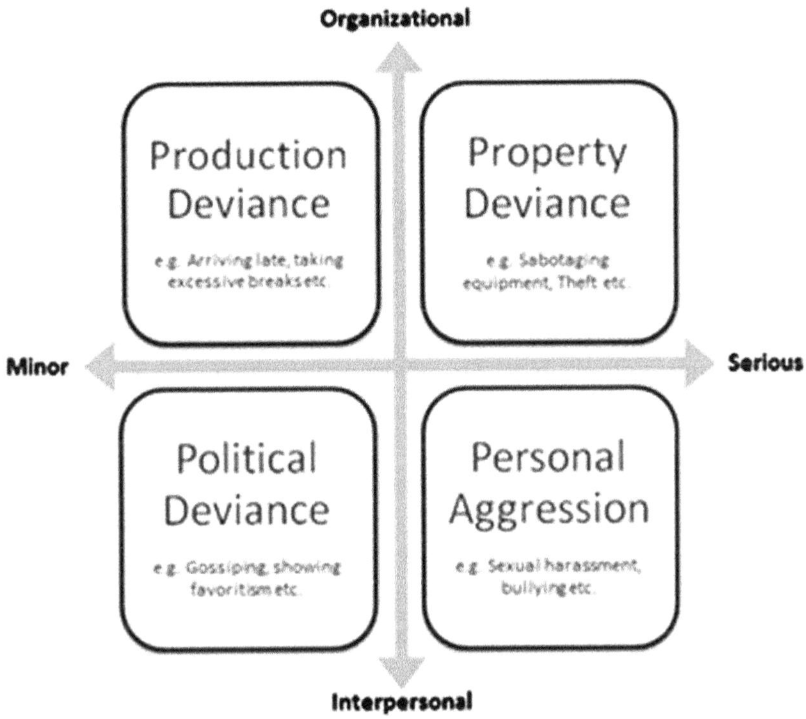

releasing confidential information etc. (Mars, 1982; Crino & Leap, 1989; Giacalone, & Knouse, 1990; Robinson & Bennett, 1995). All these above mentioned behaviors fit well into the definition of property deviance given by Hollinger & Clark (1982) i.e. property deviance is intentionally acquiring or damaging property or assets of the organization without authorization.

Political deviance is minor form of interpersonal deviance that fall into the quadrant 3 (Robinson & Bennett, 1995). Behaviors covered in the category of political deviance include gossiping, starting negative rumors, making fun of someone at work, acting rudely, showing favoritism etc. (Bennett & Robinson, 1995). It has been defined as:

Engagement in social interaction that puts other individuals at a personal or political disadvantage. (Robinson & Bennett, 1995)

Researches on political deviance are very limited and it is generally studied along with other forms of deviance. The fourth and the final quadrant of this typology consist of severe form of interpersonal deviance i.e. personal aggression. Researchers studying interpersonal deviance generally focus on personal aggression behaviors such as bullying (Einarsen, Hoel, Zapf, & Cooper, 2003; Lutgen-Sandvik, 2006). Some other behaviors that fit into the definition of personal aggression are physical and verbal abuse, sexual harassment, stealing from co-workers, destroying work of others etc. (Robinson & Bennett, 1995; Everton, Mastrangelo & Jolton, 2005).

ETHICAL MISCONDUCT IN SOCIAL WORK ORGANIZATIONS

Despite of popular belief that social workers are dedicated people who work to better human kind, there have been instances from time to time where social workers are found at wrong ends. These misconducts are even serious in nature as they affect the life of people. There has been a case in which a 14 year old girl died leading the social worker to serve a 17.5 years' imprisonment under the charges of involuntary manslaughter, child endangerment, reckless endangerment, perjury, criminal conspiracy, and forgery (Reamer, F. G. (2012). Lack of initiatives and not giving 100% in work is a common deviant behavior among social workers. There has been another unfortunate case in which a child died due to abuse and even though the case was reported at time the two social workers didn't pay attention to it and unfortunately the child died. Social workers then tried to falsify the records to prove they lead competent investigation but eventually got caught and now serving their term (Ashford & Lecroy, 2013).

Social workers despite their caring nature and noble pursuit to make a change in world at times get involved in ethical misconduct due to different reasons such as greed, desperation and personal impairment Reamer, F. G. (2012). Most of these conducts are related with delivery of services where social workers fail to perform their duties leading to the victimization of already suffered. Hence, counterproductive work behaviors are all more harmful in social work sector and therefore, steps shall be taken to curb these behaviors right when it surfaced.

COST ARISING FROM DEVIANT EMPLOYEE BEHAVIOR

One of the reasons why it is important for an organization to study, report and rectify/control the issues related to CWB is often understood in terms of the costs associated to these acts. Several empirical findings have revealed the estimated cost that organizations had to bear due to prevalent employee deviance. Henle, Giacalone & Jurkiewicz (2005) conducted a study in US according to which 95% of organizations have a reported history of deviant activities in their premises. Another study revealed that as much as 75% of employees have engaged in some sort of deviant behavior (Robinson & Bennett, 1995). It is important here to understand that not always these costs can be measured in monetary terms.

Golparvar (2015) asserted through a study that due to significant variation in reported deviant behaviors, it is very difficult to estimate the exact cost these behaviors impose on organizations. However, there have been certain studies in the past which have attempted to monetize these costs for organizations. It is shocking but true that nearly 18 years ago a study reported that organizations spent approximately $ 7.1 billon every year (in US alone) on security against cyber-attacks. Observing the growth and use of internet in past decades this figure is bound to increase many folds. Much recent studies conducted by Kidwel (2005) and Lawrence & Robinson (2007) reported the figures of 4.2 billion dollars for violent activities and nearly 40-120 billion dollars every year due to cases of stealing and robbery to American organizations.

Counterproductive work behaviors also incur several non-monetary costs including verbal and non-verbal aggressions (up to 37%), sexual harassment (approximately 25%), drugs to the members of organizations (24%) which in turn decrease the overall productivity and well-being of the organizations (Kidwell, 2005; Tepper et al. 2009). Victims of employee deviance have to bear negative consequences on their physical and mental health. Few researchers has also established the fact that victims of deviant behaviors such as verbal harassment and workplace incivility suffers from low morale, develop stress related problems and possess greater tendency to resign from their jobs (O'Leary-Kelly, Griffin, & Glew, 1996; Sharma & Singh, 2016).Organizations have to lose some of the valuable human assets in the process which cannot be always compensated through monetary resources. Therefore, it is imperative for every organization today to deal with these deviant patterns shown by certain employees as and when it is reported with due care. This chapter however is more inclined towards those factors that contribute to CWB i.e. its antecedents.

ANTECEDENTS OF CWB

As discussed above, heavy costs are usually associated with deviant behaviors at workplace and hence it is only natural that a large number of studies have been conducted overtime to understand the underlying reasons behind their occurrence. Some of the common antecedents of employee deviance are shown in Table 1. Bennett & Robinson (2003) revealed three distinct trends in the studies involving antecedents of employee deviance. These three trends are a) deviance as a reaction to one's experiences, b) due to reflection of one's personality and c) adaptation from social context.

Table 1. Antecedents of employee deviance

Antecedents	Concerned Researches
Demographic variables	Douglas & Martinko, 2001; Jang, 2007; Berry, Ones & Sackett, 2007; Anwar et al., 2011; Kumi, 2013; Sharma, Singh & Kishor, 2013; Sharma & Paluchova, 2014
Frustration	Storms & Spector, 1987; Chen & Spector, 1992; Spector, 1997; Fox & Spector, 1999; Fox, Spector, & Miles, 2001
Organizational injustice	Greenberg, 1993; Bies, 2001; Bechtoldt et al., 2007; Cohen-Charash & Mueller, 2007
Powerlessness	Perlow & Latham, 1993; Bennett, 1998; Ambrose, et al., 2002
Jobs stressors and stress	Gardner & Martinko, 1998; Spector et al., 2006
Conflict management styles	De Dreu and Gelfand, 2007
Physical conditions	Baron & Richardson, 1994; Anderson, Anderson & Deuser, 1996; Cohn & Rotton, 1997
Personal characteristics	Hollinger, 1986; Hollinger et al., 1992; Judge et al., 2006; Kemelgor et al., 2007
Employee attitudes	Magione & Quinn, 1975; Hollinger & Clark, 1982
Organizational environment	Salin, 2003; Dalal, 2005

A majority of researches who studied the antecedents of employee deviance raised concerns about the experiences that employees have at their workplace and how these experiences shape their behaviors. There are several strong empirical findings in support for the view that employee deviance is derived out of experiencing stress at workplace (Storms & Spector, 1987; Chen & Spector, 1992; Spector, 1997; Fox & Spector, 1999; Fox, Spector, & Miles, 2001). Researches have shown that experiences of perceived injustices may also trigger employee deviance activities. Distributive and procedural injustice may lead to activities such as theft (Greenberg, 1990, 1993), aggression (O'Leary-Kelly, Griffin & Glew, 1996; Skarlicki & Folger, 1997) and sabotage (Ambrose, Seabright, & Schminke, 2001) etc.

Few researches have also shown that powerlessness can also trigger employee deviances such as violence (Lam, 1993; Perlow & Latham, 1993), sabotage (Ambrose, et al., 2001) and destructive behaviors (Allen & Greenberger, 1980).

The researches supporting the view that a person's personality can be a reason for his involvement in employee deviance are very few (Bennett & Robinson, 2000). Dispositional aggressiveness in a person has been found to have a strong and direct relation with his involvement in deviant behaviors (Burroughs, Bing & James, 1999; Sablynski, Mitchell, James, & McIntyre, 2001). There are also certain other specific traits of a person that may predict his/her involvement in employee deviance

(Trevino, 1986) but to a large extent these personality variables are largely ineffective in predicting deviant intentions of employees (Robinson & Greenberg, 1998).

This chapter relates more with the third trend i.e. 'adaptation from social context'. Here the possibility of occurrence of employee deviance is based on the role of social norms, cues and constraints (Bennett & Robinson, 2000). There have been few researches in the past which supports that social norms may result in certain deviant behaviors such as sabotage (Giacalone, Riordan, & Rosenfeld, 1997), and theft (Greenberg, 1998).

SOCIAL LEARNING THEORY

In past 30 years, the social learning theory emerged as one of the most sought after theories in the field of criminology (Akers & Jensen, 2006; Akers & Sellers, 2009). Social learning theory has found strong empirical support from various researches on the regular basis (Hirschi & Stark, 1969; Gottfredson & Hirschi, 1990). Edwin Sutherland in his popular text book 'criminology' introduced the theory of differential association. He (Sutherland, 1947) advocated that criminal behaviors can be learned through interaction with certain intimate personal groups. The original theory of differential associations given by Sutherland (1947) consisted of nine major propositions which remain largely unchanged since then (Bradshaw, 2011). Out of those nine propositions, the sixth proposition proved to be the most relevant for subsequent researches and helped Burgess & Akers (1966) in development of social learning theory. The sixth proposition of theory of differential association states that:

A person becomes delinquent because of an excess of definitions favorable to violation of law over definitions unfavorable to violations of law (Sutherland, 1947).

In simpler words, this proposition insists that if a person believes that any deviant behavior is acceptable by people (based on their definition/justification of act) than he/she is likely to engage in that deviant behavior (Pantaleo, 2011). The theory of differential association is considered to be one of the major breakthrough researches of its time as most of the research then focused mainly on the psychological and biological explanations for crime rather assigning any social dimension to it (Bradshaw, 2011). However, it also drew a large number of criticisms from various researchers. Cressey (1960) argued that it is not always that a person indulges in a deviant behavior just because others approve such indulgence. One of the major statements in differential association theory was that associations cause delinquency (Sutherland, 1947) but a number of researchers proved it otherwise. They asserted through facts that it is actually this delinquency that results in the formation of such associations (Glueck & Glueck, 1950; Kornhauser, 1978; Gottfredson & Hirschi, 1990; Sampson & Laub, 1993). It also makes a logical sense as the persons who are indulged in criminal behaviors will relate and look to have a friendly relationship with such people who are also engaged in similar behaviors (Pantaleo, 2011). Another concern raised by later research was that Sutherland (1947) claims that criminal behavior can be learned through the interaction with personal groups but he did not discuss or even mentioned the process of such learning in its research (Burgess & Akers, 1966, Pantaleo, 2011). Finally due to these criticisms, it became necessary for researchers to bring in some extensions to original theory of differential associations.

Almost two decades after the theory of differential association, Burgess & Akers (1966) tabled the concept of differential association-reinforcement theory by fusing differential association theory with measures of learning & theory of reinforcement given by Skinner (1953, 1959). This theory succeeded many shortcomings of original Sutherland's theory of differential association. Akers (1973, 1977) then further refined/ revised this theory and renamed it as **social learning theory** which was widely accepted and used till date by researchers to define/describe this phenomenon. In these revisions, one of the major additions was the inclusion of 'imitation' as one of the components of social learning (Akers, 1977). Akers (1973, 1977) also claimed that social learning theory is the general explanation to all kinds of criminal, delinquent and deviant behaviors.

Simultaneously, at the time when refinements in theory of differential association as well as in social learning theory were being made by Akers and his colleagues, Bandura and his associates contributed towards the social behaviorism aspect of the deviant behaviors (Bandura & Walters, 1963; Bandura, 1973, 1977, 1986). Bandura & Walter (1963) expanded the understanding of various cognitive processes that facilitates the learning of new behaviors by people. These social behaviorism theories helped Akers and colleagues to identify the four integral components of social learning theory (Akers, 1998). These four components were identified as differential reinforcement, imitation, differential association and definitions.

COMPONENTS OF SOCIAL LEARNING THEORY

In *Differential Association*, the term associations refer to the individuals such as peers, co-workers and family members with which a person interacts. This theory principally states that individuals/groups with which a person interacts provides a social context where social learning process is facilitated. In other words, theory of differential association suggests that if these associations are involved in criminal/ deviant behaviors than the person is more likely to involve in criminal/deviant behavior himself/herself (Akers, 1998). Differential association is measured simply by asking respondents to report the number of members in his/her social group that are involved in particular deviant behavior (Akers, 1979, 1998; Agnew, 1991; Thornberry et al., 1994).

Differential reinforcement built upon the notion that anybody's involvement in a deviant behavior depends upon how that person anticipates the outcome of his/her participation. If a behavior is often rewarded or rarely punished than a person is more likely to engage in such behavior (Akers, 1998). This theory is largely based on the theory of reinforcement given by Skinner (1953, 1959). According to reinforcement theory, reinforcement can occur in two ways: positive reinforcement (rewarding for behavior) and negative reinforcement (removal of negative consequences). So if a person perceives that his wrong doings will be rewarded in some manner or he/she is less likely to be punished for deviant behavior than the person will be comfortable with engaging in such behavior (Akers and Sellers, 2004). The chances of occurrence of any deviant behavior are based upon a number of factors including amount, frequency as well as past, present and anticipated punishment/rewards associated with the specific behavior (Akers, 1998). While measuring differential reinforcement, researches claim that it is necessary to measure both negative as well as positive reinforcement in order to make the study more meaningful (Akers & Lee, 1999).

Imitation is an act by which a person observes others preforming a specific behavior and then engages in same behavior. Akers (1985) extended that imitation contributes in the initiation of a new or novel behavior in a person. Sutherland (1947) in his research commented that imitation occurs only when a person directly interacts with others but later on researchers argued that imitation can also occur when a person indirectly observes the behaviors of other people around him/her and then engage in same behavior (Bandura, 1977; Akers, 1998). Akers (1985) also argued that imitation works best in the situation when a person has never indulged in any specific behavior before and after observing some other person performing that behavior becomes motivated to repeat the gesture. However, when compared to other social learning components the effects of imitation are generally considered relatively weak (Akers, 1998). Imitation is often measured by the asking respondent to report how many people in his social group engage in a particular deviant behavior (Akers & Lee, 1999).

The element of *definitions* refers to the values, attitudes and orientation attached with a behavior in the minds of people (Akers, 1998). It is directly related to the meaning that is attached to a specific behavior through differential association (Pantaleo, 2011). So if a criminal activity/deviant behavior is rationalized by a person's peers and influenced group then the person is more likely to engage in that deviance/crime (Akers and Sellers, 2004). On the other hand if a deviant behavior is defined negative by a person's personal group then that person is less likely to involve in that employee deviance (Pantaleo, 2011). Definitions that are conducive towards employee deviance can be of two types. Positive definitions are ones in which involvement in employee deviance is clearly justified to the exhibitor while in case of neutralizing definitions, a person believed that his/her involvement in a particular deviance is either temporary or will be justified in the future. For e.g. if a person is taking some stationery items to his/her home, he might believe that it is not stealing from the workplace rather it is a borrowing and he/she will return it as soon as possible. In order to measure definitions, respondents are asked to indicate the extent to which they approve/disapprove or agree/disagree with a particular deviant behavior at workplace (Kubrin, Stucky, and Krohn, 2009).

Criticism of SLT

Social learning theory just like any other sociological/behavioral theory has gathered a lot of criticism over period of time. One of the major issues in social learning theory is that just like in the case of theory of differential association; it is not clear that whether criminal activities encourage the friendship between the criminals or is it this friendship that encourages crime.

Also in case of definitions, many researchers believe that relying on the person's perceptions towards attitude of others (regarding deviant behavior) may not be that accurate (Pantaleo, 2011).

SLT and CWB

Kubrin, Stucky, and Krohn (2009) asserted that social learning theories have a rich scope in the studies concerning crime as well as different kinds of deviance. In the past, researches have established a strong relationship between bad habits such as drinking, smoking and drug use and social learning theories (Akers, Krohn, Lanza-Kaduce, & Radosevich, 1979; Orcutt, 1987; Sellers & Winfree, 1990; Warr & Stafford, 1991; Akers & Lee, 1996). Other researches have utilized social learning theory to identify its contribution in different kinds of crimes including vandalism, physical violence, property and drug crimes etc. (Matsueda, 1982; Alarid, Burton, & Cullen, 2000). It is clear now that social learning theories can be applied in a wide variety of settings and situations of deviant and criminal behavior. Figure 2 below shows the possible relationship between social learning constructs and deviant behaviors at workplace.

A majority of researches on predecessors of counterproductive work behaviors are concerned about the experiences that employees have at their workplace and how these experiences shape their behaviors. There are several strong empirical findings in support for the view that employee deviance is derived out of experiencing stress at workplace. Social learning theory is cocooned around the theory of differential

Figure 2. Assumed relationship between social learning constructs and deviant behaviors

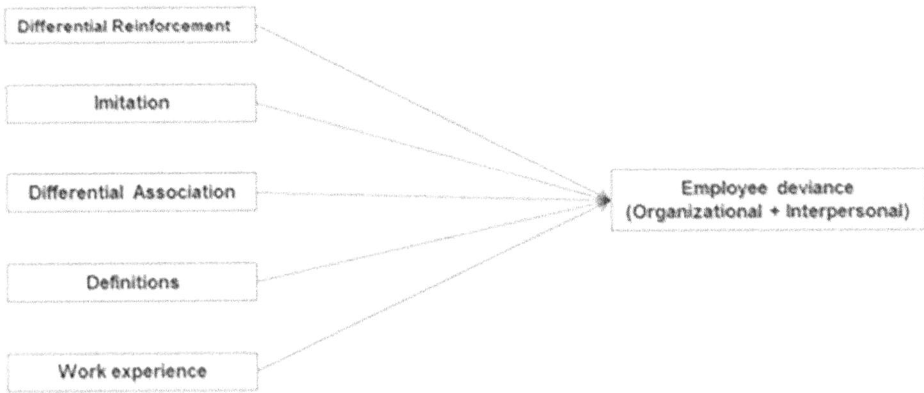

association which was proposed by Edwin Sutherland in late 1940s. Theory of differential association simply laid down the fact that criminal behaviors shown by a person are learned through his/her interaction with his personal and professional circles. Built upon the theory of differential association (Sutherland, 1947), social learning theory was coined by Ronald L. Akers in year 1973. Social learning theory begins with only one component i.e. differential association (Sutherland, 1947) but later on three more components were added by different researchers. These components are imitation (Orcutt, 1987), differential reinforcement (Akers, 1979) and definitions (Akers, 1979). There have been few researches in the past which supports that social norms may result in certain deviant behaviors such as sabotage (Giacalone, Riordan, & Rosenfeld, 1997), and theft (Greenberg, 1998). Studies pertaining social learning theory and its impact on deviant behaviors are very limited and a majority of them have only considered one social learning component i.e. differential association (Arriaga & Foshee, 2004; Haynie et al., 2006).

Several researches in the past have attempted to establish the relationship between counterproductive work behaviors with the four social learning constructs (individually) discussed above. Attempts of considering all four social learning constructs at the same time are very few. One such comprehensive studies of recent times has been conducted by Anderson et al. (2015), in which structural equation models were used to test direct, indirect, and feedback effects of social learning constructs on deviant behaviors. The study clearly establishes that social learning components have strong direct as well as indirect effect towards boasting counterproductive workplace behaviors.

CONCLUSION

Employee deviance has become a chronic disease for corporate world today and therefore in the recent past it has been studied and analyzed by various organizations across the globe. These studies/researches are significant because of the range of individuals who are affected by these counterproductive workplace behaviors. Though, many researchers have attempted to study this phenomenon under the light of personal/individual differences among employees and the strained employer/ employee relationships, this chapter highlighted the importance of social structure of an organization promoting such unethical acts in organizational premises.

It has been asserted by several past researches that all the social learning components are responsible for spreading CWB in organizations and hence managers/administrators are advised to check such deviant social interactions between employees.

To sum up the findings obtained, it is to be understood that employee deviance is an issue that is present in every organization irrespective of its size, nature or location and hence must not be overlooked. Management or administration may believe that they have a firm control over their employees (and their behavior) but there will always be few people who are willing to bend these rules and disrupt the organizational ecosystem. The management/administration thus needs to adopt a proactive approach while dealing with these deviant employees. Prevalence of such acts can be traced back throughout the human history just as chapter 3rd, 33rd verse from Bhagwad Gita says:

It means that 'even a man of knowledge acts according to his own nature that he has learned through his life experiences (involving people around him)'.

REFERENCES

Agnew, R. (1991). The interactive effects of peer variables on delinquency. *Criminology*, *29*(1), 47–72. doi:10.1111/j.1745-9125.1991.tb01058.x

Akers, R. (1985). *Deviant behavior: A social learning approach* (3rd ed.). Wadsworth.

Akers, R. L. (1973). *Deviant behavior: A social learning approach*. Belmont, CA: Wadsworth.

Akers, R. L. (1977). *Deviant behavior: A social learning approach* (2nd ed.). Belmont, CA: Wadsworth.

Akers, R. L. (1998). *Social learning and social structure: A general theory of crime and deviance*. Boston, MA: Northeastern University Press.

Akers, R. L., & Jensen, G. F. (2006). The empirical status of social learning theory of crime and deviance: The past, present, and future. *Taking Stock: The Status of Criminological Theory, 15*, 37-76.

Akers, R. L., Krohn, M. D., Lanza-Kaduce, L., & Radosevich, M. (1979). Social learning and deviant behavior: A specific test of a general theory. *American Sociological Review*, *44*(4), 636–655. doi:10.2307/2094592 PMID:389120

Akers, R. L., & Lee, G. (1996). A longitudinal test of social learning theory: Adolescent smoking. *Journal of Drug Issues*, *26*(2), 317–343. doi:10.1177/002204269602600203

Akers, R. L., & Sellers, C. S. (2009). *Criminology theories*. Academic Press.

Alarid, L. F., Burton, V. S. Jr, & Cullen, F. T. (2000). Gender and crime among felony offenders: Assessing the generality of social control and differential association theories. *Journal of Research in Crime and Delinquency*, *37*(2), 171–199. doi:10.1177/0022427800037002002

Ambrose, M. L., Seabright, M. A., & Schminke, M. (2002). Sabotage in the workplace: The role of organizational injustice. *Organizational Behavior and Human Decision Processes*, *89*(1), 947–965. doi:10.1016/S0749-5978(02)00037-7

Anderson, C. A., Anderson, K. B., & Deuser, W. E. (1996). Examining an affective aggression framework weapon and temperature effects on aggressive thoughts, affect, and attitudes. *Personality and Social Psychology Bulletin*, *22*(4), 366–376. doi:10.1177/0146167296224004

Anderson, D. R., Sweeney, D. J., Williams, T. A., Camm, J. D., & Cochran, J. J. (2015). *An introduction to management science: quantitative approaches to decision making*. Cengage Learning.

Anwar, M. N., Arif, I., Sarwar, M., & Awan, R. N. (2011). Gender differences in workplace deviant behavior of university teachers and modification techniques. *International Education Studies*, *4*(1), 193–197. doi:10.5539/ies.v4n1p193

Arriaga, X. B., & Foshee, V. A. (2004). Adolescent dating violence: Do adolescents follow in their friends, or their parents, footsteps? *Journal of Interpersonal Violence*, *19*(2), 162–184. doi:10.1177/0886260503260247 PMID:15006000

Ashford, J. B., & Lecroy, C. W. (2013). *Human behavior in the social environment: A multidimensional perspective*. Belmont, CA: Brooks/Cole.

Bandura, A. (1977). Self-efficacy: Toward a unifying theory of behavioral change. *Psychological Review*, *84*(2), 191–215. doi:10.1037/0033-295X.84.2.191 PMID:847061

Bandura, A. (1986). The explanatory and predictive scope of self-efficacy theory. *Journal of Social and Clinical Psychology*, *4*(3), 359–373. doi:10.1521/jscp.1986.4.3.359

Bandura, A., & Jeffery, R. W. (1973). Role of symbolic coding and rehearsal processes in observational learning. *Journal of Personality and Social Psychology*, *26*(1), 122–130. doi:10.1037/h0034205

Bandura, A., & Walters, R. H. (1963). *Social learning and personality development*. Academic Press.

Baron, R. A., & Richardson, D. R. (1994). *Human aggression* (2nd ed.). New York: Pleun.

Bechtoldt, M. N., Welk, C., Zapf, D., & Hartig, J. (2007). Main and moderating effects of self-control, organizational justice, and emotional labor on counterproductive behavior at work. *European Journal of Work and Organizational Psychology*, *16*(4), 479–500. doi:10.1080/13594320701662618

Bennett, J. W. (1998). Classic anthropology. *American Anthropologist*, *100*(4), 951–956. doi:10.1525/aa.1998.100.4.951

Bennett, R. J., & Robinson, S. L. (2000). Development of a Measure of Workplace Deviance. *The Journal of Applied Psychology*, *85*(3), 349–360. doi:10.1037/0021-9010.85.3.349 PMID:10900810

Berry, C. M., Ones, D. S., & Sackett, P. R. (2007). Interpersonal deviance, organizational deviance, and their common correlates: A review and meta-analysis. *The Journal of Applied Psychology*, *92*(2), 410–424. doi:10.1037/0021-9010.92.2.410 PMID:17371088

Bies, R. J. (2001). Interactional (in) justice: The sacred and the profane. *Advances in Organizational Justice*, 89-118.

Burgess, R. L., & Akers, R. L. (1966). A differential association-reinforcement theory of criminal behavior. *Social Problems*, *14*(2), 128–147. doi:10.2307/798612

Burroughs, S. M., Bing, M. N., & James, L. R. (1999). *Effects of personality and job stressors on affective reactions and aggressive work behaviors*. American Psychological Association and the National Institute for Occupational Safety and Health interdisciplinary conference on Work, Stress, and Health.

Chen, P. Y., & Spector, P. E. (1992). Relationships of work stressors with aggression, withdrawal, theft and substance use: An exploratory study. *Journal of Occupational and Organizational Psychology*, *65*(3), 177–184. doi:10.1111/j.2044-8325.1992.tb00495.x

Cohen-Charash, Y., & Mueller, J. S. (2007). Does perceived unfairness exacerbate or mitigate interpersonal counterproductive work behaviors related to envy? *The Journal of Applied Psychology*, *92*(3), 666–680. doi:10.1037/0021-9010.92.3.666 PMID:17484549

Cohn, E. G., & Rotton, J. (1997). Assault as a function of time and temperature: A moderator-variable time-series analysis. *Journal of Personality and Social Psychology*, *72*(6), 13–22. doi:10.1037/0022-3514.72.6.1322

Cressey, D. R. (1960). Epidemiology and individual conduct: A case from criminology. *Pacific Sociological Review*, *3*(2), 47–58. doi:10.2307/1388200

Crino, M. D., & Leap, T. L. (1989). What HR managers must know about employee sabotage. *Personnel*, *66*(5), 31.

Dalal, R. S. (2005). A Meta-Analysis of the Relationship Between Organizational Citizenship Behavior and Counterproductive Work Behavior. *The Journal of Applied Psychology*, *90*(6), 1241–1255. doi:10.1037/0021-9010.90.6.1241 PMID:16316277

De Dreu, C. K. W., & Gelfand, M. J. (2007). Conflict in the workplace: Sources, dynamics, and functions across multiple levels of analysis. In The psychology of conflict and conflict management in organizations (pp. 3–54). New York: Lawrence Erlbaum.

Douglas, S. C., & Martinko, M. J. (2001). Exploring the role of individual differences in the prediction of workplace aggression. *The Journal of Applied Psychology*, *86*(4), 547–559. doi:10.1037/0021-9010.86.4.547 PMID:11519640

Einarsen, S., Hoel, H., Zapf, D., & Cooper, C. (2003). Bullying at work. The way forward. In Bullying and emotional abuse in the workplace. International perspectives in research and practice (pp. 412-416). New York: Taylor & Francis.

Everton, W. J., Mastrangelo, P. M., & Jolton, J. A. (2005). Personality correlates of employees personal use of work computers. *Cyberpsychology & Behavior*, *8*(2), 143–153. doi:10.1089/cpb.2005.8.143 PMID:15938654

Fox, S., & Spector, P. E. (1999). A model of work frustration-aggression. *Journal of Organizational Behavior*, *20*(6), 915–931. doi:10.1002/(SICI)1099-1379(199911)20:6<915::AID-JOB918>3.0.CO;2-6

Fox, S., & Spector, P. E. (2005). *Counterproductive work behavior: Investigations of actors and targets*. Washington, DC: APA. doi:10.1037/10893-000

Fox, S., Spector, P. E., & Miles, D. (2001). Counterproductive work behavior (CWB) in response to job stressors and organizational justice: Some mediator and moderator tests for autonomy and emotions. *Journal of Vocational Behavior*, *59*(3), 291–309. doi:10.1006/jvbe.2001.1803

Gardner, W. L., & Martinko, M. J. (1998). An organizational perspective of the effects of dysfunctional impression management. *Monographs in Organizational Behavior and Industrial Relations, 23*, 69-126.

Geis, G., & Goff, C. (1983). Introduction. In *E.H., Sutherland. White collar crime: The uncut version*. New Haven, CT: Yale University Press.

Giacalone, R. A., & Knouse, S. B. (1990). Justifying wrongful employee behavior: The role of personality in organizational sabotage. *Journal of Business Ethics*, *9*(1), 55–61. doi:10.1007/BF00382564

Giacalone, R. A., Riordan, C. A., & Rosenfeld, P. (1997). Employee sabotage. *Antisocial Behavior in Organizations*, 109-29.

Glueck, S., & Glueck, E. (1950). Unraveling juvenile delinquency. *Juv. Ct. Judges J.*, *2*, 32.

Golparvar, M. (2015). Prediction of Organizational Citizenship Behaviors and Deviant Behaviors Through Impression Management Components. *Quarterly Journal of Social Work*, *4*(1), 3–15.

Gottfredson, M. R., & Hirschi, T. (1990). *A general theory of crime*. Stanford University Press.

Greenberg, J. (1990). Organizational justice: Yesterday, today, and tomorrow. *Journal of Management*, *16*(2), 399–432. doi:10.1177/014920639001600208

Greenberg, J. (1993). Stealing in the name of justice: Informational and interpersonal moderators of theft reactions to underpayment inequity. *Organizational Behavior and Human Decision Processes*, *54*(1), 81–103. doi:10.1006/obhd.1993.1004

Greenberg, J. (1998). The cognitive geometry of employee theft: Negotiating" the line" between taking and stealing. *Monographs in Organizational Behavior and Industrial Relations, 23*, 147-194.

Haynie, D. L., Silver, E., & Teasdale, B. (2006). Neighborhood characteristics, peer networks, and adolescent violence. *Journal of Quantitative Criminology*, *22*(2), 147–169. doi:10.1007/s10940-006-9006-y

Henle, C. A., Giacalone, R. A., & Jurkiewicz, C. L. (2005). The role of ethical ideology in workplace deviance. *Journal of Business Ethics*, *56*(3), 219–222. doi:10.1007/s10551-004-2779-8

Hirschi, T., & Stark, R. (1969). Hellfire and delinquency. *Social Problems*, *17*(2), 202–213. doi:10.2307/799866

Hollinger, R. C. (1986). Acts against the workplace: Social bonding and employee deviance. *Deviant Behavior*, *7*(1), 53–75. doi:10.1080/01639625.1986.9967695

Hollinger, R. C., & Clark, J. P. (1982). Formal and informal social controls of employee deviance. *The Sociological Quarterly*, *23*(3), 333–343. doi:10.1111/j.1533-8525.1982.tb01016.x

Hollinger, R. C., Slora, K. B., & Terris, W. (1992). Deviance in the fast-food restaurant: Correlates of employee theft, altruism, and counter productivity. *Deviant Behavior: An Interdisciplinary Journal*, *13*(2), 155–184. doi:10.1080/01639625.1992.9967906

Jang, S. J. (2007). Gender differences in strain, negative emotions, and coping behaviors: A general strain theory approach. *Justice Quarterly*, *24*(3), 523–553. doi:10.1080/07418820701485486

Judge, T., LePine, J., & Rich, B. (2006). Loving yourself abundantly: Relationship of the narcissistic personality to self- and other perceptions of workplace deviance, leadership and task performance. *The Journal of Applied Psychology*, *91*(4), 762–776. doi:10.1037/0021-9010.91.4.762 PMID:16834504

Kemelgor, B., Sussman, L., Kline, J., & Zurada, J. (2007). Who are the difficult employees? Psychopathological attributions of their co-workers. *Journal of Business & Economics Research*, *5*(10), 47–62.

Kidwell, R. E. (2005). The prevalence (and ambiguity) of deviant behavior at work. In Managing organizational deviance (pp. 1-21). Thousand Oaks, CA: SAGE Publishing. doi:10.4135/9781452231105.n1

Kornhauser, R. R. (1978). *Social sources of delinquency: An appraisal of analytic models*. Chicago: University of Chicago Press.

Kubrin, C. E., Stucky, T. D., & Krohn, M. D. (2008). *Researching theories of crime and delinquency*. Oxford, UK: Oxford University Press.

Kumi, E. (2013). Are demographic variables predictors of work deviant behavior? *International Journal of Management Sciences*, *1*(1), 1–10.

Lawrence, T. B., & Robinson, S. L. (2007). Aint misbehavin: Workplace deviance as organizational resistance. *Journal of Management*, *33*(3), 378–394. doi:10.1177/0149206307300816

Lutgen-Sandvik, P. (2006). Take this job and...: Quitting and other forms of resistance to workplace bullying. *Communication Monographs*, *73*(4), 406–433. doi:10.1080/03637750601024156

Magione, T., & Quinn, R. (1975). Job satisfaction, counterproductive behaviour and drog used at work. *The Journal of Applied Psychology*, *60*(1), 114–116. doi:10.1037/h0076355 PMID:1110252

Mars, G. (1982). *Cheats at Work: An Anthropology of Workplace Crime*. Boston: G. Allen and Unwin.

Matsueda, R. L. (1982). Testing control theory and differential association: A causal modeling approach. *American Sociological Review*, *47*(4), 489–504. doi:10.2307/2095194

O'Leary-Kelly, A. M., Griffin, R. W., & Glew, D. J. (1996). Organization-motivated aggression: A research framework. *Academy of Management Review*, *21*, 225–253.

Orcutt, J. D. (1987). Differential association and marijuana use: A closer look at Sutherland (with a little help from Becker). *Criminology*, *25*(2), 341–358. doi:10.1111/j.1745-9125.1987.tb00801.x

Pantaleo, K. (2011). *Serving up crime: A social learning perspective of employee deviance in restaurants* (Doctoral dissertation). Indiana University of Pennsylvania.

Perlow, R., & Latham, L. L. (1993). Relationship of client abuse with locus of control and gender: A longitudinal study in mental retardation facilities. *The Journal of Applied Psychology*, *78*(5), 831–834. doi:10.1037/0021-9010.78.5.831 PMID:8253634

Reamer, F. G. (2012). *Eye on Ethics*. Retrieved May 1, 2017, from http://www.socialworktoday.com/news/eoe_051712.shtml

Robinson, S. L., & Bennett, R. J. (1995). A typology of deviant workplace behaviors: A multidimensional scaling study. *Academy of Management Journal*, *38*(2), 555–572. doi:10.2307/256693

Robinson, S. L., & Greenberg, J. (1998). Employees behaving badly: Dimensions, determinants and dilemmas in the study of workplace deviance. *Journal of Organizational Behavior (1986-1998)*, 1.

Sablynski, C. J., Mitchell, T. R., James, L. R., & McIntyre, M. (2001). *Identifying aggressive individuals via conditional reasoning: An experimental study*. Academy of Management Conference, Washington, DC.

Sackett, P. R., & DeVore, C. J. (2001). Counterproductive behaviors at work. In N. Anderson, D.S. Ones, H.K. Sinangil, & C. Viswesvaran (Eds.), Handbook of industrial, work, and organizational psychology (pp. 145–164). London: Sage. doi:10.4135/9781848608320.n9

Salin, D. (2003). Ways of explaining workplace bullying: A review of enabling, motivating and precipitating structures and processes in the work environment. *Human Relations*, *56*(10), 1213–1232. doi:10.1177/00187267035610003

Sampson, R. J., & Laub, J. H. (1993). Structural variations in juvenile court processing: Inequality, the underclass, and social control. *Law & Society Review*, *27*(2), 285–311. doi:10.2307/3053938

Sellers, C. S., & Winfree, L. T. (1990). Differential associations and definitions: A panel study of youthful drinking behavior. *The International Journal of the Addictions*, *25*(7), 755–771. doi:10.3109/10826089009056217 PMID:2272721

Sharma, N., & Paluchova, J. (2014). An aerial glimpse of workplace deviance in Indian service industry. *Gurukul Business Review*, *10*, 11–16.

Sharma, N., & Singh, V. K. (2016). Effect of workplace incivility on job satisfaction and turnover intentions in India. *South Asian Journal of Global Business Research*, *5*(2), 234–249. doi:10.1108/SAJGBR-02-2015-0020

Sharma, N., Singh, V. K., & Kishor, J. (2013). Demographic differences, causes and impact of workplace production deviance on organizations: An empirical study on non-punctuality of employees in service cluster. *Research Journal of Social Science and Management*, *3*(8), 99–106.

Skarlicki, D. P., & Folger, R. (1997). Retaliation in the workplace: The roles of distributive, procedural, and interactional justice. *The Journal of Applied Psychology*, *82*(3), 434–443. doi:10.1037/0021-9010.82.3.434

Skinner, B. F. (1953). *Science and human behavior*. New York: Macmillan.

Skinner, B. F. (1959). *Cumulative record*. New York: Appleton Century Crofts.

Spector, P. E. (1997). *Job satisfaction: Application, assessment, causes, and consequences* (Vol. 3). Sage Publications.

Spector, P. E., Fox, S., Penney, L. M., Bruursema, K., Goh, A., & Kessler, S. (2006). The dimensionality of counterproductivity: Are all counterproductive behaviors created equal? *Journal of Vocational Behavior, 68*(3), 446–460. doi:10.1016/j.jvb.2005.10.005

Storms, P. L., & Spector, P. E. (1987). Relationships of organizational frustration with reported behavioural reactions: The moderating effect of locus of control. *Journal of Occupational Psychology, 60*(3), 227–234. doi:10.1111/j.2044-8325.1987.tb00255.x

Tepper, B. J., Carr, J. C., Breaux, D. M., Gieder, S., Hu, C., & Hua, W. (2009). Abusive supervision, intentions to quit and employees workplace deviance. *Organizational Behavior and Human Decision Processes, 109*(2), 156–167. doi:10.1016/j.obhdp.2009.03.004

Thornberry, T. P., Lizotte, A. J., Krohn, M. D., Farnworth, M., & Jang, S. J. (1994). Delinquent peers, beliefs, and delinquent behavior: A longitudinal test of interactional theory. *Criminology, 32*(1), 47–83. doi:10.1111/j.1745-9125.1994.tb01146.x

Trevino, L. K. (1986). Ethical decision making in organizations: A person-situation interactionist model. *Academy of Management Review, 11*(3), 601–617.

Warr, M., & Stafford, M. (1991). The influence of delinquent peers: What they think or what they do? *Criminology, 29*(4), 851–866. doi:10.1111/j.1745-9125.1991.tb01090.x

Wren, D. A., & Bedeian, A. G. (2009). *The Evolution of Management Thought.* Hoboken, NJ: John Wiley & Sons.

KEY TERMS AND DEFINITIONS

Differential Association: Sutherland's theory of differential association proposes that while interacting with others, people learn their values, attitudes, techniques and motives for criminal behavior.

Differential Reinforcement: It is the implementation of reinforcing only the behavior one wish to increase in future.

Employee Deviance/Counterproductive Work Behavior: These are the employee behaviors which are considered harmful for the organization or its people.

Imitation: It is a kind of behavior whereby a person observes and replicates someone else's behavior.

Interpersonal Deviance: Deliberate behaviors that cause harm to the people of the organization.

Organizational Deviance: Deliberate behaviors that cause harm to the organization.

Personal Aggression: An intent or motive to harm fellow workers in the organization.

Political Deviance: A minor kind of deviant behavior that is directed at a specific individual or directed to benefit or harm certain individuals in an organization.

Production Deviance: This kind of deviance includes behaviors that waste time and other useful resources of an organization affecting the overall productivity.

Property Deviance: This kind of deviant behavior includes either theft or destruction of facility or organizations' property.

Social Learning: Learning that takes place in social context and can occur also through observation or direct instruction.

Compilation of References

Abrudan, E. (2011). Ethical Expertise and Bioethics. *Journal for Study of Religions and Ideologies*, *10*(30), 399–402.

Accreditation of the social services providers. (n.d.). Retrieved from http://www.mmuncii.ro/j33/index.php/ro/comunicare/intrebari-frecvente/3575-2014-acreditarefss?highlight=WyJhY3JlZGl0YXJlIl0=

Adam, S. (2009, Nov.). Profesia de cadru didactic între reprezentare socială şi vocaţie individuală [The profession of professor between the social representation and the individual vocation]. *Revista de Cercetare în Ştiinţe ale Educaţiei, Sociologia educaţiei.*

Agheorghesei, D. T. (2011). *Etica în afaceri* [Ethics in business]. Iasi, Romania: Alexandu Ioan Cuza University Publishing.

Agheorghiesei (Corodeanu), D.T. (2013). Etica în Administrația Publică. Ed. Tritonic. București.

Agheorghiesei, D. T., Iliescu, L., Gavrilovici, C., & Oprea, L. (2013). What is to be expected from an ethics audit integrated within the accreditation process of hospitals from Romania? *Iranian Journal of Public Health*, *42*(7), 737–747. PMID:24427752

Agich, G. J. (2009). The Issue of Expertise in Clinical Ethics. *Diametros,* (22), 3–20. Retrieved from: http://www.diametros.iphils.uj.edu.pl/serwis/pdf/diam22agich.PDF?id=8055

Agnew, E. N. (2004). *From Charity to Social Work: Mary E. Richmond and the Creation of an American Profession* (Vol. 13). University of Illinois Press.

Agnew, R. (1991). The interactive effects of peer variables on delinquency. *Criminology*, *29*(1), 47–72. doi:10.1111/j.1745-9125.1991.tb01058.x

Ahmadi, N. N. (2003). Globalisation of consciousness and new challenges for international social work. *International Journal of Social Work Welfare*, *12*, 14-23.

Akers, R. L., & Jensen, G. F. (2006). The empirical status of social learning theory of crime and deviance: The past, present, and future. *Taking Stock: The Status of Criminological Theory*, *15*, 37-76.

Akers, R. L., & Sellers, C. S. (2009). *Criminology theories.* Academic Press.

Akers, R. (1985). *Deviant behavior: A social learning approach* (3rd ed.). Wadsworth.

Akers, R. L. (1998). *Social learning and social structure: A general theory of crime and deviance*. Boston, MA: Northeastern University Press.

Akers, R. L., Krohn, M. D., Lanza-Kaduce, L., & Radosevich, M. (1979). Social learning and deviant behavior: A specific test of a general theory. *American Sociological Review*, *44*(4), 636–655. doi:10.2307/2094592 PMID:389120

Akers, R. L., & Lee, G. (1996). A longitudinal test of social learning theory: Adolescent smoking. *Journal of Drug Issues*, *26*(2), 317–343. doi:10.1177/002204269602600203

Akhtar, F. N. (2012). *Mastering Social Work Values and Ethics*. Jessica Kingsley Publishers.

Alarid, L. F., Burton, V. S. Jr, & Cullen, F. T. (2000). Gender and crime among felony offenders: Assessing the generality of social control and differential association theories. *Journal of Research in Crime and Delinquency*, *37*(2), 171–199. doi:10.1177/0022427800037002002

Alexiu, M. (2003). Valori şi faze ale acţiunii în asistenţa socială [Values and phases of action in social work]. In *Tratat de asistenţă socială* [Treaty of Social Work] (pp. 319–365). Iaşi: Ed. Polirom.

Alexiu, T. M. (2011). Values and Phases of Action in Social Assistance. In *Treaty of social assistance*. Iasi: Polirom Publishing House.

Allen, A. (2016). Privacy and Medicine. In E. N. Zalta (Ed.), *The Stanford Encyclopedia of Philosophy*. Retrieved May 16, 2017, from https://plato.stanford.edu/archives/win2016/entries/privacy-medicine/

Allen, M.B. (1995). The ethics audit. *Nonprofit World*, *13*(A6), 51.

Allen, A. (1997). Genetic Privacy: Emerging Concepts and Values. In M. Rothstein (Ed.), *Genetic Secrets: Protecting Privacy and Confidentiality in the Genetic Era* (pp. 31–59). New Haven, CT: Yale University Press.

Allen, K. (2012). What is an ethical dilemma? *The New Social Worker*, *19*(2), 6–7.

Allison, S., Stacey, K., Dadds, V., Roeger, L., Wood, A., & Martin, G. (2003). What the family brings: Gathering evidence for strengths-based work. *Journal of Family Therapy*, *25*(3), 263–284. doi:10.1111/1467-6427.00248

Almason, A. L. (1997). Personal Liability Implications of the Duty to Warn Are Hard Pills to Swallow: From Tarasoff To Hutchinson v. Patel and Beyond. *The Journal of Contemporary Health Law and Policy*, *13*(2), 471–486. PMID:9212527

Ambrose, M. L., Seabright, M. A., & Schminke, M. (2002). Sabotage in the workplace: The role of organizational injustice. *Organizational Behavior and Human Decision Processes*, *89*(1), 947–965. doi:10.1016/S0749-5978(02)00037-7

American Medical Association. (1994). *Code of medical ethics (Report, Council on ethical and Judicial Affairs)*. Chicago: Author.

Anderson, D. R., Sweeney, D. J., Williams, T. A., Camm, J. D., & Cochran, J. J. (2015). *An introduction to management science: quantitative approaches to decision making*. Cengage Learning.

Anderson, C. A., Anderson, K. B., & Deuser, W. E. (1996). Examining an affective aggression framework weapon and temperature effects on aggressive thoughts, affect, and attitudes. *Personality and Social Psychology Bulletin*, *22*(4), 366–376. doi:10.1177/0146167296224004

Anderson, L., & Dedrick, R. (1990). Development of the trust in physician scale: A measure to assess interpersonal trust in patient-physician relationships. *Psychological Reports*, *67*, 1091–1100. PMID:2084735

Anwar, M. N., Arif, I., Sarwar, M., & Awan, R. N. (2011). Gender differences in workplace deviant behavior of university teachers and modification techniques. *International Education Studies*, *4*(1), 193–197. doi:10.5539/ies.v4n1p193

Apel, K.-O. (1999). *The Response of Discourse Ethics to the Moral Challenge of the Human Situation as Such and Especially Today*. Mercier Lectures, Louvain-la-Neuve, March.

Apel, K.-O. (1989). Normative Ethics and Strategical Rationality. The Philosophical Problem of Political Ethics. In R. Schurmann (Ed.), *The Public Realm. Essays on Discursive Types in Political Philosophy* (pp. 107–131). State University of New York Press.

Apel, K.-O. (1992). The Ecological Crisis as a Problem for Discourse Ethics. In A. Ofsti (Ed.), *Ecology and Ethics* (pp. 219–260). Trondheim: Nordland Academy of Arts and Sciences.

Apel, K.-O. (1993). How to Ground a Universalistic Ethics of Co-Responsibility for the Effects of Collective Actions and Activities? *Philosophica*, *52*(2), 9–29.

Apostu, I. (2012). Consensual Union in Romania. Legalization, Value, Conflict and Consequences. *European Journal of Science and Theology, 8*(Supp. 1), 303-312.

Apostu, I. (2013). The Traditionalism of the Modern Family – Social and Legal Directions and Contradictions. *Procedia: Social and Behavioral Sciences*, *92*, 46–49. doi:10.1016/j.sbspro.2013.08.635

Aristotle. (1988). *Etica Nicomahică* (S. Petecel, Trans.). Bucharest: Ştiinţifică şi Enciclopedică Publishing House.

Arriaga, X. B., & Foshee, V. A. (2004). Adolescent dating violence: Do adolescents follow in their friends, or their parents, footsteps? *Journal of Interpersonal Violence*, *19*(2), 162–184. doi:10.1177/0886260503260247 PMID:15006000

Ashford, J. B., & Lecroy, C. W. (2013). *Human behavior in the social environment: A multidimensional perspective*. Belmont, CA: Brooks/Cole.

Ashwoorth, A. (1989). Criminal Justice and Deserved Sentences. *Criminal Law Review (London, England)*, *36*, 340–355.

Atar, B., Saroiu, S., & Koutsky, L. A. (2002). Obtaining Sensitive Data through the Web: An Example of Design and Methods. *Epidemiology (Cambridge, Mass.)*, *13*(6), 640–645. doi:10.1097/00001648-200211000-00007 PMID:12410004

Australian Association of Social Workers. (2010). *Code of Ethics.* Retrieved from: https://www.aasw.asn.au/document/item/1201

Australian Association of Social Workers. (2010). *Code of Ethics.* Retrieved July 14, 2017, from: https://www.aasw.asn.au/document/item/1201

Axinn, J., & Levin, H. (1975). *Social welfare: A history of the American response to need.* New York: Harper & Row.

Bandura, A., & Walters, R. H. (1963). *Social learning and personality development.* Academic Press.

Bandura, A. (1977). Self-efficacy: Toward a unifying theory of behavioral change. *Psychological Review*, *84*(2), 191–215. doi:10.1037/0033-295X.84.2.191 PMID:847061

Bandura, A. (1986). The explanatory and predictive scope of self-efficacy theory. *Journal of Social and Clinical Psychology*, *4*(3), 359–373. doi:10.1521/jscp.1986.4.3.359

Bandura, A. (2002). Selective Moral Disengagement in the Exercise of Moral Agency. *Journal of Moral Education*, *31*(2), 101–119. doi:10.1080/0305724022014322

Bandura, A., & Jeffery, R. W. (1973). Role of symbolic coding and rehearsal processes in observational learning. *Journal of Personality and Social Psychology*, *26*(1), 122–130. doi:10.1037/h0034205

Banks, S. (1998). Professional ethics in social work—What future? *The British Journal of Social Work*, *28*(2), 213-231. https://doi.org/10.1093/oxfordjournals.bjsw.a011324

Banks, S. (2008). Critical commentary: Social work ethics. *British Journal of Social Work*, *38*(6), 1238-1249. https://doi.org/10.1093/bjsw/bcn099

Banks, S. (1995). *Ethics and Values in Social Work.* London: Macmillan. doi:10.1007/978-1-349-24145-3

Banks, S. (1998). Professional Ethics in Social Work - What Future? *British Journal of Social Work*, *28*(2), 213–231. doi:10.1093/oxfordjournals.bjsw.a011324

Banks, S. (2001). *Ethics and values in social work.* Hampshire, UK: Palgrave.

Banks, S. (2008). Critical commentary: Social work ethics. *British Journal of Social Work*, *38*(6), 1238–1249. doi:10.1093/bjsw/bcn099

Banks, S., & Williams, R. (2005). Accounting for ethical difficulties in social welfare work: Issues, problems and dilemmas. *British Journal of Social Work*, *35*(7), 1005–1022. doi:10.1093/bjsw/bch199

Barker, R. L. (2003). *The social work dictionary* (5th ed.). Washington, DC: NASW Press.

Baron, J., & Spranca, M. (1997). Protected Values. *Organizational Behavior and Human Decision Processes*, *70*(1), 1–16. doi:10.1006/obhd.1997.2690 PMID:9236161

Baron, R. A., & Richardson, D. R. (1994). *Human aggression* (2nd ed.). New York: Pleun.

BASW. (2012). *The Code of Ethics for Social Work: Statement of Principles*. BASW.

Bazemore, G. (1998). Restorative justice and earned redemption: Communities, victims, and offender reintegration. *The American Behavioral Scientist*, *41*(6), 768–813. doi:10.1177/0002764298041006003

Bazemore, G., & Umbreit, M. (2001). *A comparison of four restorative conferencing models. In Juvenile Justice Bulletin* (pp. 1–19). Washington, DC: U.S. Department of Justice.

Beauchamp, T., & Childress, J. (2009). Principles of Biomedical Ethics (6th ed.). New York: Oxford University Press.

Beauchamp, T. L., & Childress, J. F. (2001). *Principles of Biomedical Ethics* (5th ed.). New York: Oxford University Press.

Bechtoldt, M. N., Welk, C., Zapf, D., & Hartig, J. (2007). Main and moderating effects of self-control, organizational justice, and emotional labor on counterproductive behavior at work. *European Journal of Work and Organizational Psychology*, *16*(4), 479–500. doi:10.1080/13594320701662618

Beckett, C., Maynard, A., & Jordan, P. (2017). Values and Ethics in Social Work. *Sage*.

Beck, U. (1992). *The Risk Society Risk Society: Towards a New Modernity* (1st ed.). SAGE Publications Ltd.

Benn, P. (1998). *Ethics*. London: UCL Press.

Bennett, J. W. (1998). Classic anthropology. *American Anthropologist*, *100*(4), 951–956. doi:10.1525/aa.1998.100.4.951

Bennett, R. J., & Robinson, S. L. (2000). Development of a Measure of Workplace Deviance. *The Journal of Applied Psychology*, *85*(3), 349–360. doi:10.1037/0021-9010.85.3.349 PMID:10900810

Bentham, J. (1970). *Introduction to the Principles of Morals and Legislation* (2nd ed.). London: Athlone Press.

Berlin, I. (2002). *Liberty: Incorporating Four Essays on Liberty* (2nd ed.). Oxford: Oxford University Press. doi:10.1093/019924989X.001.0001

Berry, C. M., Ones, D. S., & Sackett, P. R. (2007). Interpersonal deviance, organizational deviance, and their common correlates: A review and meta-analysis. *The Journal of Applied Psychology*, *92*(2), 410–424. doi:10.1037/0021-9010.92.2.410 PMID:17371088

Bies, R. J. (2001). Interactional (in)justice: The sacred and the profane. *Advances in Organizational Justice*, 89-118.

Biestek, F. (1961). *The casework relationship*. London: George Allen and Unwin.

Blundo, R. (2001). Learning strengths-based practice: Challenging our personal and professional frames. *Families in Society*, *82*(3), 296–304. doi:10.1606/1044-3894.192

Boboc, A. (1984). *The History of Modern and Contemporaneous Philosophy* (Vol. 1). Bucharest: Academiei RSR Publishing House.

Boehm, W. W. (1959). *The social casework method in social work education. A project report of the curriculum study* (Vol. 10). New York: Council on Social Work Education.

Bogo, M., & McKnight, K. (2005). Clinical supervision in social work. *The Clinical Supervisor*, *24*(1/2), 49–67.

Bok, S. (1982). *Secrets: On the Ethics of Concealment and Revelation*. New York: Pantheon Books.

Borţun, D. (2010). *Responsabilitatea socială corporativă* [Corporative social responsibility]. Bucureşti: SNSPA.

Bostan, I., & Grosu, V. (2015). The Health Risk Management and its Legal Impact. *Revista Romana de Bioetica*, *13*(1), 37–43.

Bowen, G. N. (2008). Naturalistic inquiry and the saturation concept: A research note. *Qualitative Research*, *8*(1), 137–152. doi:10.1177/1468794107085301

Bowles, W., Collingridge, M., Curry, S., & Valentine, B. (2006). *Ethical Practice in Social Work*. Open University Press.

Boyle, D. M., Hermanson, D. R., & Wilkins, A. (2011). *Ethics Audits: Implications for Internal Auditors Internal Auditing*. ProQuest Central.

Braithwaite, J. (1989). *Crime, shame, and reintegration*. Cambridge, UK: Cambridge University Press. doi:10.1017/CBO9780511804618

Braithwaite, J. (1998). Restorative justice. In M. Tonry (Ed.), *The handbook of crime and punishment* (pp. 323–344). Oxford, UK: Oxford University Press.

Braithwaite, J. (1999). Restorative justice: Assessing optimistic and pessimistic accounts. In M. Tonry (Ed.), *Crime and justice: A review of research* (Vol. 25, pp. 1–127). doi:10.1086/449287

Braithwaite, J. (2002). *Restorative justice and responsive regulation*. New York: Oxford University Press.

Braithwaite, J. (2003). Principles of restorative justice. In A. Von Hirsch, J. V. Roberts, A. Bottoms, K. Roach, & M. Schiff (Eds.), *Restorative justice and criminal justice: Competing or reconcilable paradigms?* (pp. 1–20). Oxford, UK: Hart.

Braithwaite, J., & Strang, H. (2001). Introduction: Restorative justice and civil society. In H. Strang & J. Braithwaite (Eds.), *Restorative justice and civil society* (pp. 1–13). Cambridge, UK: Cambridge University Press.

Braithwaite, V. (1998). The value orientations underlying liberalism conservatism. *Personality and Individual Differences, 25*(3), 575–589. doi:10.1016/S0191-8869(98)00111-1

Brenden, M. A., & Shank, B. (2012). Social work for social justice: Strengthening social work education through the integration of catholic social teaching. *Social Work & Christianity, 39*(2), 128–150.

Brill, C. K. (2001). Looking at the social work profession through the eye of the NASW Code of Ethics. *Research on Social Work Practice, 11*(2), 223–234. doi:10.1177/104973150101100209

Briskman, L. (2001). A Moral Crisis for Social Work: Critical Practice and Codes of Ethics. Critical Social Work, 2(1), www.uwindsor.ca/units/socialwork/critical.nsf, (Accessed on 23 October 2008).

British Association of Social Workers (BASW). (2012). *Code of Ethics.* Retrieved July 13, 2017, from http://www.basw.co.uk/codeofethics/

Brod, M., Tesler, L. E., & Christensen, T. L. (2009). Qualitative research and content validity: Developing best practices based on science and experience. *Quality of Life Research: An International Journal of Quality of Life Aspects of Treatment, Care and Rehabilitation, 18*(9), 1263–1278. doi:10.1007/s11136-009-9540-9 PMID:19784865

Brun, C., & Rapp, R. C. (2001). Strengths-based case management: Individuals' perspective on strengths and the case manager relationship. *Social Work, 46*(3), 278–288.

Bubnys, R. (2014). Reflektavimo kompetencijos struktūra socialinio darbo studentams atliekant praktikas [The Structure of Reflection Competency during Social Work Students' Practices]. *Socialinė teorija, empirija, politika ir praktika, 9*, 50-63.

Buğra, A. (2008). *Kapitalizm, yoksulluk ve Türkiye'de sosyal politika.* İstanbul: İletişim Yayınları.

Bulgaru, M. (2012). Asistenţa socială în contextul globalizării [Social assistance in the context of globalization]. *Studia Universitatis Moldaviae. Seria Ştiinţe Sociale, 8*(58), 5-11.

Bulgaru, M. (2013). Deontologia asistenţei sociale [Deontology of social work]. *Studia Universitatis Moldavie Seria Ştiinţe Sociale, 8*(68), 3-15.

Bulgaru, M. (2013). Deontologia asistentei sociale [The deontology of social work]. *Studia Universitatis Moldaviae. Seria Ştiinţe Sociale, 8*(68), 3-15. Retrieved from http://studiamsu.eu/wp-content/uploads/01.-p.03-15.pdf

Bulgaru, M. (2013). Deontologia asistentei sociale [The deontology of social work]. *Studia Universitatis Moldaviae. Seria Ştiinţe Sociale, 8*(68), 3-15. Retrieved from: http://studiamsu.eu/wp-content/uploads/01.-p.03-15.pdf

Burgess, R. L., & Akers, R. L. (1966). A differential association-reinforcement theory of criminal behavior. *Social Problems, 14*(2), 128–147. doi:10.2307/798612

Burmeister, E., & Aitken, L. M. (2012). Sample size: How many is enough? *Australian Critical Care, 25*(4), 271–274. doi:10.1016/j.aucc.2012.07.002 PMID:22835279

Burroughs, S. M., Bing, M. N., & James, L. R. (1999). *Effects of personality and job stressors on affective reactions and aggressive work behaviors.* American Psychological Association and the National Institute for Occupational Safety and Health interdisciplinary conference on Work, Stress, and Health.

Business Integrity. (2013). Justiţia socială [Social justice]. *Jurnal de cercetare anticoruptie, 65*. Retrieved May 25, 2017, from http://www.businessintegrity.ro/content/justi%C5%A3ia-social%C4%83

Butler, I. (2002). A code of ethics for social work and social care research. *British Journal of Social Work, 32*(2), 239–248. doi:10.1093/bjsw/32.2.239 PMID:12774784

Buzducea, D., Rujoiu, V. & Lazăr, F. (2011). *International Social Work: A Supplement of Social Work Review*. Bucureşti: Editura Universităţii din Bucureşti.

Buzducea, D. (2009). *Sisteme moderne de asistenţă socială. Tendinţe globale şi practici locale* [Modern systems of social work. Global tendencies and local practices]. Iaşi: Editura Polirom.

Buzducea, D. (2017). *Risc si societate* [Risk and society]. Bucharest, Romania: Tritonic.

Campanini, A. (2013). *International perspective in Social Work – A new challenge?* Retrieved May 25, 2017, from http://scienzepolitiche.unical.it/bacheca/archivio/materiale/1862/Social%20Work%20in%20a%20globalizing%20world%20(University%20of%20Calabria,%20May%2026%20-%2031%202013)/INTERNATIONAL%20CAMPANINI%20International%20perspective%20in%20sw%20[modalit%C3%A0%20compatibilit%C3%A0].pdf

Caras (Frunză), A., & Sandu, A. (2014). Epistemic and Pragmatic Backgrounds of Supervision of Ethics. *Procedia - Social and Behavioral Sciences, 149,* 142-151. https://doi.org/10.1016/j.sbspro.2014.08.178

Caras, A., & Sandu, A. (2013). Ethical Evaluation of Social Services and the Need for Ethics Committees. *Procedia - Social and Behavioral Sciences, 92,* 142-149. https://doi.org/10.1016/j.sbspro.2013.08.650

Caras, A., & Sandu, A. (2014). The Role of Supervision in Professional Development of Social Work Specialists. *Journal of Social Work Practice: Psychotherapeutic Approaches in Health, Welfare and the Community, 28*(1), 75-94. https://doi.org/10.1080/02650533.2012.763024

Caras, A., & Sandu, A. (2014b). *Relational Autonomy – Connections Between Moral Agent Theory and Supervision of Ethics.* Presented at the ISUD Tenth World Congress, the Human Being: Its Nature and Functions, Craiova, Romania.

Caras, A. (2014). Perspectives for Reconstruction of Ethical Expertise. *Postmodern Openings*, *5*(2), 81–96. doi:10.18662/po/2014.0502.06

Caras, A., & Sandu, A. (2014a). The Role of Supervision in Professional Development of Social Work Specialists. *Journal of Social Work Practice: Psychotherapeutic Approaches in Health, Welfare and the Community*, *28*(1), 75–94.

Carroll, A., & Buchholtz, A. K. (2012). Business & society: ethics, sustainability, and stakeholder management. South-Western Cengage Learning.

Carroll, J. S., Perkowitz, W. T., Lurigio, A. J., & Weaver, F. M. (1987). Sentencing goals, causal attributions, ideology, and personality. *Journal of Personality and Social Psychology*, *52*(1), 107–118. doi:10.1037/0022-3514.52.1.107 PMID:3820064

Chapin, R., & Cox, E. O. (2002). Changing the paradigm. *Journal of Gerontological Social Work*, *36*(3-4), 165–179. doi:10.1300/J083v36n03_13

Chateauneuf, D., Ramde, J., & Avril, A. (2016). Processes Employed by Social Work Practitioners in Child Welfare for Exchanging and Using Knowledge. *Journal of Social Work Practice*, *30*(4), 397–415. doi:10.1080/02650533.2015.1116439

Chenoweth, L., & McAuliffe, D. (2005). *The road to social work and human service practice: An introductory text*. Southbank Victoria: Thomson Learning.

Chen, P. Y., & Spector, P. E. (1992). Relationships of work stressors with aggression, withdrawal, theft and substance use: An exploratory study. *Journal of Occupational and Organizational Psychology*, *65*(3), 177–184. doi:10.1111/j.2044-8325.1992.tb00495.x

Çifçi, G. E., & Gönen, E. (2011). Sosyal hizmet uygulamalarinda etik karar verme süreci. *Toplum ve Sosyal Hizmet Dergisi*, *22*(2), 149–160.

Clark, C. (2000). *Social Work Ethics*. London: Palgrave.

Clark, C. (2000). *Social Work Ethics*. London: Palgrave.

Clinical Social Work Association. (2016). *Code of ethics*. Retrieved from http://www.clinicalsocialworkassociation.org/CSWA-Ethics

Cohen-Charash, Y., & Mueller, J. S. (2007). Does perceived unfairness exacerbate or mitigate interpersonal counterproductive work behaviors related to envy? *The Journal of Applied Psychology*, *92*(3), 666–680. doi:10.1037/0021-9010.92.3.666 PMID:17484549

Cohn, E. G., & Rotton, J. (1997). Assault as a function of time and temperature: A moderator-variable time-series analysis. *Journal of Personality and Social Psychology*, *72*(6), 13–22. doi:10.1037/0022-3514.72.6.1322

Cojocaru, Ş. (2003). Reabilitarea bazată pe comunitate a persoanelor cu dizabilităţi [Community-based rehabilitation of people with disabilities]. *Revista de Cercetare şi Intervenţie Socială*, 2.

Cojocaru, Ş. (2005). *Metode apreciative în asistenţa socială. Ancheta, supervizarea şi managementul de caz* [Appreciative methods in social work. Inquiry, supervision and case management]. Iaşi: Polirom Publishing.

Cojocaru, Ş. (2010). *Evaluarea programelor de asistenţă social* [Assessing the social welfare programs]. Iasi, Romania: Polirom Publishing.

Cojocaru, D., Sandu, A., & Oprea, L. (2013). Încrederea în relaţia medic-pacient [Trust in the doctor-patient relationship]. In *Relaţia medic-pacient* [The relationship between the doctor and the patient] (pp. 95–123). Iasi, Romania: Polirom Publishing.

Cojocaru, S. (2005). *Metode Apreciative in Asistenta Sociala – Ancheta, Supervizarea si Managementul de Caz* [Appreciative Methods in Social Work – Inquiry, Supervision and Case Management]. Iasi, Romania: Polirom Publishing.

Cojocaru, S. (2005). *Metode Apreciative în Asistenţa Socială. Ancheta, Supervizarea şi Managementul de Caz* [Appreciative Methods in Social Work. Inquiery, Supervision and Case Management]. Iasi: Polirom Publishing.

Colegiul National al Asistentilor Sociali (CNASR). (2008). *Codul deontologic al profesiei de asistent social.* Publicat in Monitorul Oficial al Romaniei, Partea I, Nr. 173/6.III.2008. Retrieved from: http://www.carp-omenia.ro/wp-content/uploads/2015/07/cod_deontologic_as.pdf

Collingridge, M., Miller, S., & Bowles, W. (2008). Privacy and confidentiality in social work. *Australian Social Work, 54*(2), 3–13. doi:10.1080/03124070108414319

Comisia Europeana (C.E.). (2017). *Raport general - Activităţile Uniunii Europene. Raportul general publicat de Comisia Europeană prezintă principalele iniţiative şi realizări ale UE din anul precedent. UE în 2016.* Retrieved May 25, 2017, from https://europa.eu/european-union/documents-publications/reports-booklets/general-report_ro

Comte-Sponville, A. (1995). *Petit Traité des grandes vertus.* Paris: P.U.F.

Congress, E., & McAuliffe, D. (2006). Professional codes in Australia and the United States. *Social Work Ethics, 49*(2), 151–164. https://doi.org/10.1177/0020872806061211

Congress, E. (2000). What Social Workers Should Know About Ethics: Understanding and Resolving Practice Dilemmas. *Administration in Social Work, 1*(1), 1–26.

Congress, E. P. (1999). *Social work values and ethics: Identifying and resolving professional dilemmas.* Chicago: Nelson Hall.

Congress, E. P. (2000). What social workers should know about ethics: Understanding and resolving ethical dilemmas. *Administration in Social Work, 1*(1), 1–25.

Congress, E., & McAuliffe, D. (2006). Social work ethics: Professional codes in Australia and the United States. *International Social Work, 49*(2), 151–164. doi:10.1177/0020872806061211

Conrad, A. P. (1988). Ethical considerations in the psychosocial process. *Social Casework, 69*(10), 603–610.

CooperRiis Healing Community. (2014a). *Board operating principles*. Mill Spring, NC: Author.

CooperRiis Healing Community. (2014b). *Manual of policies, programs, procedures and practices*. Mill Spring, NC: Author.

Copoeru, I., Moldovan, S., Agheorghiesei, D. T., Ciuhodaru, T., Seghedin, E., & Iorga, M. (2013). The Inter-Agency Cooperation in Healthcare and Social Services for Substance Misuse and Addiction in Romania: A Case Study. *Revista de Asistenţă Socială, 2*, 125–133.

Corbin, J. M., & Strauss, A. (2008). *Basics of qualitative research: techniques and procedures for developing Grounded Theory* (3rd ed.). London, UK: Sage Publications Inc. doi:10.4135/9781452230153

Corey, G., Corey, M. S., & Callanan, P. (2003). *Issues and ethics in the helping profession* (6th ed.). Pacific Grove, CA: Brooks/Cole Publishing.

Corley, M. C., Minick, P., Elswick, R. K., & Jacobs, M. (2005). Nurse moral distress and ethical work environment. *Nursing Ethics, 12*(4), 382–390. doi:10.1191/0969733005ne809oa PMID:16045246

Cournoyer, B. R., & Powers, G. T. (2002). Evidence-based social work: The quiet revolution continues. In A. R. Roberts & G. Greene (Eds.), *Social workers' desk reference* (pp. 798–807). New York: Oxford University Press.

Cowger, C. D. (1998). Clientilism and clientification: Impediments to strengths based social work practice. *Journal of Sociology and Social Welfare, 25*(1), 25–37.

Cozma, C. (2001). Introducere în aretelogie, Mic tratat de etică [Introduction in aretheology. Small ethics treaty]. Iasi: "Alexandru Ioan Cuza" University Publishing.

Cressey, D. R. (1960). Epidemiology and individual conduct: A case from criminology. *Pacific Sociological Review, 3*(2), 47–58. doi:10.2307/1388200

Creswell, J. W. (2007). *Qualitative Inquiry and Research Design: Choosing Among Five Traditions* (2nd ed.). Sage Publication, Inc.

Crino, M. D., & Leap, T. L. (1989). What HR managers must know about employee sabotage. *Personnel, 66*(5), 31.

Crisp, R. (2015). Well-Being. In *The Stanford Encyclopedia of Philosophy*. Retrieved from: http://plato.stanford.edu/archives/ sum2015/entries/well-being/

Csikai, E. L. (2004). Social Workers Participation in the Resolution of Ethical Dilemmas in Hospice Care. *Health & Social Work, 29*(1), 67–76. doi:10.1093/hsw/29.1.67 PMID:15024920

Dalal, R. S. (2005). A Meta-Analysis of the Relationship Between Organizational Citizenship Behavior and Counterproductive Work Behavior. *The Journal of Applied Psychology*, *90*(6), 1241–1255. doi:10.1037/0021-9010.90.6.1241 PMID:16316277

Daley, M. R., & Hickman, S. (2011). Dual relations and beyond: Understanding and addressing ethical challenges for rural social work. *Journal of Social Work Values and Ethics*, *8*(1), 99–108.

Daly, K. (2000). Revisiting the Relationship between Retributive and Restorative Justice. In Restorative Justice: From Philosophy to Practice (pp. 33-54). Aldershot, UK: Dartmouth.

De Dreu, C. K. W., & Gelfand, M. J. (2007). Conflict in the workplace: Sources, dynamics, and functions across multiple levels of analysis. In The psychology of conflict and conflict management in organizations (pp. 3–54). New York: Lawrence Erlbaum.

De Keijser, J. W., Van Der Leeden, R., & Jackson, J. L. (2002). From moral theory to penal attitudes and back: A theoretically integrated modelling approach. *Behavioral Sciences & the Law*, *20*(4), 317–335. doi:10.1002/bsl.494 PMID:12210971

De Singly, F. (2003). *Les uns avec les autres. Quand l'individualisme crée du lien*. Paris: Ed. Hachette.

De Singly, F. (2007). *L'individualisme est un humanisme*. Paris: Éditions de l'Aube.

Decision of the Government no. 118, 11.03.2014, for the approval of the Methodological norms of application of the provisions of the Law nr. 197/2012 regarding the assurance of quality in the domain of social services, with subsequent modifications, annexes 1-30. (2014). *Official Monitor of Romania, Part I, 172*.

Decision of the Government no. 1512, 31.12.2008 for the approval of the National Program for the Establishment of the Integrated System of Social Services for 2008-2012. (2009). *Official Monitor of the Republic of Moldova, 7-9*.

Decision of the Government no. 95, 07.02.2014 for the approval of the Regulation regarding the procedure of accreditation of the social services providers.

Decision of the Government no.867, 10. 2015, for the approval of the Nomenclature of social services, as well as of the regulations-frameworks of organizing and functioning of social services, with modifications and annotations. (2015). *Official Monitor of Romania, Part I, 834*.

Decision of the Government of the Republic of Moldova nr. 1512, 31.12.2008 for the approval of the National program regarding the creation of tan integrated system of social services for 2008-2012. (2009). *Official Monitor of the Republic of Moldova, 7-9*.

Decision of the Government of The Republic of Moldova nr. 784, 09.07.2007 for the approval of the National strategy and Plan of actions regarding the reform of the residential system of child's care for 2007-2012. (2007). *Official Monitor of the Republic of Moldova, 103-106*, 832.

Deck, P. (2016). Ethics—law and social work: Reconciling conflicting ethical obligations between two seemingly opposing disciplines to create a collaborative law practice. *Western New England Law Review, 38*(2), 261–283.

Derks, L. (2005). *Social Panoramas: Changing the Unconscious Landscape with NLP and Psychotherapy*. Crown House Publishing.

Dibley, L. (2011). Analyzing narrative data using McCormacks lenses. *Nurse Researcher, 18*(3), 13–19. doi:10.7748/nr2011.04.18.3.13.c8458 PMID:21560921

Dickson, M. W., Smith, D. B., Grojean, M. W., & Ehrhart, M. (2001). An organizational climate regarding ethics: The outcome of leader values and the practices that reflect them. *The Leadership Quarterly, 12*(2), 197–217. doi:10.1016/S1048-9843(01)00069-8

Diedrich, W.W., Burggraeve, R., & Gastmans, C. (2003). Towards a Levinasian Care Ethics: A Dialogue between the Thoughts of Joan Tronto and Emanuel Levinas. *Ethical Perspectives: Journal of the European Ethics Network, 13*(1), 33-61.

DiFranks, N. N. (2008). Social workers and the NASW code of ethics: Belief, behavior, disjuncture. *Social Work, 53*(2), 167–176. doi:10.1093/sw/53.2.167 PMID:18595450

Dimitrescu, F. (1997). *Dicţionar de cuvinte recente*. Audit. LOGOS SRL.

Dolgoff, R., Harrington, D., & Loewenberg, F. M. (2012). *Ethical Decisions for Social Work Practice* (9th ed.). Brooks/Cole Cengage Learning.

Dolgoff, R., & Skolnik, L. R. (1996). Ethical decision making in social work with groups: An empirical study. *Social Work with Groups, 19*(2), 49–65. doi:10.1300/J009v19n02_05

Dominelli, L. (2002). Values in Social Work: Contested Entities with Enduring Qualities. In R. Adams, L. Dominelli, & M. Payne (Eds.), *Critical Practice in Social Work* (pp. 15–27). London: Palgrave.

Douglas, S. C., & Martinko, M. J. (2001). Exploring the role of individual differences in the prediction of workplace aggression. *The Journal of Applied Psychology, 86*(4), 547–559. doi:10.1037/0021-9010.86.4.547 PMID:11519640

DPSM. (2000). *Management Services Review Report on the Organizational Review of the Social Welfare Function of the ministry of Local Government Lands and Housing* (Approved by Cabinet). Gaborone, Botswana: Directorate of Public Service Management.

Drower, S. J. (1996). Social work values, professional unity, and the South African context. *Social Work, 41*(2), 138–146. doi:10.1093/sw/41.2.138 PMID:8851353

Drucker, P. F. (2004). *Management of Future*. Bucharest: ASAB Publishing House.

Duff, A. (2001). *Punishment, communication, and community*. Oxford, UK: Oxford University Press.

Dumond, L. (1983). *Essais sur l'individualisme. Une perspective anthropologique sur l'idéologie moderne*. Paris: Éditions du Seuil.

Durkheim, É. (1987). L'individualisme et les intellectuels. Paris: Ed. Mille et une nuits. (originally published 1898)

Durkheim, É. (2007). Diviziunea muncii sociale [The division of social work]. Bucharest: Ed. Antet. (originally published 1893)

Early, T. J., & GlenMaye, L. F. (2000). Valuing families: Social work practice with families from a strength perspective. *Social Work*, *45*(2), 118–130. doi:10.1093/sw/45.2.118 PMID:10710985

Eggleston, B. (2005). The Ineffable and the Incalculable: G.E. Moore on Ethical Expertise. In L. M. Rasmussen (Ed.), *Ethics Expertise: History, Contemporary Perspectives, and Applications* (pp. 89–102). Springer, Netherlands. doi:10.1007/1-4020-3820-8_6

Einarsen, S., Hoel, H., Zapf, D., & Cooper, C. (2003). Bullying at work. The way forward. In Bullying and emotional abuse in the workplace. International perspectives in research and practice (pp. 412-416). New York: Taylor & Francis.

Elliot, E. A. (2016). Craft consumption and consumer transformation in a transmodern era. *Journal of Business Research*, *69*(1), 18–24. doi:10.1016/j.jbusres.2015.07.016

Engel, R. J., & Schuitt, R. K. (2013). *The Practice of Research in Social Work*. Sage Publications.

Erik, B. (2006). *Ethics in Social Work. An ethical code for social work professionals*. Ersta Sköndal University College, SSR.

Everton, W. J., Mastrangelo, P. M., & Jolton, J. A. (2005). Personality correlates of employees personal use of work computers. *Cyberpsychology & Behavior*, *8*(2), 143–153. doi:10.1089/cpb.2005.8.143 PMID:15938654

Fawcett, G., & Wardman, M. (2008). Ethical governance in local government in England: A regulator's view. In Ethics and integrity of governance: perspectives across frontiers. Edward Elgar. doi:10.4337/9781848441378.00018

Fennig, S., Secker, A., Levkovitz, Y., Barak, V., Benyakar, M., Farina, J., & Fennig, S. et al. (2004). Are psychotherapists consistent in their ethical attitude to patient confidentiality? *The Israel Journal of Psychiatry and Related Sciences*, *41*(2), 82–89. PMID:15478453

Ferrell, O. C. (2016). A Framework for Understanding Organisational Ethics. In P. E. Peterson & O. C. Ferrell (Eds.), *Business Ethics: New Challenges for Business Schools and Corporate Leaders: New Challenges for Business Schools and Corporate Leaders*. London: Routledge.

Ferrell, O. C., Fraedrich, J., & Ferrell, L. (2012). *Business Ethics: Ethical Decision Making & Cases*. South-Western Publishing. SUA.

Fitoussi, J.-P., & Rosanvallon, P. (1999). Noua epocă a inegalităţilor [New era of inequalities]. Iaşi: Institutul European. (originally published 1996)

Fletcher, J. C., & Siegler, M. (1996). What Are the Goals of Ethics Consultation? A Consensus. *The Journal of Clinical Ethics*, *7*(2), 122–126. PMID:8889887

Foot, P. (1978). The problem of abortion and the doctrine of the double effect. In Virtues and Vices and Other Essays in Moral Philosophy (pp. 19-32). Berkeley, CA: University of California Press.

Foucault, M. (2005). *A supraveghea şi a pedepsi. Naşterea închisorii* [To supervise and to punish. The birth of prison]. Bucharest, Romania: Paralela 45.

Fox, S., & Spector, P. E. (1999). A model of work frustration-aggression. *Journal of Organizational Behavior*, *20*(6), 915–931. doi:10.1002/(SICI)1099-1379(199911)20:6<915::AID-JOB918>3.0.CO;2-6

Fox, S., & Spector, P. E. (2005). *Counterproductive work behavior: Investigations of actors and targets*. Washington, DC: APA. doi:10.1037/10893-000

Fox, S., Spector, P. E., & Miles, D. (2001). Counterproductive work behavior (CWB) in response to job stressors and organizational justice: Some mediator and moderator tests for autonomy and emotions. *Journal of Vocational Behavior*, *59*(3), 291–309. doi:10.1006/jvbe.2001.1803

Francis, R., & Armstrong, A. (2003). Ethics as a risk management strategy: The Australian experience. *Journal of Business Ethics*, *45*(4), 375–385. doi:10.1023/A:1024163831371

Fraser, K., & Strang, V. (2002). Decision-Making and Nurse Case Management. A Philosophical Perspective. *ANS. Advances in Nursing Science*, *27*(1), 32–43. doi:10.1097/00012272-200401000-00005 PMID:15027660

Freeman, S. J., Engels, D. W., & Altekruse, M. K. (2004). Foundations for ethical standards and codes: The role of moral philosophy and theory in ethics. *Counseling and Values*, *48*(3), 163–173. doi:10.1002/j.2161-007X.2004.tb00243.x

Friele, M. B. (2003). Do Committees Ru(i)n the Bio-Political Culture? On the Democratic Legitimacy of Bioethics Committees. *Bioethics*, *17*(4), 301–308. doi:10.1111/1467-8519.00347 PMID:14567389

Fritzche, J. (1995). Personal Values: Potential Keys to Ethical Decision-Making. *Journal of Business Ethics*, *14*(11), 909–922. doi:10.1007/BF00882069

Frunză, S. (2011). Ethical responsibility and social responsibility of organizations involved in the public health system. *Revista de Cercetare şi Intervenţie Socială, 32,* 155-171.

Frunză, A. (2016). *Către o nouă expertiză etică - deconstruind valorile etice* [Towards a new ethical expertise - deconstructing ethical values]. Iasi, Romania: Lumen Publishing.

Frunză, A. (2016). *Către o nouă expertiză etică. Deconstruind valorile etice* [Towards an ethics expertise. Deconstructing the ethical values]. Iasi, Romania: Editura LUMEN.

Frunză, A. (2017). *Supervizarea şi dezvoltarea profesională a asistenţilor sociali* [Supervision and professional development of social workers]. Iaşi, Romania: Lumen Publishing.

Frunză, M. (2011). *Expertiză etică şi acţiune socială* [Ethics expertise and social action]. Bucharest: Tritonic Publishing.

Frunză, M. (2012). *Expertiza etică şi acţiune socială* [Ethics expertise and social action]. Bucharest, Romania: Tritonic.

Frunză, S. (2011). *Comunicarea etică şi responsabilitatea socială* [Ethical Communication and Social Responsibility]. Bucharest: Tritonic Publishing.

Furlong, R. M. (1986). The Social Workers Role on the Institutional Ethics Committee. *Social Work in Health Care, 11*(4), 93–100. doi:10.1300/J010v11n04_08 PMID:3775618

Furman, R., Downey, E. P., Jackson, R. L., & Bender, K. (2002). Poetry therapy as a tool for strengths-based practice. *Administration in Social Work, 3*(2), 146–157.

Fusch, P. I., & Ness, L. R. (2015). Are we there yet? Data saturation in qualitative research. *Qualitative Report, 20*(9), 1408–1416.

Gadamer, H. G. (1999). *The Eulogy of Theory. The Heritage of Europe*. Iasi: Polirom Publishing House.

Garçia-Marza, D. (2005). Trust and Dialogue: Theoretical Approaches to Ethics Auditing. *Journal of Business Ethics, 57*(3), 209–219. doi:10.1007/s10551-004-8202-7

Gardner, W. L., & Martinko, M. J. (1998). An organizational perspective of the effects of dysfunctional impression management. *Monographs in Organizational Behavior and Industrial Relations, 23*, 69-126.

Garhart Mooney, C. (2009). *Theories of Attachment: An Introduction to Bowlby, Ainsworth, Gerber, Brazelton, Kennell, and Klaus*. Redleaf Press.

Garmezy, N. (1994). Reflections and commentary on risk, resilience, and development. In R. J. Haggerty, L. R. Sherrod, N. Garmezy, & M. Rutter (Eds.), *Stress, risk, and resilience in children and adolescents: Processes, mechanisms, and interventions* (pp. 1–18). Cambridge, UK: Cambridge University Press.

Gavriluţă, C. (2013). Ethical perspectives in sociological research of medical environment and people with vulnerabilities. *Revista Romana de Bioetica, 10*(4), 115–128.

Gehrke, P. J. (2010). Being for the Other-to-the-Other: Justice and Communication in Levinasian Ethics. *Review of Communication, 10*(1), 5–19. doi:10.1080/15358590903248769

Geis, G., & Goff, C. (1983). Introduction. In *E.H., Sutherland. White collar crime: The uncut version*. New Haven, CT: Yale University Press.

Gelman, S. R., Pollack, D., & Weiner, A. (1999). Confidentiality of social work records in the computer age. *Social Work, 44*(3), 243–252. doi:10.1093/sw/44.3.243 PMID:10348697

George, M. (2012). Migration traumatic experiences and refugee distress: Implications for social work practice. *Clinical Social Work*, *40*(4), 429–437. doi:10.1007/s10615-012-0397-y

Giacalone, R. A., Riordan, C. A., & Rosenfeld, P. (1997). Employee sabotage. *Antisocial Behavior in Organizations*, 109-29.

Giacalone, R. A., & Knouse, S. B. (1990). Justifying wrongful employee behavior: The role of personality in organizational sabotage. *Journal of Business Ethics*, *9*(1), 55–61. doi:10.1007/BF00382564

Gibelman, M. (1999). The Search for Identity: Defining Social WorkPast, Present, Future. *Social Work*, *44*(4), 298–310. doi:10.1093/sw/44.4.298

Gilligan, C. (1977). In a Different Voice: Womens Conceptions of Self and of Morality. *Harvard Educational Review*, *47*(4), 481–517. doi:10.17763/haer.47.4.g6167429416hg510

Gilligan, C. (1982). *In a Different Voice: Psychological Theory and Women's Development*. Cambridge, MA: Harvard University.

Givelber, D., Bowers, W., & Blitch, D. (1984). Tarasoff, myth and reality: An empirical study of private law in action. *Wisconsin Law Review*, *18*, 443–497. PMID:11653756

Glueck, S., & Glueck, E. (1950). Unraveling juvenile delinquency. *Juv. Ct. Judges J.*, *2*, 32.

Godden, J. (2012). *BASW/CoSW England research on supervision in social work, with particular reference to supervision practice in multi disciplinary teams*. Retrieved from http://cdn.basw.co.uk/upload/basw_13955-1.pdf

Golparvar, M. (2015). Prediction of Organizational Citizenship Behaviors and Deviant Behaviors Through Impression Management Components. *Quarterly Journal of Social Work*, *4*(1), 3–15.

Goodin, R. (2006). Utilitatea şi binele [Usefulness and good]. In P. Singer (Ed.), *Tratat de etică* [Treaty of ethics] (pp. 268–276). Iasi, Romania: Polirom.

Gormley, K. (1992). One hundred years of privacy. *Wisconsin Law Review*, *5*, 1335–1441.

Gottfredson, M. R., & Hirschi, T. (1990). *A general theory of crime*. Stanford University Press.

Goulding, C. (1999). *Grounded Theory: some reflections on paradigm, procedures and misconceptions*. Working Paper Series. Wolverhampton Business School, Management Research Centre.

Government of Botswana. (2001). *National Policy for Non-governmental Organizations*. Gaborone, Botswana: Ministry of Labour and Home Affairs. Retrieved from http://www.icnl.org/research/journal/vol3iss3/2-01.pdf

Government of Botswana. (2010). *A Social Development Policy Framework for Botswana Phase I: Situation Analysis*. Gaborone, Botswana: Ministry of Local Government. Retrieved from https://www.uea.ac.uk/documents/439774/4406128/Botswana+SD+policy+phase+I+report+26+May+10.pdf/211a67cb-3773-4822-8034-4b98e9c2bef7

Granich, S. (2012). *Duty to Warn, Duty to Protect*. Retrieved June 15, 2017 from http://www.socialworker.com/feature-articles/ethics-articles/Duty_to_Warn%2C_Duty_to_Protect/

Graumann, S. (2012). Social Services Ethics, Overview. In Encyclopedia of Applied Ethics (2nd ed.; pp. 175–181). Academic Press. doi:10.1016/B978-0-12-373932-2.00398-7

Graybeal, C. (2001). Strengths-based social work assessment: Transforming the dominant paradigm. *Families in Society*, *82*(3), 233–242. doi:10.1606/1044-3894.236

Gray, M. (2011). Back to basics: A critique of the strengths perspective in social work. *Families in Society*, *92*(1), 5–11. doi:10.1606/1044-3894.4054

Gray, M., Coates, J., & Bird, M. Y. (2008). Introduction. In M. Gray, J. Coates, & M. Y. Bird (Eds.), *Indigenous Social Work Around the World: Towards Culturally Relevant Education and Practice* (pp. 1–12). Aldershot, UK: Ashgate Publishing.

Gray, M., & Gibbons, J. (2007). There are no answers, only choices: Teaching ethical decision making in social work. *Australian Social Work*, *60*(2), 222–238. doi:10.1080/03124070701323840

Greenberg, J. (1998). The cognitive geometry of employee theft: Negotiating" the line" between taking and stealing. *Monographs in Organizational Behavior and Industrial Relations*, *23*, 147-194.

Greenberg, J. (1990). Organizational justice: Yesterday, today, and tomorrow. *Journal of Management*, *16*(2), 399–432. doi:10.1177/014920639001600208

Greenberg, J. (1993). Stealing in the name of justice: Informational and interpersonal moderators of theft reactions to underpayment inequity. *Organizational Behavior and Human Decision Processes*, *54*(1), 81–103. doi:10.1006/obhd.1993.1004

Greene, A. D., & Latting, J. K. (2004). Whistle blowing as a form of advocacy: Guidelines for the practitioner and organization. *Social Work*, *49*(2), 219–230. doi:10.1093/sw/49.2.219 PMID:15124962

Greene, G. J., Lee, M. Y., & Hoffpauir, S. (2005). The languages of empowerment and strengths in clinical social work: A constructivist perspective. *Families in Society*, *86*(2), 267–277. doi:10.1606/1044-3894.2465

Greif, G. L. (2004). When a social worker becomes a voluntary commissioner and calls on the code of ethics. *Social Work*, *49*(2), 277–280. doi:10.1093/sw/49.2.277 PMID:15124968

Groza, D. (2006). *Drepturile victimei. Recuperarea din uitare* [Victim's rights. Recovery through oblivion]. Iasi, Romania: LUMEN Publishing.

Guo, W., & Tsui, M. (2010). From resilience to resistance: A reconstruction of the strength perspective in social work practice. *International Social Work*, *53*(2), 233–245. doi:10.1177/0020872809355391

Guttmann, D. (2013). *Ethics in Social Work: A Context of Caring*. Routledge.

Habermas, J. (1991). *The Structural Transformation of the Public Sphere: An Inquiry into a Category of Bourgeois Society*. MIT Press.

Habermas, J. (2000). *Conştiinţă morală şi acţiune comunicativă* [Moral consciousness and communicative action]. Bucharest, Romania: All Educaţional Publishing.

Hall, M., Dugan, E., Zheng, B., & Mishra, A. K. (2001). Trust in phyicians and medical institutions: What is it, can it be measured, and does it matter? *The Milbank Quarterly*, *79*(4), 613–639. doi:10.1111/1468-0009.00223 PMID:11789119

Harkness, D., & Poertner, J. (1989). Research and social work supervision: A conceptual review. *Social Work*, *34*(2), 115–119.

Harrington, D., & Dolgoff, R. (2008). Hierarchies of ethical principles for ethical decision making in social work. *Ethics and Social Welfare*, *2*(2), 183–196. doi:10.1080/17496530802117680

Hawkins, P., & Shohet, R. (1989). *Supervision in the Helping Professions. An individual, group and organizational approach.* Milton Keynes, UK: Open University Press.

Haynes, R., Corey, G., & Moulton, P. (2003). *Clinical Supervision in the Helping Professions: A Practical Guide*. Pacific Grove, CA: Brookes/Cole.

Haynie, D. L., Silver, E., & Teasdale, B. (2006). Neighborhood characteristics, peer networks, and adolescent violence. *Journal of Quantitative Criminology*, *22*(2), 147–169. doi:10.1007/s10940-006-9006-y

Henle, C. A., Giacalone, R. A., & Jurkiewicz, C. L. (2005). The role of ethical ideology in workplace deviance. *Journal of Business Ethics*, *56*(3), 219–222. doi:10.1007/s10551-004-2779-8

Hesse-Biber, S. N. (2006). The practice of feminist in-depth interviewing. In S. H. Hesse-Biber & P. L. Leavy (Eds.), *The Practice of Qualitative Interviewing* (pp. 111–148). London: Sage Publishing.

Hirschi, T., & Stark, R. (1969). Hellfire and delinquency. *Social Problems*, *17*(2), 202–213. doi:10.2307/799866

Ho, A. (2008). Relational autonomy or undue pressure? Family's role in medical decision-making. *Scandinavian Journal of Caring Sciences*, *22*(1), 128-35. https://doi.org/10.1111/j.1471-6712.2007.00561.x

Hoffmann, W. (1967). Social Work Supervision. In B. McKendrick (Ed.), *Introduction to Social Work in South Africa* (pp. 206–248). Pinetown, South Africa: Owen Burgess Publishers.

Hofmann, P. (1995). Performing an ethics audit. *Healthcare Executive Journal, 10*(6).

Hofmann, P. (2006). The Value of an Ethics Audit. *Healthcare Executive Journal, 21*(2).

Hofmann, P. B. (2006). The Value of an Ethics Audit. *Healthcare Executive*, *21*(2), 44–45. PMID:17020183

Hofmann, P. B. (2012). *Fear of Conflict: Management and Ethical Costs. Healthcare Executive, 27, 1*. ProQuest Central.

Hollinger, R. C. (1986). Acts against the workplace: Social bonding and employee deviance. *Deviant Behavior*, *7*(1), 53–75. doi:10.1080/01639625.1986.9967695

Hollinger, R. C., & Clark, J. P. (1982). Formal and informal social controls of employee deviance. *The Sociological Quarterly*, *23*(3), 333–343. doi:10.1111/j.1533-8525.1982.tb01016.x

Hollinger, R. C., Slora, K. B., & Terris, W. (1992). Deviance in the fast-food restaurant: Correlates of employee theft, altruism, and counter productivity. *Deviant Behavior: An Interdisciplinary Journal*, *13*(2), 155–184. doi:10.1080/01639625.1992.9967906

Holunga, L. (2013). *Evaluation and supervision of the social services*. Alba Iulia: POSDRU.

Houston, S. (2003). Establishing Virtue in Social Work: A Response to McBeath and Webb. *British Journal of Social Work*, *33*(6), 819–824. doi:10.1093/bjsw/33.6.819

Howard, M. O., McMillen, C. J., & Pollio, D. E. (2003). Teaching evidence-based practice: Toward a new paradigm for social work education. *Research on Social Work Practice, 13*(2), 234-259. DOI: 10.1177/1049731502250404

Huby, P. (1974). Greek Ethics. In W. D. Hudson (Ed.), *New Studies in Ethics, Classical Theories* (pp. 1–71). London: Macmillan Press LTD. doi:10.1007/978-1-349-02396-7_1

Hudson, B. (1996). *Understanding Justice: An Introduction to Ideas, Perspectives and Controversies in Modern Penal Theory*. Buckingham, UK: Open University Press.

Hugman, R. (2005). Exploring the Paradox of Teaching Ethics for Social Work Practice. *Social Work Education*, *24*(5), 535–545. doi:10.1080/02615470500132772

Hutton, M. (1992). *Social Work: An extension of community*. Gaborone, Botswana: University of Botswana.

IFSW & IASSW. (2004). *Ethics in social work, statement of principles*. Retrieved from https://www.iassw-aiets.org/wp-content/uploads/2015/10/Ethics-in-Social-Work-Statement-IFSW-IASSW-2004.pdf

IFSW & IASSW. (2004). *Ethics in social work. Declaration of principles*. Retrieved May 25, 2017, from http://ethics.iit.edu/ecodes/node/3934

IFSW. (2005). *Ethics in Social Work, Statement of Principles*. Available from: http://www.ifsw.org/en/f38000032.html

IFSW. (2005). *Ethics in social work, statement of principles*. Retrieved from http://www.ifsw.org/en/f38000032.html

Iltis, A. S., & Sheehan, M. (2016). Expertise, Ethics Expertise, and Clinical Ethics Consultation: Achieving Terminological Clarity. *J Med Philos, 41*(4), 416-433. https://doi.org/10.1093/jmp/jhw014

InfoEuropa. (2012). *O soluţie pentru criza valorilor: mai multă Europă: Declaraţia Preşedintelui APCE cu ocazia Zilei Europei* [A solution for the values crisis: more Europe: Declaration of the RACE President on Europe Day]. Retrieved July 13, 2017, from http://www.infoeuropa.md/evenimente-europene-in-moldova/o-solutie-pentru-criza-valorilor-mai-multa-europa-declaratia-presedintelui-apce-cu-ocazia-zilei-europei

Ioan, B., & Gavrilovici, C. (2005). *Secretul profesional nu poate fi pus inaintea protectiei unui om* [The professional secret cannot be placed before the human protection]. Retrieved June 15, 2017 from adevarul.ro/sanatate/medicina/secretul-profesional-nu-pus-protectiei-unui-om-1_50ad2bad7c42d5a663900bf6/index.html

Iser, M. (2013). Recognition. In *The Stanford Encyclopedia of Philosophy*. Retrieved from: http://plato.stanford.edu/archives/ fall2013/entries/recognition/

Jaffee v. Redmond, 116 S. Ct. 1923 (1996).

Jagim, R. D., Wittman, W. D., & Noll, J. O. (1978). Mental health professionals attitude towards confidentialitz, privilege, and third party disclosure. *Professional Psychology*, *9*(3), 458–466. doi:10.1037/0735-7028.9.3.458 PMID:11662548

Jang, S. J. (2007). Gender differences in strain, negative emotions, and coping behaviors: A general strain theory approach. *Justice Quarterly*, *24*(3), 523–553. doi:10.1080/07418820701485486

Jankélevitch, S. (1987). Un individualisme paradoxal? In E. Durkheim (Ed.), L'individualisme et les intellectuels (pp. 45-64). Paris: Ed. Mille et une nuits.

Jeurissen, R., & van der Putten, F. P. (2007). Ethics in international business. In Ethics in business. Van Gorcum.

Johnstone, G. (2011). Restorative Justice: Ideas, Values, Debates. New York: Routledge.

Johnstone, G., & Van Ness, D. (2006). *The Meaning of Restorative Justice. The Handbook on Restorative Justice*. Cullompton: Willan Publishing.

Jonas, H. (1984). The Imperative of Responsibility. In *Search of an Ethics for the Technological Age*. Chicago: University of Chicago Press.

Jones, K., & Schroeter, F. (2012). Moral Expertise. *Analyse & Kritik*, *2*, 217–230.

Jordan, B. (2008). Social work and world poverty. *International Social Work*, *51*(4), 440–452. doi:10.1177/0020872808090238

Joseph, M. V. (1991). Standing for values and ethical action: Teaching social work ethics. *Journal of Teaching in Social Work*, *5*(2), 95–109. doi:10.1300/J067v05n02_09

Judge, T., LePine, J., & Rich, B. (2006). Loving yourself abundantly: Relationship of the narcissistic personality to self- and other perceptions of workplace deviance, leadership and task performance. *The Journal of Applied Psychology, 91*(4), 762–776. doi:10.1037/0021-9010.91.4.762 PMID:16834504

Kachigian, C., & Felthous, A. R. (2004). Court Responses to Tarasoff Statutes. *The Journal of the American Academy of Psychiatry and the Law, 32*(3), 263–273. Retrieved from http://jaapl.org/content/jaapl/32/3/263.full.pdf PMID:15515914

Kadushin, G., & Egan, M. (2001). Ethical dilemmas in home health care: A social work perspective. *Health & Social Work, 26*(3), 136-149. https://doi.org/10.1093/hsw/26.3.136

Kadushin, A. (1992). *Supervision in Social Work* (3rd ed.). New York: Columbia University Press.

Kalof, L., Dan, A., & Dietz, T. (2008). *Essentials of Social Research.* New York, NY: Open University Press.

Kant, I. (1972). *Critica rațiunii practice* [The criticism of practical reasoning]. Bucharest: Științifică Publishing.

Kaptein, M. (1998). *Ethics Management: Auditing and Developing the Ethical Content of Organizations*. Dordrecht: Kluwer. doi:10.1007/978-94-011-4978-5

Karataş, K. (1999). Sosyal refah: Kavramsal boyutu, gelişimi ve nitelikleri. In N. Koşar & V. Duyan (Ed.), Prof. Dr. Sema Kut'a armağan: Yaşam boyu sosyal hizmet (pp. 33-43). Ankara: Hacettepe Üniversitesi Sosyal Hizmetler Yüksekokulu Yayını No: 004.

Kemelgor, B., Sussman, L., Kline, J., & Zurada, J. (2007). Who are the difficult employees? Psychopathological attributions of their co-workers. *Journal of Business & Economics Research, 5*(10), 47–62.

Kenny, D. (1982). Confidentiality: The Confusion Continues. *Journal of Medical Ethics, 8*(1), 5–8. doi:10.1136/jme.8.1.9 PMID:7069738

Kidwell, R. E. (2005). The prevalence (and ambiguity) of deviant behavior at work. In Managing organizational deviance (pp. 1-21). Thousand Oaks, CA: SAGE Publishing. Doi:10.4135/9781452231105.n1

Kluckhohn, F. R., & Strodtbeck, F. L. (1961). *Variations in value orientations*. Evanston, IL: Row, Peterson.

Kornhauser, R. R. (1978). *Social sources of delinquency: An appraisal of analytic models.* Chicago: University of Chicago Press.

Kreitzer, L. (2006). Social work values and ethics issues of universality. *Currents, 5*(1).

Krell, E. (2010). How to Conduct an Ethics Audit, An ethics audit can reveal gaps in your ethics policies and practices. *HR Magazine*. Available at https://www.shrm.org/hr-today/news/hr-magazine/pages/0410agenda_social.aspx

Kubrin, C. E., Stucky, T. D., & Krohn, M. D. (2008). *Researching theories of crime and delinquency*. Oxford, UK: Oxford University Press.

Kumi, E. (2013). Are demographic variables predictors of work deviant behavior? *International Journal of Management Sciences*, *1*(1), 1–10.

Lake, P. F. (1994). Revisiting Tarasoff. *Alb. L. Rev.*, *58*, 97, 98.

Lambley, S., & Marrable, T. (2013). *Practice enquiry into supervision in a variety of adult care settings where there are health and social care practitioners working together*. Social Care Institute for Excellence.

Landman, W. A., Mouton, J., & Nevhutalu, K. H. (2001). *Chris Hani Baragwanath Hospital Ethics Audit*. Research Report No. 2. Available at https://www.tei.org.za/phocadownloadpap/Research_Reports/CHBHFinalReport.pdf

Larkin, H. (2006). Social Work as an Integral Profession. *Journal of Integral Theory and Practice*, *1*(2). Retrieved May 25, 2017, from https://www.researchgate.net/publication/251743486_Social_Work_as_an_Integral_Profession

Lasky, G. B., & Riva, M. T. (2006). Confidentiality and privileged communication in group psychotherapy. *International Journal of Group Psychotherapy*, *56*(4), 455–476. doi:10.1521/ijgp.2006.56.4.455 PMID:17040183

Law nr. 129, 08.06.2012 regarding the accreditation of the providers of social services. (2012). *Official Monitor of the Republic of Moldova, 181-184.*

Law nr. 197, 01.11.2012 regarding the assurance of quality in the domain of social services. Text actualized according to the modifying normative acts. (2013). *Official Monitor of Romania, Part I.*

Law of social work nr 547-XV, 25.12.2003. (2004). *Official Monitor of the Republic of Moldova, 42-44.*

Law of social work nr. 292, 20.12.2011, with subsequent modifications. (2013). *Official Monitor of Romania, 905.*

Law of the Republic of Moldova Law Nr. 295, 21.12.2007 for the approval of National Strategy of Development for 2008-2011. (2008). Official Monitor of the Republic of Moldova, 18-20.

Law regarding the social services nr. 123, 8.06.2010. (2010). *Official Monitor of the Republic of Moldova, 155-158.*

Lawrence, T. B., & Robinson, S. L. (2007). Aint misbehavin: Workplace deviance as organizational resistance. *Journal of Management*, *33*(3), 378–394. doi:10.1177/0149206307300816

Lees, R., & Lees, S. (1975). Social Sciences in Social Work Practice: The Case for an Action Research Approach. *British Journal of Social Work*, *5*(2), 161–174.

Lerner, A. (1981). Poetry therapy. In R. Corsini (Ed.), *Handbook of innovative psychotherapies* (pp. 138–152). New York: John Wiley and Sons.

Levinas, E. (1969). *Totality and Infinity: An Essay on Exteriority* (A. Lingis, Trans.). Pittsburgh, PA: Duquesne University Press.

Lipovetsky, G. (1996). Amurgul datoriei: Etica nedureroasă a noilor timpuri democratice [Twilight of duty. The unpainful ethics of new democratic times]. Bucharest, Romania: Babel Publishing.

Lipovetsky, G. (1983). *L'ère du vide. Essais sur l'individualisme contemporain*. Paris: Galimard.

Lipovetsky, G. (1993). *Le Crépuscule du devoir: l'éthique indeloire des noveaux temps démocratiques*. Gallimard.

Lipovetsky, G. (2007). *Fericirea paradoxală. Eseu asupra societățiide hiperconsum* [Paradoxal happiness. Essay on the society of hyperconsummerism] (M. Ungurean, Trans.). Iasi: Polirom.

Littlechild, B. (2012). Values and cultural issues in social work. *ERIS Web Journal*, *1*, 62-76. Retrieved May 25, 2017, from http://periodika.osu.cz/eris/dok/2012-01/07_values_and_cultural_issues_in_sw.pdf

Litvinova, D. (2017). Bill Decriminalizing Domestic Violence Passes First Reading in Russian Parliament. *The Moscow Time*. Retrieved June 15, 2017 from https://themoscowtimes.com/articles/bill-decriminalizing-domestic-violence-passes-first-reading-in-russian-parliament-56783

Long, J. E. (2017). Beyond Bathsheba: Managing Ethical Climates Through Pragmatic Ethics. *The Journal of Values-Based Leadership*, *10*(2), 14. doi:10.22543/0733.102.1194

Loue, S. (2016). Therapeutic farms in Europe and the U.S.: Recovery from mental illness. New York: Springer Science+Business. doi:10.1007/978-3-319-13539-7

Loue, S. (2013). Social Work, Advocacy, and Ethics: Opportunities and Challenges in Romania. *Procedia: Social and Behavioral Sciences*, *92*, 1039–1043. doi:10.1016/j.sbspro.2013.08.796

Lovat, T., & Gray, M. (2008). Towards a proportionist social work ethics: A Habermasian perspective. *British Journal of Social Work, 38*(6), 1100-1114. https://doi.org/10.1093/bjsw/bcl396

Lutgen-Sandvik, P. (2006). Take this job and…: Quitting and other forms of resistance to workplace bullying. *Communication Monographs*, *73*(4), 406–433. doi:10.1080/03637750601024156

Lyons, K. (2006). Globalization and Social Work: International and Local Implications. *British Journal of Social Work*, 36.

Magione, T., & Quinn, R. (1975). Job satisfaction, counterproductive behaviour and drog used at work. *The Journal of Applied Psychology*, *60*(1), 114–116. doi:10.1037/h0076355 PMID:1110252

Maiss, M. (2010). Ethical learning and ethical deliberation in social work. In D. Zarvisek, B. Rommelspacher, & S. Staub-Bernasconi (Eds.), *Ethical dilemmas in social work* (pp. 39–61). Ljubljana: University of Ljubljana.

Malley, J., & Fernández, J.-L. (2010). Measuring quality in social care services: Theory and practice. *Annals of Public and Cooperative Economics*, *81*(4), 559–582. doi:10.1111/j.1467-8292.2010.00422.x

Mars, G. (1982). *Cheats at Work: An Anthropology of Workplace Crime*. Boston: G. Allen and Unwin.

Matsueda, R. L. (1982). Testing control theory and differential association: A causal modeling approach. *American Sociological Review*, *47*(4), 489–504. doi:10.2307/2095194

Mattison, M. (2000). Ethical decision making: The person in the process. *Social Work, 45*(3), 201-212. https://doi.org/10.1093/sw/45.3.201

Maxwell, J. A. (2013). *Qualitative research design: An interactive approach (3rd ed.)*. London: Sage Publication.

McAuliffe, D. (2002). *Social Work Ethics Audits: A New Tool for Ethical Practice*. Retrieved from http://citeseerx.ist.psu.edu/viewdoc/download?doi=10.1.1.202.1345&rep=rep1&type=pdf

McAuliffe, D. (n.d.). *Social Work Ethics Audits: A New Tool for Ethical Practice*. Retrieved from http://citeseerx.ist.psu.edu/viewdoc/download?doi=10.1.1.202.1345&rep=rep1&type=pdf

McAuliffe, D. (2005). I'm still standing: Impacts and consequences of ethical dilemmas for social workers in direct practice. *Journal of Social Work Values and Ethics*, *2*(1), 1–10.

McAuliffe, D. (2005, December). Putting ethics on the organisational agenda: The social work ethics audit on trial. *Australian Social Work*, *58*(4), 357–369. doi:10.1111/j.1447-0748.2005.00232.x

McAuliffe, D., & Ferman, T. (2002). *Meeting the Challenges of Designing Ethics Education for Social Work*. Melbourne: RMIT, Faculty of Education, Language & Community Services.

Mcbeath, G., & Webb, S. A. (2002). Virtue Ethics and Social Work: Being Lucky, Realistic, and not Doing ones Duty. *British Journal of Social Work*, *32*(8), 1015–1036. doi:10.1093/bjsw/32.8.1015

McClain, W. H. (1907). Relations existing between defective characteristics and dependence. *Proceedings of the National Conference of Charities and Correction*, 347-354.

McDonald, G., & Nijhof, A. (1999). Beyond codes of ethics: an ntegrated framework for stimulating morally responsible behaviour in organisations. *Leadership and Organization Development Journal*, *20*(3), 133-146. Available from Deakin Research Online: http://hdl.handle.net/10536/DRO/DU:30024095

McDonald, G. M. (2009). An anthology of codes of ethics. *European Business Review*, *21*(4), 344–372. doi:10.1108/09555340910970445

McFatter, R. M. (1978). Sentencing strategies and justice: Effects of punishment philosophy on sentencing decisions. *Journal of Personality and Social Psychology*, *36*(12), 1490–1500. doi:10.1037/0022-3514.36.12.1490

McFatter, R. M. (1982). Purposes of punishment: Effects of utilities of criminal sanctions on perceived appropriateness. *The Journal of Applied Psychology, 67*(3), 255–267. doi:10.1037/0021-9010.67.3.255 PMID:7107551

McIntosh v. Milano, 403 A.2d 500 (N.J. Super. Ct. Law Div.1979)

McLeod, C. (2015). Trust. In E. N. Zalta (ed.), *The Stanford Encyclopedia of Philosophy*. Retrieved May 16, 2017, from https://plato.stanford.edu/archives/fall2015/entries/trust/

McMillen, J. C., Morris, L., & Sheraden, M. (2004). Ending social work's grudge match: Problems versus strengths. *Muskie School of Public Service*, 5. Retrieved from http://digitalcommons.usm.maine.edu/muskie/5

Menzel, D. C. (2007). *Ethics management for public administrators: building organizations of integrity*. Armonk, NY: M.E. Sharpe.

Menzel, D. C. (2016). *Ethics Management for Public and Nonprofit Managers: Leading and Building Organizations of Integrity*. Routledge.

Miftode, V. (2011). *Tratat de asistenta Sociala. Protectia populatiilor specifice si automarginalizate* [Social Work Treaty. Protection of specific and self-marginalized populations]. Iasi: Lumen Publishing.

Miles, M. B., & Huberman, A. M. (1994). *Qualitative data analysis: An expanded sourcebook*. Thousand Oaks, UK: Sage Publication.

Mill, J. S. (1871). *Utilitarianism* (4th ed.). London: Longmans, Green, Reader, and Dyer.

Mitrache, C. (1994). Drept penal român: partea generală [Romanian Penal Justice: the general part]. Bucharest, Romania: Casa de Editură şi Presă.

Moore, G. E. (1993). *Principia Ethica*. Cambridge, UK: Cambridge University Press.

Morar, V. (2006). Etica şi afacerile. Morală elementară şi responsabilitate socială [Ethics and business. Elementary morals and social responsibility]. Bucharest: Universităţii Publishing.

Motsamai, M. (2016). Code of conduct for social workers in offing. *Botswana - Daily News*. Retrieved June 18, 2017, from http://www.dailynews.gov.bw/mobile/news-details.php?nid=31693&flag=

Murdach, A. D. (2011). Is social work a human rights profession? *Social Work, 56*(3), 281–293. doi:10.1093/sw/56.3.281 PMID:21848092

Mureşan, V. (2007). Este etica aplicată, o aplicare a eticii? [Is applied ethics and appliance of ethics?]. *Revista de Filosofie Analitică, I*(1), 70–108.

Murray, D. J. (1995). *Ethics in organisations*. London: Kogan Page.

Mwansa, L.-K. J., Malinga-Musamba, T., Ntshwarang, P. N., & Maripe, K. (2012). *Report on the tracer study project: University of Botswana 1998-2008 social work graduates (1998-2008)* (Unpublished report). Gaborone, Botswana: Office of Research and Development, University of Botswana.

Mwansa, L.-K. (2011). Social work education in Africa: Whence and whither. *Social work education, 30*(1), 4–16. doi:10.1080/02615471003753148

Nash, M. (1998). *People, policies and practice: Social work education in Aotearoa New Zealand 1949-1995* (PhD thesis). Massey University.

NASW. (1996). *Code of ethics - Approved by the 1996 NASW Delegate Assembly and revised by the 2008 NASW Delegate Assembly.* Retrieved July 2, 2017, from http://www. naswdc. org/pubs/code/code

NASW. (1999). *Code of Ethics*. Washington, DC: National Association of Social Workers. Retrieved from http://www.socialworkers.org/pubs/code/default.asp

NASW. (2008). *Code of Ethics*. Retrieved from http://www.socialworkers.org/pubs/code/code.asp

NASW. (2008). *Code of Ethics*. Retrieved from: http://www.socialworkers.org/pubs/code/code.asp

NASW. (2008). *Code of Ethics*. Retrieved May 13, 2017, from: http://www.socialworkers.org/pubs/code/code.asp

National Association of Social Workers (NASW). (2008). *Code of Ethics*. Retrieved May 25, 2017, from http://www.socialworkers.org/pubs/code/code.asp

National Association of Social Workers. (1996). *Code of Ethics*. Washington, DC: NASW Press.

National Association of Social Workers. (2008). *Code of ethics*. Retrieved from https://www.socialworkers.org/pubs/code/code.asp?print=1&print=1&pr

Naumann, S. E., & Bennett, N. (2000). A case for procedural justice climate: Development and test of a multilevel model. *Academy of Management Journal, 43*(5), 881–889. doi:10.2307/1556416

Neamțu, G. (2011). *Treaty of social assistance*. Iasi: Polirom Publishing House.

Neamtu, G. (2012). The specific of professional education in social work adjusted to labour marketplace. *Revista de Cercetare şi Intervenţie Socială, 39,* 39-58.

Nemțoi, G., & Ignătescu, C. (2014). National Citizenship as Representative of European Citizenship. *Procedia Social and Behavioral Sciences, 149*, 653-658. Retrieved May 25, 2017, from http://www.sciencedirect.com/science/article /pii/S1877042814049568

Neuman, W. L. (2007). *Basics of Social Research: Quantitative and Qualitative Approaches*. Boston: Allyn and Bacon Publishing.

Nobel, C. (1982). Ethics and Experts. *The Hastings Center Report*, *12*(3), 7–8. doi:10.2307/3561822 PMID:7107239

Norbert, E. (1991). La société des individus. Paris: Librairie Arthème Fayard. (originally published 1939)

Norman, E. (2000). *Resiliency enhancement: Putting the strengths perspective into social work practice*. New York: Columbia University Press. doi:10.7312/norm11800

Nthomang, K. (2007). *Provisions of services and poverty reduction: The case of Botswana. Geneva: UNRISD*. Retrieved October 15, 2013 from http://www.unrisd.org/8025 6B3C005BCCF9/(httpAuxPages)/B8AFAF7E9C8AEB33C1257AF600305225/$file/Botswana%20Nthomang%20web.pdf

O'Leary-Kelly, A. M., Griffin, R. W., & Glew, D. J. (1996). Organization-motivated aggression: A research framework. *Academy of Management Review*, *21*, 225–253.

O'Brien, M. (2013). Social work registration and professionalism: Social justice and poverty – fellow travellers or discarded passengers? *Aotearoanew Zealand Social Work Issue, 25*(3), 50-59. Retrieved May 25, 2017, from http://anzasw.nz/wp-content/uploads/Social-Work-Review-Issue-25-Number-3-Aticles-OBrien.pdf

ODonoghue, K., Yuh Ju, P. W., & Tsui, M. S. (2017). Constructing an evidence-informed social work supervision model. *European Journal of Social Work*, 1–11. doi:10.1080/13691457.2017.1341387

Ojasoo, M. (2016). CSR Reporting, stakeholder engagement and preventing hypocrisy through ethics audit. *Journal of Global Entrepreneurship Research*, *6*(1), 14. doi:10.1186/s40497-016-0056-9

Olaughlin, B. (1998). Missing men? The debate over rural poverty and women-headed households in Southern Africa. *The Journal of Peasant Studies*, *25*(2), 1–48. doi:10.1080/03066159808438665

O'Neill, O. (2002). *Autonomy and Trust in Bioethic*. Cambridge, UK: Cambridge University Press. doi:10.1017/CBO9780511606250

O'Neill, O. (2006). Etica lui Kant. In P. Singer (Ed.), *Tratat de etică* [Treaty of ethics] (pp. 204–215). Iasi: Polirom.

Onofrei, A. (2013). Modernization of social services in the Republic of Moldova – key factor to an effective system of social work. *Studia Universitatis Moldavie. Seria Ştiinţe Sociale, 8*(68), 2013, 26-29.

Orcutt, J. D. (1987). Differential association and marijuana use: A closer look at Sutherland (with a little help from Becker). *Criminology*, *25*(2), 341–358. doi:10.1111/j.1745-9125.1987.tb00801.x

Osei-Hwedie, K. (1993). The challenge of social work in Africa: Starting the indigenisation process. *Journal of Social Development in Africa*, *8*(1), 19–30.

Osei-Hwedie, K. (2000). Culture as a Tool for Social Work Practice. *Social Work Africa*, *1*(1), 11–18.

Osmo, R., & Landau, R. (2001). The need for explicit argumentation in ethical decision-making in social work. *Social Work Education*, *20*(4), 483–492. doi:10.1080/02615470120064723

Özateş, S. Ö. (2010). Sosyal hizmet etiğinin felsefi temelleri. *Toplum ve Sosyal Hizmet Dergisi*, *21*(1), 85–97.

Pantaleo, K. (2011). *Serving up crime: A social learning perspective of employee deviance in restaurants* (Doctoral dissertation). Indiana University of Pennsylvania.

Parker, J. (2004). *Effective Practice Learning in Social Work*. London: Learning Matters Ltd.

Pellegrino, E. (1991). Trust and Distrust in Professional Ethics. In E. D. Pellegrino, R. Weatch, & J. Lagan (Eds.), *Ethics, Trust and the Professions*. Washington, DC: Georgetown UP.

Pence, G. (2006). Teoria virtuții. In P. Singer (Ed.), *Tratat de etică* [Treaty of ethics] (pp. 277–288). Iasi: Polirom.

Perlow, R., & Latham, L. L. (1993). Relationship of client abuse with locus of control and gender: A longitudinal study in mental retardation facilities. *The Journal of Applied Psychology*, *78*(5), 831–834. doi:10.1037/0021-9010.78.5.831 PMID:8253634

Pettit, P. (2006). Consecințialismul. In P. Singer (Ed.), *Tratat de etică* [Treaty of ethics] (pp. 258–268). Iasi: Polirom.

Platonova, E. A., Kennedy, K. N., & Schewchuck, R. M. (2008). Understand patient satisfaction, trust, and loyalty to primary care physicians. *Medical Care Research and Review*, *65*(6), 696–712. doi:10.1177/1077558708322863 PMID:18723450

Pope, K. S., Tabechnik, B. G., & Keith-Spiegel, P. (1988). Good and poor practices in psychotherapy. National survey of belief of psychotherapy. *Professional Psychology, Research and Practice*, *19*(5), 547–552. doi:10.1037/0735-7028.19.5.547

Popper, K. R. (2000). Individualism versus colectivism. In K. R. Popper (Ed.), Filosofie socială şi filosofia ştiinţei [Social philosophy and philosophy of science] (pp. 362-374). Bucharest: Trei Publishing. (originally published 1945)

Powers, M. (2005). Bioethics as Politics: The Limits of Moral Expertise. *Kennedy Institute of Ethics Journal*, *15*(3), 305–322. doi:10.1353/ken.2005.0023 PMID:16250118

Qreferat. (2006). Standarde profesionale în domeniul asistenței sociale. *Chişinău*, pp. 7-15. Retrieved May 25, 2017, from http://www.qreferat.com/referate/psihologie/Standardele-profesionale-in-do258.php

Quality of Social Services in Europe. (n.d.). Retrieved from http://www.epr.eu/images/EPR/documents/policy_documents/2014policypapers/Quality_of_Social_ServicesinEurope.pdf

Ramamoorti, S., & Luke, E.R. (2011, Aug. 1). The corporate ethics audit: to prevent and detect management fraud, internal auditors must have a sound understanding of human behavior. *Internal Auditor*.

Rapp, C. A., Saleebey, D., & Sullivan, W. P. (2005). The future of strengths-based social work. *Administration in Social Work*, *6*(1), 79–90.

Rasmussen, A. (2005). *In Search of Ethics Expertise in Ethics Expertise. History, Contemporary Perspectives and Applications*. Springer. https://doi.org/10.1007/1-4020-3820-8

Rasmussen, L. M. (2016). Clinical Ethics Consultants are not "Ethics" Experts—but They do Have Expertise. *J Med Philos*, *41*(4), 384-400. https://doi.org/10.1093/jmp/jhw012

Rawls, J. (2012). O teorie a dreptăţii (H. Târnoveanu, Trans.). Iaşi, Romania: Alexandu Ioan Cuza University Publishing.

Rawls, J. (2012). O teorie a dreptății [A theory of justice]. Iasi, Romania: Alexandu Ioan Cuza University Publishing.

Reamer, F. G. (1987). *Ethics Committees in Social Work, Faculty Publications*. Retrieved from: http://works.bepress.com/frederic_reamer/8

Reamer, F. G. (2000). The Social Work Ethics Audit: A Risk-Management Strategy. Social Work, 45(4), 355–366. Available at http://www.jstor.org/stable/23718779

Reamer, F. G. (2003). Boundary Issues in Social Work: Managing dual relationships. *Social Work, 48*(1), 121-133. https://doi.org/10.1093/sw/48.1.121

Reamer, F. G. (2012). *Eye on Ethics*. Retrieved May 1, 2017, from http://www.socialworktoday.com/news/eoe_051712.shtml

Reamer, F. G. (2012). Social Work. In Encyclopedia of Applied Ethics (2nd ed.; pp. 189–197). Academic Press. doi:10.1016/B978-0-12-373932-2.00415-4

Reamer, F. (1998). *Ethical strandards in social work: A critical review of the NASW code of ethics*. Washington, DC: NASW Press.

Reamer, F. (2001). *The Social Work Ethics Audit: A Risk Management Tool*. NASW Press.

Reamer, F. G. (1982). *Ethical dilemmas in social service*. New York: Columbia University Press.

Reamer, F. G. (1982). *Ethical Dilemmas in Social Service*. New York: Columbia University Press.

Reamer, F. G. (2005). Documentation in social work: Evolving ethical and risk-management standards. *Social Work*, *50*(4), 325–334. doi:10.1093/sw/50.4.325 PMID:17892242

Reamer, F. G. (2006). *Social Work Values and Ethics* (3rd ed.). New York: Columbia University Press.

Reck, B. (2003). *Between Democracy and Technocracy. The Role of Expertise for the European Parliament.* Stuttgart: Ibidem- Verlag.

Reidenbach, R. E., & Donald, P. R. (1990). Toward the Development of a Multidimensional Scale for Improving Evaluations of Business Ethics. *Journal of Business Ethics*, *9*(8), 639–653. doi:10.1007/BF00383391

Rhodes, M. L. (1986). *Ethical Dilemmas in Social Work Practice*. London: Routledge and Kegan Paul.

Rice, D. (1975). The Code: A voice for approval. *Social Work Today*, *18*, 381–382.

Richmond, M. (1917). *Social diagnosis*. New York: Sage.

Rîjicova, S., & Grigoraş, S. (2017). *Mecanismul de supervizare profesională în asistenţa socială. Ghid de implementare practică* [The mechanism of professional supervising in social work. Guide for practical implementation]. Retrieved from http://www.mmpsf.gov.md/sites/default/files/document/attachments/usaid_2_ghid_supervizare_rom.pdf

Robinson, S. L., & Greenberg, J. (1998). Employees behaving badly: Dimensions, determinants and dilemmas in the study of workplace deviance. *Journal of Organizational Behavior (1986-1998)*, 1.

Robinson, S. L., & Bennett, R. J. (1995). A typology of deviant workplace behaviors: A multidimensional scaling study. *Academy of Management Journal*, *38*(2), 555–572. doi:10.2307/256693

Rosanvallon, P. (1998). *Noua problemă socială* [The new social problem]. Iaşi: European Institute. (Original work published 1995)

Rossiter, A. (2005). *Discourse Analysis in Critical Social Work: From Apology to Question*. Retrieved May 25, 2017, from http://www1.uwindsor.ca/criticalsocialwork/discourse-analysis-in-critical-social-work-from-apology-to-question

Rosthorn, J. (2000). Business Ethics Auditing – More Than a Stakeholders Toy. *Journal of Business Ethics*, *27*(1/2), 9–19. doi:10.1023/A:1006414502730

Rubin, A., & Babbie, E. (2014). *Research Methods for Social Work*. Pacific Grove, CA: Brooks Cole.

Sablynski, C. J., Mitchell, T. R., James, L. R., & McIntyre, M. (2001). *Identifying aggressive individuals via conditional reasoning: An experimental study*. Academy of Management Conference, Washington, DC.

Sackett, P. R., & DeVore, C. J. (2001). Counterproductive behaviors at work. In N. Anderson, D.S. Ones, H.K. Sinangil, & C. Viswesvaran (Eds.), Handbook of industrial, work, and organizational psychology (pp. 145–164). London: Sage. doi:10.4135/9781848608320.n9

Saleebey, D. (1996). The strengths perspective in social work practice: Extensions and cautions. *Social Work*, *41*(3), 296–305. PMID:8936085

Saleebey, D. (1997). The strengths perspective: Possibilities and problems. In D. Saleebey (Ed.), *The strengths perspective in social work practice* (2nd ed.; pp. 231–248). New York: Longman.

Saleebey, D. (2002). *The strengths perspective in social work practice* (3rd ed.). New York: Longman.

Saleebey, D. (2006). Power in the people: Introduction. In D. Saleebey (Ed.), *The strengths perspective in social work practice* (4th ed.; pp. 1–24). Boston: Allyn & Bacon.

Salin, D. (2003). Ways of explaining workplace bullying: A review of enabling, motivating and precipitating structures and processes in the work environment. *Human Relations*, *56*(10), 1213–1232. doi:10.1177/00187267035610003

Sampson, R. J., & Laub, J. H. (1993). Structural variations in juvenile court processing: Inequality, the underclass, and social control. *Law & Society Review*, *27*(2), 285–311. doi:10.2307/3053938

Sandu, A. (2010). Freedom as a hermeneutical pretext. *Revista Românească pentru Educaţie Multidimensională, 2*(3), 5-24.

Sandu, A. (2015). Etică profesională şi transparenţă în administraţia publică [Professional ethics and transparency and public administration]. Bucharest, Romania: Didactică şi Pedagogică-RA Publishing.

Sandu, A. (2015). *Etică profesională și transparență în administrația publică* [Professional ethics and transparency in public administration]. Bucharest, Romania: Didactică şi Pedagogică Publishing.

Sandu, A. (2015). *Etică profesională și transparență în administrația publică*. Bucharest, Romania: Editura Didactică şi Pedagogică.

Sandu, A. (2016). From distributive to procedural justice. Justice as a constitutive value of public administration. *Annals of "Ştefan cel Mare" University of Suceava Philosophy, Social and Human Disciplines Series*, *1*, 43-58. Retrieved from http://www.apshus.usv.ro/arhiva/2016I. pdf#page=45

Sandu, A. (2016). Social Protection of Abused Children: A Socio-legal and Ethical Analysis. In Multidimensional Education and Professional Development. Ethical Values (pp. 461-466). Editografica.

Sandu, A. (2016b). Cadre normativ-instituţionale ale construcţiei sociale a profesiei de consilier de probaţiune în zona de Nord-Est a României şi în Republica Moldova [Normative-institutional frameworks of the social construction of the probation counseling profession in the North-East of Romania and the Republic of Moldova]. *Sociologie Românească, 14*(1), 23-44.

Sandu, A., & Caras (Frunză), A. (2014). Some Considerations on the Construction of Ethics Policies. Shared Ethics and Communicative Action. *Procedia - Social and Behavioral Sciences, 149*, 846–854. https://doi.org/10.1016/j.sbspro.2014.08.325

Sandu, A. (2012). *Appreciative ethics. A constructionist Version of Ethics*. Lap Lambert Acad. Publ. GmbH & Co. KG.

Sandu, A. (2013). *Asistenţa socială aplicată. Tehnici de cercetare şi modele de intervenţie* [Applied Social Work. Research techniques and intervention patterns]. Iasi, Romania: Lumen Publishing.

Sandu, A. (2014). *Elemente de sociologie. Sociologie generală, juridică şi metodologia cercetării sociale* [Elements of sociology. General and legal sociology, and the methodology of social research]. Bucharest, Romania: Tritonic Publishing.

Sandu, A. (2015). Philosophical Practice and Values Based Ethics: Rethinking Social Action and Core Values, Philosophical Practice. *Journal of the American Philosophical Practitioners, 10*(3), 1618–1631.

Sandu, A. (2016). *Etică și practică socială* [Ethics and social practice]. Iasi, Romania: Lumen Publishing.

Sandu, A. (2016a). *Social Construction of Reality as communicative Action*. Cambridge Scholars Publishing.

Sandu, A. (2016a). *Social Construction of Reality as Communicative Action*. Cambridge Scholars Publishing.

Sandu, A. (2016b). A Levinasian Opening on the Affirmative Ethics of Care. *Journal for the Study of Religions and Ideologies, 15*(43), 28–47.

Sandu, A. (2017). *O etică centrată pe valori în sfera publică* [An ethics centered on values in the public sphere]. Iasi: Lumen Publishing.

Sandu, A., & Caras (Frunză), A. (2014). Some Considerations on the Construction of Ethics Policies. Shared Ethics and Communicative Action. *Procedia: Social and Behavioral Sciences, 149*, 846–854. doi:10.1016/j.sbspro.2014.08.325

Sandu, A., & Caras, A. (2013). Deconstruction of charity. Postmodern ethical approaches. *Journal for the Study of Religions and Ideologies, 12*(36), 72–99.

Sandu, A., & Caras, A. (2013). Philosophical Practice and Social Welfare Counselling and Supervision of Ethics. *Journal of the APPA Philosophical Practice, 8*(3), 1287–1296.

Sandu, A., Cojocaru, D., Gavrilovici, C., & Oprea, L. (2013). Trust: An Ethical Dimension of Healthcare in Chronic Disorders. *Revista Romana de Bioetica, 11*(1), 190–205.

Sandu, A., & Damian, S. (2012). Applying Appreciative Inquiry Principles in the Restorative Justice Field. *Postmodern Openings, 3*(2), 37–52.

Sandu, A., & Unguru, E. (2013). Supervision of social work practice in North-Eastern Romanian rural areas. *Procedia: Social and Behavioral Sciences, 82*, 386–391. doi:10.1016/j.sbspro.2013.06.280

Sandu, A., & Unguru, E. (2014). *Acțiune comunicativă, justiție deliberativă și restaurativă. Perspective socio-juridice asupra medierii și probațiunii* [Communicative action, deliberative and restorative justice. Social-legal perspectives on mediation and probation]. Bucharest, Romania: Tritonic Publishing.

Sapouna, L. (2007, May). *Progress report on the Slí Eile housing project.* Cork, Ireland: Department of Applied Social Studies, University College Cork.

Schicktanz, S., Schweda, M., & Wynne, B. (2012). The Ethics of Public Understanding of Ethics—Why and How Bioethics Expertise Should Include Public and Patients Voices. *Medicine, Health Care, and Philosophy*, *15*(2), 129–139. doi:10.1007/s11019-011-9321-4 PMID:21448745

Schneider, B. (1990). The climate for service: An application of the climate construct. In B. Schneider (Ed.), *Organizational climate and culture* (pp. 383–412). San Francisco: JosseyBass.

Schoeman, F. D. (1984). Privacy: philosophical dimensions of the literature. In F. D. Schoeman (Ed.), *Philosophical Dimensions of Privacy* (pp. 1–33). Cambridge, MA: Cambridge University Press. doi:10.1017/CBO9780511625138.002

Schumann, P. L. (2001). A Moral Principles Framework for Human Resource Management Ethics. *Human Resource Management Review*, *11*(1-2), 93–111. doi:10.1016/S1053-4822(00)00042-5

Sears, B. P. (1993). *Auditing business ethics. The Internal Auditor, 50(3),* 38. ProQuest Central.

Seedhouse, D. (2005). *Values-Based Decision-Making for the Caring Professions.* Chichester, UK: Wiley.

Seleka, T., Siphambe, H., Ntseane, D., Mbere, N., Kerapeletswe, C., & Sharp, C. (2007). Social Safety Nets in Botswana: Administration, Targeting and Sustainability. Gaborone, Botswana: Lightbooks - Lentswe La Lesedi (PTY).

Sellers, C. S., & Winfree, L. T. (1990). Differential associations and definitions: A panel study of youthful drinking behavior. *The International Journal of the Addictions*, *25*(7), 755–771. doi:10.3109/10826089009056217 PMID:2272721

Sharma, N., & Paluchova, J. (2014). An aerial glimpse of workplace deviance in Indian service industry. *Gurukul Business Review*, *10*, 11–16.

Sharma, N., & Singh, V. K. (2016). Effect of workplace incivility on job satisfaction and turnover intentions in India. *South Asian Journal of Global Business Research*, *5*(2), 234–249. doi:10.1108/SAJGBR-02-2015-0020

Sharma, N., Singh, V. K., & Kishor, J. (2013). Demographic differences, causes and impact of workplace production deviance on organizations: An empirical study on non-punctuality of employees in service cluster. *Research Journal of Social Science and Management*, *3*(8), 99–106.

Sharpe, V. A. (2005). Perspective: Privacy and Security for Electronic Health Records. *The Hastings Center Report*, *35*(6), 18. doi:10.2307/3528564 PMID:16396204

Singer, P. (1972). Moral Experts. *Analysis*, *32*(4), 115–117. doi:10.1093/analys/32.4.115

Singer, P. (1979). *Practical Ethics*. Cambridge, UK: Cambridge University Press.

Singer, P., & Wells, D. (1984). *The Reproductive Revolution: New Ways of Making Babies*. Oxford, UK: Oxford University Press.

Skarlicki, D. P., & Folger, R. (1997). Retaliation in the workplace: The roles of distributive, procedural, and interactional justice. *The Journal of Applied Psychology*, *82*(3), 434–443. doi:10.1037/0021-9010.82.3.434

Skinner, B. F. (1953). *Science and human behavior*. New York: Macmillan.

Skinner, B. F. (1959). *Cumulative record*. New York: Appleton Century Crofts.

Smalley, R. E. (1967). *Theory for social work practice*. New York: Columbia University Press.

Snyder, M., Schactman, L., & Young, S. (2015). Rates and correlations of change in three dimensions of recovery within a recovery model oriented therapeutic community. *The Psychiatric Quarterly*, *86*(1), 123–136. doi:10.1007/s11126-014-9318-2 PMID:25294276

Södergren, C. (2014). *Organisations: A Battle for Life, in the Name of Globalisation. Communication for Development One-year Master, 15 Credits, Spring 2014, Supervisor: Michael Krona, Faculty of Culture and Society*. Malmö University.

Solove, D. (2004). *The digital person: Technology and Privacy in the Information Age*. New York: University Press.

Solove, D. J. (2008). *Understanding Privacy*. Cambridge, MA: Harvard University Press.

Soulet, M.-H. (2004). Ce valori, ce practici ale solidarităţii? [What values, what practices of solidarity?]. In A. Vilbrod & I. Ionescu (Eds.), *Asistenţa socială în tranziţie* [Social work in transition] (pp. 23–33). Iaşi: European Institute.

Spector, P. E. (1997). *Job satisfaction: Application, assessment, causes, and consequences* (Vol. 3). Sage Publications.

Spector, P. E., Fox, S., Penney, L. M., Bruursema, K., Goh, A., & Kessler, S. (2006). The dimensionality of counterproductivity: Are all counterproductive behaviors created equal? *Journal of Vocational Behavior*, *68*(3), 446–460. doi:10.1016/j.jvb.2005.10.005

Spencer, H. (1891). Principes de sociologie. Paris: Ed. Felix Alcan.

Spencer, H. (1996). Individul împotriva statului [The individual against the state]. Iaşi: Timpul Publishing. (originally published 1884)

Staniforth, B. (2010). *Past, present and future perspectives on the role of counselling in social work in Aotearoa New Zealand* (PhD thesis). Massey University.

Staudt, M., Howard, M. O., & Drake, B. (2001). The operationalization, implementation and effectiveness of the strengths perspective: A review of empirical studies. *Journal of Social Service Research, 27*(3), 1–21. doi:10.1300/J079v27n03_01

Stokic, P. L., & Bajec, J. (2014). European Social Policy Network (ESPN). Thematic Report on Social Investment Serbia 2015. European Union.

Storms, P. L., & Spector, P. E. (1987). Relationships of organizational frustration with reported behavioural reactions: The moderating effect of locus of control. *Journal of Occupational Psychology, 60*(3), 227–234. doi:10.1111/j.2044-8325.1987.tb00255.x

Streets, F. J. (2008). Religion and Social Work: Dilemmas and Challenges in Practice. *Journal of Jewish Communal Service, 83*(2/3), 170.

Strom-Gottfried, K. (2000). Ensuring ethical practice: An examination of NASW code violations, 198697. *Social Work, 45*(3), 251–261. doi:10.1093/sw/45.3.251 PMID:10803079

Swedish Code of Ethics. (2006). Retrieved October 15, 2017, from http://cdn.ifsw.org/assets/Socialt_arbete_etik_08_Engelsk_LR.pdf

Szabo, A. (2010b). From Restorative Justice to Restorative Practices: Applicability in the Field of Social Work. *Revista de Asistenţă Socială, 1.*

Szabo, A. (2010a). Greşeală, vinovăţie şi pedeapsă: despre reabilitarea persoanelor care au comis infracţiuni [Mistake, guilt and punishment: on rehabilitating the persons who have committed crimes]. In *Asistenţa socială a grupurilor de risc* [Social care of groups of risk] (pp. 455–482). Iasi, Romania: Polirom Publishing.

Tarasoff v. Regents of the University of California, 551 P.2d 334 (Cal. 1974)

Tarasoff v. Regents of University of California. (n.d.). Retrieved June 15, 2017 from http://www.casebriefs.com/blog/law/torts/torts-keyed-to-dobbs/the-duty-to-protect-from-third-persons/tarasoff-v-regents-of-university-of-california/2/

Taubman, S. (2012). *Dangerousness to Self and Others in Social Work Practice. School of Social Welfare Field Preparation Panel.* University of California. Retrieved June 15, 2017 from http://socialwelfare.berkeley.edu/sites/default/files/docs/Handouts__Dangerousness_to_Self_and_Others_in_Social_Work_Practice.pdf

Tenbrunsel, A. E., Smith-Crowe, K., & Umphress, E. E. (2003). Building Houses on Rocks: The Role of the Ethical Infrastructure in Organizations. *Social Justice Research, 16*(3), 285-307. https://doi.org/10.1023/A:1025992813613

Tepper, B. J., Carr, J. C., Breaux, D. M., Gieder, S., Hu, C., & Hua, W. (2009). Abusive supervision, intentions to quit and employees workplace deviance. *Organizational Behavior and Human Decision Processes, 109*(2), 156–167. doi:10.1016/j.obhdp.2009.03.004

Terec-Vlad, L. & Cucu, M. (2016). Ethics and Organizational Culture – Key Elements regarding the Development of Economic Activities. *Ecoforum Journal, 5*(8), 192-198.

Terec-Vlad, L. (2016). The Principle of Responsibility towards the Human Non-Presence or the Non-Human Presence. *Postmodern Openings*, *7*(2), 79–89. doi:10.18662/po/2016.0702.06

The Official Monitor of Romania. (2008). *Codul deontologic al profesiei de asistent social* [The deontological code of the profession of social worker of Romania]. Code nr.1/2008. The Official Monitor of Romania. Part I, nr.173 din 06.03.2008. Retrieved May 25, 2017, from http://www.carp-omenia.ro/wp-content/uploads/2015/07/cod_deontologic_as.pdf

The Policy, Ethics and Human Rights Committee. (2014). *The Code of Ethics for Social Work. Statement of Principles*. Retrieved from http://cdn.basw.co.uk/upload/basw_95243-9.pdf

The Policy, Ethics and Human Rights Committee. (2014). *The Code of Ethics for Social Work. Statement of Principles*. Retrieved from: http://cdn.basw.co.uk/upload/basw_95243-9.pdf

Thomson v. County of Alameda, 614 P.2d 728 (Cal. 1980)

Thornberry, T. P., Lizotte, A. J., Krohn, M. D., Farnworth, M., & Jang, S. J. (1994). Delinquent peers, beliefs, and delinquent behavior: A longitudinal test of interactional theory. *Criminology*, *32*(1), 47–83. doi:10.1111/j.1745-9125.1994.tb01146.x

Timms, N. (1983). *Social Work Values, An Enquiry*. London: Routledge and Kegan Paul plc.

Tomlinson, T. (1999). Ethics Consultant: Problem Solver or Spiritual Counselor*? Human Studies*, *22*(1), 43–52. doi:10.1023/A:1005408718236

Topuz, S., & Öz, M. (2012). Türkiye'de sosyal hizmet eğitimi veren yükseköğretim kurumları, mezunların istihdam durumları ve öngörüler. In V. Işıkhan, T. Tuncay & E. Erbay (Ed.), 50. yılında Türkiye'de sosyal hizmet eğitimi: Sorunlar, öncelikler ve hedefler (pp. 239-246). Ankara: Sosyal Hizmet Araştırma ve Geliştirme Derneği Yayını.

Tosatia, S., Lawthongb, N., & Suwanmonkhab, S. (2015). Development of an Appreciative Inquiry and Assessment Processes for Students Self-Knowing and Self-Development. *Procedia: Social and Behavioral Sciences*, *191*, 753–758. doi:10.1016/j.sbspro.2015.04.422

Trevino, L. K. (1986). Ethical decision making in organizations: A person-situation interactionist model. *Academy of Management Review*, *11*(3), 601–617.

Treviño, L. K., & Nelson, K. A. (2011). *Managing business ethics: Straight talk about how to do it right*. Wiley.

Tsui, M. S. (2008). Adventures in re-searching the features of social work supervision in Hong Kong. *Qualitative Social Work: Research and Practice*, *7*(3), 349–362. doi:10.1177/1473325008093706

Turnage, B. F., Jacinto, G. A., & Kirven, J. (2003). Reality therapy, domestic violence survivors, and self-forgiveness. *International Journal of Reality Therapy*, *22*(2), 24–27.

Ungureanu, S. Autoritatea Națională de Management al Calității în Sănătate (ANMCS). (2017). *Managementul riscului clinic componentă esențială a siguranței pacientului în unitățile sanitare. Auditul Clinic*. Available at www.sanatateromania.ro

Valentine, S., & Godkin, L. (2016). Ethics policies, perceived social responsibility, and positive work attitude. *Irish Journal of Management, 35*(2), 114–128. doi:10.1515/ijm-2016-0013

Van Beek, G. (2010). *Common Quality Framework for Social Services of General Interest.* Brussels: Prometheus.

Verweij, M., Brom, F. W., & Huibers, A. (2000). Do's and Dont's for Ethics Committees: Practical Lessons Learned in the Netherlands. *HEC Forum, 12,* 344–357. https://doi.org/10.1023/A:1008997605664

Vitelli, R. (2014). Revisiting Tarasoff. Should therapists breach confidentiality over a patient's violent threat? *Psychology Today*. Retrieved June 15, 2017 from https://www.psychologytoday.com/blog/media-spotlight/201407/revisiting-tarasoff

Von Hirsh, A. (1976). *Doing Justice: The Choice of Punishment.* New York: Hill and Wang.

Waring, C. G., & Daugherty, C. A. (2004). Auditing Ethics-Make Them an Offer They Can't Refuse Waring. *The Journal of Government Financial Management, 53*(1), 34. ProQuest Central.

Warr, M., & Stafford, M. (1991). The influence of delinquent peers: What they think or what they do? *Criminology, 29*(4), 851–866. doi:10.1111/j.1745-9125.1991.tb01090.x

Weick, A., Rapp, C., Sullivan, W. P., & Kisthardt, W. (1989). A strengths perspective for social work practice. *Social Work, 34*(4), 350–354. doi:10.1093/sw/34.4.350

Weinstein, B. D. (1994). The possibility of Ethical Expertise. *Theoretical Medicine, 15*(1), 61–75. doi:10.1007/BF00999220 PMID:8059434

WHO. (2006). *From Access Adherence: The challenges of antiretroviral treatment, studies from Botswana, Tanzania and Uganda.* Geneva, Switzerland: World Health Organization. Retrieved from http://apps.who.int/medicinedocs/pdf/s13400e/s13400e.pdf

Wieland, J. (2003). Standards and audits for ethics management systems: the European perspective: with 4 tables. Springer. doi:10.1007/978-3-662-05107-8

William Glasser Institute. (2010a). *Choice theory.* Retrieved from http://www.wglasser.com/the-glasser-approach/choice-theory

William Glasser Institute. (2010b). *Reality therapy.* Retrieved 16 July 2015 from http://www.wglasser.com/the-glasser-approach/reality-therapy

Worrall, A., & Mawby, R. C. (2014). Probation worker cultures and relationships with offenders. *Probation Journal, 61*(4), 346 – 357. https://doi.org/10.1177/0264550514548251

Wren, D. A., & Bedeian, A. G. (2009). *The Evolution of Management Thought.* Hoboken, NJ: John Wiley & Sons.

Wu, M.-H., Liao, C.-H., Chiu, W.-T., Lin, C.-Y., & Yang, C.-M. (2011). Can we accredit hospital ethics? A tentative proposal. *Journal of Medical Ethics*, *37*(8), 493-7.

Yoder, S. D. (1998). The Nature of Ethical Expertise. *The Hastings Center Report*, *28*(6), 11–19. doi:10.2307/3528262 PMID:9868604

Young, S., Schactman, L., & Snyder, M. (2014). Early report on the effectiveness of a recovery model oriented therapeutic community for individuals with complex and persistent recovery challenges. *The Psychiatric Quarterly*, *85*(3), 329–343. doi:10.1007/s11126-014-9292-8 PMID:24615555

Young, S., Snyder, M., & Schactman, L. (2015). Early recovery from psychotic spectrum disorder within a therapeutic community: Significance and effects. *Psychosis*, *7*(1/2), 37–47. doi:10.1080/17522439.2014.926387

Zaner, R. M. (2004). *Ethics and the Clinical Encounter*. Lima: CSS Publishing.

Zwart, H. (2012). Ethical Expertise in Policy. In R. Chadwick (Ed.), *Encyclopedia of Applied Ethics* (2nd ed.; pp. 157–164). San Diego, CA: Academic Press. doi:10.1016/B978-0-12-373932-2.00006-5

About the Contributors

Antonio Sandu is Professor PhD at "Stefan cel Mare" University of Suceava, Romania, and Senior Researcher at the LUMEN Research Center in Social and Humanistic Sciences, Iasi, Romania. His main areas of interest include ethics, bioethics, social work and social philosophy. The original contributions of the author's scientific activities start from the social construction of reality and social constructionism as seen from a semiological perspective. He analyses the social construction of reality by developing his very own version of social constructionism operating at the intersection between the constructionist paradigm and the theory of communicative action. He is the author of the book: Social Construction of Reality as Communicative action, published at Cambridge Scholar Publishing (2016), and also of "Social Work Practice: Research Techniques and Intervention Models: From Problem Solving to Appreciative Inquiry", "Appreciative Ethics: A constructionist version of ethics" and "Social-Constructionist Epistemology: A transmodern overview", all three published by Lap Lambert between 2012 and 2013. He has also authored more than 20 volumes in Romanian and English language.

Ana Frunză obtained a PhD in philosophy at Al. I. Cuza University of Iasi, in 2014, presenting a thesis entitled "A deconstructive approach to ethical values. Ethics expertise". She obtained an MA degree in Supervision and Social Planning in 2011, with a Bachelor's degree in Social Work in 2009. She is Scientific Researcher III at the LUMEN Center for Social and Humanistic Research. Her main scientific interests are applied ethics, applied philosophy, social work, supervision and ethics expertise. She is associated university assistant PhD "Stefan cel Mare" University from Suceava, Faculty of Law & Administrative Sciences, Romania. Ana Frunza is currently working on defining a new model of ethics expertise – the supervision of ethics, in conjunction with Professor Antonio Sandu, Doctor in Philosophy at LUMEN Center for Social and Humanistic Research from Iasi, Romania. She is the author of three books, "Etica şi dezvoltarea comunitară/Ethics and community development" and "Către o nouă expertiză etică. Deconstruind valorile etice/Towards a new ethics expertise – deconstructing the ethical values", "Supervizarea şi dezvoltarea profesională a asistenţilor sociali/The supervision and the professional development of the social workers" published by LUMEN Publishing House between 2013 and 2017. Her research interests are ethics, research ethics, ethics expertise, supervision of ethics, applied philosophy. During 2014 and 2016 she also studied bioethics and research ethics within the Advanced Certificate Program in Research Ethics for Central and Eastern Europe, sponsored by the Fogarty International Center of the National Institutes of Health under Award Number R25TW007085.

* * *

Daniela-Tatiana Agheorghiesei is a professor at Faculty of Economics and Business Administration, Management, Marketing and Business Administration Department, Alexandru Ioan Cuza University, Iasi, Romania.

Dan Ioan Dascalu is an associate professor at the "Stefan cel Mare" University of Suceava. He teaches sociology and social psychology courses in the social work and political science study programs. He is a part of the Department of Human Disciplines, Social and Political Science. He is licensed in sociology at the University of Bucharest, Faculty of History and Philosophy and has received his PhD in psychology at the "Al. I. Cuza" University of Iasi in 2001. His research focuses are on totalitarianism, political social psychology and the dimensions of contemporary individualism. His publications include the 2002 volume „Totalitarian personality", the 2007 volume "Consumer behavior", and the 2006 collective volume "Violence in sports".

Tatiana Focsa is a University lecturer and researcher in Social Work and Law, working on developing a new concept named "Procedure of establishing the child's residence in public law". Scientific activities and interests based on researching and expanding topics as: "Considerations regarding the notions of 'family', 'child', 'minor' in the context of the national and international regulations"; "national and international normative framework of regulating the concepts of family and child's rights"; "The Procedural Practices of Establishing the Child's Residence in the Republic of Moldova"; "Mediation in the cases of establishment the child's residence and the role of foster authorities in these situations", etc. Besides the scientific activity, I'm working as Expert in accrediting the providers of social services.

Svetlana Haraz is a University lecturer and researcher in Social Psychology and Social Work, working on the research regarding "The prevention of social exclusion of parents caring for children with special needs". Scientific activities and interests based on researching and expanding topics as: "Child's disability as a factor that places the family at risk of social exclusion", "Inclusive education", "Social unadaptation and social inclusion", "Diagnosing and solving social problems". Expert in child protection; National Expert in accreditation of social services; Author and co-author of publications (5 book chapters, 3 guides, 6 booklets and 30 referred articles in national and international journals.) and training curricula.

Masego Lecha is a hospital social work practitioner. She holds a Bachelors Degree in Social Work from the Nelson Mandela Metropolitan University in Port Elizabeth, South Africa, and a Diploma in Social Work from the University of Botswana. She has worked in the hospital setting for the past eighteen years and had served in various multi-disciplinary committees aimed at improving service delivery in health settings. As part of her role in the hospital, she works in multidisciplinary teams to assist clients to adapt and adjust after diagnosis and during hospitalization. She also engages in clients' needs assessment, advocacy to ensure that clients receive timely and quality services, and linking clients with community resources upon discharge.

Sana Loue serves as the Vice Dean for Faculty Development and Diversity and is a professor in the Department of Bioethics of Case Western Reserve University School of Medicine. She holds secondary appointments in Psychiatry, Epidemiology and Biostatistics, and Global Health. Dr. Loue holds degrees in epidemiology (PhD), medical anthropology (PhD), social work (MSSA), secondary education (MA), public health (MPH) and theology (MA). She is a licensed lawyer, a licensed independent social worker and an ordained interfaith minister. Her sandplay practice focuses on individuals with severe mental illness, including schizophrenia, gender identity.

Tumani Malinga is a doctoral candidate at the School of Social Work, University of Illinois at Urbana-Champaign and holds a teaching position in the Department of Social Work, University of Botswana. She received her Master in Social Work (MSW) from the University of Utah, Salt Lake City. Post MSW, she worked directly with clients in the hospital setting in Botswana to help them adjust and adapt post hospitalization; link clients with community resources; and in advocating for clients' rights and needs. She has also worked with disciplinary committees aimed at improving service delivery in health settings. Her research interests include low income women, gender issues, and mental health. She is also interested in social work ethics and social work practice issues.

Sorin-Tudor Maxim, PhD Stefan cel Mare University of Suceava (Romania). His areas of competence are moral philosophy and political philosophy. His studies are focused on elements of prospective ethics, moral conscience issues, moral responsibility and tolerance. He has published more than 10 books as author and coordinator and more than 100 studies in prestigious volumes from home and abroad, such as "Constiinta morala" Editura Junimea, Iasi, 1999; "Toleranta. Dreptul la diferenta", Editura Didactica si Pedagogica, Bucharest, 2004; "Peripatethice" Editura PIM, Iasi, 2010, "Elemente de logica si teoria argumentarii, Editura LUMEN, 2014."

Poloko Ntshwarang is a lecturer in the department of social work at the University of Botswana and currently pursuing her PhD at the University of KwaZulu-Natal, South Africa. She completed her Masters of Social Work degree (majoring in health) from the University of Utah, U. S.A. in 2004. She also has a Bachelors of Social Work from the University of Botswana, which she acquired in 2001. After completing her studies Mrs. Ntshwarang worked in the health services before joining the University. She worked in two hospitals in Botswana as a Social Worker. She also worked at Botswana Red Cross Society in the Refugee Health Program as a Social Welfare officer. In these agencies, she got exposure and experience in Health issues such as HIV and AIDS and how they impacted the people's wellbeing. She is interested in issues pertaining to social work practice and research but with specific interest on health, children's and gender issues.

Liranso Selamu is a Ph.D. scholar in Social Work and an author of many world class books and research journals.

Naman Sharma is currently working as Assistant Professor with Amity University. Dr. Naman Sharma has received his PhD in Management (Organizational Behavior/HR). His areas of research are employee relations, unethical behavior and deviant behaviors in organizations.

Mohan S. Singhe is an Assistant Professor in the Department of Social Work, Mangalore University, India.

Elena Unguru is a PhD Candidate at the Doctoral School of Sociology, University from Oradea. Legal Adviser for LUMEN Association, in Iasi. She graduated from MA studies in Supervision and Family Planning, at the Faculty of Philosophy and Social Political Sciences from Al. I. Cuza University in Iasi. She has a BA in Law and Social Work. Fields of interest: sociology, law, social sciences, public relations and communication.

Teodor Vicol is a National Council of Accreditation for the Provider of Social Services, Republic of Moldova.

Oğuzhan Zengin is an Assistant Professor, PhD, is a full time faculty member in the Department of Social Work at Çankırı Karatekin University. He joined the School of Social Work at Hacettepe University in 2011 as a research assistant. Prior to joining the academy, he has worked as a social worker in the fields of family and children, disability, poverty and medical social work. His academic studies are usually about medical social work, social work education, children and young people and solution focused brief therapy in social work settings. Specifically, he conducts studies on psychosocial aspects of chronic illnesses, and on developing, and implementing social work interventions to improve their psychosocial health and well-being.

Index

G

I

M

O

P

S

T

U

V

W

www.ingramcontent.com/pod-product-compliance
Lightning Source LLC
LaVergne TN
LVHW081341300926
849161LV00008B/2046